Credits

EXECUTIVE EDITOR
Chris Webb

SENIOR ACQUISITIONS EDITOR
Sharon Cox

ACQUISITIONS EDITOR
Katie Feltman

PROJECT EDITOR
Marcia Ellett

COPY EDITOR
Gabrielle Chosney

EDITORIAL MANAGER
Ami Frank Sullivan

VICE PRESIDENT AND EXECUTIVE GROUP PUBLISHER
Richard Swadley

VICE PRESIDENT AND EXECUTIVE PUBLISHER
Bob Ipsen

EXECUTIVE EDITORIAL DIRECTOR
Mary Bednarek

PROJECT COORDINATOR
Maridee Ennis

GRAPHICS AND PRODUCTION SPECIALISTS
Sean Decker, Melanie DesJardins, Kelly Hardesty, Stephanie D. Jumper, Shelley Norris, Laurie Petrone, Jacque Schneider, Rashell Smith, Julie Trippetti, Jeremey Unger

QUALITY CONTROL TECHNICIANS
John Bitter, Andy Hollandbeck, Susan Moritz, Angel Perez, Carl Pierce, Linda Quigley

PROOFREADING AND INDEXING
TECHBOOKS Production Services

About the Authors

Norbert Pohlmann is a founding member and Chairman of TeleTrusT, an organization dedicated to establishing cryptography standards, and serves on the management boards of several other security companies in Germany. Mr. Pohlmann is the recipient of two awards for security work from *IT Services Magazine* as well as the Aachen Prize for Innovation in Technology, and is a frequent conference speaker on security topics. This book is updated and adapted from his German-language bestseller, *Firewall-Systeme,* now in its fourth edition.

Tim Crothers is Chief Security Engineer for ITM Technologies, a leading Internet security-managed services provider. Tim has worked professionally as a computer engineer for over 17 years. He is a CNE, MCSE, MCT, CIW, and CCNA specializing in Internet security and TCP/IP. He splits his time between consulting for Fortune 100 companies, research and development, teaching and speaking about Internet security, and writing. His primary areas of security focus are penetration testing, security infrastructure design, intrusion detection, and forensic analysis. Tim is probably best known for his "in the trenches" approach and his innovative solutions to security problems.

Firewall Architecture for the Enterprise

Firewall Architecture for the Enterprise

Norbert Pohlmann and Tim Crothers

FIREWALL MEDIA
(An Imprint of Laxmi Publications Pvt. Ltd.)
BANGALORE • CHENNAI • COCHIN • GUWAHATI
HYDERABAD • KOLKATA • LUCKNOW • RANCHI
NEW DELHI

Wiley Publishing, Inc.
Best-Selling Books • Digital Downloads
• e-Books • Answer Networks
• e-Newsletters • Branded Web Sites
• e-Learning

Published by :
FIREWALL MEDIA
(An Imprint of Laxmi Publications Pvt. Ltd.)
113, Golden House, Daryaganj,
New Delhi-110002

Phone : 011-43 53 25 00
Fax : 011-43 53 25 28

www.laxmipublications.com
info@laxmipublications.com

Economy Edition Price : **Rs. 839.00** *Only.* *Edition* : 2009

OFFICES

India

© **Bangalore**	080-26 61 15 61
© **Chennai**	044-24 34 47 26
© **Cochin**	0484-239 70 04
© **Guwahati**	0361-254 36 69, 251 38 81
© **Hyderabad**	040-24 65 23 33
© **Jalandhar**	0181-222 12 72
© **Kolkata**	033-22 27 43 84
© **Lucknow**	0522-220 95 78
© **Mumbai**	022-24 91 54 15, 24 92 78 69
© **Ranchi**	0651-221 47 64

USA

Boston
11, Leavitt Street, Hingham,
MA 02043, USA

FFI-2723-839-FIREWALL ARCHITECTURE **C—16057/08/06**

Printed at : Ajit Printers, Delhi.

For the crew at ITM: John, Rik, Jerry, Mike, Ron, Sean, Tim, Todd, Dan, Big Mike,
Brian, John H, Jim, Len, Greg, Larry, and Mark.
You guys make work mostly fun.

Preface

The Internet can be a crazy place. The misconception of anonymity on the Internet inspires people to act in ways that are unheard of "in the real world." A firewall is first line of defense to the sort of mischief that can occur. Of course, implementing solid security is never as easy as simply buying and installing a firewall program. You can choose from a seemingly endless array of features and implementations. The end result in many organizations is poor security, poor performance, and hampered users. The good news is that you don't have to suffer with "poor anything" when using a firewall.

This book helps you sort through the issues that you face in choosing and implementing a firewall. Firewalls, when implemented properly, can deliver a significant amount of security. To that end, this book takes you through the components that make up the modern firewall. You learn how they work together so that you can decide how best to assemble them for your organization's security needs.

Firewalls can be a bit daunting at first, but they are really just a collection of several smaller security components, such as encryption, packet filtering, and application gateways. You can mix and match the components that suit your organization's needs to achieve a tailored solution.

Bear in mind that security is ultimately about balance – achieving sufficient security to keep the bad guys out, while still allowing your organization to get its work done. Understanding when *not* to use a firewall is almost as important as understanding when you should use one. Hopefully, you will know both of these things by the end of this book.

Acknowledgments

A book like this is the result of work by far more than just the authors. I'm fortunate to get to work with some of the best and extend to them my heartfelt gratitude. My family – Lori, Emily, Ben, and Jacob – patiently dealt with Dad being locked in his study, typing away for hours on end. Norbert Pohlmann wrote the initial book on which this is based. It served as an excellent foundation on which to build new material. Marcia Ellett and Gabrielle Chosney had the onerous task of shaping my writing into something comprehensible. Being the professionals they are, they make it look easy. Katie Feltman, the acquisitions editor, weathered numerous delays with her usual good humor and kept us all to task so we actually got the book completed in good order.

Contents at a Glance

Contents

Chapter 1

Business Transformation, IT Security, and Introduction to the Firewall

THIS BOOK IS ABOUT SECURITY SOLUTIONS, specifically, firewalls that protect IT systems against threats from insecure networks such as the Internet. Security is not just a matter of technical and organizational controls, but should also be viewed in the context of social issues. Historically, one might even argue inevitably, every technological advance has been the target of those who would exploit or subvert it. Given the reliance of modern business on the IT systems that deliver increased efficiency and capabilities, it should come as no surprise that those systems are under an increasing number of attacks.

To lend some perspective to the subject of security, this chapter begins with a brief historical overview. IT security is an increasingly complex topic. Not long ago you could foil external attackers with a simple filter. Now you need a complex defense as evidenced by this book. An understanding of the history of information security quickly reveals that the need for security is accelerating. Because the Internet has connected all organizations' systems together, the sooner organizations master the current defenses and keep pace with the new threats, the better for all.

This chapter finishes with an explanation of the general objectives of a firewall system by means of analogies, and explains the idea behind the operation of a firewall system and the concept of a *Common Point of Trust.*

Developments in Information Technology and IT Security

Technological progress has always influenced every aspect of society (Volt, 95). Penicillin replaced folk medicine, automobiles replaced covered wagons, electric typewriters replaced manual typewriters, and so on. From the consequential to the mundane, technological advances bring constant change to our lives.

Indeed, the very structure of life changed from an agrarian to an industrial society due to the advance of technology. As each technological breakthrough occurred, the pace at which new developments were found increased as well.

The modern world is shifting from industrial to largely information and communication-based. More and more people work to produce services rather than products. Technology has progressed so much that our very lives depend on its proper functioning and distribution. Security is one of the vital tools for protecting that technology and, more importantly, the information housed in it. As a result, security is becoming a central facet of everyday life.

The following list details the development of Information Technology and IT security since 1938:

- In 1938, German born Konrad Zuse developed the first mechanical computer. The first digital computers were developed during World War II. Using a computer based on vacuum tubes, the British succeeded in breaking the ENIGMA encryption system used by the German military, which had previously been viewed as unbreakable. In 1948, Claude Shannon laid the foundation of information theory when he introduced the *bit* (binary digit) as the smallest unit of information. In effect, one of the very first computer uses was specifically for security.
- In 1950, the invention of the transistor provided a basis for computers with far greater capabilities than those possible with vacuum tubes at a fraction of the cost. The transistor quickly superseded vacuum tube technology, which was slow, vulnerable, bulky, and required considerable power to operate. With the advent of mainframe systems, which were fed with punched cards and could process unbelievable quantities of data, silicon was hailed as the *new steel*. The issue of *Electronic Data Processing (EDP) security* was raised for the first time, and was regulated by a combination of physical (controlled access to the computer center) and administrative (dividing tasks between system administrator, users, and data input staff) measures.
- In the 1960s, networking developed when increasingly capable terminals were connected to mainframes. IT security had finally ceased to be physically secluded. Before long, there were distributed networks such as SNA and DECnet with Ethernet topology based on the ISO reference model. The ISO reference model and TCP/IP and Ethernet technology were developed; not long after, decentralized military and company networks, such as SNA, DECnet and the global IBM network, followed. In 1973 the Arpanet, a precursor of the Internet, was born. In 1991 it became public and, with the World Wide Web, the age of the Internet began.
- Paralleling advances in information technology, cryptography was also being developed. Important algorithms evolved, including the U.S. Data Encryption Standard (DES, 1976), RSA (1977), IDEA (1990), Phil Zimmermann's PGP (1991), and the Advanced Encryption Standard (AES, 2000) using the Rijndael algorithm.

◆ The next technology leap was the advent of the (home) PC, with its own operating system and fast processor board, with ever higher-capacity hard disks, floppy disk drives and, later, ZIP, CD, and DVD drives for data exchange. The data media were already mobile, and with miniaturization, mobile laptops and palmtops became possible also. As PCs became steadily less expensive and more powerful, integration of audio and video became possible. Today, a significant proportion of the population in the industrial nations possesses their own multimedia PC, often with numerous peripheral devices (scanner, printer, and so on). Companies, like private individuals, equipped their PCs with modems to provide access to mailboxes and later to online services over the telephone network. The only security issue that received much attention related to PCs was computer viruses. This preoccupation with viruses allowed other data abuses, such as information theft, to flourish behind the scenes for a long time.

◆ Today, communications and information technology have merged. On one hand, the bandwidth of the cable-linked networks is expanding; on the other hand, high-bandwidth wireless radio links are being created (terrestrial and satellite-based networks). Stationary and mobile networking with high data rates will soon be possible from anywhere in the world.

The Internet Revolution

In just a few years, the Internet has established itself as a universal, bidirectional, and global communications medium. The "network of networks" is free of the physical and temporal restrictions that curb the flow of information using the classical print, radio, and television media.

The drive towards greater and greater use of the Internet has undoubtedly been spurred by the technological hegemony of the U.S., and no doubt this will continue to be the case.

Characteristics of the Internet as the Global Data Network

The TCP/IP protocol that the Internet is based on is arguably not the best choice for protocols, yet the Internet managed to supplant virtually all other public networks in a decade. Several characteristics of the Internet contribute to its domination:

◆ **Simple and inexpensive access.** From the notebook through PCs and workstations to mainframes, any computer can be connected simply and inexpensively.

◆ **Uniform standard.** No country-specific peculiarities exist because TCP/IP technology is network-independent and available for every operating system.

- **Global network, shared infrastructure.** Hundreds of thousands of networks link up over 100 million connected computer systems in more than 240 countries. In virtually any country in the world, you can dial in to any suitably connected remote access gateway over the telephone network via AOL or CompuServe or connect directly to the Internet via an Internet provider such as UUNet or AT&T Worldnet.
- **Increasing acceptance.** As of February 2002, the current estimates from Nielson/Net Ratings put the active Internet user population at over 80 million people. These active users are on the Internet an average of 3 hours 44 minutes per week. In contrast, Global Reach put the current English-speaking Internet user count at 220 million. Regardless which figure is correct, a common usage of the Internet is clear.
- **Extranet, intranet, Web Services.** Enterprise-wide intranets are accessible to company staff via technology such as VPNs. Extranets are used to share selected internal information with specific partners via the Internet. A major push is now underway to consolidate many services – Internet, intranet, or extranet – through a new infrastructure called Web Services that is being pushed by Microsoft and many other significant companies. If Web Services takes off, you'll see an even tighter integration of services from different companies in a fashion much more transparent to the users of those services.
- **Beneficial to international business relations.** Sales employees of an enterprise can access the computer systems at Head Office over the Internet from any country around the world. The advantages are obvious: prices, delivery times, and new information can be retrieved rapidly, and orders can be entered and processed immediately. There is no need to switch media, and the information only has to be entered once. This enables efficient and rational processing of ever more complex tasks.

Electronic Services

The Internet offers a multitude of electronic services that are indispensable to everyday dealings involving computer systems:

- **Electronic mail (e-mail).** The possibilities of this type of communication are virtually without bounds: it is possible to send electronic mail in a simple manner from a PC to any Internet subscriber in the world. Messages are received almost at once (without any delay from the postal service) on computer systems and can be further processed without having to switch to a different medium. The text message contained in an *electronic letter* can be expanded by appending attachments (files) in any file format.

  E-mail is the application used most frequently on the Internet and is even more popular than surfing in the multimedia World Wide Web.

- **Multimedia.** The possibilities for commercial exploitation are endless. The graphical user interface is extremely user-friendly.

  The Web offers companies an inexpensive showcase for their products and services. Customers can easily enter their requirements.

  For official bodies, there is no easier, cheaper, or more comprehensive means of fulfilling their duty to provide information.

- **File transfers (FTP).** Information of any kind can be copied easily to one's own computer system. Here it can be processed further without having to change media.

  Software houses can make new releases of their products available quickly and without complication, at considerable savings.

- **Worldwide forums (news, chat).** You can find offline forums on thousands of subject areas, covering virtually every conceivable topic. For example, software developers who work with particular tools can exchange notes and help each other resolve problems.

  In online forums (chat rooms), you can meet like-minded individuals for a discussion.

- **Online connection to computer systems (Telnet/remote login).** From your computer system, you can access any other computer system in the world as if it were your own. This means, for example, that software houses can perform maintenance work remotely or that a high-performance computer can be used from a remote location.
- **Peer-to-Peer service sharing.** Napster created a sensation with its revolutionary approach to information sharing on the Internet. Although Napster appears to have come to an end, the technique pioneered by Napster is here to stay, with numerous replacement services using and expanding on the peer-to-peer sharing protocols.
- **Transparent service usage.** In its early stages, Web Services holds much promise to further simplify and integrate the resources available on the Internet in a manner that should deliver increased availability, flexibility, and ease of access. It should be noted that, by definition, increased access means reduced security. Balancing the benefits of increased accessibility with the threats of their misuse promises to bring new challenges to the security profession.

The Internet as a World-Wide Source of Information

In today's information society it is important, and in many areas even crucial, to have the right information at the right time, as in the following examples:

- Organizations need information about products and services quickly so that they can complete their tasks within the period stipulated.
- Banks need to detect and interpret stock market movements rapidly so that they can take appropriate action.
- Journalists often require up-to-date background information about the day's events.
- Developers need specific information from software houses to progress their development work smoothly – for example, to update software that contains errors.
- Customers can receive information about product ranges, demand, and prices through online services, giving them a worldwide-market view of all products.

Dangers from the Internet

Communication over the Internet offers advantages that no organization can afford to lose if it is to keep up with the times and take advantage of future developments. However, a heavy price is often paid for the undisputed advantages of the Internet, because connection to a public network is not a one-way street. It opens up a channel by which intruders can invade a company.

Figure 1-1 illustrates a direct connection to an insecure network such as the Internet. Any of the workstations on the Internet (the insecure network) can access the workstation on the private network (the protected network). The private workstation can also access any of the workstations on the Internet. Any of the workstations in this illustration can be used to attack any other workstation. The standard Internet applications do not incorporate any security mechanisms, making the transmission of sensitive data by e-mail, for example, extremely risky.

Every single computer system in the network must be protected against attacks from the Internet. In small organizations, the number of affected computer systems may be small (perhaps no more than ten), but in large organizations with a large number of computer systems, over 10,000 such systems could be affected.

What forms do the dangers from the Internet take? Which networked computer systems or computer systems connected to the Internet are at risk?

- High-tech spies can steal the knowledge or strategic plans of third parties and make a profit by selling them to the competition.
- Hackers can break into companies' local networks or official bodies and falsify data or plant incorrect information.
- Crackers can paralyze organizations' computer systems, costing them millions.

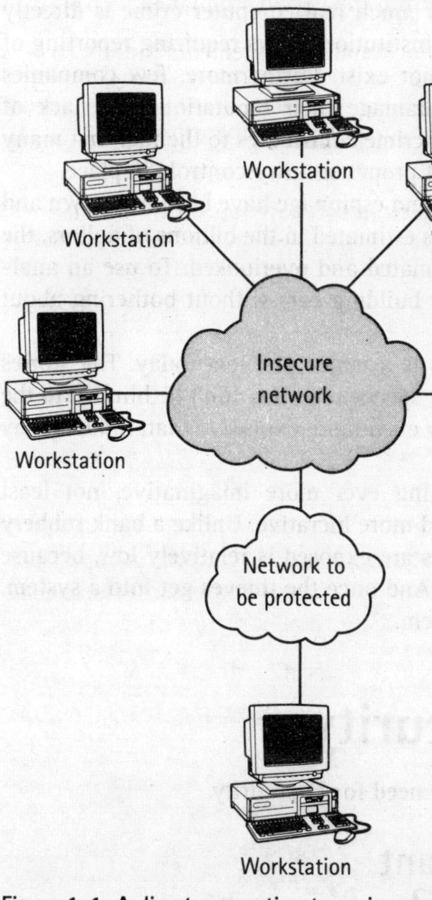

Figure 1-1: A direct connection to an insecure network

The risk of an attack is very high, because there is no hierarchy on the Internet and no Internet police. Anyone can romp around on the *data highway*, data surfing to his heart's content.

Most Internet users today are not security savvy. If Internet services are to be used professionally, then they must be made secure and controllable so that their benefits can be calculated.

General Threats from the Internet

The term *hacker* once referred to someone who was extremely talented with computers. The media has long since changed public perception to associate the term hacker with computer criminals. Whether you call them hackers, crackers, or thieves, the reality is the same. Their sophistication and skill levels have increased far more quickly than the means to curtail them.

It is difficult to pin down precisely how much real computer crime is directly related to the Internet. Outside of financial institutions, laws requiring reporting of computer crime to federal authorities do not exist. Furthermore, few companies report hacking incidents because it may damage their reputation. This lack of understanding the true amount of computer crime contributes to the fact that many organizations think they can get by without proper security controls in place.

Although many cases of computer crime and espionage have become known and the damage caused by electronic break-ins is estimated in the billions of dollars, the subject of security has long been underestimated and overlooked. To use an analogy, it is as if the automobile industry was building cars without bothering about seat belts, crunch zones, or air bags.

The misuse of communication networks is a major problem today. The stories that make it to the press may be particularly spectacular, but don't be blinded to the fact that the question of security is probably even more explosive than indicated by the break-ins and abuse that are reported.

Hackers and their methods are becoming ever more imaginative, not least because their crimes are becoming more and more lucrative. Unlike a bank robbery in the real world, the risk to which crackers are exposed is relatively low, because their crimes are very difficult to prosecute. And once the thieves get into a system, it is virtually impossible to keep track of them.

The Need for IT Security

Several points can be made to establish the need for IT security.

Why is Security So Important in Information Technology?

Today's modern workstation has the same capability that an entire classical computer center had only a few years ago. In those computer centers, organizational and personnel-related security measures were sufficient. They included the following:

- Access control to buildings and rooms in computer centers
- Controlled and defined work flows and corresponding job processing
- Separation between personnel in specialist departments (users) and IT staff (programmers, operators, and so on)

Data processing was partitioned off in a separate building so that external threats were obvious and the host's operating system was responsible for protecting resources from unauthorized access.

Modern information technology concepts, such as client/server technology, outsourcing, Internet, intranet, and the like, in which information is exchanged over a network that can be attacked, mean that the hardware and software in these networks are particularly vulnerable. The extent of their vulnerability is not always readily apparent. Outsourcing and cooperation between suppliers in particular can lead to not-so-obvious vulnerability paths. For example, many organizations provide extranets and limited VPN access to partners for purposes of exchanging information. The access granted to the partner results in additional vulnerability. If an attacker penetrates security at the partner's location, they can use the partner's connection to access your organization's systems through the trusted access of the VPN or extranet. This vulnerability does not stop at the direct partner, however. Just as you could be compromised through one of your partners, your partners could also be compromised through one of theirs. This compromise at a tertiary partner, probably completely unknown to you, can eventually result in your compromise. Essentially, your security level is directly tied to your partner's security level, as their security level is tied to all of their partners. The U.S. trusted system classification of A through D was established because of the understanding that allowing another organization access to your computer systems means that the effective level of your security is potentially decreased by the level of security at another organization. A competent attacker can turn small compromises into steppingstones that lead from one place to another. Indeed, NASA continues to be a prime target of attackers, not for the purpose of accessing NASA information, but for using NASA's networks as a steppingstone to access military networks via private communications mechanisms.

Moreover, the IT safeguards available for workstations, especially for PCs, are significantly weaker than was the case with classic mainframes. Today, a workstation user can be simultaneously end-user, operator, or programmer – a situation that brings new problems.

Today's distributed computer systems can no longer be protected by organizational measures alone. Additional *technical security mechanisms* are necessary to enable secure and controllable processing of information. This requires strategic security concepts that establish and maintain *confidentiality*, *integrity*, and *availability* of computer systems, data, programs, and persons as essential elements of organizations. In addition, wherever necessary, the binding character and accountability of procedures and actions must be guaranteed.

What Role Does IT Security Play in the Information Society?

In recent years, the value of information – and thus the need to protect that information – has grown considerably.

The increasing value of information that is held on an organization's computer systems has become an important economic factor, if not the most important one. Information often contained in an organization's computer system includes the following:

- **Complete development and production documentation.** Many organizations possess hardware worth thousands of dollars on which information worth millions is stored.

- **Financial and operating results, and strategic plans.** If such results or plans were to be disclosed, it could, for example, cause changes in stock valuations, which could precipitate significant financial loss.
- **Logistics information.** If computer systems or data were to become unavailable, no one would know how much inventory is in the warehouse, what needs to be produced, which customers have ordered what products, and which goods are to be delivered to whom.
- **Customer data.** Customer information, such as credit card numbers, personal information, and buying habits, is particularly valuable and in need of protection.

Modern computer systems enable people to work efficiently and tasks to be performed in a logical manner, and in many areas the tasks cannot be performed effectively by any other means. Society has become so dependent on computer systems that its economic capability is endangered if the functional capability of computer systems cannot be appropriately guaranteed.

Global Expansion and Changing Business Processes

In the past, most business transactions occurred on paper (for example, price quotes, order forms, and customer receipts) or in person (for example, in visits to customers). These processes can be designed far more efficiently if human and material resources are replaced by electronic procedures. All the business processes in the preceding list can be carried out and electronically transmitted by computer systems, relieving the need to switch media.

Companies today are in a Catch 22. No company can manage without adapting electronic business processes or networking computer systems, but doing so makes their computer systems all the more attractive to potential attackers. Company data and relationships with business partners must be protected against theft and willful destruction.

Department stores regularly employ security guards, detectives, and use video cameras. However, only recently have organizations begun to appreciate that data should also be protected against unauthorized access, because it represents considerable value and often constitutes the bulk of an organization's assets.

Information technology has created the wherewithal to conduct industrial espionage conveniently with computer systems. This new form of espionage does not require any walls to be torn down or safes to be cracked, and the perpetrators can happily perform their deeds from their living rooms. The tools and directions for such activities are available on the software market or can even be downloaded free of charge from the Internet.

Experts estimate that the economic damage resulting from computer crime already amounts to billions of dollars and is on the rise.

Industrial and Economic Espionage

IT criminality is growing as methods of communication become more varied; industrial espionage is a major problem in the business world today. The potential benefits of espionage are obvious. If it costs 10 million dollars to develop a new technology but the technology can be stolen for 100,000 dollars, those without ethics see an easy choice. The proliferation of the Internet makes theft of information more accessible and viable as an option.

Economic Liability

Given the increased interdependence of organizations on the proper functioning and security of other organizations on the Internet, a new development is starting to emerge on the Internet: security liability. Multiple cases of lawsuits alleging liability for damages resulting from inadequate security controls are in place. In other words, company A sues company B because company A was damaged as a result of company B's improper security controls. The massive Distributed Denial-of-Service attacks against eBay, Yahoo, and others in February 2000 illustrate the issue well. The DDOS zombies installed at other companies on the Internet were used to impair the functioning of Yahoo, eBay, and others. Had the source companies properly configured their systems and security, the attack would not have been possible. With the increase of worms and other Internet-wide attacks due to inadequate security, it seems only a matter of time before security liability lawsuits are commonplace.

IT Security in Context

Security is concerned with the protection of assets against attack, where the objective of the attacker is to use these assets for his own purposes or to harm the owner of the assets (Comm, 98). Figure 1-2 demonstrates the complexities of IT security.

The owner of an asset is responsible for protecting it. Attackers (or *threat agents*) seek to use these assets to their own advantages and work to the detriment of the owner of the assets. For the owner of the assets, a successful attack means a reduction in the value of his assets.

Attacks on IT assets generally (but not necessarily) involve one or more of the following:

- **Loss of confidentiality.** The attacker gains unauthorized possession of assets (information).
- **Loss of integrity.** The attacker is able to manipulate assets (information) without authorization.
- **Loss of availability.** The attacker prevents the owner from enjoying the access to his assets (information, resources, and services) to which he is entitled.

- **Loss of binding character.** The binding character of the transaction can be repudiated (that is a person is able to deny having sent or received assets or information).
- **Loss of authenticity.** The communication partner is not who he purports to be; there is no certainty as to the origin of the information (data).

In protecting an organization's assets, it's all too easy to impair the organization's own use of those assets. Striking a balance between adequate protection and adequate use of assets is the main challenge for information security.

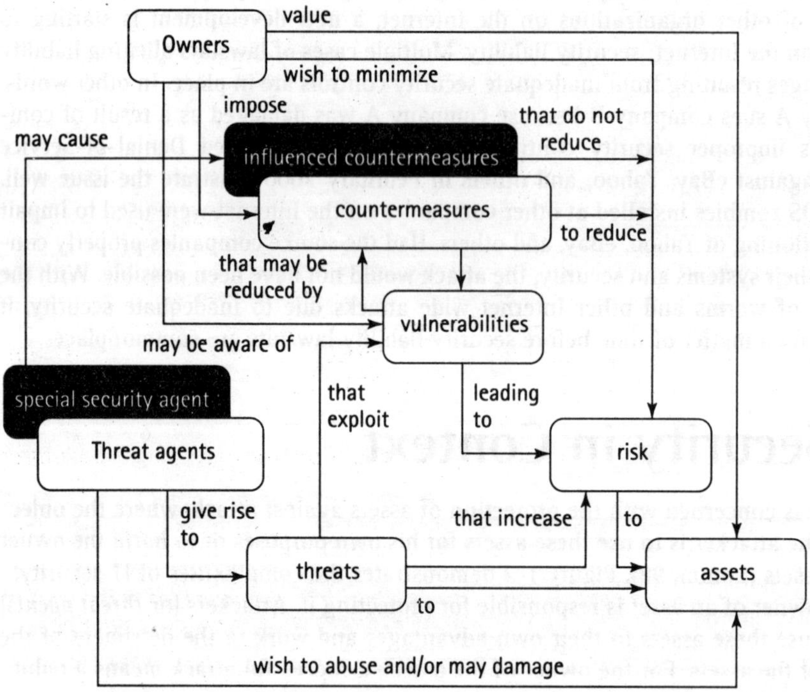

Figure 1-2: IT security complexities

Opportunities and Risk

The owner of the assets must perform an analysis to identify which types of attack are relevant to his system and which types he can ignore. This analysis of attack types will help him select appropriate countermeasures that will reduce his risk of vulnerability to an acceptable level. Countermeasures are, by definition, anything that reduces some sort of risk. Examples of countermeasures include firewalls, intrusion detection, door locks, and video cameras.

The countermeasures implemented reduce the vulnerability and must be compatible with the asset owner's security policy.

Even after the countermeasures have been implemented, a residual vulnerability remains that can be further reduced with yet more measures (Zurf, 99). Each additional countermeasure reduces risk to a lesser degree than the previous countermeasure. Each additional countermeasure further reduces the efficiency and availability to the legitimate users of a system.

Figure 1-3 shows how business success is maximized when a policy of *best practice* is pursued.

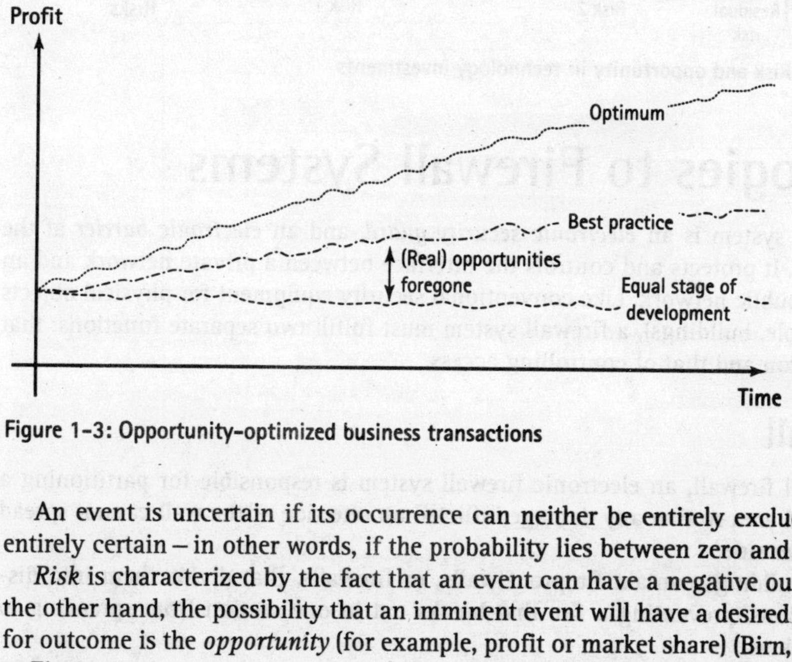

Figure 1-3: Opportunity-optimized business transactions

An event is uncertain if its occurrence can neither be entirely excluded nor is entirely certain – in other words, if the probability lies between zero and one. *Risk* is characterized by the fact that an event can have a negative outcome. On the other hand, the possibility that an imminent event will have a desired or hoped-for outcome is the *opportunity* (for example, profit or market share) (Birn, 96). Refer to Figure 1-4.

Companies and organizations should use the opportunities that information technology offers (for example, by making full use of the Internet). At the same time, they must make the appropriate investment in suitable countermeasures (firewall systems, VPN, intrusion detection systems, anti-virus software, and so on) to reduce the extent of vulnerability. With adequate security measures in place, you can conduct your business in a responsible fashion and enhance your capability, profit, and market share so that the business and the economy as a whole may thrive.

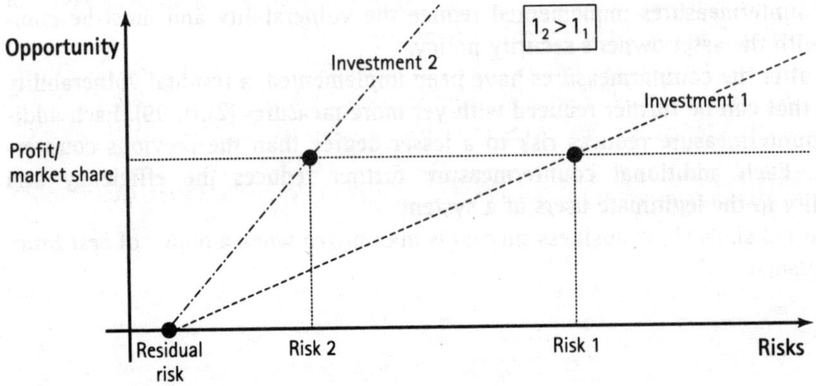

Figure 1-4: Risk and opportunity in technology investments

Analogies to Firewall Systems

A firewall system is an *electronic security guard,* and an *electronic barrier* at the same time. It protects and controls the interface between a private network and an insecure, public network. Like conventional security equipment for physical objects (for example, buildings), a firewall system must fulfill two separate functions: that of protection and that of controlling access.

Firewall

Like a real firewall, an electronic firewall system is responsible for partitioning a designated area so that any damage inflicted on one side of the wall cannot spread to the other side.

Most buildings contain fireproof walls, or firewalls, that divide them into discrete sections, preventing a fire that breaks out in one section from spreading to other sections.

In communication networks, the firewall system isolates the network to protect it from threats from the insecure network. Only a single, especially secure interface (similar to a door guarded by a security guard) is implemented between the two subnets.

Security Guard

Like a building security guard, a firewall system has the task of controlling access to an organization so that any person who desires entry must identify and authenticate himself. Persons identified as members of staff are allowed in after having their IDs checked. Visitors are registered as visitors, and a link is established between visitors and the persons in the organization with whom they are visiting. A check is performed as to which objects staff and visitors are allowed to take into the building and, above all, what they are allowed to carry out.

Finally, a log is maintained of all the events occurring at the building entrance – for example, the time each visitor arrived and left and the name of the person he visited. Any irregularities that occur can be retrospectively uncovered using this information.

The electronic equivalent of the security guard is a firewall system that does the following:

- Checks whether someone is allowed to access the organization's protected network from the insecure network
- Monitors which protocols and services are used
- Checks the computer systems with which communications are allowed

A firewall is essentially a tool for enforcing an organization's rules on traffic to and from the Internet (or any other network). The secure operation of a firewall system entails technical, personnel-related, organizational, and infrastructural security mechanisms.

Firewall systems must be integrated to secure and control the business processes conducted over communication networks. In essence, an organization's firewall system is the implementer of its security policy.

Firewalls are Not Automatic Protection

A firewall system doesn't provide automatic protection; rather, protection is possible only if a firewall system is correctly operated.

Companies must know in advance against what or whom they are protecting their networks, what should be allowed, and what should be prohibited. In principle, a security policy must be developed and implemented before a firewall system can be used. Define in advance over which protocols and resources access to the organization's network is to be allowed, just as a security guard only allows certain types of visitors into the building. For example, the security policy may specify that visitors who arrive with their names on a preexisting list are allowed in, but visitors who walk in without an appointment are denied entry.

XREF

Refer to Chapter 10 for a more detailed discussion of the nontechnical activities required to properly implement a firewall.

Reducing access in this way increases security and simplifies control and administration of a firewall system.

The firewall will only be successful if you understand the following about your assets:

- What assets need to be protected?
- In what ways are the assets vulnerable to attack?
- How can the firewall protect those assets?
- How *can't* the firewall protect those assets?

Failure to understand these issues and implement the firewall accordingly is the primary reason firewalls fail to protect organizations.

Purpose of a Central Firewall System

A firewall system is inserted as a barrier between the network to be protected and the insecure network in such a way that all the data traffic between the two networks must pass through the firewall system. Security mechanisms that make this interface secure and controllable are implemented on the firewall system. To this end, the firewall system does the following:

- Analyzes the communication data
- Controls the communications environment and communications partners
- Regiments communication in accordance with the security policy
- Logs security-relevant events
- Alerts the security administrator to any significant breaches

A firewall system constitutes a *Common Point of Trust* for bridging different networks – that is, the only route possible between the networks runs in a controlled manner through the firewall.

Firewall systems, like the one shown in Figure 1-5, can be used to structure a company's own network and create security domains with different protection requirements within it.

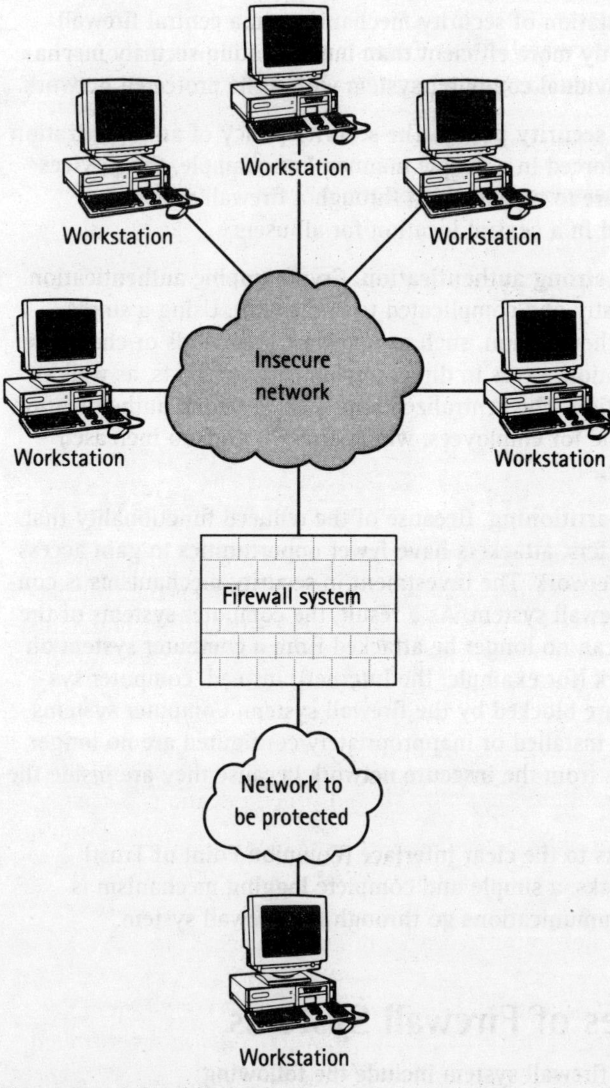

Figure 1-5: A firewall system

Advantages of the Common Point of Trust Method

Using a single point of communication between the organization's private network and the Internet, rather than several points of communication, has several benefits:

- **Cost.** The implementation of security mechanisms in a central firewall system is significantly more efficient than implementing security mechanisms on every individual computer system within the protected network.
- **Implementation of security policy.** The security policy of an organization can be centrally enforced in a simple manner. For example, the services and protocols that are to be permitted through a firewall system are defined and checked in a central location for all users.
- **Implementation of strong authentication.** Cryptographic authentication tends to be both costly and complicated to implement. Using a single point for strong authentication, such as one-time passwords or challenge-response authentication, saves in direct implementation costs, as well as reduced administration. The centralized approach to strong authentication can reduce the hassle for employees, which directly leads to increased employee utilization.
- **Security through partitioning.** Because of the reduced functionality that a firewall system offers, attackers have fewer opportunities to gain access from the insecure network. The investment in security mechanisms is concentrated on the firewall system. As a result, the computer systems of the protected network can no longer be attacked from a computer system on the insecure network (for example, the Internet); instead, computer systems from outside are blocked by the firewall system. Computer systems that are incorrectly installed or inappropriately configured are no longer targets for attackers from the insecure network because they are inside the firewall.
- **Auditability.** Thanks to the clear interface (Common Point of Trust) between two networks, a simple and complete logging mechanism is available, as all communications go through the firewall system.

General Objectives of Firewall Systems

The general objectives of a firewall system include the following:

- **Access control at the network level.** A check is performed to determine which computer systems may communicate with each other through the firewall system.
- **Access control at the user level.** The firewall system controls which users are allowed to send communications to, or receive communications from, the Internet. This entails establishing the authenticity of the user.
- **Access control at the data level.** The firewall system governs what data belonging to a defined user is allowed. This entails establishing the authenticity of the data using digital signatures.

- **Access rights management.** Access rights management entails establishing with which protocols and services and at what times communications may pass through the firewall system.
- **Control at the application level.** The firewall system filters out any commands used or data content transmitted that does not belong to the defined scope of the application.
- **Isolation of services.** Services are isolated to prevent implementation errors, weaknesses, and design errors in the services from providing opportunities for attacks.
- **Securing evidence and log analysis.** Connection data and security-relevant events are logged and can be analyzed to provide lasting evidence of user actions and enable security violations to be detected.
- **Alarm function.** Any user activity can be designated to be recorded and transmitted to the security management station for appropriate administrative response.
- **Concealment of the internal network structure.** The aim is to conceal the structure of the protected network from the insecure network. From the insecure network, it should not be possible to see whether the protected network contains 10, 100, 1,000, or 10,000 computer systems.
- **Confidentiality of communications.** Messages cannot be read in plaintext. This ensures the confidentiality of data during transmission over insecure networks.

Additional Objectives of a Firewall System

A firewall needs to be capable of more than just traffic evaluation to be fully effective today. The firewall needs to be especially resilient to direct attacks. If an attacker can take control of a firewall system or bypass its evaluations in some manner, it ceases to function as a firewall and simply becomes a router.

In addition to providing basic logging and security, alerting many organizations requires detailed usage information. Examples include tracking what users and IPs connect to what services and performance of the firewall system. The detailed usage information can be used for security purposes as well as other organizational needs.

The explosive growth of the Internet rapidly resulted in a shortage of IP addresses. To allow for continued expansion of the Internet, the interim solution, Network Address Translation (NAT), was invented. NAT allows a company to use a huge range of reserved IP addresses internally while communicating with the Internet at large through a smaller range of public IP addresses. A typical company might use only 16 addresses for dozens of computers. Although initially designed for address conservation, NAT was found to be a security boon almost immediately. Because the internal addresses can't be addressed directly from the Internet, remote attackers are forced to go through the firewall to communicate with internal computers.

For many companies, performance of critical servers is more important than security in several respects. If an organization's Web servers deliver three million dollars in revenue daily, a security incident has to exceed three million dollars in damages to warrant disconnection from the Internet for a day. Poor performance because of firewall systems can directly translate to lost sales and opportunities. The value of the lost sales and opportunities can easily exceed the cost of prevented security incidents. Bear in mind that one of the key purposes for firewalls is to prevent disruption to the business.

Some firewalls require significant changes to an organization's infrastructure to be implemented. While an occasional restructuring might be acceptable, in most cases it will not be. The firewall needs to posses the ability to adapt and grow with the needs of the environment to derive full benefit and cost savings from it. Examples of flexibility in firewalls include the ability to upgrade hardware and be extended with support for new application protocols.

Summary

The international economic expansion of many organizations – manifested, for example, by the fusion of Daimler-Benz and Chrysler, or by the biggest merger of all time between AOL and Time Warner in 2000 – depends on networked IT structures and a communications platform such as the Internet. The Internet penetrates many public and private aspects of daily life and is opening up new legal, social, and ethical problems that need to be addressed. Political and legal instruments to counter technology abuse effectively are not yet available, so the implementation of firewalls becomes all the more critical.

The actual implementation details of firewalls vary greatly with specific firewalls and organizational needs. However, the core objectives apply to the vast majority of firewalls. Surprisingly, some firewall products fail to meet core needs. Outside of very specialized circumstances, these products should be passed over. Knowing the core objectives of firewalls is critical to understanding what a firewall can and can't do for an organization.

Chapter 2

TCP/IP Technology for the Internet and Intranet

THE INTERNET ENCOMPASSES a unique, worldwide infrastructure of networked networks and the software technologies on which those networks are based. Transmission Control Protocol/Internet Protocol (TCP/IP) technology is the real heart of the Internet. Its widespread use has made networking global computer systems down to the smallest PC in the remotest area possible.

NOTE: TCP/IP technology is not fixed, but consists of various services and applications that have been continuously developed over the years. The TCP and IP protocols are, strictly speaking, only two components of the complete communications architecture, but in everyday usage, they are understood to refer to the whole protocol suite.

Advantages of TCP/IP Technology

TCP/IP technology offers a number of critical advantages:

- Every user can access all the information he is authorized to access within the entire network. In addition, any connected user can communicate with any other connected computer system. Applications have already been developed that enable worldwide telephoning or videoconferencing from one computer system to the next. In this way, the exchange of information between users is assured.
- Because TCP/IP protocols were designed to be independent of the network technology used, the Internet offers the possibility of connecting new technological developments with existing structures. Ongoing development of technology in the fields of computing and communications enables proven technology to be transferred to new developments, while at the same time remaining able to communicate with older systems.

- Because Internet technology today is extensive, a wide range of compatible network components is available. Because most software variants can also be replaced by implementations from other vendors, there is little dependence on a particular manufacturer. The extensive distribution of software within the Internet also makes products increasingly inexpensive.
- The individual protocol specifications are standardized and accessible to all at no cost. This means that implementations for new or special systems can be developed or modified easily at any time.

The OSI Reference Model

The Open System Interconnection (OSI) Reference Model has a clear architecture and is well suited for the representation of a communications architecture and the principles of the layer model. To specify a uniform structure for present and future developments of network technologies, the *OSI Reference Model* (refer to Figure 2-1) was adopted as a standard in 1983 by the International Organization for Standardization. This model assumes that a communications protocol consists of several modules, each of which has different tasks to perform during a communications operation.

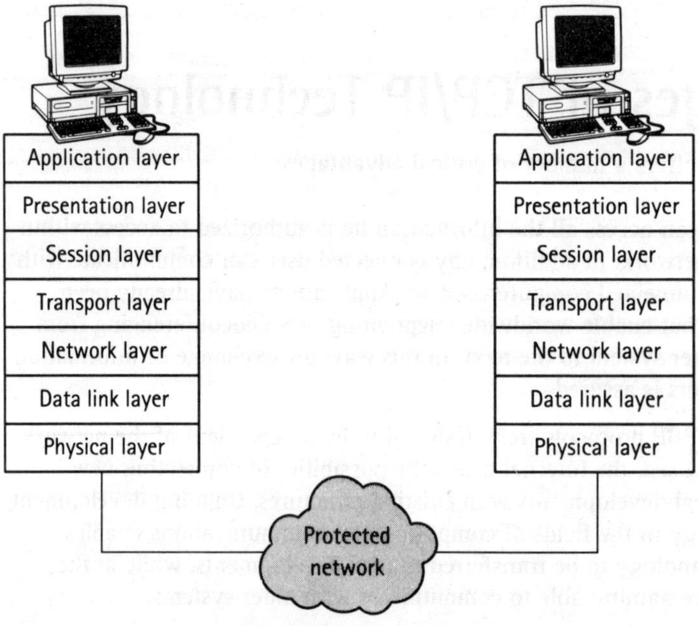

Figure 2-1: The OSI Reference Model

According to the OSI Reference Model, when a connection exists between two computer systems, their corresponding layers can communicate with one another. For example, between computer systems A and B, each layer of computer system A can communicate with the same layer of computer system B. To this end, certain bit patterns are placed in a header in front of the data in each layer or added to a trailer at the end. These bit patterns contain *protocol information* that imparts the following:

- Who sent the data?
- For whom is the data intended?
- Which path should the data take during transmission?
- How might the data be further processed?
- How should the receiver handle the data?

Each additional layer takes the data packets of the layer immediately above it and may add its own protocol information in another header or trailer if necessary for the flow of communication. At the receiver's end, the protocol data is evaluated only in the equivalent layer – that is, the data in a higher layer is not interpreted or evaluated by a lower layer. Figure 2-2 depicts communication between two computers.

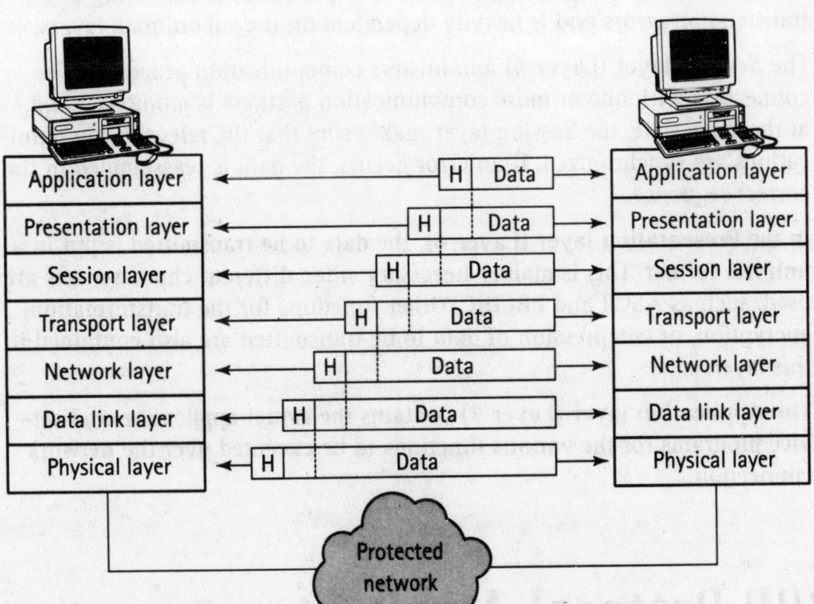

Figure 2-2: Communication between two computers

The OSI Reference Model comprises seven major layers:

- **The Physical layer (Layer 1)** specifies how the data should be physically transmitted. The parameters of this first layer include information about the transmission media used (for example, copper cable, fiberglass, infrared, or radio transmission) and the specifications of interfaces with voltage levels, connecting sockets, and data transmission rates.
- **The Data Link layer (Layer 2)** secures transmission between two adjacent stations (for example, routers) within a network. For this purpose, the bits to be transmitted are collected together in frames and provided with a checksum. If, after comparing the checksum, the receiver finds that a frame was only partially transmitted or was destroyed, the receiver requests that the sender resend the corresponding frame.
- **The Network layer (Layer 3)** determines the transmission routes for the data between two computer systems. For this purpose, information like transmission time, loading of the transmission route, and so on is used to establish a connection according to a set of predefined rules, called the *routing protocol.* The data transported within this layer is transmitted in data blocks referred to as *packets.*
- **The Transport layer (Layer 4)** provides a kind of virtual connection between the two computer systems. It is responsible for correcting any transmission errors and is heavily dependent on the subordinate layers.
- **The Session layer (Layer 5)** administers communication processes. The connection with one or more communication partners is monitored and, at the same time, the Session layer makes sure that the relevant communications are synchronized. If an error occurs, the data is reassembled in the correct sequence.
- In the **Presentation layer (Layer 6)**, the data to be transmitted is put in a uniform format. This is mainly necessary when different character sets are used, such as ASCII and EBCDIC. Other functions for the transformation, encryption, or compression of data to be transmitted are also contained in this layer.
- **The Application layer (Layer 7)** contains the actual application and service programs for the various functions to be executed over the network connection.

TCP/IP Protocol Architecture

Although there is no generally agreed-upon special TCP/IP layer model, one can say that it is constructed out of fewer layers than the OSI Reference Model (refer to Figure 2-3). The next few sections therefore refer to a four-layer model.

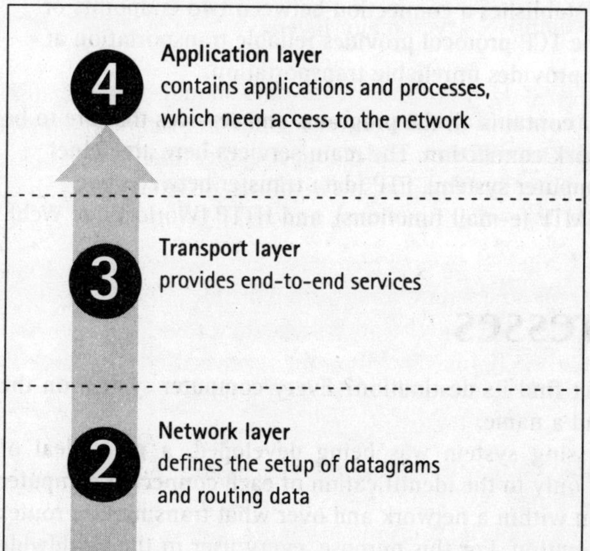

Figure 2-3: Layers in the TCP/IP protocol architecture

This model, like the OSI Reference Model, embodies various communication layers that pass data from a higher layer to the next lower layer. Each communication layer adds its own control information to the data until it is sent over the network. The receiver then passes this data upward layer-by-layer, each layer evaluating only the data that is relevant to the layer and extracting the data from the packet before passing the packet on to the next higher layer.

- The *Network Access layer* enables a computer system to transmit data to another computer system within the directly connected network (for example, an Ethernet). This requires detailed knowledge of the underlying network structure. The Network Access layer covers the two bottom layers of the OSI model and contains the encapsulation of IP packets in network frames and the assignment of IP addresses to physical network addresses, such as MAC addresses.
- The *Network layer* defines the structure of IP packets and determines the route by which the data is transmitted through the network (routing).

- The *Transport layer* establishes a connection between two endpoints or computer systems. The TCP protocol provides reliable transportation at this layer, while UDP provides unreliable transportation.
- The *Application layer* contains all the programs and services that are to be passed over the network connection. The main services here are Telnet (logon to another computer system), FTP (data transfer between two computer systems), SMTP (e-mail functions), and HTTP (World Wide Web).

Internet Addresses

How does data in the Internet find its destination? Every computer system on the Internet has an IP address and a name.

When the Internet addressing system was being developed, a great deal of importance was attached not only to the identification of each connected computer system but also to its location within a network and over what transmission routes the data could reach its destination. For this purpose, every user in the worldwide network is given a unique 32-bit (4-byte) Internet address (IPv4 address logic) consisting of a network identifier and a computer system identifier, which are represented as four decimal numbers separated by a period. For example, 11000011.10010011.00111000.11101101 corresponds to 195.147.56.237.

This address logic is divided into five classes (class A through E), which are distinguished by the first bits of the IP address. Each class has a different length of network identifier and computer system identifier (see Figure 2-4). The left octets determine how many network ranges are available. The right octets are the host identifiers. Class D address ranges are used for multi-cast addresses. Multi-cast addresses (Class D) can be used by many hosts at once. Class A, B, and C addresses must be unique. Class E addresses are reserved for experimental purposes and are not routed on the Internet at large.

Many users who have an Internet connection through a provider are only occasionally connected to the Internet. It is not necessary to assign a permanent IP address for these computer systems. In this case, automatic assignment of IP addresses is used. If a customer wishes to access the Internet, he initially dials a dial-in host of a provider in his neighborhood. The service provider's computer system has a number of IP addresses reserved for this purpose, which are automatically assigned to the relevant caller and are only valid for the current session. This procedure is known as *dynamic IP addressing.*

Given the continued growth of Internet use, endeavors have been under way since 1995 to extend the address length to 128 bits or 16 bytes (IPv6 or IPnG, next generation). Old IP addresses will continue to be valid and usable even after the new standard is adopted. It must be assumed that the transition from IPv4 to IPv6 will require some time to complete, with both systems continuing in parallel for that period.

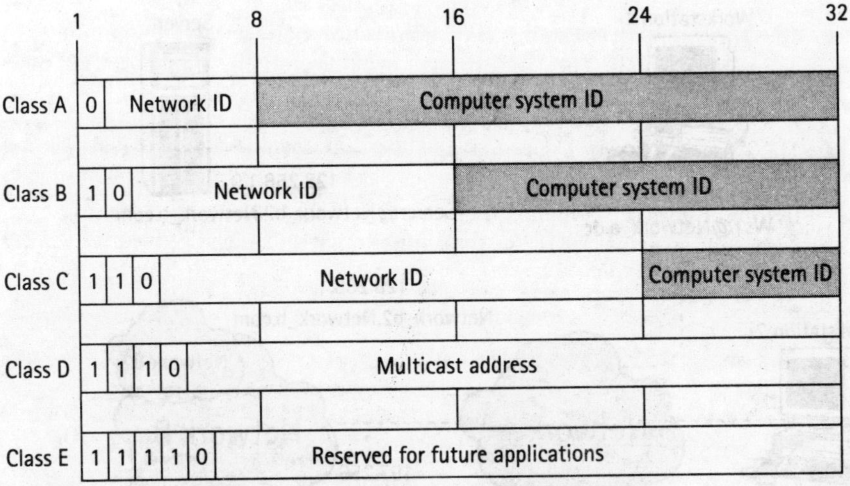

Figure 2-4: Structure of Internet addresses and division into classes

Today, companies generally use only a few official IP addresses, working instead with concealed, internally reserved IP addresses and considerably reducing the address problem.

XREF For more information on internally reserved IP addresses, refer to the discussion of NAT in Chapter 11.

The IP address logic is eminently suitable for technical systems. However, experience has shown that this procedure is too complicated and non-transparent for many users. Anyone who has surfed the World Wide Web has noticed that certain computer systems are invoked not by their IP address but by one or more symbolic names. Figure 2-5 illustrates the correlation between IP addresses and domain names.

Every network connected to the Internet can be given a domain name in addition to an IP address area. Within this domain, the network operator can create further subdomains for subordinate networks, in order to structure his network. Domain names are granted and administered centrally by the Network Information Center (NIC) and its subsidiary organizations. If an organization wishes to be assigned its own domain name, it or its provider must apply to the responsible subsidiary organization of the NIC. The top-level domains have a permanent assignment granted by the NIC and are divided into different user profiles or local groups, as listed in Table 2-1.

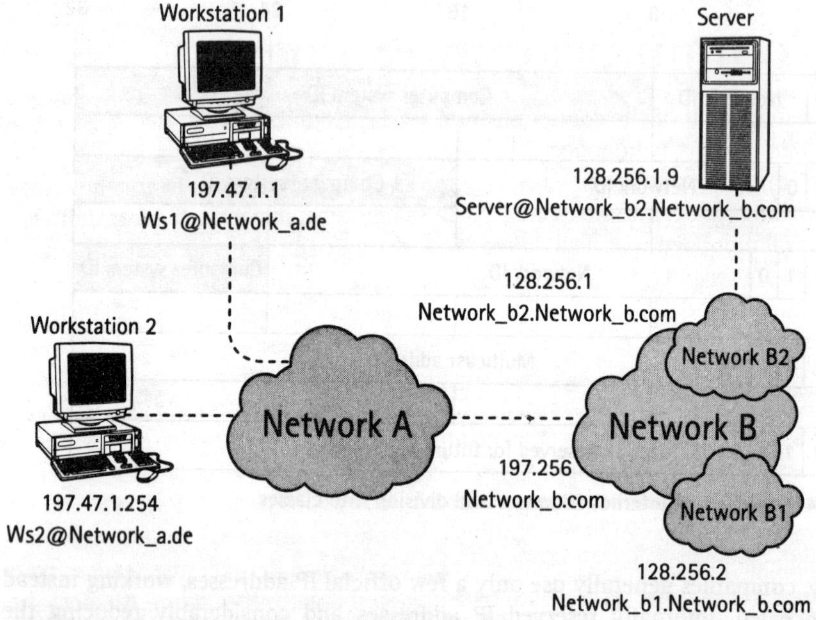

Figure 2-5: IP and domain name addressing

TABLE 2-1 INTERNET TOP LEVEL DOMAINS

Domain Extension	Acceptable Usage
.arpa	For specific establishments
.com	For commercial organizations from industry and trade
.edu	For universities and schools
.gov	For government departments and state establishments
.mil	For military establishments of the U.S. armed forces
.org	For noncommercial establishments
.de	For establishments in Germany
.uk	For establishments in the United Kingdom
.name	For personal name domains
.biz	For business domains (to extend the range beyond just .com)
.info	For general informational domains

The Communication Protocols

The following account of the communication protocols and services used most frequently on the Internet is intended to serve as a guide to what information may be transmitted in each protocol. This information is extremely important for the data transport within and between networks. At the same time, however, the transmitted data can be manipulated and, if handled incorrectly, it can generate vast amounts of damage at the receiver's end.

In principle, two different types of communication protocols can be distinguished. *Connectionless* protocols can be compared to telegrams. The sender sends the data to the network, but during transmission it can be lost, duplicated, or delayed without the sender's knowledge. This kind of information unit is also referred to as a *datagram*. This type of communication can be compared to traditional parcel service. Once the parcel is given up at the post office, the way it gets transported to its destination is outside of the sender's control.

By contrast, *connection-oriented* protocols establish communication following a particular schema. First, a virtual connection is established between the sender and the receiver. After the mutual exchange of predetermined information, the actual data transfer occurs. Only when both sides have confirmed that they have received the data in the proper fashion is the connection terminated. This case is rather like a telephone connection: one person establishes the connection, and when the other person picks up the handset, the conversation can begin.

Internet Protocol

Internet protocol (IP) is a connectionless protocol used in the Network layer. An IP header consists of several fields that have the following significance or functions:

- **Version.** Version number of the IP protocol used to create the IP packet (datagram).
- **Header length.** This field determines the length of the IP header in 32-bit units.
- **Type of service.** This field can be used to specify the importance of an IP packet and determine how or by what route this IP should be transmitted – for example, with little delay, with high data throughput, or over a secure route.
- **Total length.** The length of the entire IP packet in bytes.
- **Identifier.** During transmission, an IP packet can be split into several fragments. Each IP packet is given an identifier. Using this identifier and the source address, the fragmented IP packet is reassembled at the destination computer system.

- **Flags.** Single bits represent the flags. The first bit specifies whether an IP packet may be fragmented during transmission. The second bit is important for the reassembly of a fragmented message. It determines exactly where in the original message the data contained comes from.
- **Fragment offset.** If a message is split into several fragments, the fragments are numbered in sequence and sent. Because the individual IP packets can take different routes within the network, they do not always arrive at the destination computer system in the correct order. The various parts of a message can only be reassembled into a complete message when all parts of the message have been received.
- **Time to live (TTL).** It is not absolutely essential that the destination computer system be accessible at the moment an IP packet is sent to the network from the source computer system. In such a case, the IP packet would circulate around the network until the destination computer system was ready to receive the IP packet. To prevent this from happening, the source computer system defines a *time to live* in seconds for each IP packet. Every time the IP packet is forwarded from an intermediate station (for example, a router or a network node), the value of this field is reduced. When the field reaches the value 0, the IP packet is discarded.
- **Protocol.** This field designates the other protocols that are incorporated in the IP packet (TCP, UDP, ICMP, and so on).
- **Header checksum.** To ensure the integrity of a header, a checksum is calculated from the other fields and stored in this field by the source computer system. When the IP packet is forwarded or arrives at the destination computer system, the checksum is recalculated and compared with the original value.
- **Source address.** This field contains the IP address of the source computer system (sender).
- **Destination address.** This field contains the IP address of the destination computer system (receiver).
- **IP options.** This field is used mainly for testing networks and troubleshooting. You can specify particular options in this field. For example, this field can contain restrictions or information on the forwarding of the data. In this way, information on source routing is added so that each intermediate station of a connection is specified in detail prior to transmission.

Figure 2-6 shows the header of an IP data packet.

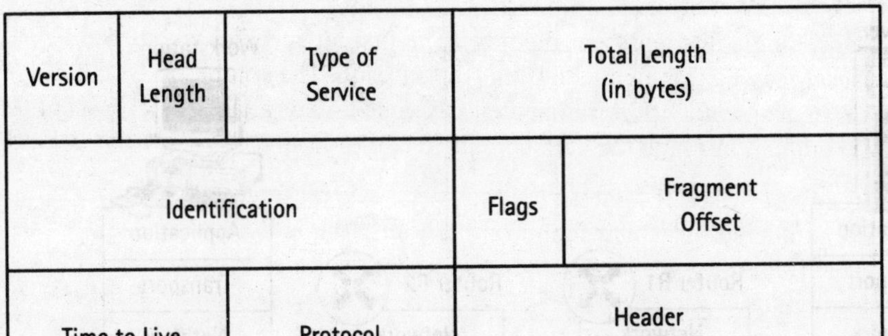

Figure 2-6: Header of an IP data packet

Routing Protocols

In a complex network such as the Internet, there are many different ways of getting data from a source to its destination. The process by which the transmission paths within networks are specified is known as *routing* (refer to Figure 2-7).

Special computer systems, known as *routers* or *gateways*, are used at the junction of two or more networks. The routers determine which route the data should take according to predefined rules. Each router uses its own routing tables to determine the routes. Routing tables contain details of all of the computer systems directly connected to the network and the gateways to adjacent networks. These tables can change at any time depending on certain factors, such as network loading or the availability of particular computer systems or networks. This procedure is known as *dynamic routing.*

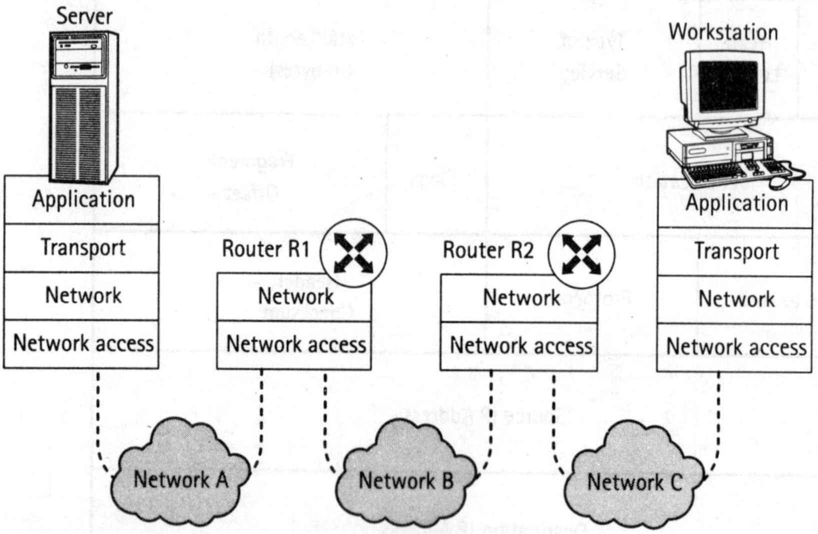

Figure 2-7: Routing over different networks

Routing protocols such as Routing Information Protocol (RIP) or Open Shortest Path First (OSPF) serve as a means of communicating changes in the routes to the systems concerned. An attacker could generate false RIP information and insert undesirable routes or intermediate stations. One of these intermediate stations could then allow him to intercept information or tamper with it.

Static routing, on the other hand, has proved significantly more secure. With this method, the individual routers are not allowed to decide which path the data should take. The transmission path is specified in detail in advance and inserted in the data packets. Static routing over the Internet is not possible due to its dynamic nature. However, in a protected intranet it can ensure a higher level of security.

Compared with computer systems in which the data flows through all the protocol layers, systems that contain routers only forward data up to the Network layer. The routers use of only the bottom three layers results in much better performance in getting the packets to their intended destination.

Internet Control Message Protocol

A connectionless protocol has no means of informing the sender if the data packet has exceeded its defined life (time to live), if the receiver cannot be contacted, or if the data has gotten lost or been destroyed en route. Yet a way to exchange this kind of information between computer systems is needed. For this reason, the Internet Control Message Protocol (ICMP) was integrated into the IP protocol. The ICMP is a critical element of the Internet protocol suite and cannot be omitted in any Internet application. Figure 2-8 shows the header of an ICMP data packet.

Normally, routers and computer systems evaluate these messages automatically and arrange certain actions or reconfigurations. By sending false ICMP information, an attacker can influence the system and/or generate reactions that enable him to impair its functional capability or break into the system later.

> **XREF** Refer to Chapter 3 for more information about methods of attack based on the TCP/IP protocols.

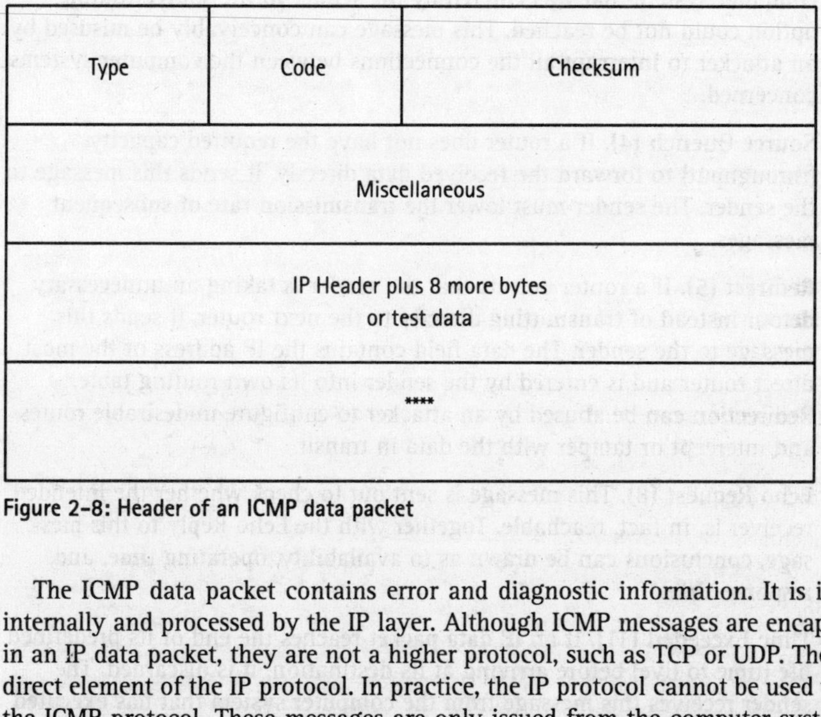

Figure 2-8: Header of an ICMP data packet

The ICMP data packet contains error and diagnostic information. It is initiated internally and processed by the IP layer. Although ICMP messages are encapsulated in an IP data packet, they are not a higher protocol, such as TCP or UDP. They are a direct element of the IP protocol. In practice, the IP protocol cannot be used without the ICMP protocol. These messages are only issued from the computer system that has sent or triggered the error and are sent directly to the original sender of the data.

Several different types of ICMP message may be distinguished. These are characterized by a number in the header of an ICMP packet (type) and can contain different data depending on the ICMP data type. The most important types are as follows:

> **NOTE** The numbers in parentheses in the following bulleted list represent the ICMP protocol number.

- **Echo Reply (0).** This message is triggered as soon as an Echo Request message is received from another computer system. Test data that provides information on availability, operating time, and so on is sent in the data field of this packet.
- **Destination Unreachable (3).** If a message does not arrive at its intended destination, the sender receives this notification. It's possible that a network, a host, a protocol, or a port was not available. Or perhaps the data packet needed to be fragmented during the transmission, but the setting of the fragmentation bit in the IP packet header prohibited fragmentation. The Destination Unreachable message may also result because a particular computer system that was entered by the sender in the source routing option could not be reached. This message can conceivably be misused by an attacker to interrupt all the connections between the computer systems concerned.
- **Source Quench (4).** If a router does not have the required capacity (throughput) to forward the received data directly, it sends this message to the sender. The sender must lower the transmission rate of subsequent messages.
- **Redirect (5).** If a router detects that the sender is taking an unnecessary detour instead of transmitting directly to the next router, it sends this message to the sender. The data field contains the IP address of the most direct router and is entered by the sender into its own routing table. Redirection can be abused by an attacker to configure undesirable routes and intercept or tamper with the data in transit.
- **Echo Request (8).** This message is sent out to check whether the intended receiver is, in fact, reachable. Together with the Echo Reply to this message, conclusions can be drawn as to availability, operating time, and response time.
- **Time Exceeded (11).** If an IP data packet reaches the end of its predefined life (time to live) before arriving at its destination, it is discarded. The sender receives this message from the computer system that has executed the process.
- **Parameter Problem (12).** If an IP data packet has been discarded due to an error in the header entries, this message is sent to the sender of the packet.

The Ping command used on most computer systems is an example of ICMP message use. This command is generated at the user level and sends one or more ICMP messages to the receiver. The commands Echo Request and Echo Reply are used here, and the sender receives information on the following:

- The IP address of the receiver and whether the computer system is reachable or not

- The MAC address of the next router or computer system
- Routing entries
- Operating time of the data
- Data losses

Port Numbers

Ports provide a vital function in the Transport layer. Ports identify packets with the services (such as WWW, FTP, e-mail) for which they are intended. A computer system (for example, a server) must be able to communicate with more than one computer system at the same time. Otherwise, while a connection is being established with one system, none of the other computer systems will be able to reach the server. Certain applications also require the simultaneous establishment of two or more connections – for example, one for command transmission and another for data transmission. For this purpose, every computer system has various port numbers at its disposal, which, together with the network identifier and the computer system identifier, form a communication endpoint (port). The use of IP address and port is designed rather like a telephone number. The network identifier may be compared with the area code, the computer system identifier with the call number, and the port number with the extension. Figure 2-9 illustrates the use of IP address and port number to create a communication endpoint.

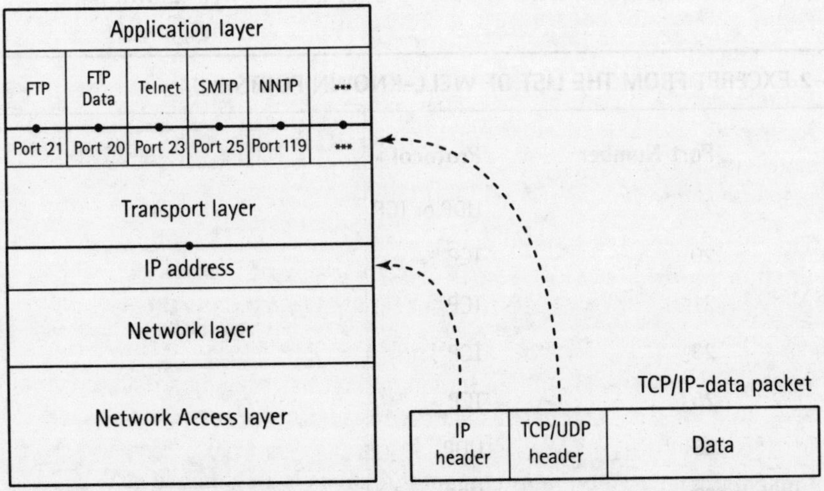

Figure 2-9: Unique identification of the communication endpoint through IP address and port number

Because a port number consists of 16 bits, a computer system with an IP address is theoretically able to establish 65,535 connections to other communication endpoints at the same time. In practice, however, the computer system cannot do this, because the different communication protocols, such as TCP or UDP, use different address spaces that can have identical port numbers but are not physically identical.

The services of the Application layer (for example, Telnet or FTP) require an existing virtual connection between two computer systems, as shown in Figure 2-10. However, in order to establish this connection at all, at least one port must be known to the active computer system (client) receiving the contact, and the corresponding service of the passive computer system (server) must be reachable on this port.

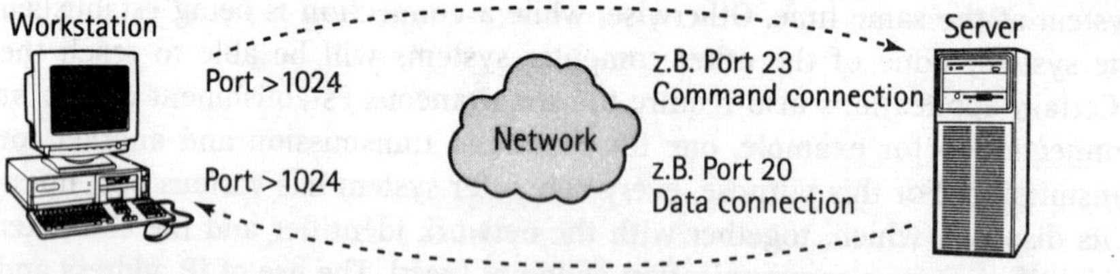

Figure 2-10: Connection between two computers (for example, FTP connection)

Specific port numbers (*well-known ports*) were defined that are routinely available for corresponding services. A client wanting to communicate with a specific server sends a connection request to the service port. The client's port is set as the source port in the connection request. Refer to Table 2-2 for a list of well-known ports.

TABLE 2-2 EXCERPT FROM THE LIST OF WELL-KNOWN PORTS

Service	Port Number	Protocol
Echo	7	UDP or TCP
ftp-data	20	TCP
ftp	21	TCP
telnet	23	TCP
Smtp	25	TCP
Dns	53	UDP
Tftp	69	UDP
Finger	79	TCP
http	80	TCP
nntp	119	TCP

User Datagram Protocol

The User Datagram Protocol (UDP) is a connectionless communication protocol for the Transport layer. It uses the subordinate IP protocol to transport messages from one computer system to another. When supplementing the IP protocol, it can distinguish between several application services (ports) of the receiver.

The crucial advantage of UDP is the low overhead, which makes it suitable for transmitting small quantities of data. In this case, resending the data when an error occurs is easier than establishing a connection that is guaranteed to be error-free. This requires a question-answer dialog between two computer systems. If no answer has arrived from the destination computer system after a specified length of time, the data packet is sent again. Another possibility is to leave the error check functions to a higher application, making monitoring the data transmission twice unnecessary. Figure 2-11 shows the header of a UDP data packet.

Source port number	Destination port number
Length	Checksum
Data	

Figure 2-11: Header of a UDP data packet

The UDP protocol does not generate any transport acknowledgments or implement any other security measures aimed at confirming that transmission occurred in the correct fashion. No information is sent back to the source computer system.

- If the data has been split into several fragments en route to the destination computer system, these fragments can take different routes. Data can arrive in the destination computer system in the wrong order. The UDP protocol passes the data unsorted to the higher application.
- If the data arrives more quickly than the destination computer system or any other computer system in the network can process it (because it is overloaded, for example), data can get lost. There is no information that can control or monitor the data flow between the computer systems.
- The header contains two 16-bit port numbers that are independent of the port numbers used by the TCP protocol.

◆ In principle, this form of data transmission is not very reliable and is also easy to manipulate. On exposed computer systems to which there is public access, the UDP protocol should be avoided unless a higher layer (for example, the Application layer) takes over the control functions.

Transmission Control Protocol

The Transmission Control Protocol (TCP) is the most important transport protocol after the IP protocol. The TCP Protocol is a connection-oriented communication protocol used in the Transport layer. Before the data is sent from the source to the destination, a virtual connection is established that functions in both directions (in other words, in *duplex mode*). The data is transmitted in the form of fixed packets, and correct transmission is ensured through various procedures. Figure 2-12 shows the header of a TCP data packet.

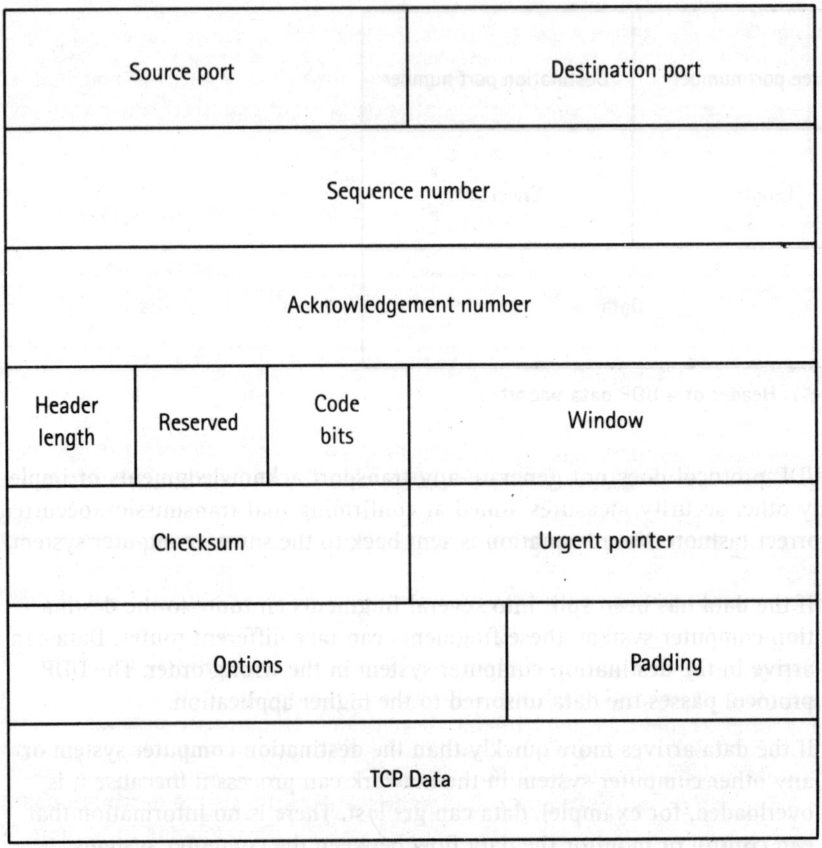

Figure 2-12: Header of a TCP data packet

- The header of a TCP data packet contains, among other things, two 16-bit port numbers that are used to identify the communication endpoints of source and destination. The different services of the Application layer can establish connections with each other using the standard assignments (well-known ports).
- Following connection setup, each TCP unit generates a start sequence number. These numbers are exchanged and reciprocally confirmed. Each data segment sent contains a serial, unique sequence number. With the aid of these sequence numbers, the data can be put together in the correct sequence at the destination, regardless of the time at which the segments arrive.
- The acknowledgement number is transmitted from the destination computer system to the computer system from which the data originated. The acknowledgement number is always one higher than the last sequence number that was correctly received. With this number, the source computer system can delete the packets from its data buffer that it holds in case the transmission needs to be repeated.
- The header length field determines the length of the protocol header in 32-bit words and hence the beginning of the payload data.
- The code bits or flags trigger reactions in the TCP protocol.
- A source computer system must not send more data than a destination computer system can process or forward. For this reason, the destination computer system designates the amount of data it can temporarily store in its buffer for immediate processing in the *Window Size* field.
- Every data segment contains a checksum that is formed from the header and payload data. The destination computer system similarly calculates a checksum from the data received and compares it with the data field in the data segment header. If the two values are identical, then the destination computer system sends a positive confirmation to the source computer system. A damaged data segment is initially ignored and, after a certain wait period, is requested once again.
- For some services, an indicator is available within the application protocol so the server can execute urgent instructions (for example, the transmission of a <Ctrl+C> or break in a Telnet session) even though not all of the input data has yet been processed. This is achieved via the *urgent data pointer*, which points to the data byte prior to the urgent message.
- Normally only the Maximum Segment Size option is used in a TCP packet. With this option, the source computer system informs the destination computer system of the maximum size of the data segments to be sent. The other options are No Operation and End of Option List.
- The *Padding* field is used to even out the length of the option field, so the overall size of the header is always a multiple of a 32-bit word.

Every segment contains a time-out mechanism that requires a destination computer system to send an acknowledgement of the packets received to the source computer system after a certain time. If a source computer system has not received an answer after the acknowledgement time has expired, the corresponding data segment is resent.

The following sections consider the protocols and services of the Application layer in detail.

Domain Name Service

In order to assign corresponding IP addresses to computer system names, it was originally necessary to regularly update a list of computer system names from a central server by data transfer to each computer system. In light of the meteoric expansion of the Internet, this method is no longer practical. Instead, the Domain Name Service (DNS) was developed. In this system, computer system names are no longer registered on each individual computer system, but on servers specially provided for this service within each subnet. Individual computer systems send queries as required to these name servers, which return the corresponding IP address or the associated computer system name by way of reply.

Any organization wanting Internet users to connect to its servers must implement a Domain Name Server with name references for its systems' IP addresses. Among other things, these databases contain two tables, enabling the associated IP address to be assigned to a particular computer system name and vice versa.

All information provided by the DNS can be misused, as this information is not encrypted in any way. To obtain access to a computer system in a network, an intruder first needs to know its IP address, which he can obtain either by guessing blindly or, more easily, by analyzing the DNS information. With this information the intruder can feign an address (IP spoofing) and obtain access to computer systems inside the protected network.

Telnet

The Telnet protocol allows a user (client) to have a terminal session on a remote computer system (server). For this purpose, a TCP connection is established between client and port 23 of the server. A login sequence is then performed, in which the user identifies and authenticates himself by entering a user name and password. Figure 2-13 shows an example of a Telnet session.

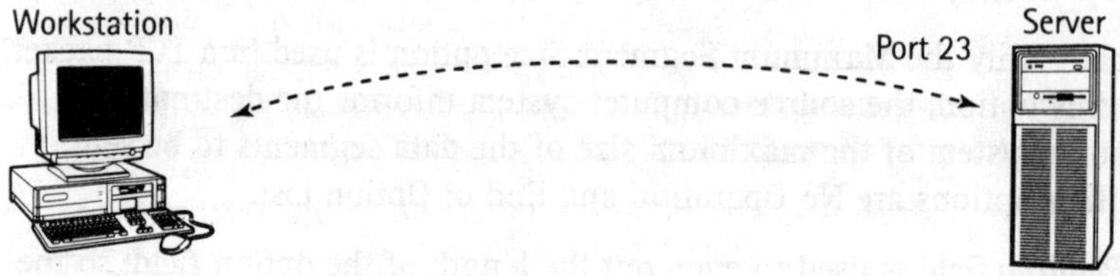

Figure 2-13: Example of a Telnet session

During this authentication procedure over the Telnet service, the password is transmitted in plaintext. An attacker may penetrate an authorized Telnet connection on the transmission route in order to intercept security-relevant information (for example, passwords), or to enter his own commands into the Telnet connection. The attacker could then log on to this server, entering the intercepted identity (masquerade attack) in order to spy on, tamper with, or delete certain data of interest to him.

File Transfer Protocol

The File Transfer Protocol (FTP) enables the exchange and transmission of files between remote computer systems, rather like a File Manager. The use of FTP entails two different connections. First, the client establishes a connection to port 21 of the server from any other port. The client sends the commands to the server over this connection. The client informs the server over which port it should transmit the data using the Port command. Using this data, the server establishes a TCP connection from port 20 to the stated port of the client, and transmits the requested data. Figure 2-14 shows an example of an FTP connection.

To enable the exchange of commands between computer systems with different FTP servers, a number of standardized commands were defined for FTP. These are not identical to the commands of the user interface. The FTP client translates the user interface commands into the relevant standard commands for the communication. For a firewall system, the standardized FTP commands are relevant, as only these are transmitted over a TCP/IP connection.

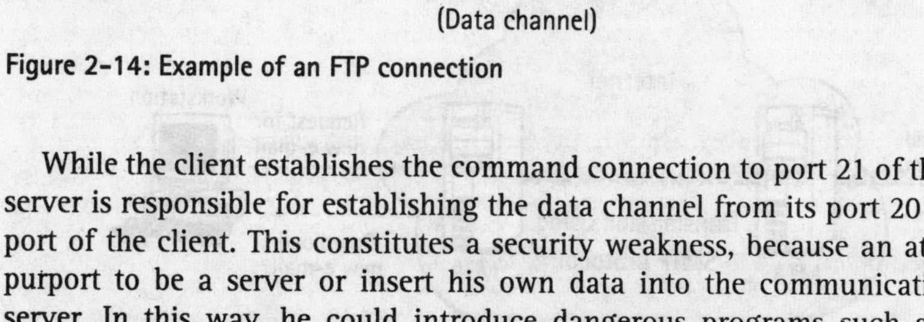

Figure 2-14: Example of an FTP connection

While the client establishes the command connection to port 21 of the server, the server is responsible for establishing the data channel from its port 20 to any other port of the client. This constitutes a security weakness, because an attacker could purport to be a server or insert his own data into the communication with the server. In this way, he could introduce dangerous programs such as viruses or Trojan horses into the computer system, which could access or destroy data. One remedy here is the passive FTP method, in which the client initiates the data connection to the server on TCP port 20 rather than the server connecting to the client.

Passive FTP was added to the FTP protocol primarily due to firewalls. Because most client computers are shielded behind firewalls using private IP addresses, an FTP server can't initiate a connection to the client. Passive FTP solves this problem by allowing the client to initiate the connection. Passive mode FTP is now the default method of operation for most FTP servers.

XREF For more information on passive FTP, refer to Chapter 4.

Simple Mail Transport Protocol

The Simple Mail Transport Protocol (SMTP) transmits electronic messages (e-mail) through the Internet or an intranet. The e-mail system contains the following two components:

- Message Transfer Agent (MTA)
- Mail User Agent (UA)

The MTA is installed by the relevant Internet provider or intranet operator and forwards the electronic mail over the subnets to its destination. UA is the e-mail software used to compose, send, and receive e-mail, depending on the particular program the user has. The electronic mail is stored on the MTA until the user downloads it on the local computer system with the aid of his software. Figure 2-15 illustrates the interaction between these components.

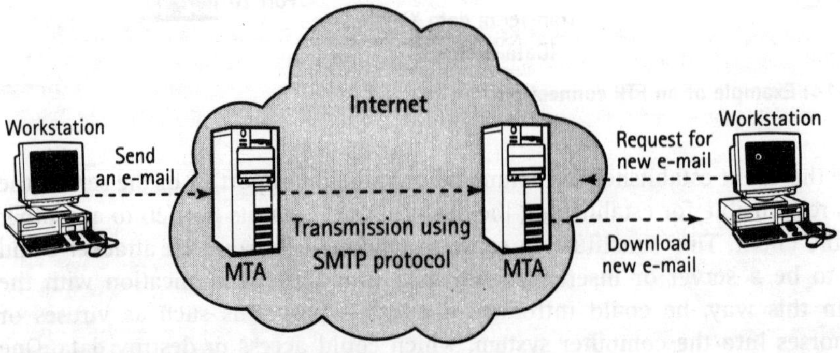

Figure 2-15: How the e-mail service works

Messages are transmitted over the Internet with the aid of the SMTP protocol with no encryption. You can't check the identity of the sender, which means that messages can be distributed over the Internet using any sender name, including a false name (mail spoofing). A user can only protect himself by using cryptographic methods such as digital signatures with encryption.

XREF

For more information on using digital signatures with encryption, refer to Chapter 6.

Another weakness of the e-mail system is the Sendmail program, which is the most widely used implementation of a Message Transfer Agent using the SMTP protocol. Its complexity and extensive capability make Sendmail both error-prone and difficult to configure. As a result, security loopholes allowing data to be copied, tampered with, or destroyed by attackers have been discovered at regular intervals in recent years.

Hypertext Transfer Protocol

A user employs a browser to reach the Internet from his computer system. The browser, among other things, enables HyperText Markup Language (HTML) documents to be displayed. HTML is a standard that defines the structure and format of the pages that are characteristic of the World Wide Web. All of the following can be transmitted at the same time:

- Text
- Graphics
- Sounds
- Animation
- Videos

In order to transmit information, a special communication protocol called the *HyperText Transfer Protocol (HTTP)* was developed.

HTTP does not work in a session-oriented manner – that is, an HTML document is transmitted independently of any previously transmitted HTML document. As with other communication protocols in the Application layer (for example, FTP or Telnet), a virtual connection (TCP) is first established between the client and server. However, instead of continuing to exist for several requests from the client, the connection is terminated by the server immediately following the sending of the reply. Figure 2-16 shows the functioning of an HTTP connection.

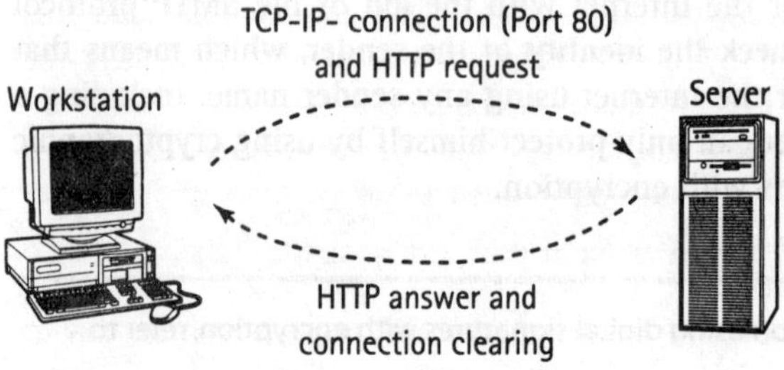

Figure 2-16: Principle of an HTTP connection

When a user retrieves a given page on a server, the browser reads the HTML document and builds the text according to the formatting specified (size, color, font, and so on). If a Web page contains additional information, such as graphics, sound, or videos, the precise location of this file is specified in the HTML document. The browser then establishes another connection over the HTTP protocol and fetches the graphics, sound file, video, or other information from the server. Following completion of the transmission, this information is displayed or reproduced by the browser directly on the user's computer system. Most browsers can be configured to display only information the user wants. For example, if the connection to the Internet is very slow, you can forego viewing large amounts of data (graphics, perhaps), and only display the text information.

ACTIVE ELEMENTS

Active elements are small autonomous programs that are loaded onto the user's computer system, using the HTTP protocol, and executed. Active elements include Java applets, ActiveX controls, and JavaScript commands.

A danger exists that these active elements may not simply represent a graphical sequence, but may also be able to access elementary system resources. For example, they might be able to delete files or directories, manipulate data or collect information, and independently send the collected information over the Internet.

For more information on active elements, refer to Chapter 12.

COOKIES

Not quite as dangerous are *cookies*, data structures that are downloaded by the Web server onto the client and stored there temporarily for use at a later time. The cookie mechanism was developed by the Netscape Corporation as a reaction to the stateless nature of the HTTP protocol: each time a browser asks the Web server for the URL of an Internet page, this operation is viewed as a new action. That this query may only be the last of many queries of this type as the user surfs the Internet is not registered by the HTTP protocol.

While this feature of the HTTP protocol ensures that the worldwide Net is used more efficiently, it also makes it extraordinarily difficult to implement functions such as virtual shopping carts on the Internet, because these require a user's actions to be tracked over an extended period.

Cookies can only be used to store information that was present at a particular point in time. For example, if you state your favorite color on a data input screen, this information can be processed in a cookie by the server and sent to your browser. The next time you visit this site, the browser will send back the cookie, enabling the server to change the background color of the page to reflect your favorite color.

However, cookies can also be used for other, controversial purposes: each time a browser retrieves a page on the Internet, information about the user is left behind. Over a period of time, this information becomes ever more comprehensive. The information gathered can include the following:

- The name and IP address of the computer
- The browser used
- The operating system of the computer
- The URL of the Internet site visited

Without cookies, it is virtually impossible to systematically collect accurate information about the user and his habits; with the assistance of cookies, however, it becomes child's play to collect and evaluate these "electronic footprints."

Errors made by the Netscape developers in the design of the cookie mechanism have meant that users must be very careful when handling cookies. Cookies are normally sent back, not only to the server from which they were originally loaded on the client system, but to all the computers in the same domain to ensure the possibility of controlling clusters of Web servers belonging to much-visited providers using cookies. The decision as to whether a computer belongs to the cookie sender's domain is based solely on the periods in the name. For example, `computer1.utimaco.de` belongs to the same domain as `computer2.utimaco.de` because the names are the same after the first period. However, this mechanism, which is also implemented in Microsoft Internet Explorer, does not work in countries with extended domain structures. The computer named `computer1.company1.co.uk` does not belong to the same domain as `computer2.company2.co.uk`, but the cookies are still sent to it.

Cookies should never be enabled indiscriminately. They should either be completely disabled or the option "Accept only cookies that are sent back to the originating server" should be selected.

Another advantage of HTML documents is their use of Uniform Resource Locators (URLs), addresses that contain additional information. URLs do not have to be other HTML documents – they could contain any other data format. A URL contains the following information:

- The protocol to be used in order to access the corresponding information
- The precise Internet address of the server with specification of the port number
- The name of the file in which the information is stored, together with the path

With this information, you can switch to different services of the Application layer (FTP, Telnet, e-mail, and so on) within a Web page in order to execute the corresponding services.

A firewall system used to protect a network must be able to analyze the commands of an HTTP packet and restrict them using filters. The data transmitted must be distinguishable and examinable for certain information.

SERVER EXTENSIONS

While not communications protocols, several programming languages operating at the Web server have the ability to control activities at the client computer level, including the following:

- ActiveX
- Java
- Javascript

Javascript and ActiveX are both designed to have limitations. For example, Javascript uses the term *sandbox* to refer to the limitation of activities that can be performed by the server on the client. This sandbox, or controlled environment, is a small subset of the client computer's capabilities. The purpose of a sandbox is to limit what a server can execute on a client computer system. Unfortunately, people are constantly finding ways around these limitations, so it's best not to trust these sandbox limitations too much. A malicious individual can create malign scripts and cause them to perform all sorts of things. Examples include installing Trojan horses, transferring files or data to remote servers, or doing actual damage to the system.

Network News Transfer Protocol

Because of its enormous size, the Internet offers a wealth of information. As developments race ahead in virtually all areas of knowledge, one relies on having the latest information available. One way to achieve this is to use a *news server*.

Many news servers specialize in very narrow subject areas due to the large amount of information that is available.

To remain up-to-date, news servers exchange new contributions among themselves at regular intervals. Within the Internet, this data exchange is accomplished using an independent protocol. The Network News Transfer Protocol (NNTP) sends new contributions to the news server. The news server then forwards the current information to the next server, and so on. This process is referred to as *news feed.* Because some of these servers forward the information not just to one server, but to several servers at the same time, it is possible for new information to spread through the entire Internet within a period of a few days.

The NNTP protocol used today has a mechanism that enables only those articles that are not yet present on the receiver's computer system to be transmitted.

Other Common Network Protocols

A modern network is rife with a wide array of protocols to meet the user's base needs.

SIMPLE NETWORK MANAGEMENT PROTOCOL

Simple Network Management Protocol (SNMP) communicates device, system health, and status information to a central management console. SNMP was designed for internal network use and, as such, the security parameters are extremely weak. SNMP client agents work by sending status messages, *traps* in SNMP protocol terms, to the console indicating condition parameters. This occurs on UDP port 162. The management console communicates with client systems through TCP port 161. Security in SNMP is based solely on a community name. Given that the community name is exchanged in plaintext, it is easily intercepted. In most networks, interception is even easier because the default community name is not changed from its default value of public. SNMP must be protected because it exposes all system configuration information. On many systems, such as NT, this includes access to vital information, including user names and encrypted passwords.

SECURE SHELL

Secure Shell (SSH) is an encrypted replacement for both Telnet and the "r" services (RSH, REXEC, RLOGIN). The SSH protocol can also transfer files via a subset protocol called SFTP. SSH supports several encryption algorithms. Version 2 of SSH has proven to be a very secure protocol and, as such, is an excellent replacement for Telnet and the "r" services. SSH uses TCP port 22 for communication by default. An additional capability that really enhances the versatility of the SSH protocol is its ability to tunnel other protocols, effectively making it a Virtual Private Network (VPN) protocol. This is very convenient for using protocols such as X-Windows remotely in a secure fashion.

"R" SERVICES

RSH, REXEC, and RLOGIN are less common than they once were but are still quite popular due to their convenience. The "r" protocols use source IP addresses for authentication rather than a user ID and password. This means that once the services are set up, they can be used without the hassle of having to log in each time. This convenience comes at the price of extremely poor security. Given the availability of the SSH protocol as a replacement to the "r" services that offers the same convenience without the security risks, there is no real reason to utilize the "r" protocols – except perhaps in embedded systems, where they cannot be replaced. REXEC uses TCP port 512 for communications, RLOGIN uses TCP port 513, and RSH uses TCP port 514.

REMOTE PROCEDURE CALL

The Remote Procedure Call (RPC) protocol is used for process-to-process communications on different systems. RPC is used for a wide variety of other programs and protocols such as NFS. RPC is a common target of attacks on UNIX systems given the wide variety of programs that are accessible through the RPC protocol. RPC uses TCP port 111 for communications.

POST OFFICE PROTOCOL

Post Office Protocol (POP) is used for retrieving e-mail from remote mail servers. POP uses TCP port 110 for communications. The primary downside of POP is that it is purely a plaintext protocol. User IDs and passwords are not encrypted, allowing for relatively easy interception.

INTERNET MAIL ACCESS PROTOCOL

The Internet Mail Access Protocol (IMAP) extends the capabilities offered by POP to add support for server-based folders. Unfortunately, a severe security vulnerability was discovered in most IMAP implementations shortly after the protocol gained widespread acceptance. As a result, thousands of computer systems were compromised. Consequently, IMAP servers were taken offline, and most companies went back to POP. IMAP never fully recovered from the setback and is not commonly deployed today. IMAP uses TCP port 143 for communications.

NETBIOS

Microsoft's Server Message Block (SMB) protocol uses an extension of the NetBIOS protocol originally written by IBM. Microsoft operating systems use NetBIOS for all authentication, file sharing, and printing functionality on a network. NetBIOS uses UDP 137 and 138, as well as TCP port 139 for communications. NetBIOS is susceptible to several types of attack, from brute force to those crafted to take advantage of the protocol's backwards-compatibility with the LAN server protocols.

NETWORK FILE SYSTEM

Network File System (NFS) is a simple UDP-based protocol for file sharing. Given that NFS uses IP addresses for authentication, like the "r" services, it's susceptible to the same security problems. Typically, most security compromises tied to NFS are a result of server misconfiguration rather than actual exploitation of the protocol itself.

X-WINDOWS

X-Windows is the Graphical User Interface (GUI) for UNIX/Linux systems. X-Windows uses TCP ports 6000 through 6099 for communications, but primarily TCP port 6000. Counterintuitive to its graphical nature, X-Windows is a plaintext protocol. X-Windows authentication can be configured in several manners, including authenticating solely by IP address. Successful access to X-Windows allows for many different types of attacks. One of the more popular attacks against X-Windows captures keystrokes remotely. The deviousness of this attack lies in the fact that the keystroke capture occurs transparently in the background.

TUNNELING PROTOCOLS

Point-to-Point Tunneling Protocol (PPTP) and Layer 2 Forwarding Protocol (L2TP) are both extremely popular VPN protocols. L2TP is most often used for tunneling the IP Secure (IPSEC) protocol because IPSEC is primarily a Network layer protocol. PPTP is Microsoft's secure VPN protocol. The first implementation of PPTP experienced some problems that resulted in certain security vulnerabilities that allowed remote attackers to obtain user name and password combinations. PPTPv2 corrected these issues and is now widely used. PPTP uses TCP port 1723 for communications and L2TP uses UDP port 1701.

DATABASE PROTOCOLS

Databases used in the modern business environment all rely on their own protocols for communications between clients and the database server. None of these protocols should be exposed directly to the Internet, because that allows remote users to interact directly with the database server as if they were local clients. Given the types of data stored on corporate database servers, such as client credit cards and personal information, these database servers represent a potential gold mine to external attackers. Microsoft SQL server uses TCP port 1433 for communications, Oracle uses TCP port 1521, Lightweight Directory Access Protocol (LDAP) servers use TCP port 389, and Notes servers use TCP port 1352.

VIDEO AND AUDIO

Other types of protocols, such as streaming video and audio, are finding their way into corporate networks. Applications include training and videoconferencing. H.323 is an example of a popular audio/video protocol used for a variety of applications. H.323 uses TCP port 1723 for communications. Another popular protocol is the Real Audio protocol; it uses TCP ports 554 and 7070.

INSTANT MESSAGING PROTOCOLS

The ICQ (ICQ is not an acronym but is intended to be sounded out and means "I Seek You") application started a massive popularity for instant text message communications. Since then, numerous applications have sprung up in order to capitalize on the immense popularity of instant messaging. While not yielding obvious business benefits in most environments, they are still commonly found installed on individual user systems. The instant messaging protocols work by connecting to a central server and indicating their station information, such as IP address and readiness to receive messages. Table 2-3 lists some popular instant messenger applications and the ports they use to communicate.

TABLE 2-3 POPULAR INSTANT MESSENGER APPLICATIONS AND THEIR PORTS

Application	Ports
ICQ	A dynamic TCP port and UDP port 4000
AOL Instant Messenger	TCP port 5190
Yahoo Messenger	TCP port 5050
MSN Messenger	TCP port 1863

PEER-TO-PEER SHARING PROTOCOLS

As with instant messaging, Peer-to-Peer sharing protocols such as Napster seemed to instantly gain a huge implementation base. Despite the fact that Napster and other protocols of this sort currently render no business application, they are quite commonly found installed on the systems of corporate users. Napster has been suspended for now due to legal problems, so newer, non-centralized protocols, such as GNUTella, have superseded it. Napster used TCP ports 7777 and 8888, while GNUTella uses TCP ports 6346 and 6347.

GAME PROTOCOLS

Gaming protocols are also commonly found on corporate networks. The first significant game of this type was called Doom. It used TCP port 666 (with intentional Biblical allusions) and has since been included in almost all computer games. It is extremely rare to see a computer game nowadays that doesn't support network play. Table 2-4 lists common games and the ports they utilize:

TABLE 2-4 COMMON GAMES AND THEIR PORTS

Game	Ports
Quake	TCP port 26000
Blizzard Battle .Net	TCP ports 4000 and 6112-6119
MSN Gaming Zone	TCP ports 28800-29000
Direct X-based games	TCP ports 47624 and 2300-2400

Summary

Ultimately, the versatility of the Internet is expressed in the wide variety of protocols it exhibits. New protocols are continually being created and can be adopted on a large scale seemingly overnight. The diversity of the use of protocols is huge. While a good cross-section of the more common protocols has been touched on in this book, the discussion has in no way been comprehensive. Many applications, such as PC/Anywhere and Palm Network Hotsync, are very specialized in nature. All of these protocols can potentially create significant security exposure, and it's important to start with a solid understanding of what protocols are being used on your specific network.

Chapter 3

Threats in Networks

THIS CHAPTER DESCRIBES the potential threats to be found in intranets and in networks such as the Internet. Deliberate attacks based on TCP/IP technology are also introduced, along with the main possibilities for countering them with the help of firewall systems.

Attack Possibilities in Communication Systems

The most serious threats to IT systems target the communication system – that is, the messages exchanged over communication systems such as the Internet and intranets. This chapter defines the various types of attack and classifies the types of damage that can arise through attacks.

A receiver responds to a message (one or more IP packets) with a particular behavior. An attacker who intercepts a communication link can interpret the behavior of the receiver and the transmitter. If the attacker has the opportunity to repeat, alter, delete, or add to a message, he can influence the response of the receiver in a targeted manner.

Based on this consideration, two types of threats can be distinguished: passive attacks and active attacks.

Passive Attacks

In a passive attack, neither the messages transmitted nor the operation of the communication system is altered. Attackers execute passive attacks deliberately and selectively to obtain information to which they are not entitled.

For example, passive attacks can be carried out by attaching clips or induction loops to the line, or by intercepting signals using directional radio and satellite connections.

The following types of passive attack may be identified:

- Data interception. By intercepting messages, an attacker gains direct possession of the messages and can use them for his own purposes. For example, an attacker could listen to the login procedure on an IP connection between a Telnet server and client and obtain the identity and password of a user, which he could then use on another occasion to gain unauthorized access to the server system. Other examples are the interception of confidential information, such as development documents relating to new products, or the interception of data covered by the Data Protection Act. These attacks can be perpetrated quite easily using freely accessible LAN connections.

- **Interception of users' identities.** The eavesdropper discovers which parties (users or computer systems) set up connections and exchange data. Just by knowing who has exchanged information with whom at a given time, the eavesdropper can often draw conclusions as to the content of the message or the behavior of the participant. If, by observation, you determine that someone placing an order always visits a particular URL and receives an order confirmation by e-mail, then a user switching to SSL and receiving e-mail connections from the mail server indicates an order has likely been placed. Even though the SSL connection is encrypted, by understanding the pattern of connections you can still ascertain much of the content.
- **Traffic flow analysis.** Even if the data is encrypted, an eavesdropper can obtain certain information – such as the scale, times, frequency, and direction of a data transfer – from a *traffic flow analysis*. This information could be useful for certain specific applications (for example, stock market transactions). If, for example, a stock sale confirmation message always originates from a particular server with a specific size range, any packets matching those parameters indicate a stock sale has occurred.

Special Dangers Related to the Use of Local Area Networks

Local area networks (LANs) are exposed to special passive attacks, because they generally use broadcast media in which all messages are sent to all users, with the assumption that users will only access those messages that are intended for them. In practice, it is customary to install extra network connections (for example, Ethernet jacks) to ensure flexibility in the event of office relocations, installation of additional computer systems, and so on. These additional connections are not blocked as long as they are not used, and can therefore be abused at any time to connect analysis devices and follow the entire message stream.

However, LANs are also designed so that extra connections and computer systems can be added during ongoing operations without disturbing the traffic. This flexibility and robustness is a disadvantage in terms of data security. Due to the desire for flexibility and robustness, connecting additional, unauthorized, and unnoticed computer systems is possible. Even authorized users' workstations can be used to intercept the entire message stream. The sniffing software will run on any station on which it can be installed.

Using simple tools such as protocol sniffers (one example is LAN Watch), it is possible to read all the packets on the LAN from any computer system.

Because many organizations perform system administration of computer systems remotely, *root* passwords can be read so that additional attacks can be carried out using them.

Log of a Telnet Session

The Telnet session log shown in Figure 3-1 covers the login phase. The software used to log the events can run on any ordinary PC connected to the LAN. There are no special requirements regarding the computer system used to make the recording.

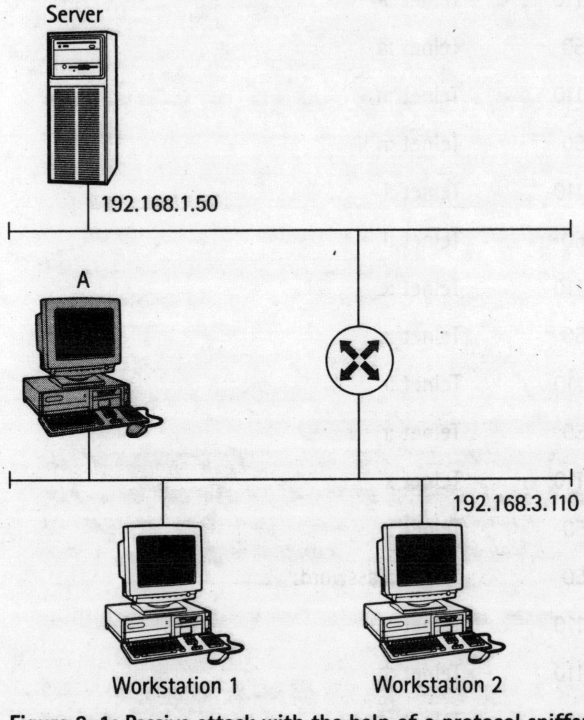

Figure 3-1: Passive attack with the help of a protocol sniffer

The user on Workstation 2 (WS 2) has logged on to the server. He entered *Spanier* as his user ID. This entry was echoed by the server as required by the protocol specifications, and for this reason, the individual letters appear twice in the log. The password that user Spanier entered is *1beutlin* (see Table 3-1). Because the letters of the password are not echoed by the server, they only appear once (this fact makes it easier to find the password in logs). If this program is used in the morning when everyone is logging on to this server, it is possible to determine all the passwords.

TABLE 3-1 RECORDING OF A TELNET SESSION

Destination	Source	Message
192.168.3.110	192.168.1.50	Telnet :login:
192.168.1.50	192.168.3.110	Telnet :s
192.168.3.110	192.168.1.50	Telnet :s
192.168.1.50	192.168.3.110	Telnet :p
192.168.3.110	192.168.1.50	Telnet :p
192.168.1.50	192.168.3.110	Telnet :a
192.168.3.110	192.168.1.50	Telnet :a
192.168.1.50	192.168.3.110	Telnet :n
192.168.3.110	192.168.1.50	Telnet :n
192.168.1.50	192.168.3.110	Telnet :l
192.168.3.110	192.168.1.50	Telnet :l
192.168.1.50	192.168.3.110	Telnet :e
192.168.3.110	192.168.1.50	Telnet :e
192.168.1.50	192.168.3.110	Telnet :r
192.168.3.110	192.168.1.50	Telnet :r
192.168.1.50	192.168.3.110	Telnet :.
192.168.3.110	192.168.1.50	Telnet :..
192.168.3.110	192.168.1.50	Telnet :Password:
192.168.1.50	192.168.3.110	Telnet :1
192.168.1.50	192.168.3.110	Telnet :b
192.168.1.50	192.168.3.110	Telnet :e
192.168.1.50	192.168.3.110	Telnet :u
192.168.1.50	192.168.3.110	Telnet :t
192.168.1.50	192.168.3.110	Telnet :l
192.168.1.50	192.168.3.110	Telnet :l
192.168.1.50	192.168.3.110	Telnet :n
192.168.1.50	192.168.3.110	Telnet :.

Destination	Source	Message
192.168.3.110	192.168.1.50	Telnet :..
192.168.3.110	192.168.1.50	Telnet :Last login: Tue Apr 29 14:05:20 from merry...

Carelessness about keeping information confidential is a major problem in local networks, because the inadequate security of normal controls regulating access to server systems and any resources in the local networks are linked with this inadequate security. The majority of common controls simply have too little security for modern networks.

Other danger points in local networks at which messages can be intercepted are bridges, routers, brouters, and gateways.

Active Attacks

Besides being threatened by data interception, communication systems are also compromised by active attacks, which could result in manipulation of the message flow and/or the use of a communication session. For example, some active attacks split open the transmission lines or use transmission protocol emulations.

Active attacks can be divided roughly into two categories: attacks perpetrated by third parties and attacks performed by communication partners. Threats from third parties include the following:

- **Replay or delay of information.** A replay or delay of information can irritate the receiver or induce him to take inappropriate action. Examples include multiple transfers of a sum of money or retransmission of an intercepted login.
- **Insertion and deletion of data.** To manipulate a system, an attacker inserts data into messages or deletes data from them. The suppression of critical information or receipt of additional information sometimes induces the receiver to behave in an inappropriate manner. For example, in an e-mail that contains the words "Do not buy this share," the words "do not" could be deleted during transmission so that the receiver gets the instruction "Buy this share."
- **Modification of data.** This type of threat involves modification of data that is not detected by the communication partners. By changing the data during transmission, an attacker can induce the receiver to take inappropriate action (Pohlmann and Ring, 1995). For example, a change in the

account number related to a money transfer causes the money to go to a person other than the intended recipient.

- **Boycott of the communication system (denial of service).** If the scope of data inserted or suppressed is too big or if data that is oriented towards real-time use is withheld for too long, the entire communication system can be boycotted as a result. For example, a permanent connection to a particular server can have the effect of blocking and isolating the server.

Threats from communication partners include the following:

- **Taking on someone else's identity (masquerade attack).** By pretending to be someone else, an attacker can obtain information intended for another party or initiate actions that only the other party is allowed to initiate. For example, a user could obtain unauthorized access to a database.
- **Repudiating communications (especially transactions resulting from communications).** The growing use of data communication to process contractually relevant processes means that neither communication partner can deny having sent a message or having received a message, as appropriate. If you order goods over the Internet, the merchant doesn't want you to be able to deny the order once you have received goods.
- **Man-in-the-middle attack.** A *man-in-the-middle* waits near a node (router or computer system) in the Internet and becomes active when a connection between two other participants is set up. Following authentication of the legitimate user, the connection is used for the attacker's purposes. Man-in-the-middle attacks allow computer systems that cannot be accessed to be manipulated and authentication processes (even cryptographic methods) to be circumvented. Figure 3-2 illustrates a man-in-the-middle attack.

The user on Workstation 1 wants to use a service of Server X on the Internet. To do this, the user establishes a connection to Server X and goes through the necessary login procedure (identification and authentication). An attacker (Computer System A) who has actively penetrated the communication connection in the Internet follows this procedure and waits until the server sends confirmation of a successful login. However, instead of this confirmation being sent to Workstation 1, the attacker causes the connection to be terminated. The attacker effectively cuts off Workstation 1 without the latter noticing the attack. The attacker can now use the authenticated connection for himself in pursuit of his own objectives. This attack method is possible even when the authentication procedure is encrypted.

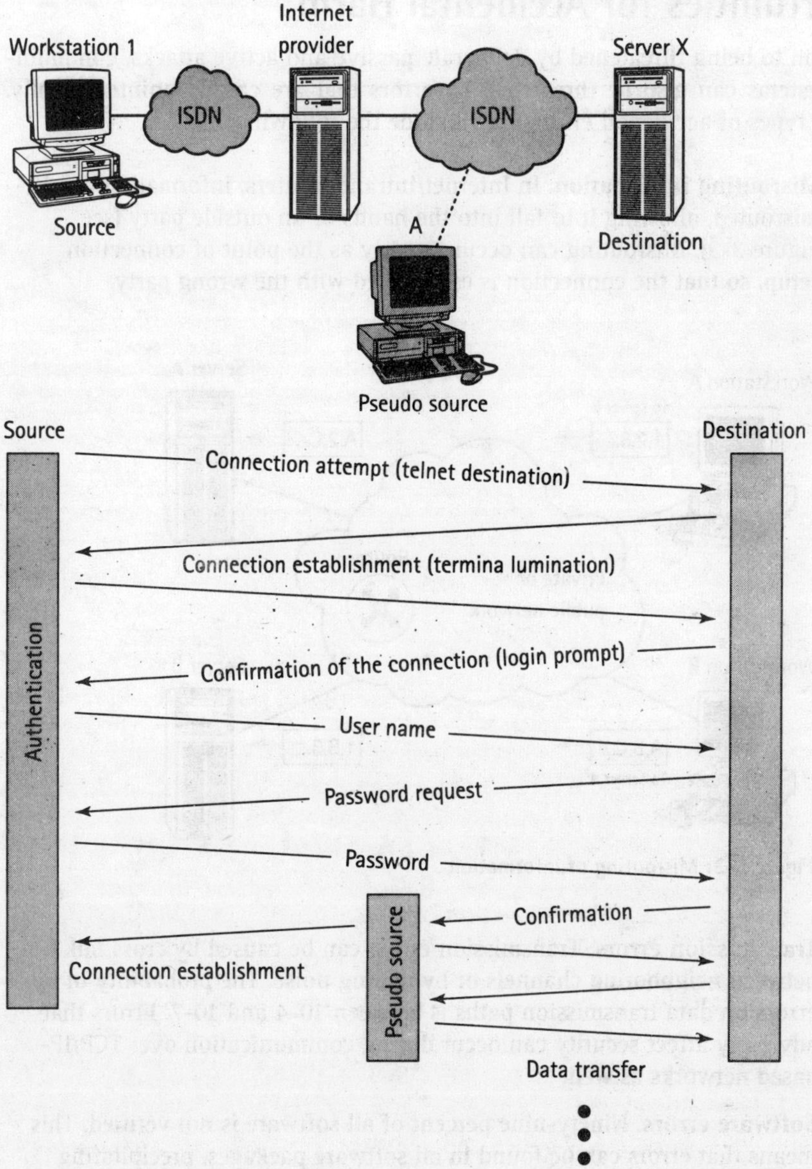

Figure 3-2: Man-in-the-middle attack

Opportunities for Accidental Harm

In addition to being threatened by deliberate passive and active attacks, communication systems can also be threatened by errors that are caused unintentionally. Different types of accidental errors may include the following:

- **Misrouting information.** In Internet/intranet routers, information can be misrouted, allowing it to fall into the hands of an outside party (see Figure 3-3). Misrouting can occur as early as the point of connection setup, so that the connection is established with the wrong party.

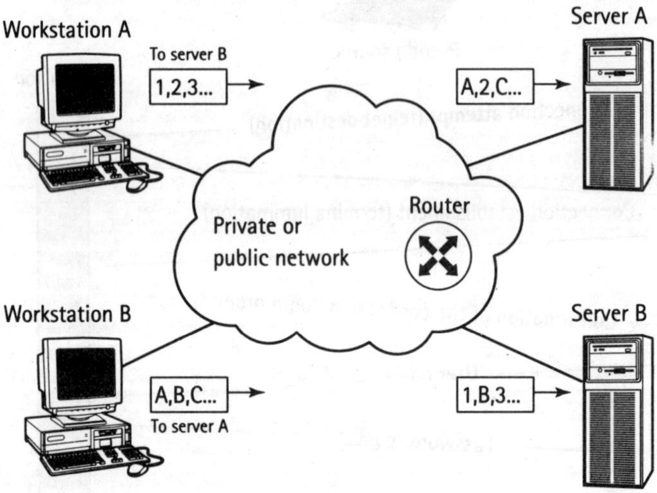

Figure 3-3: Misrouting of information

- **Transmission errors.** Transmission errors can be caused by cross talk between neighboring channels or by dialing noise. The probability of bit errors on data transmission paths is between 10-4 and 10-7. Errors that adversely affect security can occur during communication over TCP/IP-based networks as well.
- **Software errors.** Ninety-nine percent of all software is not verified. This means that errors can be found in all software packages, precipitating malfunctions in certain situations. For example, due to an internal error, the software could dial the wrong person and inadvertently send him confidential data.
- **Hardware faults due to environmental influences.** Environmental influences such as electromagnetic emissions can cause bit inversion in a computer system, which makes it behave incorrectly. For example, due to the

inversion of a bit (perhaps in the router) a confidential IP packet might be sent on a different logical channel to another party.

- **Human error.** The user initiates actions he did not intend. For example, the user might dial the wrong person and accidentally send him confidential information.

As with active attacks, preventing accidents and chance occurrences is virtually impossible. However, if you understand these errors, you are better equipped to take them into account in the design of your communication system and contain the potential extent of the damage.

Other Aspects of Potential Threats in Communication over the Internet

All providers of telecommunication services strive to maintain telecommunication secrecy. In other words, providers of telecommunication services ensure their communication systems (nodes, network management, and so on) are protected to prevent manipulation from outside.

The level of telecommunications protection is quite high in North America and Europe. The same cannot be said globally. Due to the way in which telecommunication calls occur, it is quite possible for phone connections to occur through insecure links in other countries. This routing through less secure telecommunications channels means that all telecommunications must be viewed as potentially suspect.

Communication Paths of IP Packets in the Internet

Packets can be passed over many network nodes over which the user has no influence, and the possibility of an organized attack should not be underestimated. E-mail can be especially problematic as a result of this routing. Given that e-mail is normally sent in plaintext, any node in between the source and destination can view the contents of the e-mail. Even if the desktop and server are in the same geographical location, the use of different ISPs can result in the packets going through multiple nodes in several major cities before arriving at the destination.

Attack Tools from the Internet

You can retrieve a number of tools (ISS and SATAN, for example) from the Internet that enable the network weaknesses of systems based on TCP/IP technology to be analyzed and that even allow targeted attacks to be carried out. With these tools, any user can carry out an attack, even if he does not have any specialized knowledge. Figure 3-4 shows how private communications flow through the Internet.

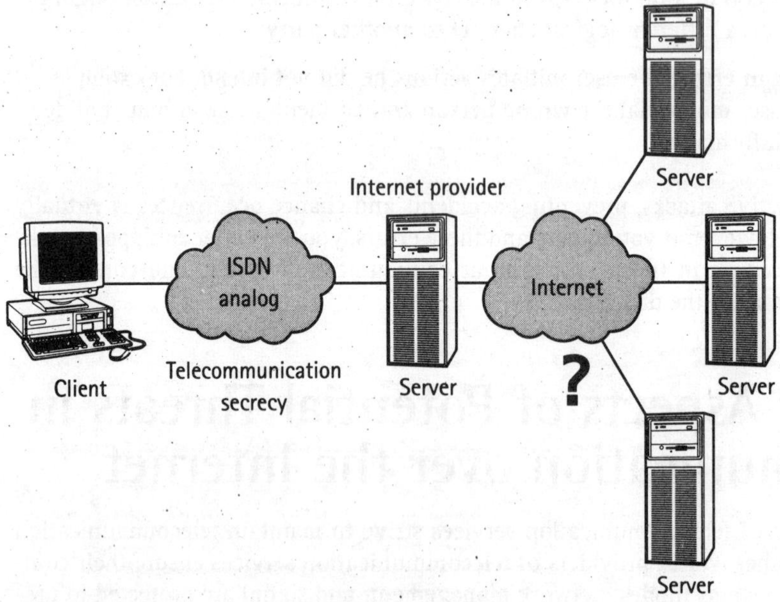

Figure 3-4: Internet and privacy of communication

Implementation Errors in Applications and Incorrect Configurations

Applications such as Sendmail have been found to incorporate implementation errors that allow any privileged commands to be executed on a remote IT system. Attacks can then be performed using these privileged commands.

For every service that is to be enabled over a network access, a daemon process exists that is incorrectly configured or faulty, once again enabling attacks to be carried out. Most daemon processes default to enabling all protocol options. Some of these options need to be disabled in order to achieve the desired level of security appropriate for a particular organization. Examples for Sendmail specifically include allowing mail relaying (SPAM) and enabling some of the options in the sendmail.cf, such as flags=9. These and other configuration options lead to security exposures ranging from annoyances to root-level compromises.

How High Is the Risk?

When assessing the risk of attack, three factors play a significant role:

- The local situation
- The value or usability of the data
- The amount of technical and material resources needed to perpetrate an attack

For example, in office buildings occupied by more than one company, the data lines of one company either run through the premises of other companies, or they are located in a cabling area that can be accessed by anyone. It is therefore quite easy to find a suitable spot to place a wiretap on the cable (see Figure 3-5).

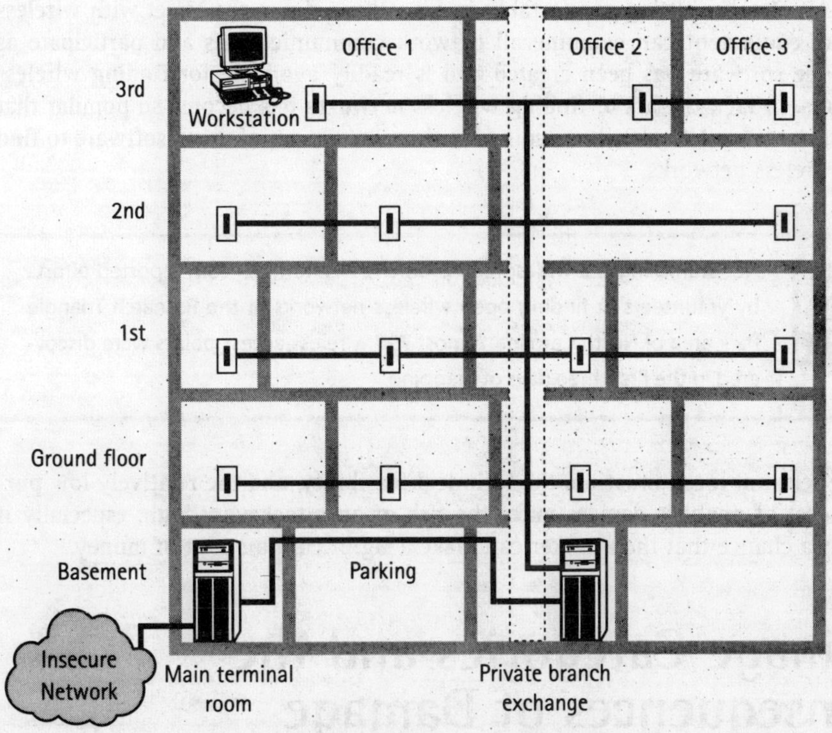

Figure 3-5: Local circumstances that increase the risk of attack

Possible points of attack are corridors, cable shafts, underground car garages, and the points at which utility supplies enter buildings (telephone junction boxes, for example, which are often located in accessible areas). An easy and relatively risk-free accessibility of data lines to potential attackers increases the danger, especially if the value of the data appears to make an attack on the computer system worthwhile.

Technically, tapping lines is no problem even for a layperson. An analysis device capable of intelligently analyzing the communication data costs between 2,400 and 5,000 dollars. Furthermore, as previously mentioned, tools suitable for carrying out intelligent attacks on computer systems are available free-of-charge on the Internet.

Network monitoring is becoming even easier today due to the wide implementation of wireless networking technology. Unfortunately, a poor implementation of the encryption in the 802.11b protocol known as Wireless Encryption Protocol (WEP) renders it worthless. The encryption algorithms themselves are solid, but the way the encryption session occurs allows for recovery of the encryption keys in a matter of minutes – if, of course, encryption is being utilized at all (in most cases, it isn't). An attacker sitting comfortably in his vehicle down the street with wireless network equipment can examine all network communications and participate as well. Free software has been created and is readily available for finding wireless networks. In fact, the act of finding wireless networks has become so popular that the term *net stumbling* has been coined to describe the act of using software to find open wireless networks.

NOTE: Net stumbling is a widespread problem. Netstumbler.com reported efforts by volunteers at finding open wireless networks in the Research Triangle Park area of North Carolina. Almost 790 wireless access points were discovered in the first three days of mapping.

The relevant local situation, the technical feasibility, and the relatively low purchase cost of analysis devices make the risk of an attack very high, especially if there is a chance that the attacker can make a significant amount of money.

Damage Categories and the Consequences of Damage

To estimate the possible loss or damage to an organization more accurately, some typical damage categories are discussed in the following section (BSI, 1999). These categories refer to the basic parameters of confidentiality, data integrity, and system availability.

Violation of Laws, Regulations, or Contracts

Violations of this kind can result from the loss of confidentiality, integrity, or availability. The severity of damage often depends on whether the violation is trivial or whether it has legal consequences for the organization.

In the United States for example, the laws, regulations, and contracts that are relevant to computer crime include the following:

- Fraud and related activity in connection with access devices (18 USC 1029)
- Computer Fraud and Abuse Act (18 USC 1030)
- Economic Espionage Act (18 USC 1831 & 1832)
- Identity Theft and Assumption Deterrence Act (18 USC 2028)
- Electronic Communications Privacy Act (18 USC 2510)

In addition, the following other areas must be observed:

- International law
- Bilateral and multilateral agreements

Physical Injury

The malfunctioning of a computer system can directly result in a wide range of injuries, even death. An attacker might damage software controlling the doses of radiation administered by a cancer treatment machine, for example. The resulting injuries could be quite severe and require months of additional medical treatments to correct. The extent of the damage in cases like this stems from both direct costs (such as the medical treatment) and indirect costs (increased insurance rates resulting from lawsuits). These damage costs can't be quantified very accurately without assessing them on the basis of actual injuries.

Impaired Performance of Duties

The loss of availability of a computer system or of the integrity of data can significantly impair an organization's ability to continue its work. Here, the severity of the loss or damage depends on the duration of the impairment and the extent to which the services offered are constrained.

Some of the typical losses resulting from impairment of systems include:

- Delay in the processing of administrative processes
- Late delivery due to delayed processing of orders
- Incorrect delivery quantity due to wrong control parameters
- Inadequate quality assurance due to the failure of a measuring system

Negative Effects on External Relationships

The loss of one of the basic parameters in a computer system (confidentiality, integrity, availability) can have a number of negative effects on external relationships, including the following:

- Damage to an organization's reputation
- Damage to business relations between partner organizations
- Loss of consumer confidence in an organization
- Loss of consumer confidence in the quality of work produced by an organization
- Leaking of confidential data to the press or to the competition
- Loss of competitive position

The extent of the damage is determined by the severity of the loss of confidence and the extent to which the damaging effects have spread. Such damage may cause a variety of adverse situations:

- An organization may be unable to act due to the failure of an IT system.
- A publication could contain incorrect information because data has been tampered with.
- Orders may be incorrectly placed due to faulty stock control programs.
- The duty to maintain confidentiality may be breached.

The possible loss or damage that results from negative effects on external relationships can be very large in many organizations. This is illustrated by the following cases, in which material presented over the Internet by public organizations was manipulated:

- On November 5, 1999, the daily newspapers reported that the Romanian Finance Ministry's Web site had been hacked. The Web site was changed to include an announcement about "taxes on stupidity."
- In January 2000, Chinese hackers succeeded in systematically hacking the Internet sites of various Japanese official bodies and mounting a protest against the Nanking massacre of 1937. This breach was viewed in "high-tech Japan" as a major humiliation.
- Around 1997, hackers renamed the American Department of Justice the "U.S. Department of Injustice" on its home page. Swedish hackers altered the CIA home page to read the "Central Stupidity Agency" and inserted hot links to sex and music sites. The CIA suffered another embarrassment when unknown persons altered its logo to the "Central Idiots Agency." The altered logo remained on the Web for four days.

Financial Consequences

Direct or indirect financial loss can result from the failure of confidentiality of sensitive data, alteration of data, or the failure of a computer system.

Common losses include the following examples:

- Unauthorized release of the results of research and development
- Manipulation of financial data in an account settlement system
- Obtaining knowledge of marketing strategy papers or sales figures
- Legal liabilities stemming from the use of improperly secured company assets
- Cessation of production due to a computer failure, resulting in lost sales

The extent of the overall loss or damage is equal to the sum of the direct financial loss and the resulting pecuniary damage.

Methods of Attack and Principle Countermeasures Based on the TCP/IP Protocols

Thanks to TCP/IP technology, every user can theoretically establish a communication link with any other user. This complete connectivity produces many problems, the scale of which can be significantly reduced or even eliminated with the aid of firewall systems.

This section presents a few examples of attacks on computer systems in a protected network and discusses the possible options for countering the attacks with the aid of a firewall system.

Idea Behind an Attack

An attacker attempts selectively and deliberately to access one or more computer systems in a protected network in order to do one or more of the following:

- Gain access to particular information not intended for him
- Initiate actions he is not authorized to initiate
- Use resources that he is not permitted to use

The attacker may or may not use the information he steals for financial gain. In any case, an attacker may be motivated by any of the following:

- **The desire to harm a (random) victim.** The motivation is similar to that which underlies vandalism or arson.
- **Pure boredom (in other words, the attacker is hacking the system "for fun").** The attacker may be insufficiently challenged at his place of employment or school, as was the case, for example, with Kevin Mitnick.
- **An inferiority complex.** In other words, the attacker may be trying to compensate for a lack of self-confidence, lack of recognition, or unrequited love.
- **Pure passion for risk, even an addiction to risk.** The attacker may be hunting for the ultimate hacking experience or a virus program that will result in its "creator" making the headlines. The attacker is often acting out of youthful high spirits (for example, *script kiddies* who adapt "proven" programs) to achieve fame, the way graffiti artists leave traces (clues) and live with their tags (characters) in a subculture – in this case, the "hackers' community" – that is incomprehensible to us. The act of hacking serves as a game of sorts with potentially huge risk (prison). The search for and creation of tools is seen as a means of staying ahead of the "good guys" and, in effect, thumbing their noses at authority.
- **Idealistic or political reasons (the fight against the "Establishment" or intolerance of particular lifestyles).**

The following section considers some attacks that can be used to access computer systems in a protected network.

Analysis of the Network Using Scanner Programs

Using a scanner program, an attacker can determine the structure of the network to be protected: IP addresses (computer systems), users, and services.

ANALYSIS OF THE NETWORK AND COMPUTER SYSTEMS

Several types of scanning programs exist for collecting information about potential target systems. A typical example can be seen in Figure 3-6. The scanning software is used to find potential weaknesses in the security of target systems, much like a bank robber might "case the joint" before a bank robbery.

- **Computer systems.** A network's active IP addresses can be analyzed (using the Ping command, for example). An attacker sends the Ping command to all the possible IP addresses in an address range. In a class C network, this means that a Ping command is sent to IP addresses A.B.C.1 through A.B.C.254. From the answers received, the attacker determines which IP addresses represent a connected computer system.

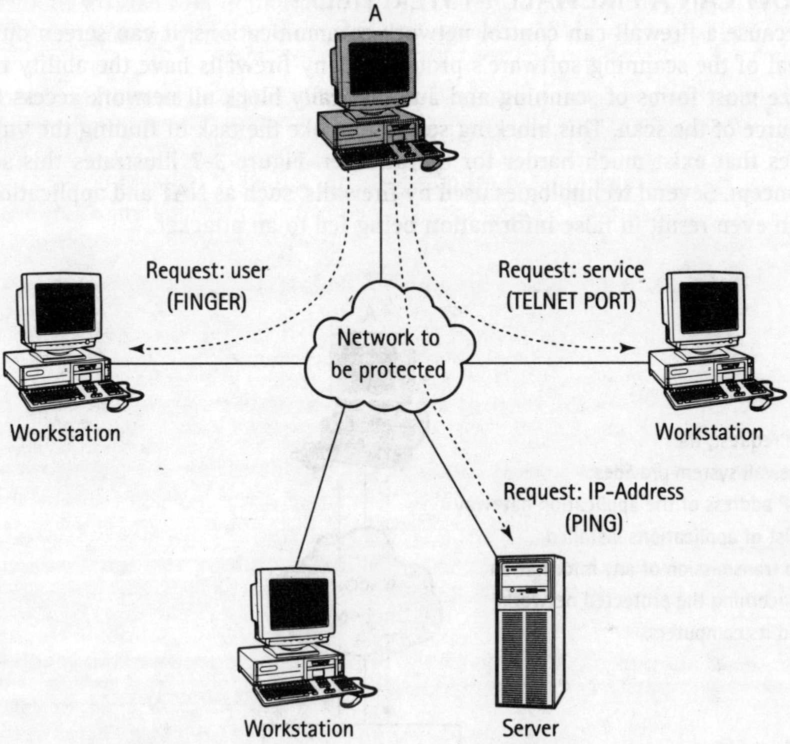

Figure 3-6: Analysis of the network using scanner programs

- **Active users.** With the Finger command, an attacker can determine which users are active on a given computer system at a particular time, whether they have already read the e-mails they have received, and so on.
- **Active services.** By addressing individual ports, an attacker can analyze which services have a daemon process installed on the corresponding computer system.
- **Vulnerability analysis on individual computer systems.** With additional tools such as ISS or SATAN, the attacker can perform a targeted vulnerability analysis. This analysis entails checking, for example, whether an attack on the computer system is possible due to errors in the configuration of daemon processes of the active services or through the use of old software versions that contain errors.

EXPLOITATION OF THE IDENTIFIED WEAKNESSES

The next step performed by the attacker is to resolutely exploit the weaknesses he has identified.

HOW CAN A FIREWALL SYSTEM HELP?

Because a firewall can control network communications, it can screen out a good deal of the scanning software's probing. Many firewalls have the ability to recognize most forms of scanning and automatically block all network access from the source of the scan. This blocking serves to make the task of finding the vulnerabilities that exist much harder for the attacker. Figure 3-7 illustrates this screening concept. Several technologies used by firewalls, such as NAT and application proxy, can even result in false information being fed to an attacker.

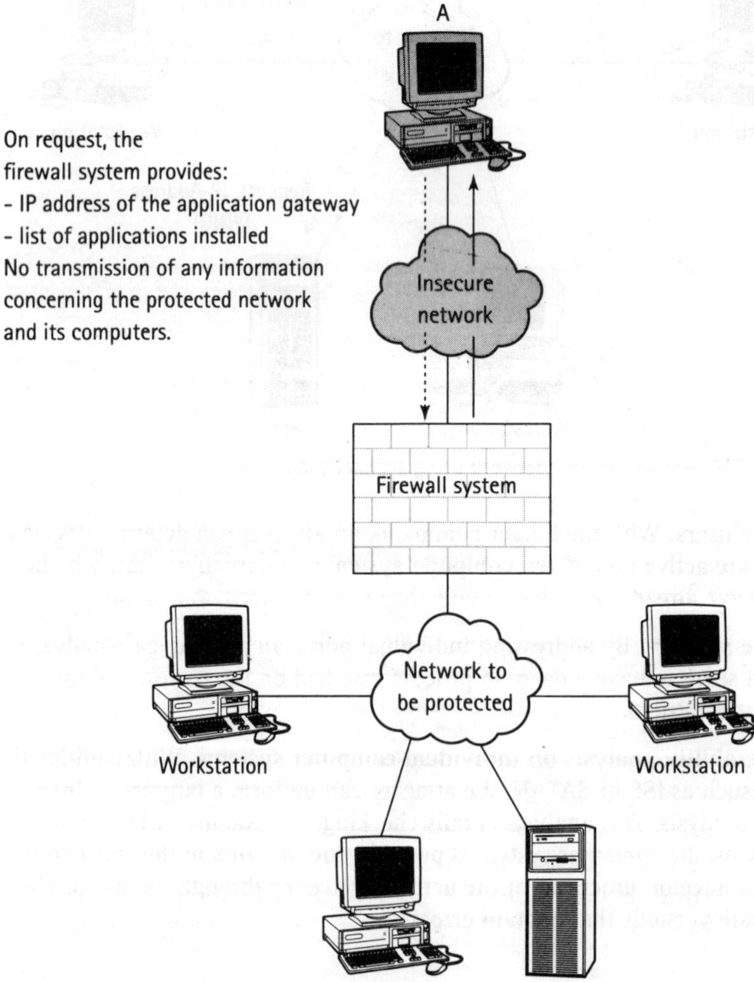

Figure 3-7: Firewall system with the security service "Hiding the internal network structure"

If a firewall system that hides the internal network structure is integrated, analysis of the protected network can be reduced. An attacker can then only analyze the IP addresses of the firewall system and establish what services would be possible over the firewall system after successful authentication.

In this case, determining how many computer systems are connected in the protected network (1, 10, 100 or 1000?) and what services are activated on the computer systems is much more difficult. This slows down the information-gathering process, which in turn allows more opportunity to detect and respond appropriately to the attacker's activities.

Password Snooping and IP Masquerade

The fact that user names and passwords are transmitted in plaintext and that everyone can assume any IP address when using the TCP/IP protocols and services (for example, Telnet or FTP) constitutes a major potential threat.

In a preliminary phase, the attacker uses an analysis program (for example, DSniff or TCPDump) to read the IP address and password used to gain access to a service by the authorized user. Programs such as DSniff and TCPDump work by placing a connected computer network card into "promiscuous mode." When a computer network card is in promiscuous mode (commonly referred to as "sniffing") it sees all network traffic local to it. Any protocol using plaintext can be viewed in real-time as it is transmitted. Specialized programs such as DSniff specifically search for information, such as user names and passwords, and print them to the screen or log them in a file.

USE OF IP ADDRESS AND PASSWORD

After the authorized communication is terminated, the attacker assumes the IP address of the *legitimate* computer system (known as *IP masquerade*). He then initiates communication with the computer systems on which he wishes to work illegally, using the password he has intercepted.

The attacker can now carry out his attack as desired, using the rights of the user whose password he has stolen (see Figure 3-8).

HOW CAN A FIREWALL SYSTEM HELP?

When a firewall system with the security service "Access control at the user level" is integrated, a *uniform cryptographic authentication* procedure controls access to all the internal computer systems in the protected network.

Because a cryptographic authentication protocol is used, only authorized users can authenticate themselves to the firewall. A user can only correctly identify himself cryptographically if he has the correct secret key.

This procedure is based on the assumption that reading the information that is transmitted (random number and cryptogram) will not help an attacker subsequently gain access to the protected network through the firewall system.

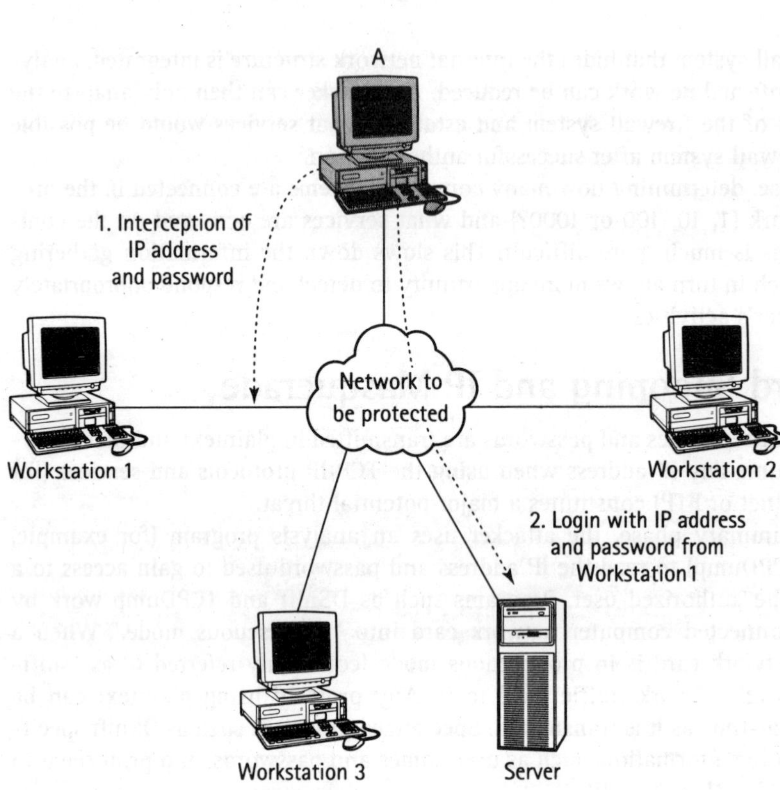

Figure 3-8: Password snooping and IP masquerade

XREF

Refer to Chapter 7 for more information on methods of authentication.

Unequivocal identification and authentication of a user means that the logbook data generated by a firewall system during communication can be unequivocally attributed to this user. Refer to Figure 3-9.

NOTE

Bear in mind that attribution of logs to specific users is the ideal result. In actual practice, the results will probably be less than perfect. Users tend to share passwords with each other for various reasons (often legitimate in their minds). This practice means that the accuracy of the authentication is not truly unequivocal. The second challenge stems from the fact that some software and organizational requirements may prevent the authentication from being implemented throughout an organization. Firewall authentication works extremely well for standard applications like Web and e-mail. However, proprietary applications typically cannot use firewall authentication successfully.

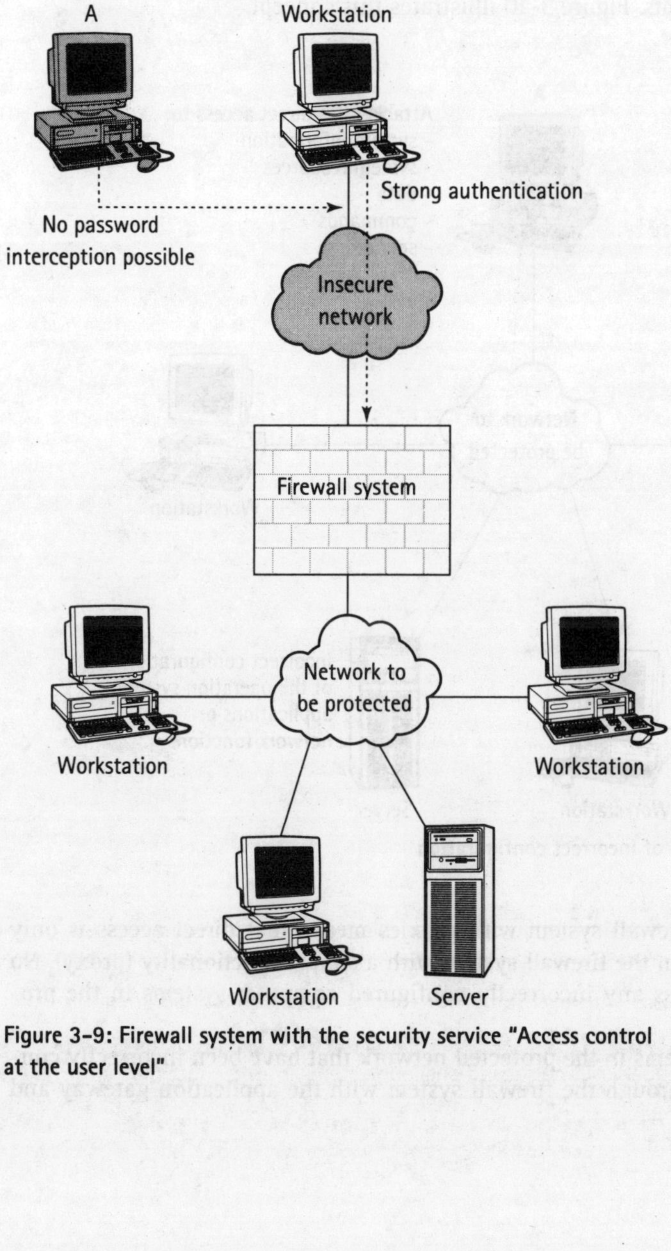

Figure 3-9: Firewall system with the security service "Access control at the user level"

Exploitation of Incorrect Configuration

For every service that is to be enabled through network access, a daemon process exists. This process can be incorrectly configured or installed so that privileged commands enabling an attack to be carried out can be executed on the remote computer system.

An attacker can exploit the fact that the computer has been configured incorrectly in order to acquire the root user rights for a computer system as a means of achieving his objectives. For example, a Web server might operate with root rights and defective CGI scripts. Figure 3-10 illustrates this concept.

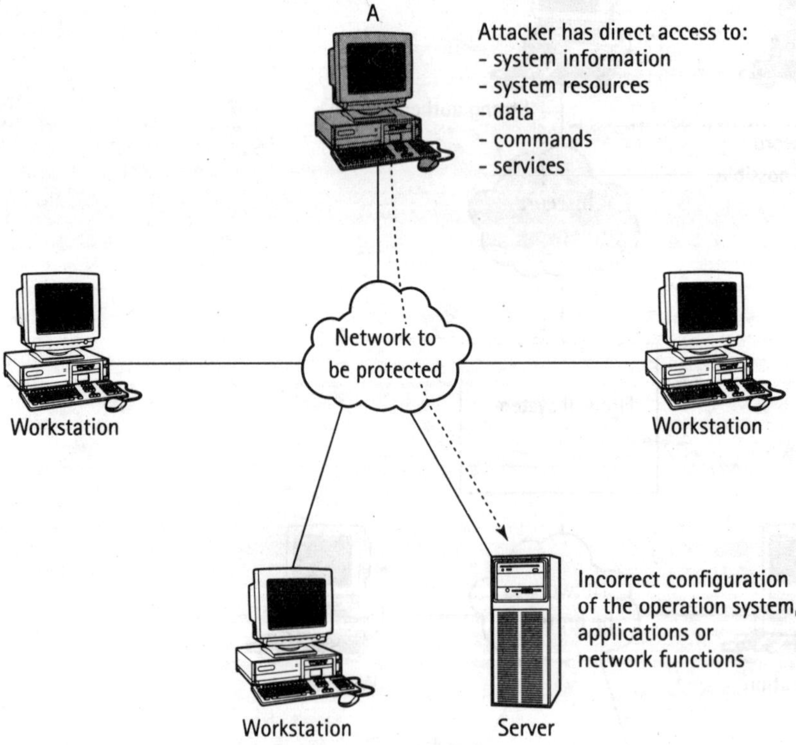

Figure 3-10: Exploitation of incorrect configuration

Integration of a firewall system with proxies means that direct access is only possible to a service on the firewall system with a simple functionality (proxy). No one can directly access any incorrectly configured computer systems in the protected network.

Any computer systems in the protected network that have been incorrectly configured are isolated through the firewall system with the application gateway and proxy (refer to Figure 3-11). In this scenario, the firewall prevents communications that originate from external networks. The firewall does not stop internal users from originating the communications. To get around this block, hackers resort to techniques such as infecting internal systems with Trojan horse software. Once installed internally, the software initiates outbound communications and establishes a connection with the hackers' systems. Fortunately, this type of bypass is relatively difficult to achieve and is not commonly seen.

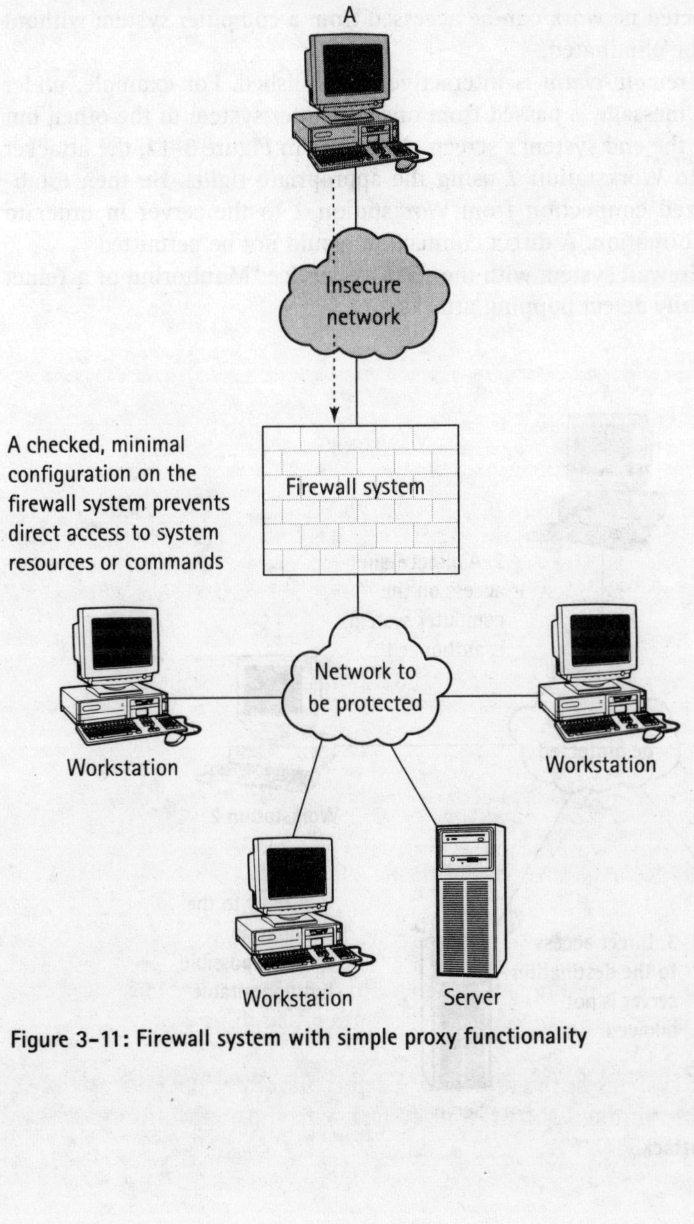

Figure 3-11: Firewall system with simple proxy functionality

Hopping

Hopping is the unauthorized relaying of a connection from one remote computer system to another in the protected network. One system is compromised. The compromised system is used to compromise another system and so on. Hopping is the process of going from one system to another. As each system is compromised, the attacker takes advantages of trust between systems to gain access to the next.

In many applications – for example, in software maintenance – allowing remote access to computer systems is sensible. However, the possibility that other computer systems in the protected network can be accessed from a computer system without authorization must be eliminated.

With hopping, a *remote chain* is interactively established. For example, under Telnet the attacker's message is passed from one computer system to the other, but is only displayed on the end system's screen. As shown in Figure 3-12, the attacker (user) gains access to Workstation 2 using the appropriate rights. He then establishes an unauthorized connection from Workstation 2 to the server in order to access important information. A direct connection would not be permitted.

Integration of a firewall system with the security service "Monitoring of a Telnet session" can *potentially* detect hopping attacks.

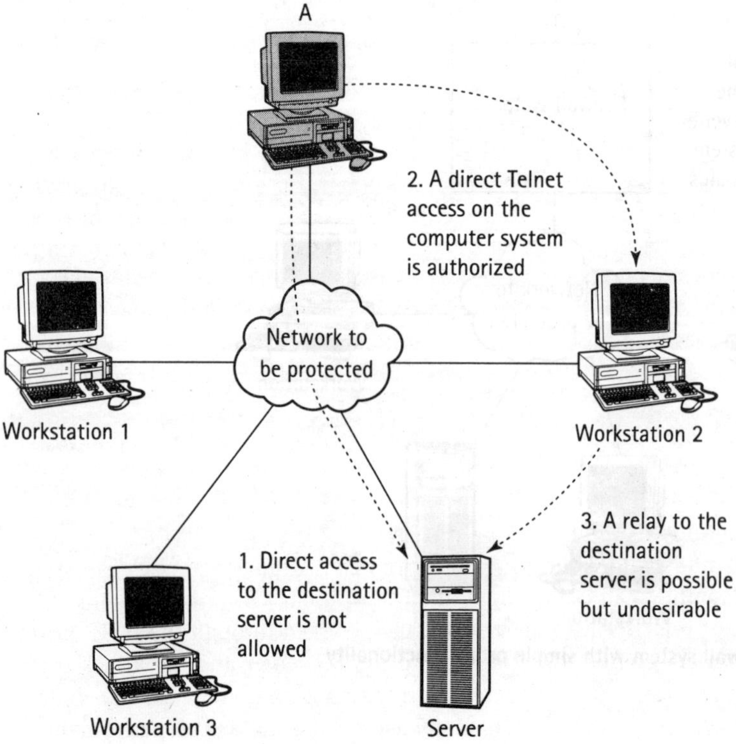

Figure 3-12: Hopping attack

The response to the attack is to close the connection, log the security-relevant event and, optionally, send a spontaneous message to the security management system.

Although many firewalls can be configured to protect against hopping attacks, they frequently aren't because it is very difficult for firewalls to differentiate between hopping attacks and legitimate user activity. In fact, implementing protections against hopping attacks often causes unacceptable levels of interference with legitimate user activity. Hopping is one of the most significant techniques in an attacker's arsenal. Most competent attackers will not attack their true target directly; instead, they will attack a target with trusted access to the true target. An attacker may hop ten or more times before he gets to the true source. Making multiple hops is not viewed negatively by attackers because doing so has the added benefit of making tracing their activities and their true source much more challenging. Figure 3-13 illustrates a firewall configured to prevent hopping.

Exploitation of Implementation Errors in Applications such as Internet Information Server

The programs used in TCP/IP communications are very complex. Programming and function errors that were repeatedly used to perpetrate attacks continue to be prevalent. In reality, it is not possible to test programs that contain more than 10,000 lines sufficiently or comprehensively to prove that errors cannot occur in any operating state. For this reason, you should assume that the programs contain security risks that could be exploited for attacks.

For example, complex applications such as Internet Information Server (IIS) have been shown to contain implementation and design errors that enable privileged commands to be executed on the remote computer system. These commands are used to carry out attacks. An attacker uses an attack against IIS to start up a program on the relevant computer system. This enables him to read information from computer systems in the protected network, as illustrated in Figure 3-14.

Integration of a firewall system with the security service "Decoupling of insecure services" prevents an attacker from perpetrating an attack against application errors from the outside.

Programs on the computer systems in the protected network that contain errors are isolated through the firewall system, so that they cannot be accessed directly but only through proxies. Figure 3-15 shows the application attack blocked by an appropriately configured firewall.

Using proxies is not a total solution to this problem. Although proxies can stop many of the attacks, they can't stop them all. The original RDS attack against IIS is a good example of this. Because the entire attack worked through the HTTP protocol, the firewall proxy passed the attack on to the IIS server and the attack was executed successfully. The other challenge to proxies is that they usually exact a significant performance overhead. In many cases, the degree of performance degradation precludes the use of proxies.

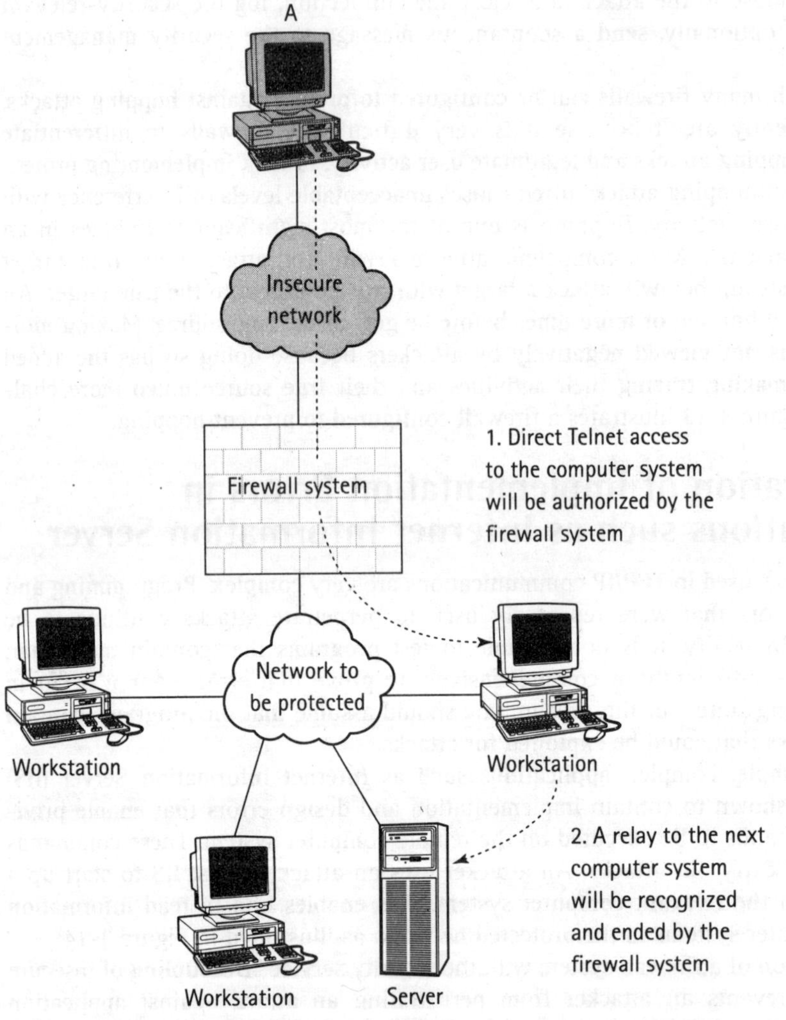

Figure 3-13: Firewall system with the security service "Monitoring of a Telnet session"

IP Address Spoofing

In address spoofing attacks, the attacker falsifies the transmitter IP address of the IP packets he wishes to send without authorization to the protected network, using an existing internal IP address of the protected network. In an unprotected network, the remote access gateway does not check whether the IP packet comes from outside or inside the network.

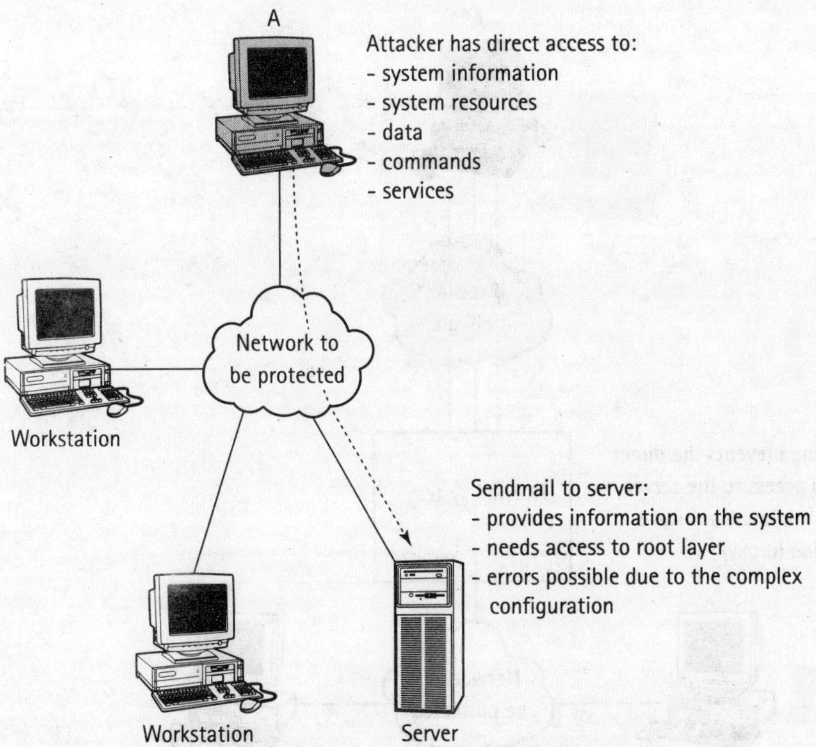

Figure 3-14: Exploitation of implementation errors in applications

In this way, the attacker can communicate with a computer system in the protected network from outside the network.

Many firewall systems have experienced problems with this type of attack. Prevention of this type of attack requires the firewall to be configured specifically to stop spoofing. While this is available in virtually all firewalls today, as with all other security functions, it must be enabled to be effective. Figure 3-16 shows an attacker spoofing an internal address due to lack of firewall protection.

Integration of a firewall system with the security service "Unequivocal recognition of the party from which an IP packet was received and corresponding access rights management" is a simple but effective defense against IP address spoofing attacks.

The spoofing prevention service works by identifying the origin of a packet. A packet with an internal network source address can't come from the insecure network. After a packet is determined to originate internally, it is allowed to pass based on further rules set by the firewall administrator. Packets with an internal source address originating from the insecure network are denied.

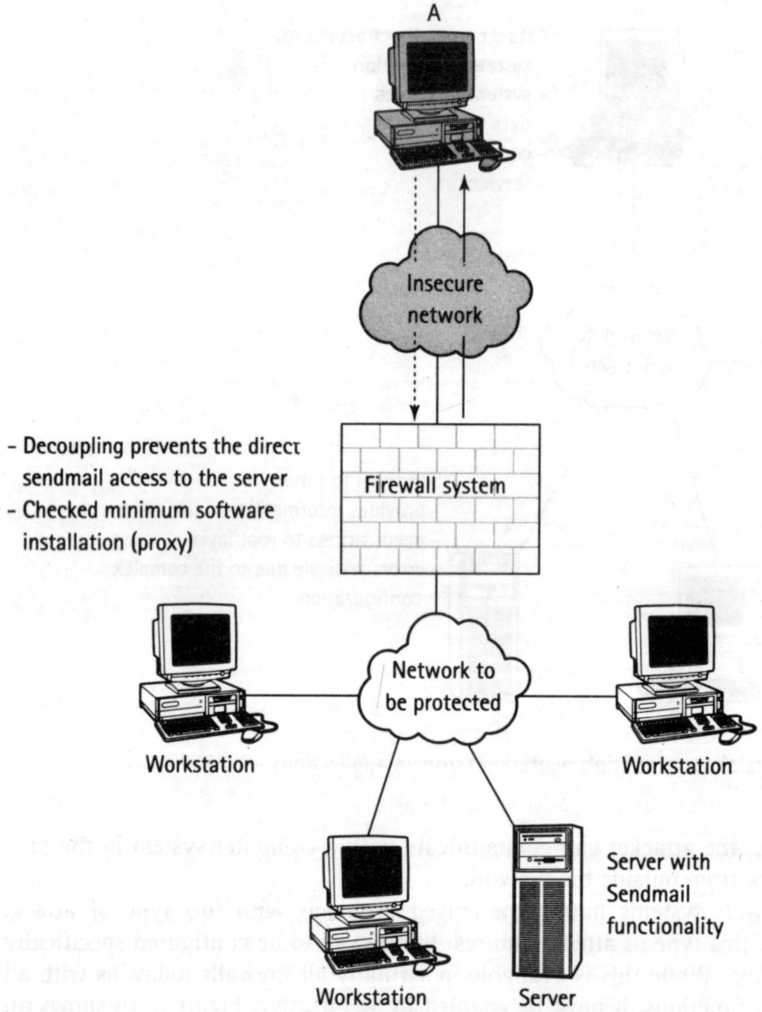

Figure 3-15: Firewall system with the security service "Decoupling of insecure services"

ICMP Attacks

The ICMP protocol, as an integrated element of the TCP/IP protocol stack, is used (among other things) to display error messages to the transmitter of IP packets if any network problems occur. The transmitter can then respond to the error. With many implementations, an automatic response is initiated immediately from the TCP/IP stack whenever certain messages occur. An attacker who transmits false ICMP protocol elements can deliberately manipulate computer systems in the protected network.

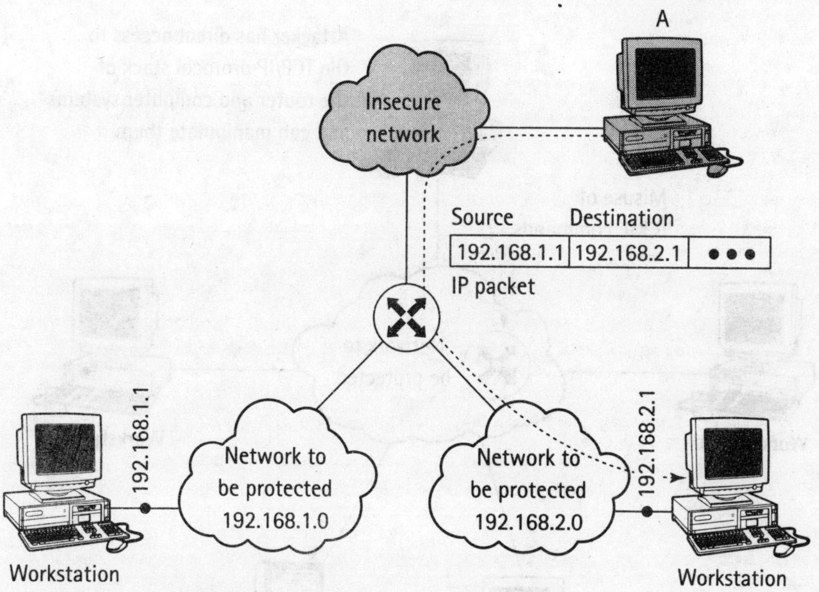

Figure 3-16: IP address spoofing

The following could be aims of an ICMP attack:

- To damage the functional capability of IP networks (perhaps through insertion of the command Fragmentation Needed, Destination Unreachable, or Source Quench), or
- To change the switching paths using the command Redirect

Figure 3-17 illustrates an attacker using an ICMP attack against the protected network's router to redirect traffic to an internal server.

Possible ICMP attacks include the following:

- **Improper use of the Destination Unreachable command.** If IP packets cannot be transmitted to the desired receiver, the last computer system in the switching system transmits the ICMP Destination Unreachable command to the transmitter. Generally, the transmitter responds by terminating the connection. By sending false Destination Unreachable commands, an attacker can terminate existing TCP/IP connections.
- **Improper use of the Fragmentation Needed command.** Transmission of the ICMP Fragmentation Needed command enables an attacker to trigger the fragmentation of IP packets in any computer system, causing the data to fragment (divide up) into small packets. Such an attack increases the network loading.

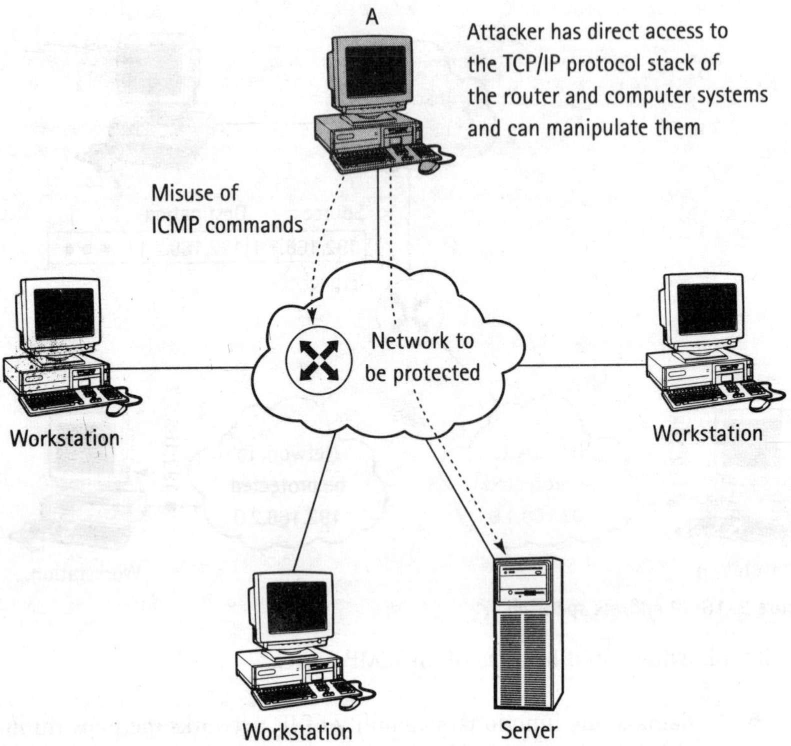

Figure 3-17: ICMP attacks

- **Improper use of the Source Quench command.** Using the ICMP Source Quench command can reduce the transmission rate of the transmitter's computer system. By improperly sending excessive numbers of artificially generated Source Quench packets, an attacker can disrupt communication.
- **Improper use of the Redirect command.** By sending targeted ICMP Redirect commands, an attacker can alter the routing tables of a network's routers in such a way that the IP packets of a communication link are transmitted over other computer systems where the data can be tampered with or read.

Integration of a firewall system with the security service "Administration of ICMP command rights" prevents an attacker from perpetrating the attacks previously described from outside (see Figure 3-18).

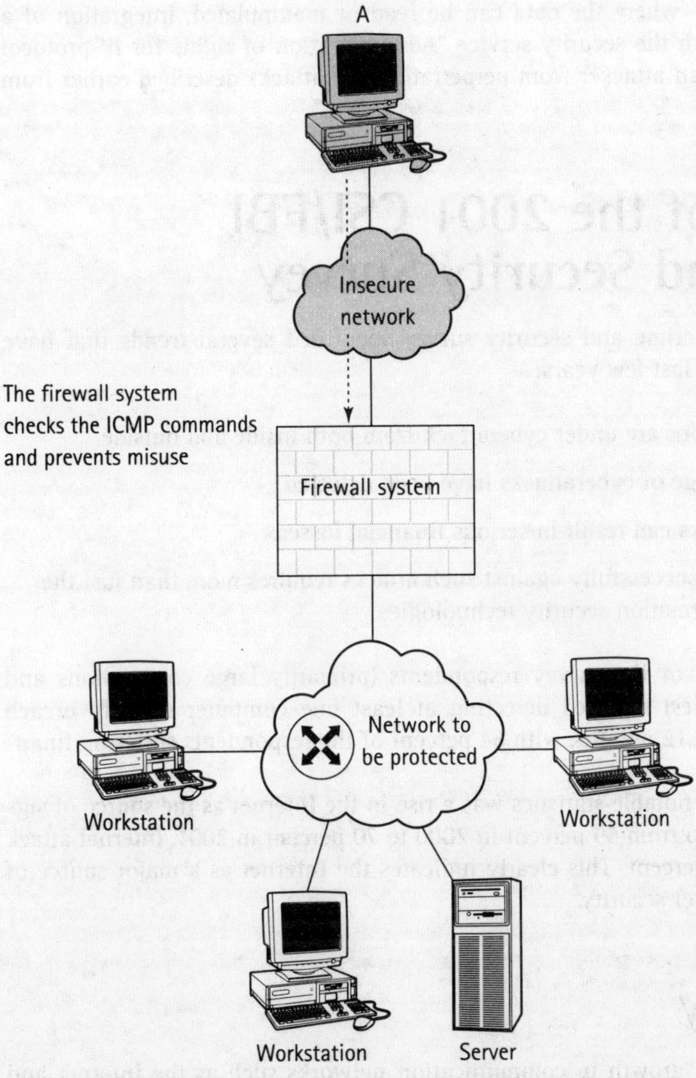

Figure 3-18: Firewall system with the security service "Administration of ICMP command rights"

Internet Routing Attacks

Various additional functions can be used in the IP header if the appropriate options are selected. The *Loose Source Routing* and *Strict Source Routing* options enable an attacker to carry out attacks on the protected network from outside by predefining the route. Under the Strict Source Routing option, all switching nodes to be passed through are specified in a prescribed sequence. This means that an attacker can arrange for the communication to pass through a particular computer system – his own, for example – where the data can be read or manipulated. Integration of a firewall system with the security service "Administration of rights for IP protocol options" prevents an attacker from perpetrating the attacks described earlier from outside.

Results of the 2001 CSI/FBI Crime and Security Survey

The 2001 CSI/FBI crime and security survey identified several trends that have developed over the last few years:

- Organizations are under cyberattack from both inside and outside.
- A wide range of cyberattacks have been detected.
- Cyberattacks can result in serious financial losses.
- Defending successfully against such attacks requires more than just the use of information security technologies.

Over 91 percent of the survey respondents (primarily large corporations and government agencies) reported detecting at least one computer security breach within the previous 12 months, with 64 percent of the respondents suffering financial loss.

One of the more notable statistics was a rise in the Internet as the source of significant attacks – up from 59 percent in 2000 to 70 percent in 2001. Internal attack sources fell to 31 percent. This clearly indicates the Internet as a major source of concern for computer security.

Summary

With the enormous growth in communication networks such as the Internet and intranets, the risk of data manipulation or data theft is also increasing, and with it, the possibility of loss or damage to the organization. Although you are not in a position to eliminate these threats, you can take steps to ensure that your vulnerability is reduced. Designing your communication systems more securely, and enabling trustworthy and controllable communications to be implemented is becoming increasingly important.

Active defense mechanisms such as security audit systems and intrusion detection and response systems are steadily gaining in importance. In the end, it is not acceptable for major organizations' IT operations to be put out of action simply because someone is scanning the systems, for instance.

On the other hand, comprehensive protective measures leaving a small residual risk will always remain. Every organization should draw up contingency plans that detail procedures and responsibilities for that "hypothetical disaster." These plans should also be tested from time to time in a practice run to prevent panic and additional damage in the event of a real disaster. The description of the various threats in this chapter is not exhaustive. To obtain additional information, you can consult various Web forums.

Chapter 4

Elements of a Firewall System

THIS CHAPTER DESCRIBES the basic elements of which firewall systems are composed. It explains how technical security mechanisms can be implemented for firewall elements, what options for assuring security exist, how those options work, and where those options' limitations lie.

A distinction is made between firewall elements that actively intervene in communications between the protected network and the insecure network and the Security Management firewall element. The latter is responsible for administration of the active firewall elements, and contains the organization's security policy as defined in the ruleset.

In practice, the packet filter and application gateway active firewall elements each address specific security needs. Each takes a different approach to integration into the network and in the possibilities for analysis and logging.

Table 4-1 defines some of the essential firewall elements discussed throughout the rest of this chapter.

TABLE 4-1 FIREWALL ELEMENT DEFINITIONS

Firewall Element	Significance
Packet filter	Packet filters analyze and control the transmitted packets from the Network Access layer and Network layer through to the Transport layer and, in the case of state-oriented packet filters, through to the Application layer.
Application gateway	Application gateways analyze and control the packets in the Application layer and offer more extensive scope for the logging of actions.
Security Management	Security Management directs and administers the active firewall elements.

Active Firewall Elements

This section defines the basic structure of the active firewall elements that are integrated in the communications interface between the insecure network and the protected network (refer to Figure 4-1).

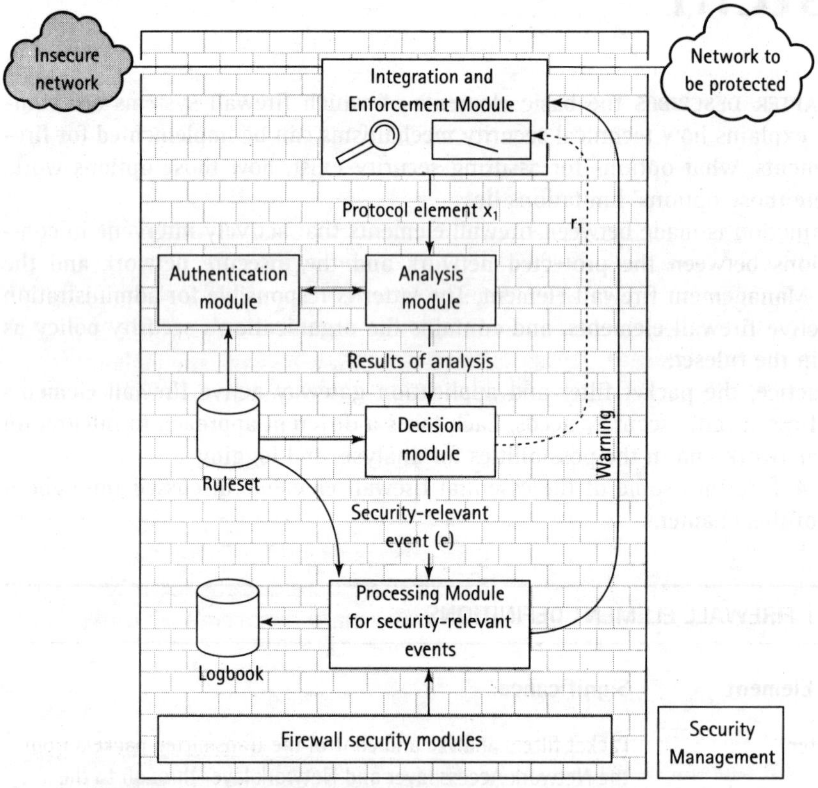

Figure 4-1: Structure of an active firewall element

Architecture of Active Firewall Elements

All active firewall elements need the following components in order to deliver the security services for which they are used.

INTEGRATION MODULE

The Integration Module implements the integration of the active firewall element into the communication system. Integration is usually accomplished through device drivers integrated into the operating system protocol stack. With a packet filter, this integration is above the Network Access layer; with an application gateway for the proxies, it is above the ports (Transport layer).

ANALYSIS MODULE

In the Analysis Module, the communication data is analyzed in terms of the capabilities of the active firewall element. In other words, the analysis module analyzes packet header data for the packet filtering element and application protocol information for the application gateway. The results are passed to the Decision Module. The depth of analysis – that is, the level of detail – is critical to security.

DECISION MODULE

The Decision Module evaluates and compares the results of the analysis with the security policy definitions laid down in the ruleset. A check is performed using access lists as to whether or not the communication data arriving is allowed to pass through the firewall. If it is, then the Integration Module allows it through. Otherwise, the communication data is not allowed through, and the event is classified as security-relevant and processed further as appropriate.

PROCESSING MODULE FOR SECURITY-RELEVANT EVENTS

This Processing Module processes all security-relevant events that are generated in the active firewall element. Depending on the ruleset and the configuration settings, a security-relevant event plus the associated log data is written to the logbook, and the alarm function ensures that Security Management is notified with a spontaneous message.

AUTHENTICATION MODULE

The Authentication Module is responsible for the identification and authentication of the instances (processes in the computer systems, users, and so on) and/or data that communicate through the active firewall element. Here, the security of the cryptographic algorithms and methods used is relevant to the overall security of the firewall system.

RULESET

The ruleset covers all the information necessary to make a decision for or against transmission of the communication data through the active firewall element. The ruleset also defines which security-relevant events should be logged and for which ones Security Management should be notified through the alarm function.

LOGBOOK

All the log data related to security-relevant events occurring during operation of an active firewall element, and for which the ruleset requires that a record be maintained, is entered in the logbook. Here, it is especially important that the log data be secure.

SECURITY MANAGEMENT

The security management module provides the interface where administrators enter and maintain the firewall ruleset. Security management also allows the log data for the security-relevant events to be analyzed from the logbooks. Security management often runs as a separate program on a management station or management server. The security management module usually communicates with the firewall system through encrypted communications. Given the sensitivity of data access through security management, it must be able to withstand attacks.

FIREWALL PROTECTION MODULE

Concealed in the Firewall Protection Module are active security enforcing functions that ensure the reliable operation of the active firewall element. These include the following security mechanisms:

- **Integrity test.** This security mechanism ensures that changes to the software (operating system, firewall applications, security mechanisms, and so on), the ruleset, and the logbook are detected. This integrity checking is implemented, for example, through regular and/or spontaneous checksum testing of the software and data (ruleset).
- **Authentication mechanism.** This security mechanism ensures that only appropriately authorized Security Management can influence the ruleset and read logbook data.
- **Operational security mechanisms.** Operational security mechanisms ensure the secure operation of the active firewall elements. For example, they monitor the logbooks and storage media (hard disks, and so on) to ensure that they are not in danger of overflowing and check to see whether the software is in a defined state (machine state).

Design Concept for an Active Firewall Element

A secure design concept for active firewall elements is described in this section. The more these security criteria are taken into account, the more effective and correct the security services of an active firewall element will be.

MINIMAL SOFTWARE

In addition to providing security services, the active firewall element itself must be able to withstand attacks, and should, therefore, use only error-free software. The firewall element must have a clear structure, design, and implementation. However, because any program can potentially contain security weaknesses, only those programs essential to the provision of the firewall functionality should be installed on the active firewall element (for example, it should not have any router functionality, or run other applications).

Unnecessary or superfluous processes in the background frequently result in security weaknesses.

SECURE INTEGRATION INTO THE COMMUNICATION SYSTEM

The security of an active firewall element depends on how well the security mechanisms have been integrated into the communication system (network software, operating system, and so on). Steps must be taken to ensure that the firewall security-enforcing functions cannot be circumvented via the operating system or the communication software used (TCP/IP software, network access drivers, and so on).

When IP forwarding (a kernel functionality) is used, it is possible for communications to bypass the firewall element, making the security mechanisms ineffective.

SEPARATE SECURITY MANAGEMENT

The requirement to install only the minimal amount of software on the active firewall elements means that Security Management must be implemented separately from the actual security-enforcing functions of the active firewall element, so that the highest possible degree of security can be ensured.

A separate Security Management implementation can be achieved using a separate computer system or a removable hard disk that is only used for the purpose of specifying the ruleset.

SIMPLE, RELIABLE, AND AUTHORIZED USE OF SECURITY MANAGEMENT

Security Management should be reliable and easy-to-use so that the rules can be entered without errors. Check for contradictions within the rules that might inadvertently result in entries that place security at risk.

To prevent Security Management from being used by attackers to permit communications through the active firewall element, only an authorized administrator should be able to access the active firewall elements via Security Management.

By adhering to this system architecture and design concept and by performing an evaluation according to recognized criteria – such as ITSEC or the Common Criteria (CC) – you can successfully implement the technical basis for the security and trustworthiness of firewall systems.

The goal of this section is to show how technical security mechanisms can be implemented for firewall elements, specific ways of ensuring security, how they work, and where their limitations lie. A firewall system may be composed of the following basic elements:

- Packet filter
- Stateful inspection
- Application gateway
- Proxies
- Network address translation
- Virtual private network
- Adaptive proxies

Packet Filters

A *packet filter* is an active firewall element that analyzes and controls the inbound and outbound packets in the Network Access, Network, and Transport layers. It records and analyzes the packets (for example, Ethernet or token ring) that are transmitted over the physical cable. The interposition of the packet filter between the networks keeps them physically separate. A packet filter normally behaves like a simple bridge. Packet filters are not confined to TCP/IP protocols.

A packet filter interprets the content of the packets and checks whether the data in the corresponding communication layer headers complies with the defined rule base. The rules are defined so that only necessary communication is allowed and settings known to pose a risk to security, such as IP fragmentation, are avoided. The packet filters occur at the network level so they are transparent to users.

The functions of a packet filter can be compared to those of a security guard. When a supplier's truck drives up to the factory gates with a delivery, the "packet filter security guard" examines the logo on the side of the vehicle to see if it is familiar to him. If the vehicle passes this summary inspection, the packet filter security guard allows the truck to pass through the gate without checking the shipping manifest.

Packet Filter General Mode of Operation

Figure 4-2 illustrates the general manner in which packet filters work. It is important to know what information from the packets is used in the analysis.

Different checks can be performed in the different communication layers as determined by the specific firewall capabilities and ruleset in place.

- The party from whom the packet is received is checked (this information is obtained from the Integration Module).
- In the Network Access layer, the following checks are performed:
  - The source and destination addresses
- The protocol type used
- In the Network layer, depending on the protocol, the following checks are performed:
  - IP protocol (for example, the source and destination addresses and the layer 4 protocol, as well as the checkbox and flags)
  - ICMP protocol, such as ping and network redirect
  - IPX protocol (for example, network/node)
  - OSI protocol (the OSI network address)
- In the Transport layer, the following checks are performed:

- With UDP/TCP, the port numbers (source and destination ports). Services such as FTP, Telnet, and http have fixed port numbers associated with them.
- With TCP, the direction of the connection setup

◆ In addition, a check can be performed on packets as to whether access through the packet filter occurs within predefined time bands (for example, Monday through Friday between 7 a.m. and 7 p.m., Saturdays between 7 a.m. and 1 p.m., Sundays not allowed).

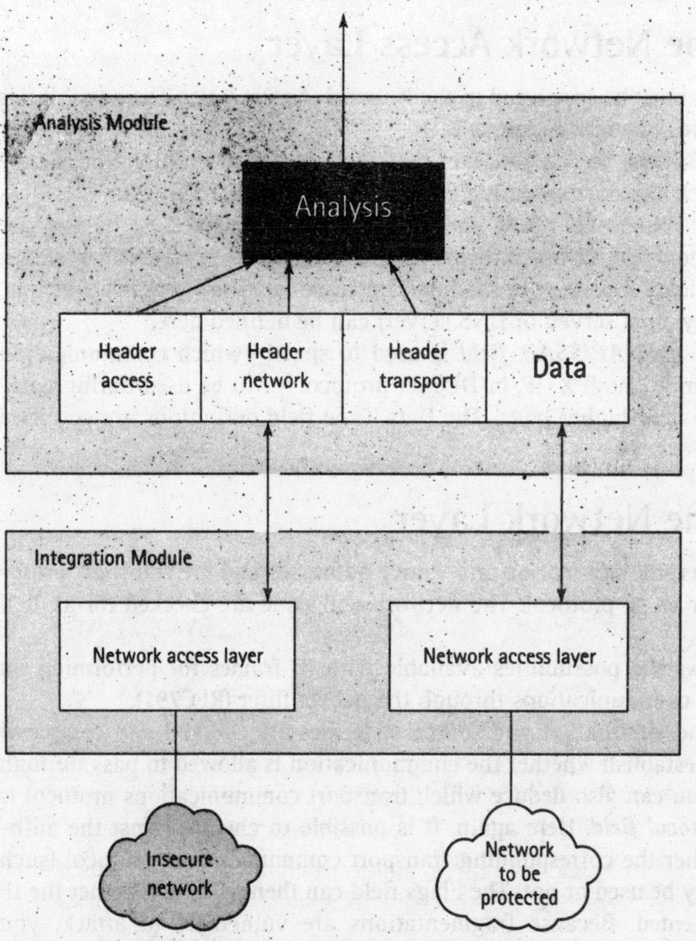

Figure 4-2: General mode of operation of a packet filter

The verification information is taken from the ruleset (access list, authorization list) and compared with the analysis results. If the rules have been violated, a security-relevant event is logged, and, if the relevant option has been set, a spontaneous message is sent to Security Management with the log data related to the security-relevant event so appropriate and prompt action can be taken.

The following sections explain in greater detail what checks can be performed in the various communication layers. With intranets, checks in the Network Access layer are generally performed in the local area, while in the Network and Transport layers, checks are aimed at controlling communications over the Internet and intranets.

Checks in the Network Access Layer

Different standards must be supported in the Network Access layer. The possibilities with an Ethernet are shown in Figure 4-3.

With Ethernet packets, the packet filter can analyze the destination and source addresses and check the corresponding ruleset to see whether the computer systems, servers, and routers to which the addresses (MAC addresses) belong are allowed to pass a communication through the packet filter. With firewall systems, the direct communication partner in the lowest communication layer (for example, application gateway, mail server, or DNS server) can be defined here.

The *Data Type*, or *DSAP/SSAP, field* is used to specify which communication protocol – for example, the IPX, IP, or DECnet protocol – will be used during communications in the next higher layer. The Data Type field definitions are specified in RFC1700.

Checks in the Network Layer

In the Network layer, the destination and source addresses and the transport protocol are checked for an IP protocol. The network and node are checked for an IPX protocol.

Figure 4-4 shows the possibilities available with IP frames for performing an analysis to control communications through the packet filter (RFC791).

With an IP frame, destination and source addresses are checked and compared with the ruleset to establish whether the communication is allowed to pass through the packet filter. You can also deduce which transport communications protocol is used from the *Protocol field*. Here again, it is possible to check against the authorization list whether the corresponding transport communications protocol (such as TCP or UDP) may be used or not. The Flags field can then tell you whether the IP packets are fragmented. Because fragmentations are vulnerable to attack, you should prohibit them by defining the rights appropriately.

The Options field determines which options (source routing, and so on) are allowed through the packet filter. Source routing can and should be forbidden, as it is possible for attacks to be carried out using this function.

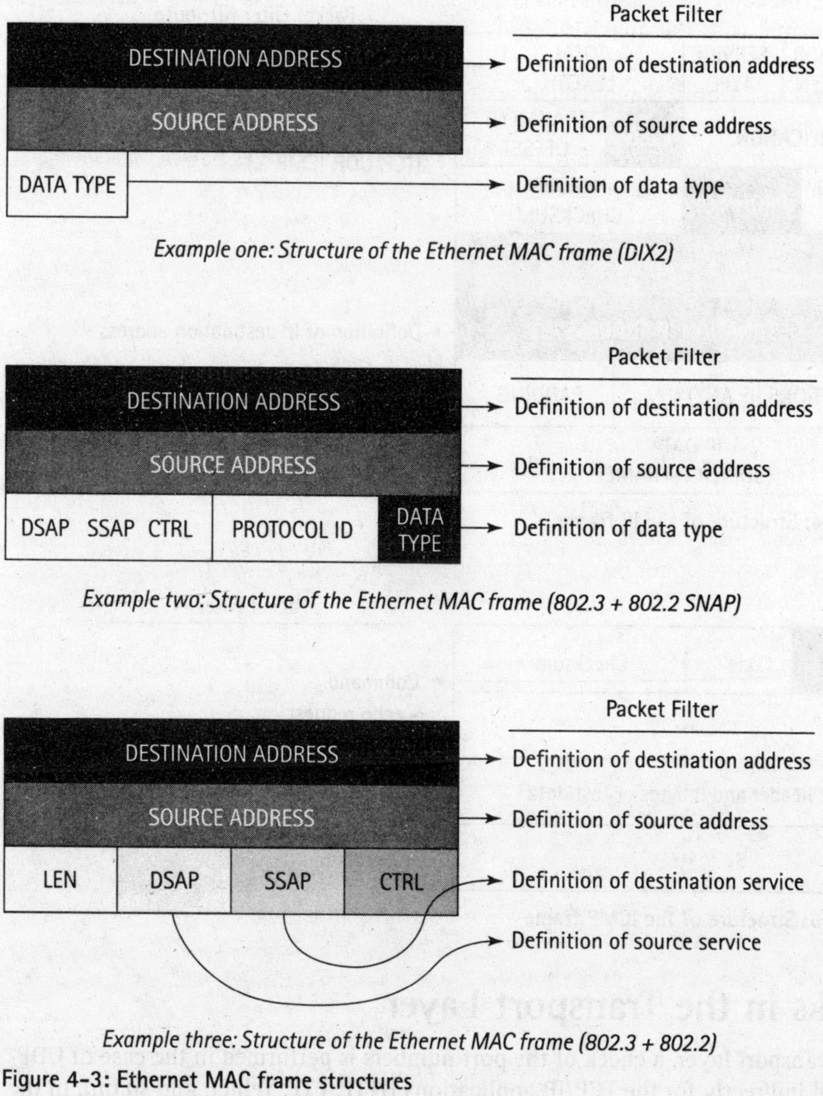

Figure 4-3: Ethernet MAC frame structures

With ICMP (RFC792) it is possible to analyze the Type field in which the commands are defined. Here, commands such as EchoRequest, EchoReply, Redirect, and Destination Unreachable can be either allowed or forbidden (refer to Figure 4-5). For example, EchoRequest and EchoReply, which are used for the Ping command, might be permitted, but the Redirect command, which can be used for attacks, should be forbidden. The commands are defined in RFC792.

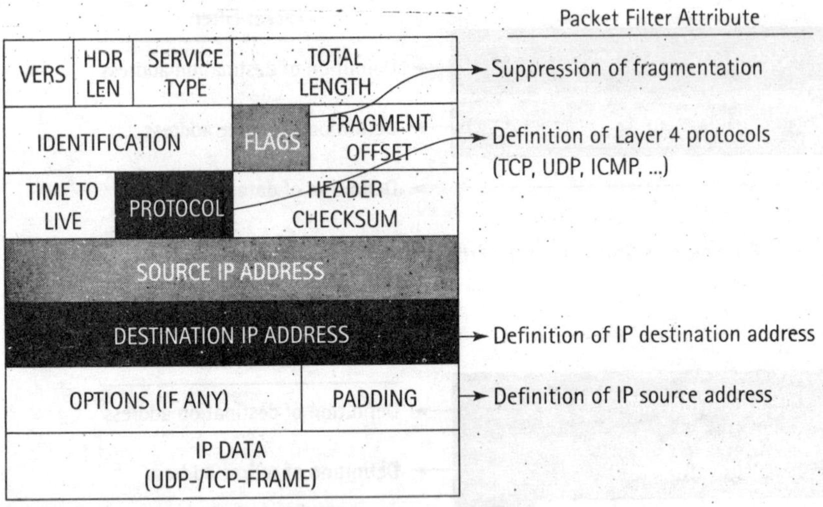

Figure 4-4: Structure of the IP frame

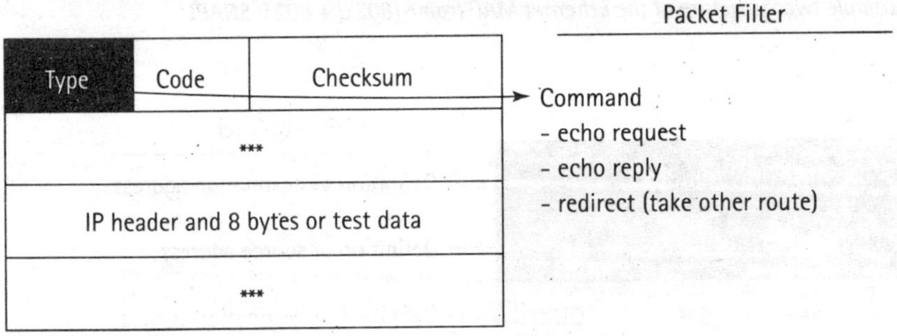

Figure 4-5: Structure of the ICMP frame

Checks in the Transport Layer

In the Transport layer, a check of the port numbers is performed in the case of UDP/TCP (and indirectly for the TCP/IP applications HTTP, FTP, Telnet, and so on). In the case of TCP, the direction of the connection setup is also checked.

THE UDP TRANSPORT PROTOCOL

UDP is a connectionless communications protocol (see Figure 4-6). In other words, the UDP packets are transmitted independently of each other, with no guarantee or check that the packets are delivered correctly. No distinction is made between a new UDP connection setup and the packets within an existing UDP connection.

With the UDP frame (RFC768), the packet filter can analyze the source and destination ports. Using an authorization list, it is possible to specify which services can be run over UDP (for example, SNMP, TFTP, and so on).

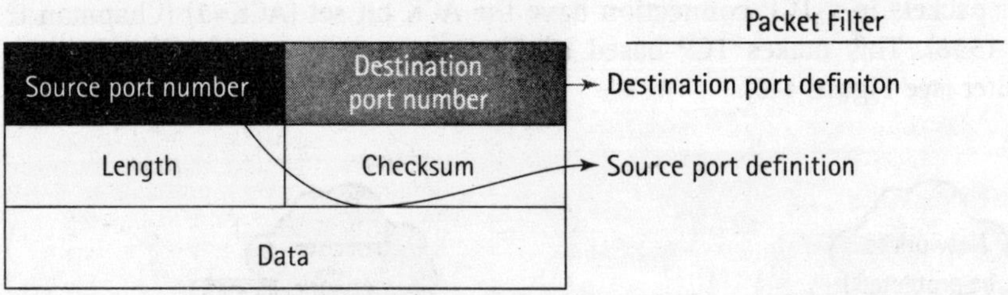

Figure 4-6: Structure of the UDP frame

As a rule, prohibit UDP packets if possible, because they can be used to carry out numerous attacks.

THE TCP TRANSPORT PROTOCOL

Figure 4-7 shows what information can be analyzed and checked with a TCP frame.

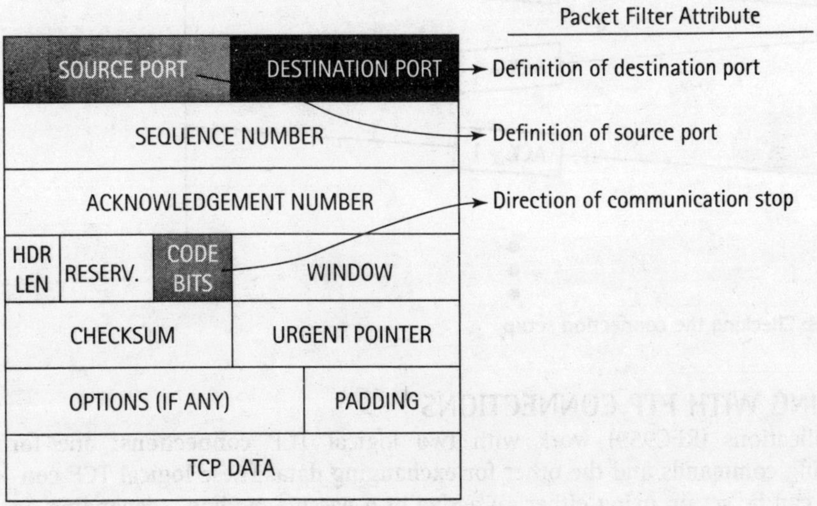

Figure 4-7: Structure of the TCP frame

With the TCP frame (RFC793), the packet filter can analyze the source and destination ports. Services allowed through the packet filter (at particular times) are specified in an authorization list. Moreover, the direction in which the connection has been established can be identified from the Code Bits field through interpretation of the ACK (acknowledge) bit. In this way, connections can be established in only one direction for security reasons.

CHECKING THE CONNECTION SETUP

TCP is a connection-oriented communications protocol. During connection setup, TCP always works without the ACK bit in the Code Bits field (that is, ACK=0). All the other packets in a TCP connection have the ACK bit set (ACK=1) (Chapman & Zwicky, 1996). This makes TCP-based applications easier to control through a packet filter (see Figure 4-8).

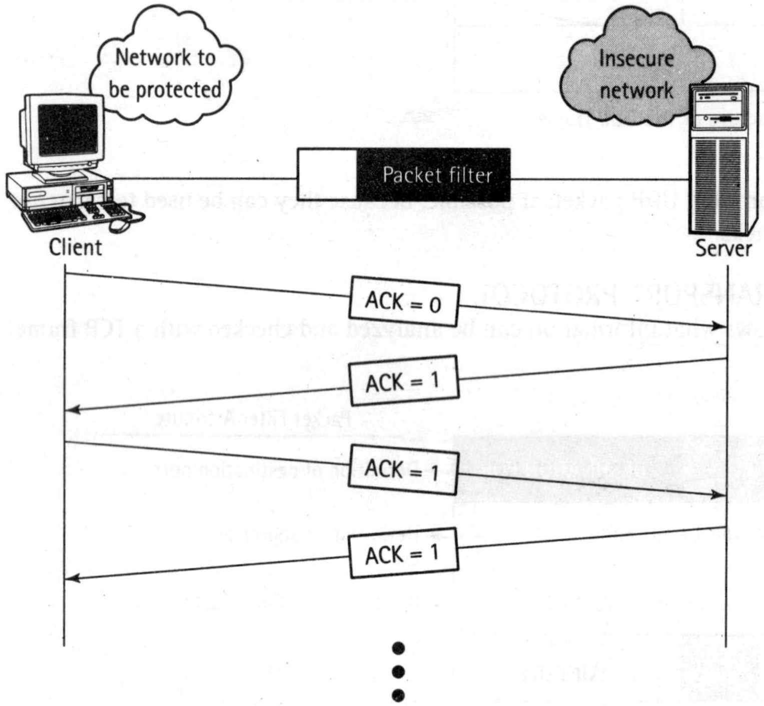

Figure 4-8: Checking the connection setup

FILTERING WITH FTP CONNECTIONS

FTP applications (RFC959) work with two logical TCP connections: one for exchanging commands and the other for exchanging data. These logical TCP connections can be set up using either an active or a passive method – depending on the viewpoint of the FTP client (Chapman & Zwicky, 1996).

FTP CONNECTION SETUP

During an FTP connection setup, the client uses two port numbers above 1024 (for example, 4320 and 4321). The client establishes the TCP connection for the commands over the first port (for example, 4320). The server receives the commands over the defined port 21.

The two methods by which the data channel can be established by the computer systems with FTP applications are described below.

ACTIVE METHOD

With the command `PORT 4321`, the client tells the server the number of the port over which it intends to process the data. The server sends the data from its defined port 20 to the client's port, number 4321 (see Figure 4-9).

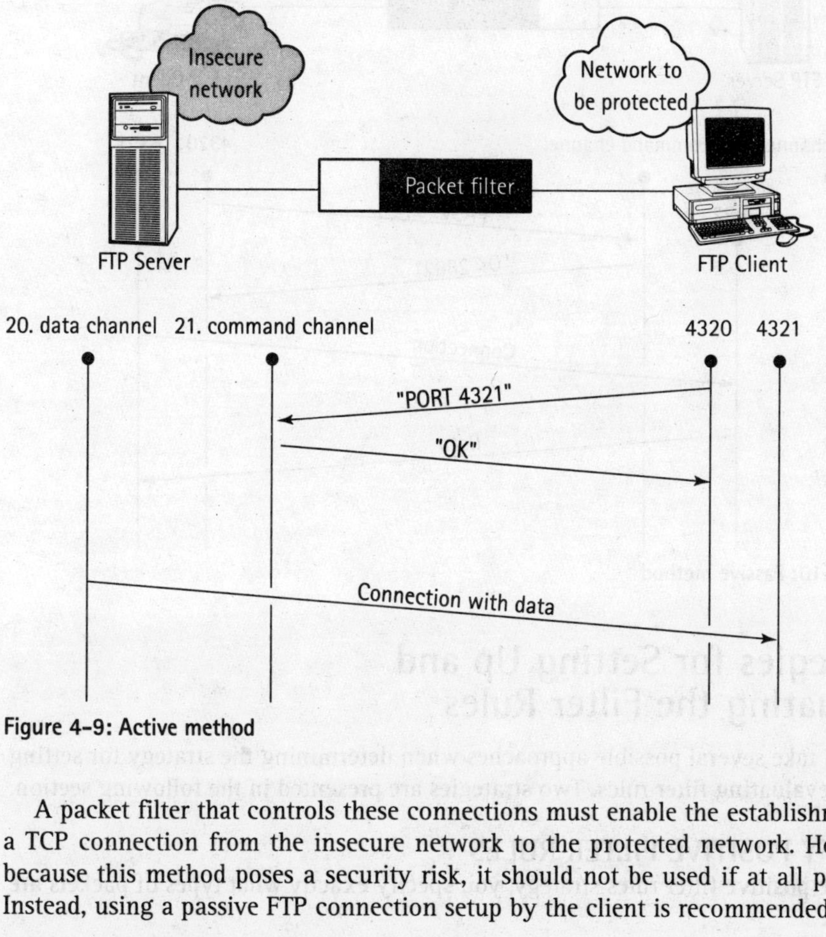

Figure 4-9: Active method

A packet filter that controls these connections must enable the establishment of a TCP connection from the insecure network to the protected network. However, because this method poses a security risk, it should not be used if at all possible. Instead, using a passive FTP connection setup by the client is recommended.

PASSIVE METHOD

With the passive method, the client establishes the TCP connection. When combined with a packet filter, this method can result in a higher level of security. The passive method is illustrated in Figure 4-10.

Keep in mind that the passive method is not offered by all client/server FTP implementations.

OTHER POSSIBLE STIPULATIONS

The times that each filter rule applies should be specified in the packet filters (for example, Mondays to Fridays from 8 a.m. and 5 p.m., Saturdays from 8 a.m. to noon, and at no time on Sundays).

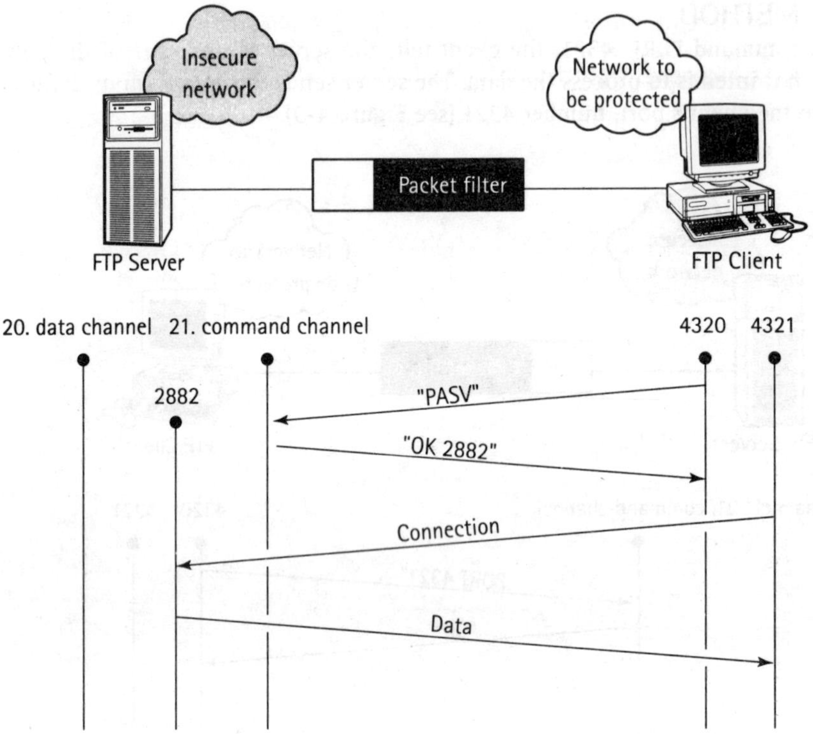

Figure 4-10: Passive method

Strategies for Setting Up and Evaluating the Filter Rules

You can take several possible approaches when determining the strategy for setting up and evaluating filter rules. Two strategies are presented in the following section.

SPECIFY POSITIVE FILTER RULES

With the positive filter rules strategy, you specify exactly what types of packets are allowed.

- You must specify exactly what is to be allowed.
- Everything that is not explicitly allowed is automatically forbidden.
- The firewall element only allows what is explicitly characterized as "allowed" in the access list.

SPECIFY NEGATIVE FILTER RULES

With the negative filter rules strategy, you specify exactly what packets are denied.

- Begin with the principle that everything is allowed.
- Using specific entries, specify what is to be forbidden.
- The packet filter only prohibits what is explicitly characterized as "not allowed" in the access list.

EVALUATION

Positive filters are preferable, as it is not possible using this strategy to leave out an entry (prohibiting something) through carelessness and thereby create a security problem. Negative filters must be handled with caution, because inept stipulations or failure to remember entries that are required can result in settings that pose a security risk.

Example of the Use of a Packet Filter

Security can be implemented between two networks that have different protection requirements with the aid of packet filters.

Figure 4-11 shows two networks: Network X, with the IP address range 192.168.3.X, and Network Y, with the IP address range 192.168.5.Y. The two networks are independent of each other and no link exists between them. The administrator of Server 1 in Network X is working at Workstation A in Network Y and wants to access Server 1 of Network X remotely. The two networks are to be connected by a packet filter in such a manner that only a Telnet session from Workstation A in Network Y to Server 1 in Network X is permitted.

CHARACTERISTICS OF THE TELNET COMMUNICATION SERVICE

The remote terminal protocol, telnet, has the following characteristics:

- Telnet is based on TCP.
- The standard port number used by the Telnet server is 23 (TCP destination port number).
- The TCP source port number used by the Telnet client is any port number greater than 1023.

NOTE: The packet filter operates with positive filter rules. In other words, it is necessary to specify what should be permitted, and everything that is not explicitly permitted is automatically forbidden.

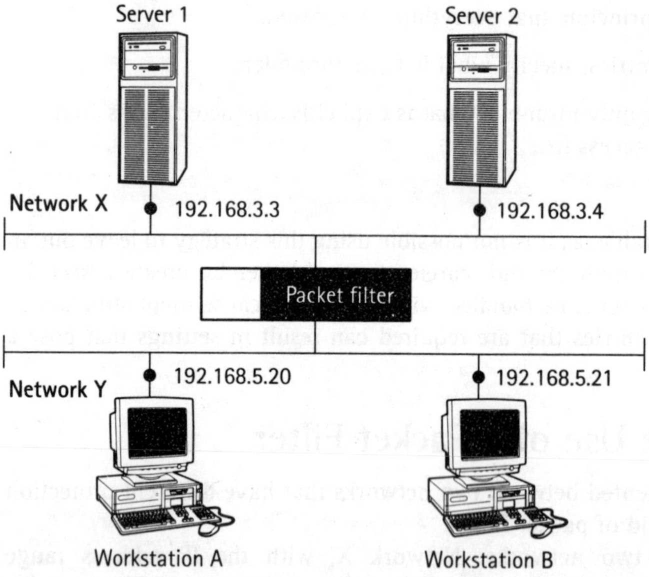

Figure 4-11: Example of the use of a packet filter

REQUIRED TELNET FILTER RULES

Here is an example of specific filter rules for telnet.

- Workstation A can use the Telnet service on Server 1 on weekdays between 7 a.m. and 5 p.m. and establish this connection under the following additional conditions:
  - Workstation A must use the IP address 192.168.5.20.
  - Server 1 must use the IP address 192.168.3.3.
  - The transport protocol used is TCP.
  - The Telnet port on Server 1 must be 23.
  - The source port on Workstation A must be greater than 1023.
- Workstation A cannot do the following:
  - Use the Telnet service on Server 1 at any time other than the times specified.
  - Use any services other than those specified.
  - Access any other computer systems in network X – for example, Server 2.
- Workstation B can't access Servers 1 or 2.

The filter rules that are necessary to specify the preceding conditions are presented in Table 4-2.

TABLE 4-2 REQUIRED FILTER RULES

Computer System	Source Address	Destination Address	Transport Protocol	Source Port	Destination Port	Connection Setup Allowed	Weekdays	Time Window
A with S1	192.168.5.20	192.168.3.3	TCP	> 1023	23	Yes	Mon–Fri	7 a.m. to 6 p.m.
S1 with A	192.168.3.3	192.168.5.20	TCP	23	> 1023	No	Mon–Fri	7 a.m. to 6 p.m.

These filter rules specify which source address Workstation A can use to access which destination address of Server 1 over TCP. In addition, precise rules specify the timeframe (days, times) within which access is permitted. The reply is specified precisely in the packet filter, from which source address and to which destination address Server 1 may communicate with Workstation A using the TCP communication protocol, to the source and destination ports. Connection setup is only permitted from Workstation A to Server 1.

RESULT

With the aid of the packet filter, you can specify that workstation A can have a Telnet session with Server 1 at particular times, but that all other communications links are actively forbidden. Communication remains transparent to the administrator, Workstation A, and Server 1 – that is, the packet filter is not "visible" and does not need any other instructions.

LIMITATIONS OF PACKET FILTERS

Any other service that has been activated on Server 1 on port 23 can also pass through the packet filter. The packet filter can't determine whether port 23 is being used for a Telnet session or for another application. This potential weakness must be considered in a manner appropriate to the potential threat. An insider could perpetrate an attack. The only way to deter an attack that exploits this packet filter weakness is for the communication partners (the users of workstation A and Server 1) to work together.

Dynamic Packet Filters

This section describes how dynamic packet filters work. With connectionless communications links, such as UDP, determining the exact place from which a connection is being established is not possible. In the case of the UDP protocol, dynamic packet filters also take note of the IP addresses and source and destination ports for UDP packets sent "to the outside," only allowing "replies" from virtual connections whose parameters match those values. In other words, only reply packets that arrive from the same computer system and the same port to which the original UDP packet was sent are allowed through, while outgoing reply packets are sent back to the same computer system and the same port from which the original UDP packet was sent. Packet filters that possess this property are described as *dynamic* because the filter rules are adapted internally dynamically. The rules adapted for a given reply apply only temporarily, and if no reply arrives within a defined period, the dynamic rules are automatically deleted by the dynamic packet filter.

Figure 4-12 shows what information (source address, source port, destination address, destination port, and time at which the packet was transmitted) is held in the dynamic packet filter so that an accurate assignment can take place. This property can also be used for TCP connections (Chapman & Zwicky, 1996).

Services such as SNMP can be provided more securely through packet filters that possess this property.

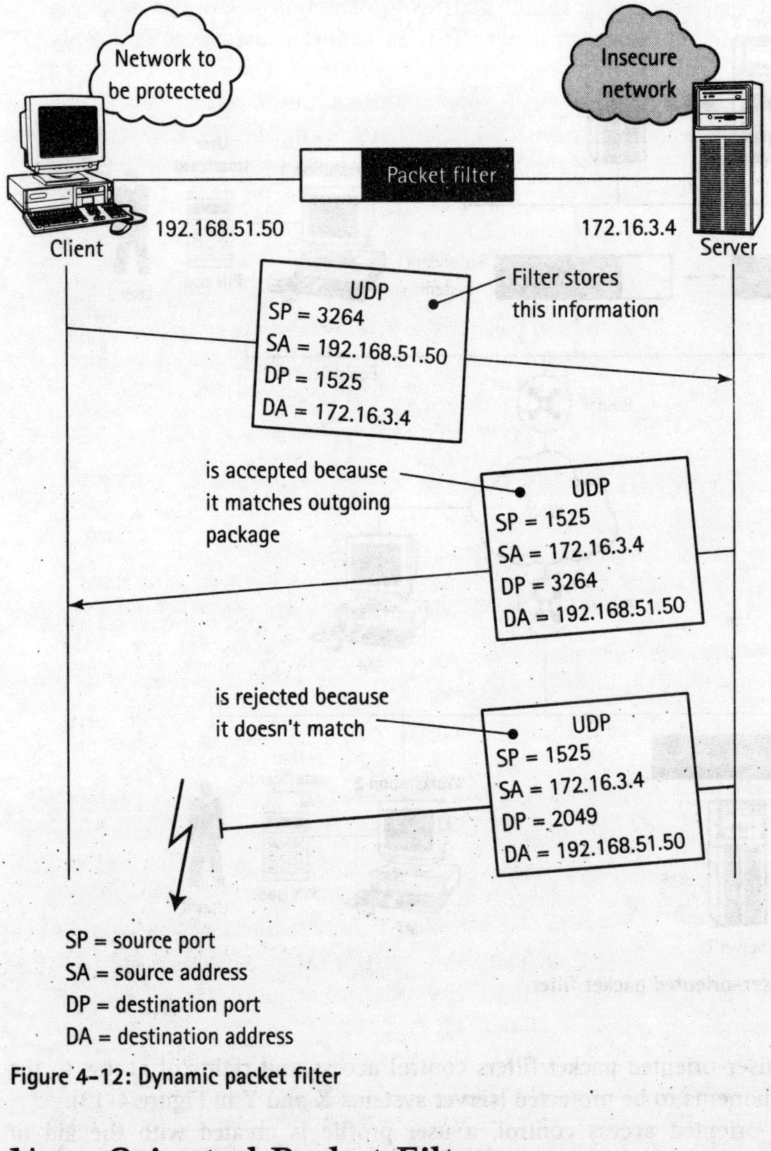

Figure 4-12: Dynamic packet filter

User-Oriented Packet Filters

Packet filters generally work in an address-oriented manner – that is, they are oriented to the IP addresses of the computer systems. However, certain packet filters can also assign connections to users. These packet filters are then known as *user-oriented packet filters*. In this case, the access control and access rights management in a network are defined in a user-oriented way with the aid of authentication procedures. Figure 4-13 illustrates an example of a user-oriented packet filter.

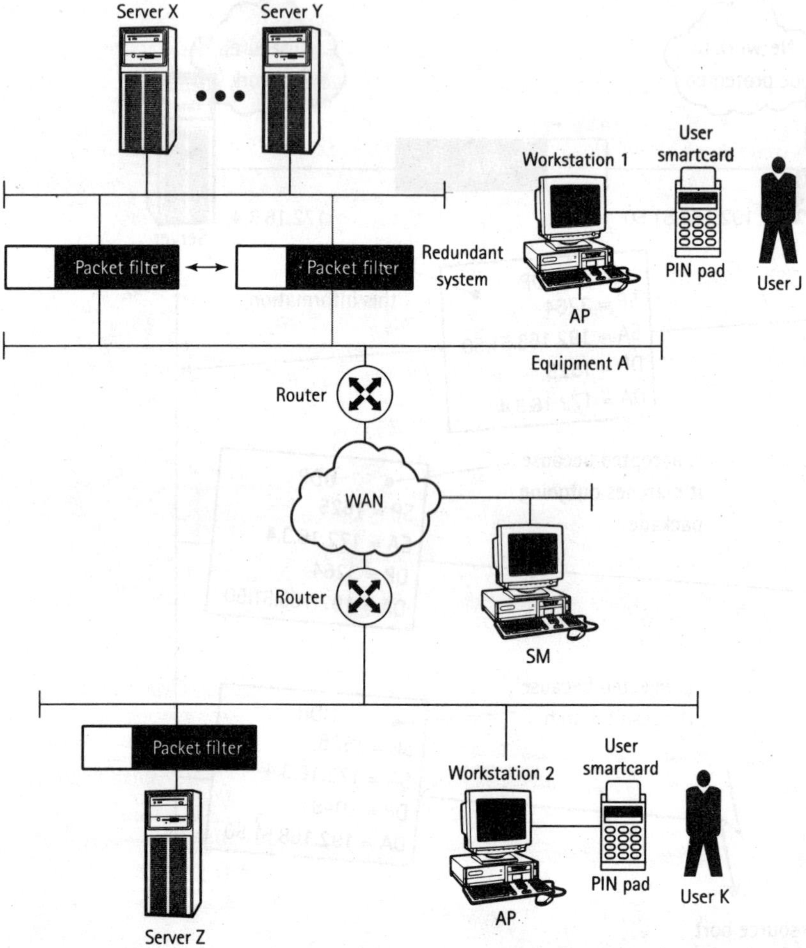

Figure 4-13: User-oriented packet filter

Here, the user-oriented packet filters control access and rights of access to the network components to be protected (server systems X and Y in Figure 4-13).

With user-oriented access control, a user profile is created with the aid of Security Management for every user who will be allowed to access a network component protected by a packet filter. This user profile specifies what communications protocols and applications can be used, and at what times and on what computer systems they may be used.

A user who wants to access a protected computer system (server X or server Y) must first activate his smart card, using a PIN (personal identification number), for example. An Authentication Process (AP) then carries out an authentication dialog with the packet filter with the aid of the smart card. If the authentication dialog completes successfully, the packet filter, acting on behalf of the protected computer systems (servers X and Y), identifies and authenticates the user. The communication profile of the user is dynamically loaded from the security database (SMIB) into the packet filter. This enables the user to access the protected computer system (server X or server Y) – assuming he has the appropriate access rights – using the defined communications protocols of the computer system from which he has authenticated himself (refer to Figure 4-14).

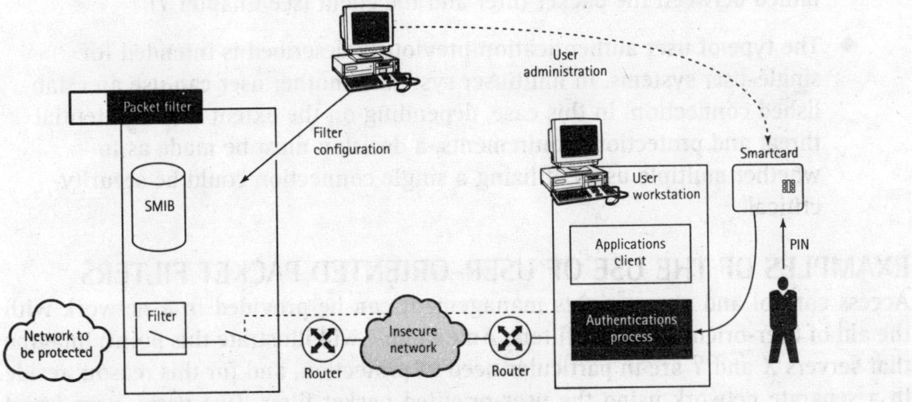

Figure 4-14: Access control and access rights management

The packet filter actively prevents the use of nonpermitted communications protocols. If defined by the administrator, a spontaneous message would be sent to Security Management, or the event would be logged accordingly in the packet filter logbook. Following a successful authentication, a reauthentication can be repeated at defined time intervals, either between authentication process and packet filter or between activated smart card and packet filter.

It is also conceivable to use the smart card for other applications — for example, for access control to the building and for the local security of the computer system. Some organizations use smart cards that allow the implementation of different applications.

REDUNDANCY SYSTEM

To increase the resiliency of packet filters, it should be possible to operate them redundantly, so that their overall availability increases. Higher availability can be achieved by switching a second packet filter in parallel to the active packet filter and operating it in Standby mode as a redundancy system. Standby mode means that the second packet filter is operated with the same configuration as the active packet filter; thus, if the active packet filter fails, the redundancy packet filter can spontaneously replace it. Communication between the two packet filters is effected over a separate additional connection. All configuration changes performed on the active packet filter are communicated to the redundancy packet filter over this connection, resulting in real-time adjustment of the access rights data in the two packet filters.

Other aspects of a user-oriented packet filter are as follows:

- If the connection is encrypted, continuous authentication can be maintained between the packet filter and the client (see Chapter 7).
- The type of user authentication previously described is intended for single-user systems. In multiuser systems, another user can use an established connection. In this case, depending on the extent of the potential threat and protection requirements, a decision must be made as to whether multiple users utilizing a single connection could be security-critical.

EXAMPLES OF THE USE OF USER-ORIENTED PACKET FILTERS

Access control and access rights management can be provided in a network with the aid of user-oriented packet filters. An example will illustrate this point: Imagine that servers X and Y are in particular need of protection, and for this reason, reside in a separate network using the user-oriented packet filter. Two users, user J and user K, are individual users on the network. Each user performs different tasks so needs a specific set of access rules.

DEFINITION OF FILTER RULES

User K can do the following:

- Send files to server X from workstation 2 using FTP.
- Only access server X on Wednesdays between 8 a.m. and 12 p.m.

User J can do the following:

- Use the Novell server Y from workstation 1 with the IPX communication protocol.
- Use the network from Mondays to Fridays between 7 a.m. and 7 p.m.

Some assumptions need to be made to complete the scenario:

- Users Y and J both have personal smart cards.
- Workstations 1 and 2 have smart card readers and authentication software with which authentication with the packet filters can be implemented.
- Source and destination computer systems can be addressed via defined addresses.

- Server X is accessed using an IP address.
- Server X is accessed using an IPX address.
- Server X uses standard port numbers for FTP.

The filter rules that are necessary to specify the preceding conditions are presented in Table 4-3.

TABLE 4-3 FILTER RULES

Users	Source Computer	Destination Computer	Protocol	Application	Weekdays	Time Window
K	Workstation 2	Server X	IP	FTP	Weds.	8 a.m. to 12 p.m.
J	Workstation 1	Server Y	IPX	*	Mon–Fri	7 a.m. to 7 p.m.

RESULT

With a user-oriented packet filter, it is possible to precisely specify the users that may communicate in the protected network: from particular computer systems at particular times and days of the week, using defined protocols, via applications (services) to be configured, with servers to be specified.

Security-Relevant Information in a Packet Filter

In a packet filter, violations of the filter rules can be logged in the various communications layers as security-relevant events. They constitute an important security mechanism for the detection of attacks (see Chapter 13).

When a security-relevant event occurs, the following information should be entered in the logbook of the packet filter:

- Date and time at which the event occurred
- Sequence counter(s) for the continuous numbering of events
- Type of security-relevant event that occurred
- IP addresses and port numbers (service)
- Any record of the information contained in the IP packet

It should be possible to operate the following modes for the logbook, in compliance with the relevant security policy:

FREE RUN MODE

The logbook functions like a circular buffer – that is, when the logbook overflows, the oldest logbook entry is overwritten.

In this mode, the latest security-relevant events are always determined. However, there is a danger that an attacker could retrospectively cover up an attempted attack by generating other, new events.

SINGLE SHOT MODE

In this mode, if the logbook should overflow, then new logbook entries are rejected and older security-relevant events are retained.

One danger is that an attacker could successfully cover up an attack by generating other events in advance of his attack.

BLOCK IF FULL

In this mode if the logbook overflows, the packet filter is switched to Block mode – no additional packets are allowed through.

The advantage of this method is that no security-relevant events can be lost. However, an attacker could prevent communications through the packet filter by generating security-relevant events, rendering the protected network unavailable from outside.

NOTE: The preceding dangers can be eliminated by specifying that a spontaneous message be sent to Security Management if the logbook is in danger of overflowing (for example, when it is 75 percent full). This spontaneous message causes Security Management to read the logbook immediately, thus making room for new entries of security-relevant events with the appropriate logged data. In this way, it is not possible to lose information and the packet filter is not blocked.

Packet filters should be configurable so that it is possible to define which security-relevant events should be entered in the logbook and which should not (perhaps because they are not of interest for a given organization).

Methods of Implementing Packet Filters

Packet filter functionality can be implemented in a number of ways. The most common approaches either integrate the packet filter functionality into a router or provide it as a separate security component.

PACKET FILTER IMPLEMENTATION IN THE ROUTER

Many routers intended to protect networks offer rudimentary packet filter functionality. The security-enforcing functions integrated in such routers are adequate for internal applications that are not particularly security-relevant, and in these cases, they constitute a less expensive solution than separate security components. However, routers with packet filter functionality exhibit a number of weaknesses:

- The depth of analysis is generally shallower than with a dedicated packet filter.
- Most routers, because they are not security products, do not provide the necessary facilities to administer the security-enforcing functions properly; because no Security Management exists, the wrong settings are often made, resulting in security loopholes.
- Routers generally have only incomplete logging facilities and do not possess any alarm mechanism to alert the administrator to security-relevant events.
- Routers are poorly equipped against attacks directed at the security mechanisms themselves. No security mechanisms are available to counter such attacks; thus, it is often possible to deactivate the packet filter functionality or to modify the rules from outside, using management functions.
- Routers are required to convey packets quickly and in the optimal manner. The software that is needed for this optimized packet handling is very complex and hence vulnerable to implementation errors.
- In practice, when security-enforcing features are activated, performance of some routers declines so markedly that it is not possible for the router's main tasks to be performed at the required speed.
- A new router that is procured expressly for the task of packet filtering is more expensive than a separate security component.
- Often, responsibility for operation of the routers lies in a different area (another department or a different company – for example, a network service provider) that can render compliance with the security policy difficult or even impossible.

PACKET FILTERS AS SEPARATE SECURITY COMPONENTS

When packet filters are used as separate security components, their primary task is to implement security between an insecure network and a network to be protected.

The advantages of using a separate security component for packet filtering are:

- Packet filters can fulfill the secure design criteria of active firewall elements more easily than routers because they do not need any additional software for other functions.
- With packet filters, a clear delineation exists between communication requirements and security requirements.

- Packet filters generally offer separate Security Management facilities that can also be used centrally to administer several packet filters, so that a uniform security policy can be implemented in a simple and controlled fashion.
- Separate security components are more flexible than routers with packet filter functionality, as they are independent of other functions.

The following are disadvantages to using independent packet filtering security components:

- Packet filters are often more expensive than software add-ons in the router.
- A packet filter means extra hardware, which always has the effect of reducing the availability of the network services.

PACKET FILTER IN A MICROCHIP

Some vendors offer packet filter functionality in the form of microchips, which achieve very high performance and can be integrated quite easily into communications equipment (modems, routers, and so on).

Application Areas of Packet Filters

A firewall system that relies exclusively on packet filters is unsuitable for connecting a network requiring protection to the Internet, as the protection requirements of most such networks exceed the controlling capabilities of a packet filter.

Packet filters are used to establish high-level security firewall systems and for controlled communications in the Intranet. For these applications, packet filters that simultaneously encrypt the data are a particularly effective security component, enabling Internet and intranet applications to be implemented in a secure and controlled fashion.

CAPABILITIES, ADVANTAGES, AND SPECIAL ASPECTS OF PACKET FILTERS

Packet filters provide several advantages over other types of security mechanisms.

- Transparent (that is, invisible to the user and the computer systems, operating without any positive action being required, except where authentication is necessary)
- Easy to upgrade to accommodate new protocols or services
- Can be used for protocol families other than TCP/IP, such as IPX, OSI, DECnet, and SNA

- High-performance through optimized mechanisms (operating system, drivers, and so on)
- Easy to implement, as they are not complex

DISADVANTAGES AND LIMITATIONS OF PACKET FILTERS

Packet filters have definite limits beyond which they are not appropriate to use. The limitation of packet filters include the following:

- Data above the Transport layer is generally not analyzed.
- There is no security for the applications (FTP, HTTP, and so on) such that, for example, when SMTP (port 25) is in use, attacks can be carried out based on Sendmail.
- Because permitted communications links provide direct access to the computer system, incorrectly configured programs on computer systems in the protected network can be used from the outside.
- Typical packet filters cannot conceal the structure of the network to be protected.
- Log data is only provided up to the Transport layer.

State-Oriented Packet Filters

Having the packets interpreted in higher communication layers can extend the scope of packet filters. In this case, the packets are also interpreted, for example, in the Application layer, and status information for each current connection is assessed and held in the different communication layers.

Security Guard Analogy

The use of a security guard for physical security has several similarities tp the functioning of state-oriented packet filters in firewalls. When a delivery arrives, the security guard does not just examine the address on the label. He also looks at the manifest to make sure that the packet does not contain any prohibited items. This is good, but not as reliable as actually opening the packet and examining its contents. If the packet seems acceptable, then the security guard opens the gate and allows the truck driver to enter the premises.

The status information can be held in the form of *states* with the corresponding information. For example, a communication layer can be in a state of connection setup, transfer state, or disconnection. In each state, it is possible to interpret the communications data in a special way. Firewall marketing literature refers to such extended state-oriented packet filters as ***stateful inspection, smart filtering,*** or ***adaptive screening.*** With this extended functionality, they are often offered as user-oriented packet filters. Figure 4-15 illustrates state-oriented packet filters.

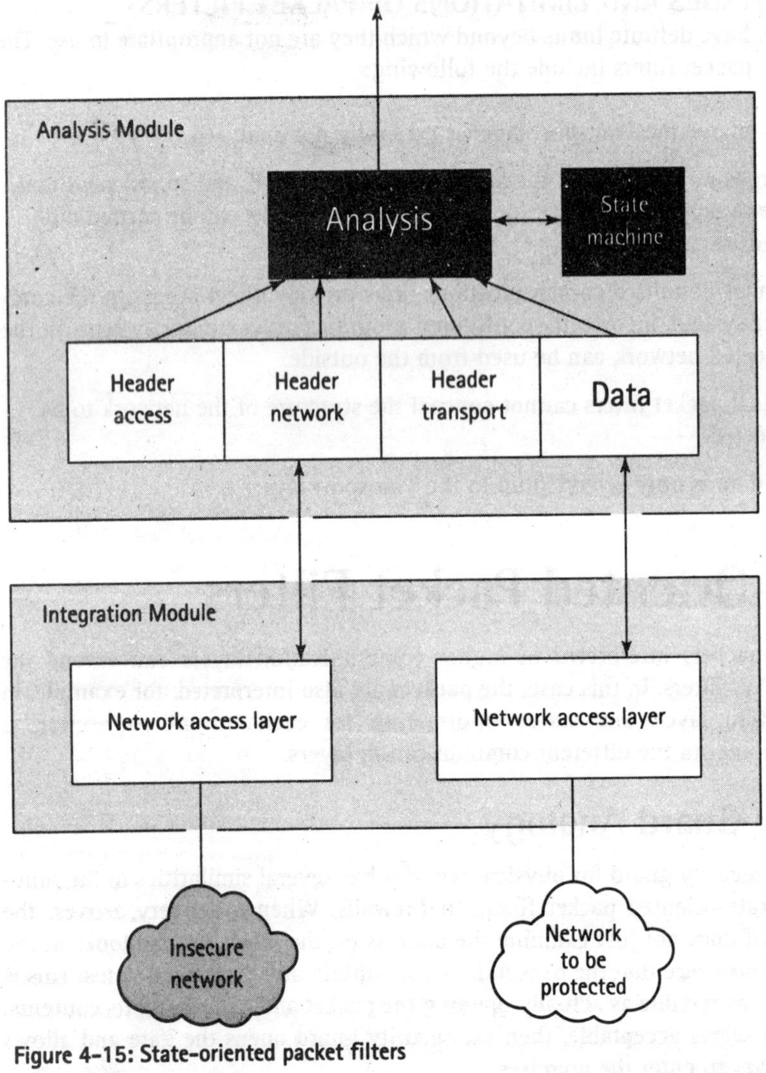

Figure 4-15: State-oriented packet filters

State-oriented packet filters have the same advantages as packet filters, but they can also check the applications. Some risks remain because the services are not directly isolated from each other.

Because it is a complex matter to simultaneously hold and interpret the communications data in the different communications layers, state-oriented packet filters generally have a shallower depth of analysis, or they are particularly prone to errors connected with their very powerful software. Basically, you can't test the complex software of state-oriented packet filters sufficiently or comprehensively to prove that errors cannot occur in any operating state. For this reason, one must continue to assume that the complex programs contain potential security risks that could be used to perpetrate an attack.

A better and more secure way to analyze the application data is to use application gateways with proxies. This approach is described in the next section.

Network Address Translation

As its name implies, *NAT (Network Address Translation)* works by using one set of addresses for communications on the Internet and a separate set of addresses for communications on the internal network. To fully support this translation, the IANA set aside three ranges of IP addresses in RFC 1918:

- 10.0.0.0 through 10.255.255.255 (10.0.0.0/8)
- 172.16.0.0 through 172.31.255.255 (172.16.0.0/12)
- 192.168.0.0 through 192.168.255.255 (192.168.0.0/16)

These addresses are reserved for internal use only and, as a consequence, are nonroutable on the Internet. Attempts to communicate with any of these ranges through the Internet result in ICMP "network unreachable" errors.

An organization implementing NAT uses one of the preceding ranges for their internal network addressing. The external interface of the firewall is assigned a normal routable IP address. When the firewall transmits a packet from the internal network to the Internet, it actually creates a new packet destined for the same address but originating from the external address(es) of the firewall. This packet is then transmitted to the destination. The firewall keeps a table of current communications so that when the return communications reach the firewall, they are taken and placed into a new packet destined for the internal computer and transmitted internally.

The NAT process affords a substantial degree of security. Since all direct communications are prevented (as long as the systems are properly configured), an external attacker is forced to compromise the firewall or find a means of passing his communications through it successfully rather than attacking the internal host directly. Given the firewall protection module and hardening, this is a relatively significant challenge.

Not inconsequentially, NAT prolongs the life expectancy of IPv4 on the Internet. Were it not for address translation, the supply of Internet addresses would have been exhausted long ago. Using NAT, a company with hundreds of internal computers can communicate fully with the Internet using only a handful of routable addresses.

In addition to being used dynamically, NAT is also used in a static translation mode. *Static translation NAT* uses a one-to-one correspondence of an external routable address to an internal nonroutable address. It is used for application servers such as Web, e-mail, DNS, and FTP where externally originated communications are necessary. By using NAT in these circumstances, the firewall is still required to be a bridge between the internal server and the Internet, thus requiring the attacker to deal with the firewall in addition to the host security of the protected server.

XREF Some of the challenges posed by NAT are covered in Chapter 11.

Application Gateways and Proxies

This section describes how the application gateway firewall element works. The distinguishing feature of the application gateway is that it separates the two networks logically and physically, as shown in Figure 4-16.

In some firewall configurations, the application gateway is the only computer system that can be accessed from the insecure network (for example, the Internet); thus, the application gateway requires particular protection. For this reason, the computer system on which the application gateway is implemented is also referred to as a *bastion host.*

The application gateway – implemented as a dual-homed gateway – has two network interfaces, one in the network to be protected and the other in the insecure network. The term "dual-homed" refers to the fact that the application gateway has complete control over the packets that are to be passed between the insecure network and the network to be protected.

The application gateway can also be operated as single-homed – in other words, operated with only one network interface. In this case, however, an attacker could bypass the application gateway.

ANALOGY TO THE SECURITY GUARD

The "application gateway security guard" does not just inspect the addresses of inbound deliveries. He also opens every packet, examines its contents, and checks the shipping documents prepared by the originator against a clearly defined set of evaluation criteria. After he has completed his detailed security check, the security guard signs the delivery note and sends the truck on its way again. This time, however, he arranges for a trustworthy driver from his own company to take the packets to the actual recipient. The security check at this point is significantly more reliable than just packet filtering, and the driver of the outside company does not see the company premises. It is true that the check takes longer, but as a result, any activities that threaten security can be ruled out.

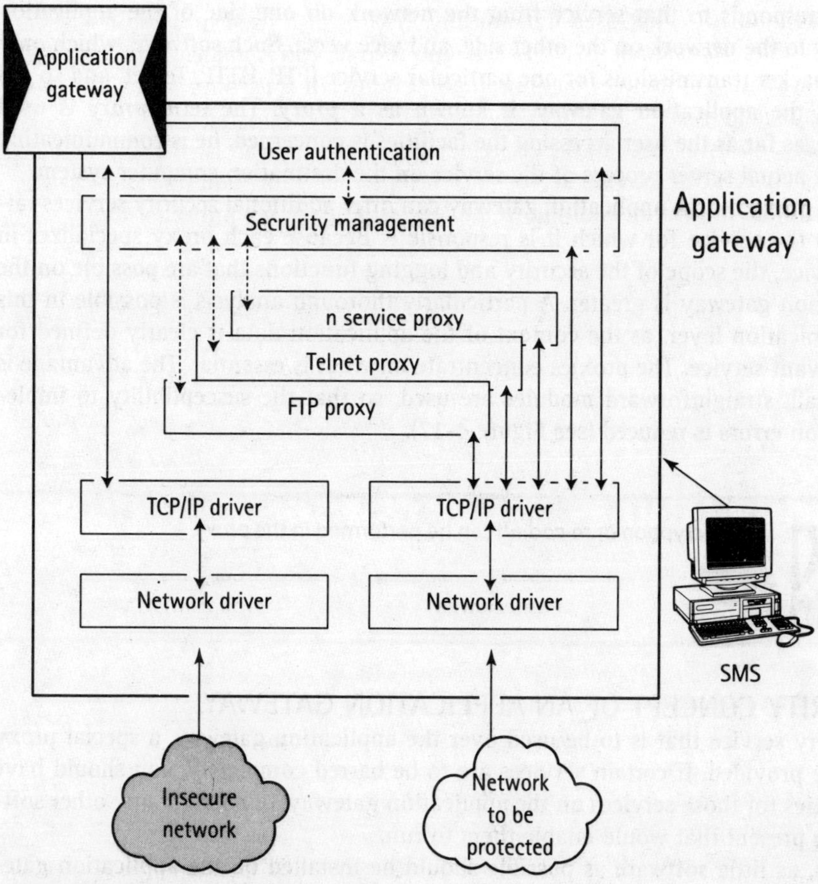

Figure 4-16: Application gateway

How Application Gateways Work

A user who wants to communicate through the application gateway must first identify himself and undergo authentication. Application gateways generally offer different authentication procedures.

To authenticate, the user first establishes a connection with the application gateway. The direct communication partner is not the destination computer system but the application gateway. However, once identification and authentication are complete, the application gateway is transparent so that the user has the impression of working directly on the destination computer system.

BASIC APPROACH

The application gateway receives the packets via the network access and TCP/IP drivers on the appropriate ports. If only one service is to be allowed on a given port, software must be available on the application gateway that will transfer the packet that corresponds to that service from the network on one side of the application gateway to the network on the other side, and vice versa. Such software, which only allows packet transmissions for one particular service (FTP, HTTP, Telnet, and so on) through the application gateway, is known as a *proxy*. The term *proxy* is used because, as far as the user accessing the facilities is concerned, he is communicating with the actual server process of the service on the destination computer system.

Each proxy on the application gateway can offer additional security services tailored to the service for which it is responsible. Because each proxy specializes in one service, the scope of the security and logging functions that are possible on the application gateway is greater. A particularly thorough analysis is possible in this communication layer, as the context of the application data is clearly defined for the relevant service. The proxies concentrate on what is essential. The advantage is that small, straightforward modules are used, so that the susceptibility to implementation errors is reduced (see Figure 4-17).

NOTE: Re-encryption or re-coding can be performed in the proxy.

SECURITY CONCEPT OF AN APPLICATION GATEWAY

For every service that is to be used over the application gateway, a special proxy must be provided. If certain services are to be barred completely, you should have no proxies for those services on the application gateway, nor should any other software be present that would enable them to run.

Thus, as little software as possible should be installed on the application gateway to avoid the possibility that, either by mistake or deliberate introduction by an attacker, some other software can adopt the role of proxy (packet transmission in the application gateway) for a service that ought not to be allowed.

Security Management is intended to make work as easy as possible for the user and is therefore supplied with powerful software (X-Terminal, database, and so on). However, for purposes of security, it should not be run on the same computer system (or at least not at the same time) as the application gateway.

To prevent the possibility that the proxies will be bypassed, application gateways should, for security reasons, have no routing functionality.

Since the application gateway is linked during communication to both the computer system of the insecure network and to the computer system of the protected network, the application gateway provides Network Address Translation. The application gateway has an IP address in the insecure network (for example, an official Internet IP address such as 194.173.3.1) and an IP address in the network to be protected (for example, a private IP address such as 192.168.1.60 that is reserved for this purpose). During communication with computer systems in the insecure network, the application gateway uses the IP addresses of the insecure network; during communication with computer systems on the network to be protected, it uses the IP addresses of that particular network.

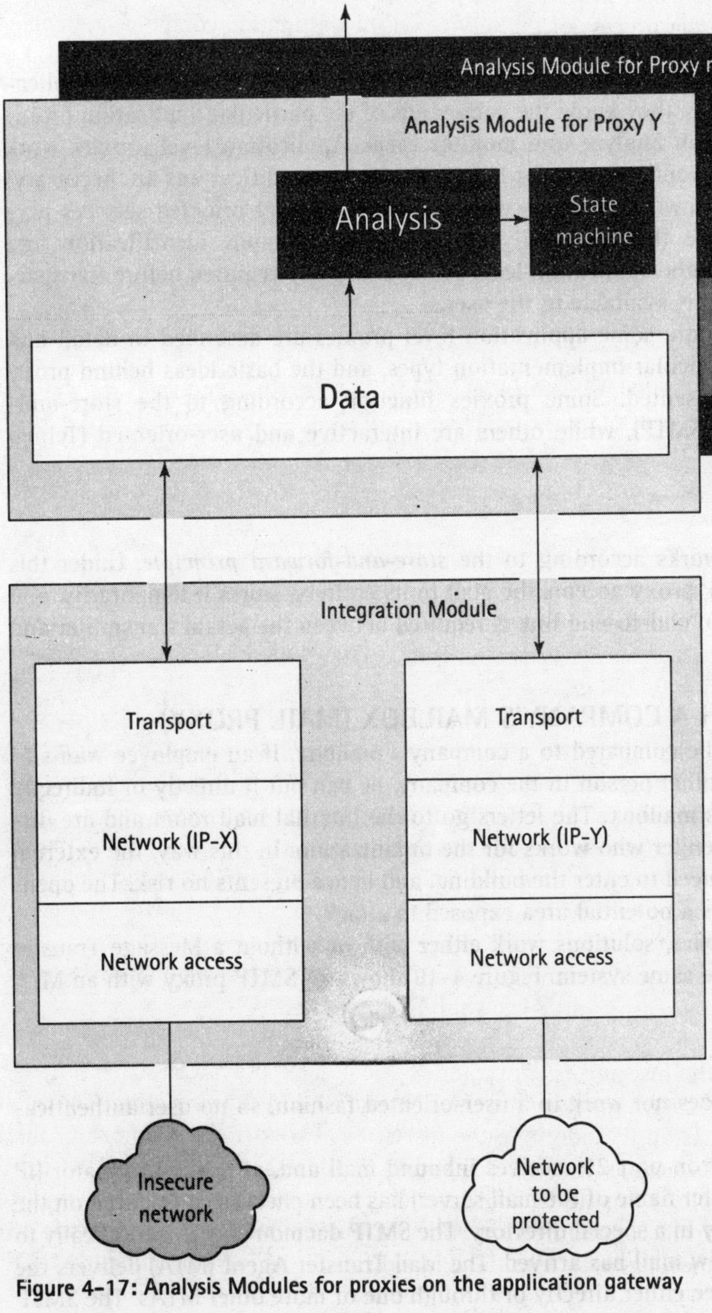

Figure 4-17: Analysis Modules for proxies on the application gateway

The Proxies

A distinction can be made between application level proxies and circuit level proxies in their implementation.

APPLICATION LEVEL PROXIES

Application level proxies are implemented for particular services and/or applications. In other words, they know the commands of the particular application protocol involved and can analyze and monitor them. Application level proxies work with the standard client software for FTP or Telnet (no modifications are necessary) or with browsers. However, the procedure followed for user-oriented services may differ from the one that is usually followed. For example, identification and authentication with the application level proxy is initially required before transparent communication is available to the user.

In the next section, some application level proxies are described in detail and illustrated with particular implementation types, and the basic ideas behind proxy technology are presented. Some proxies function according to the store-and-forward principle (SMTP), while others are interactive and user-oriented (Telnet, FTP, and HTTP).

SMTP PROXY

An SMTP proxy works according to the *store-and-forward principle*. Under this principle, the SMTP proxy accepts the mail in its entirety, stores it temporarily, and then forwards it. No end-to-end link is required between the actual transmitter and the receiver.

ANALOGY WITH A COMPANY'S MAILBOX (MAIL PROXY)

A mail proxy can be compared to a company's mailbox. If an employee wants to send a letter to another person in the company, he can put it directly or indirectly into the company's mailbox. The letters go to the internal mail room and are distributed by a messenger who works for the organization. In this way, the external mailman does not need to enter the building, and hence presents no risk. The opening to the outside is a potential area exposed to attack.

With SMTP proxies, solutions work either with or without a Message Transfer Agent (MTA) on the same system. Figure 4-18 shows an SMTP proxy with an MTA available.

DESCRIPTION

The SMTP proxy does not work in a user-oriented fashion, so no user authentication is required.

An SMTP proxy on port 25 receives inbound mail and, after the originator (IP address and computer name of the mail server) has been checked, it is stored on the application gateway in a special directory. The SMTP daemon checks periodically to see whether any new mail has arrived. The Mail Transfer Agent (MTA) delivers the mail to the addressee either directly or through one or more other MTAs. The SMTP proxy thus prevents direct access to the internal MTA from the insecure network.

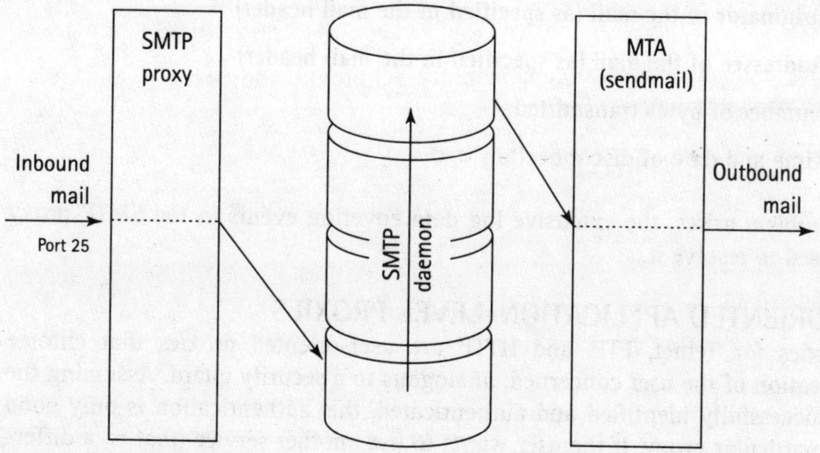

Figure 4-18: SMTP proxy

One example of a commonly used MTA is Sendmail, which is known to exhibit a number of security weaknesses and implementation errors.

An SMTP proxy only processes the following commands, which are security-neutral:

- It processes HELO, MAIL, RCPT, DATA, QUIT, RSET, NOOP.
- Some additional commands are supported with standard replies in order to make communication possible: HELP, VRFY, and EXPN.

Security-relevant commands, such as DEBUG, can send a spontaneous message to Security Management. If the DEBUG command is detected in an SMTP proxy, no resulting error can occur because the SMTP proxy does not react to it. However, if an outsider attempts to execute a DEBUG command, the fact can be interpreted to mean that it is concealing an attempted attack. This information on an attempted attack can be important.

With the store-and-forward principle, it is possible to neutralize the complex and error-prone Sendmail program (MTA). In this way, attacks known to exploit the shortcomings of Sendmail are prevented, as it is possible to prevent Sendmail from being addressed directly and ensure that only the substitute software of the SMTP proxies can be accessed. The SMTP proxy is straightforward and thus the software is easy to test.

LOGBOOK

With an SMTP proxy or MTA, the following log data can be recorded in the application gateway's logbook:

- IP address and name of the source computer system
- Time and date of connection setup

- Originator of the mail (as specified in the mail header)
- Addressee of the mail (as specified in the mail header)
- Number of bytes transmitted
- Time and date of disconnection

If a problem arises, the extensive log data covering events in the SMTP proxy can be used to resolve it.

USER-ORIENTED APPLICATION-LEVEL PROXIES

The proxies for Telnet, FTP, and HTTP are user-oriented proxies that enforce authentication of the user concerned, analogous to a security guard. Assuming the user is successfully identified and authenticated, this authentication is only good for that particular proxy. If the user wants to use another service (that is, a different proxy), he must undergo identification and authentication again. The advantage of user-oriented proxies is that the user and IP address are, without exception, correctly assigned to the desired service.

PROCESS OF COMMUNICATIONS THROUGH AN APPLICATION PROXY

The following example presents a connection setup over the application gateway with the aid of a simple password procedure for user-oriented services (refer to Figure 4-19).

- **Phase 1: Establishing a Connection to the Application Gateway.** The user attempts to establish a connection from his source computer system to a desired destination computer system over the application gateway. The application gateway accepts the connection setup and asks the person seeking access to undergo identification and authentication.
- **Phase 2: User Authentication.** The user enters his user identification and the destination computer system (name or address). A check is performed on the application gateway as to whether the user is allowed to access the desired destination computer system from his source computer system and what restrictions apply to such access. In this case, the user is then asked to enter his password. A check is performed on the application gateway as to whether the user has entered the correct password (as with the security guard).

  Authentication in firewall systems can be implemented in a number of ways. For example, one can use a standard password procedure, a one-time password, or Challenge/Response. Authentication procedures that make use of cryptographic algorithms require the user to have a security token or smart card. The particular authentication procedure that is used generally depends on the protection requirement and the direction of communication through the firewall system. Communication through the firewall system can be implemented from a network to be protected to an insecure network with a simple authentication procedure, or even without one. Where communication is directed from an insecure network to a network to be protected, encryption (involving a security token or smart card) should always be used.

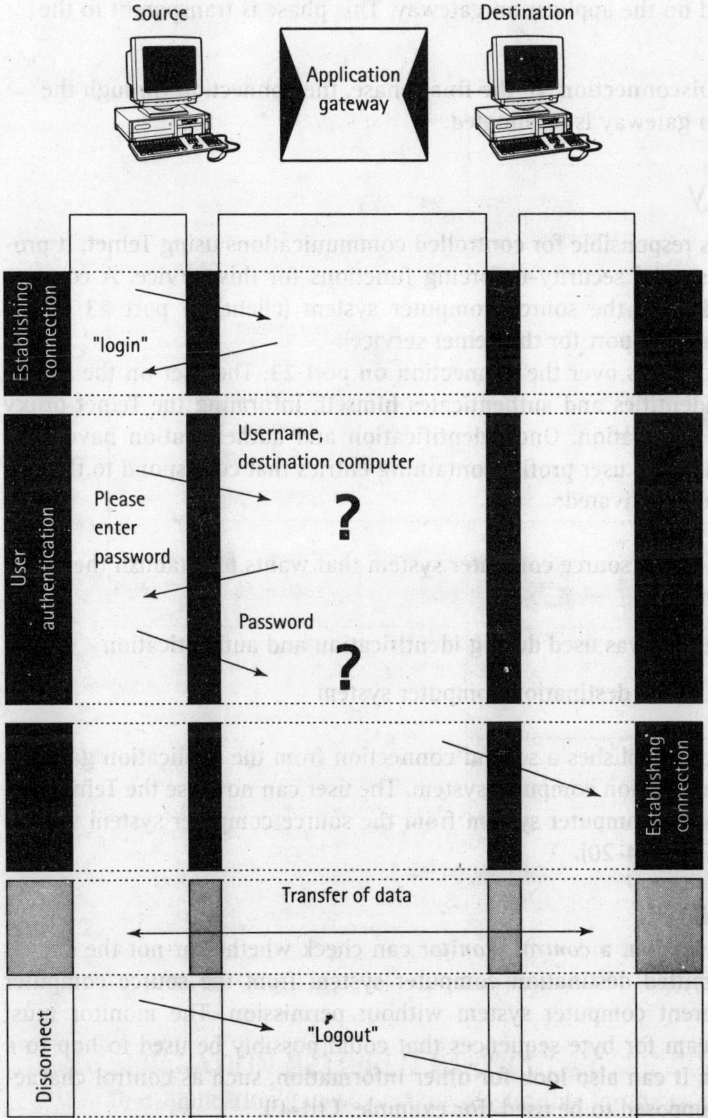

Figure 4-19: Communication over an application-level proxy

- **Phase 3: Establishing a Connection to the Destination Computer.** After the user seeking access has been successfully identified and authenticated, a second connection is established from the application gateway through the proxy to the desired and permitted destination computer system.
- **Phase 4: Data Transfer.** Data transfer occurs. Depending on the proxy concerned, the transfer of data through the proxy is monitored, controlled, and logged on the application gateway. This phase is transparent to the user.
- **Phase 5: Disconnection.** In the final phase, the connection through the application gateway is terminated.

Telnet Proxy

The Telnet proxy is responsible for controlled communications using Telnet. It provides appropriate special security-enforcing functions for this service. A connection is established from the source computer system (client) to port 23 of the application gateway (the port for the Telnet service).

The Telnet proxy takes over the connection on port 23. The user on the source computer system identifies and authenticates himself, informing the Telnet proxy of the connection destination. Once identification and authentication have been successfully completed, a user profile containing entries that correspond to the following information is activated:

- IP address of the source computer system that wants to establish the connection
- User name that was used during identification and authentication
- IP address of the destination computer system

The Telnet proxy establishes a second connection from the application gateway to port 23 of the destination computer system. The user can now use the Telnet service of the destination computer system from the source computer system via the Telnet proxy (see Figure 4-20).

CONTROL MONITOR

During the Telnet session, a *control monitor* can check whether or not the user is accessing the permitted destination computer system from the source computer system, or a different computer system without permission. The monitor must check the data stream for byte sequences that could possibly be used to hop to a different computer. It can also look for other information, such as control characters, that are not supposed to be used (for example, Ctrl+C).

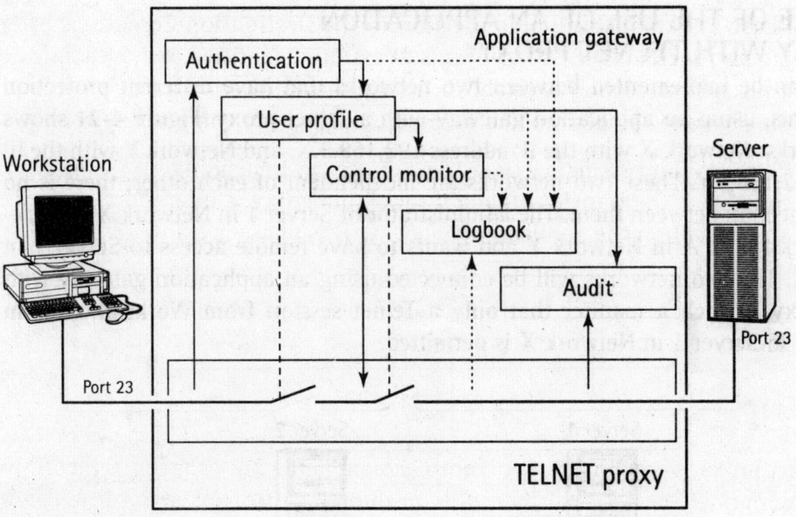

Figure 4-20: Telnet proxy

LOGBOOK

The Telnet proxy can write the following protocol entries to the logbook of the application gateway:

- IP address and name of the source computer system
- IP address and name of the destination computer system
- Time and date of connection setup
- Name of the user
- Number of bytes transmitted
- Time and date of disconnection

With a Telnet connection, it is often appropriate to make a recording of the complete communication for audit purposes. This security-enforcing function not only permits subsequent analysis of the recording, but also exercises a warning effect that should not be underestimated.

EXAMPLE ILLUSTRATING THE USE OF THE AUDIT TRAIL

The audit security mechanism can be agreed upon in the service contract with a company, perhaps in a case where remote maintenance is being provided. With this mechanism in place, the employee who performs the maintenance knows that everything he does will be recorded and will thus be motivated to perform only those actions that are required to complete the job. Should anything untoward occur, the log can be used to identify any impermissible or unnecessary actions that were carried out via remote access. In other words, the employee's actions can be reliably determined after the event.

EXAMPLE OF THE USE OF AN APPLICATION GATEWAY WITH TELNET PROXY

Security can be implemented between two networks that have different protection requirements, using an application gateway with a Telnet proxy. Figure 4-21 shows two networks: Network X with the IP address 192.168.3.X, and Network Y with the IP address 192.168.5.Y. These two networks are independent of each other; there is no direct connection between them. The administrator of Server 1 in Network X is working at Workstation A in Network Y and wants to have remote access to Server 1 in Network X. The two networks will be connected using an application gateway with Telnet proxy in such a manner that only a Telnet session from Workstation A in Network Y to Server 1 in Network X is permitted.

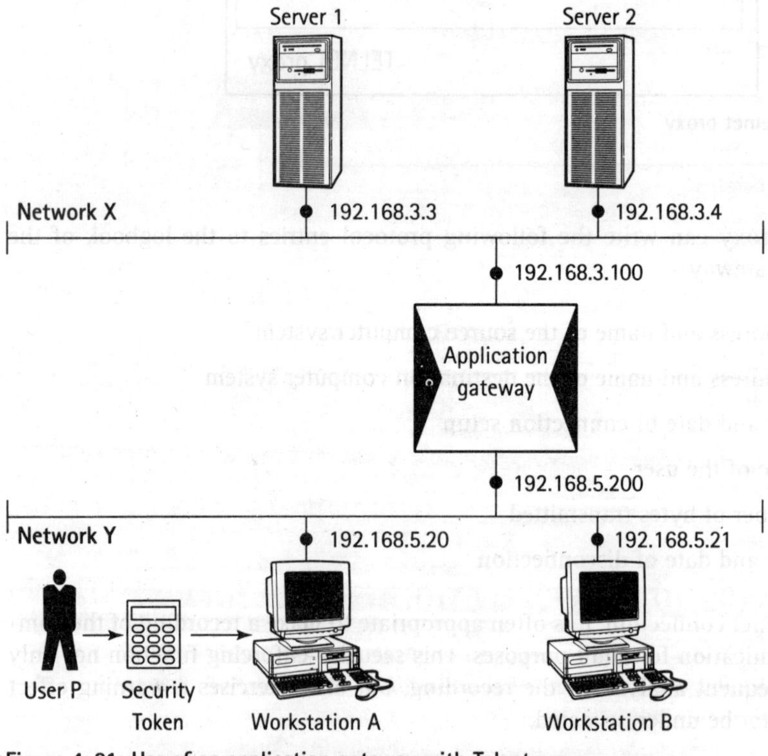

Figure 4-21: Use of an application gateway with Telnet proxy

CHARACTERISTICS OF THE TELNET COMMUNICATION SERVICE

Telnet communications has the following attributes:

- Telnet is based on TCP.
- The standard port number used by Telnet servers is 23 (TCP destination port number).

- The TCP source port number used by Telnet clients is any port number greater than 1023.

FILTER RULES SPECIFIED FOR USER P

Here are some typical rules that might apply to a user.

- P can only use the Telnet service on server 1 on working days between 7 a.m. and 6 p.m.
- P can establish this connection under the following conditions:
  - Workstation A must use IP address 192.168.5.20.
  - Server 1 must use IP address 192.168.3.3.
  - The transport protocol used is TCP.
  - The Telnet port on server 1 must be 23.
  - The source port on workstation A must be greater than 1023.
- P must authenticate himself using a security token.
- The complete connection should be logged.
- The actions that take place during connection should be monitored (control monitor).
- User P can only use the Telnet service at the specified times, and cannot use any other services.
- User P can't access any other computer systems in network X (for example, server 2).

OTHER USERS

Different users in an organization have different rights to access systems and data. Continuing the example rules, users other than P might be subject to the following limitations:

- Cannot access servers 1 or 2.
- Other users cannot obtain any information as to what computer systems exist in the other network.

Table 4-4 shows the filter rules for the Telnet proxy that are necessary to achieve the sample rules just outlined.

TABLE 4-4 FILTER RULES

User	Source Address	Destination Address	Authentication Procedure	Audit	Monitor	Weekdays	Time Window
P	192.168.5.20	192.168.3.3	Security token	Yes	Yes	Mon–Fri	7 a.m. to 6 p.m.

These filter rules specify precisely with which source address workstation A may access which destination address of server 1. In addition, precise rules specify the time frame within which access is permitted. Finally, the authentication procedure and complete logging (audit) and monitoring of actions (control monitor) are also specified.

RESULT

Using an application gateway, you can precisely specify that workstation A can have a Telnet session with server 1 at particular times; no other communications links through the application gateway are possible.

The Telnet proxy detects whether any other service has been activated on server 1 on port 23, so that this other service cannot be passed through the application gateway with the Telnet proxy. The IP addresses of networks X and Y remain concealed.

Furthermore, user P can only communicate through the application gateway with Telnet after he has been authenticated. Since all actions are logged on the application gateway, the actions of user P can be traced from the logbooks. The procedure is different for user P than when he is communicating without an application gateway, as he must authenticate himself to the proxy before he is granted access to server 1. Once the authentication phase is complete, however, operation of the Telnet proxy is transparent.

FTP PROXY

The FTP proxy is responsible for controlled communications using FTP and provides appropriate special security-enforcing functions for this service.

The connection for the command channel is established from the source computer system (client) to port 21 (the FTP command port) of the application gateway. The user on the source computer system identifies and authenticates himself, informing the FTP service of the connection destination. Once identification and authentication have been successfully completed, a user profile containing entries that correspond to the following information is activated:

- IP address of the source computer system that wants to establish the connection

- User name used during authentication
- IP address of the destination computer system

The FTP proxy now establishes a second command channel from the application gateway to port 21 of the destination computer system (see Figure 4-22).

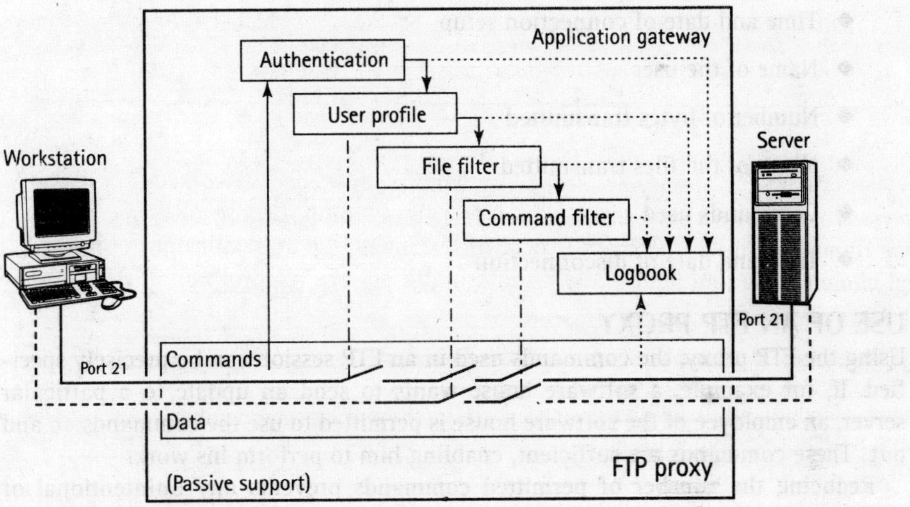

Figure 4-22: FTP proxy

COMMAND FILTER

The command filter analyzes and checks all the FTP commands entered by the user to ensure that they are all entered in the access rights file (user profile). For example, for the FTP proxy, you can define which commands (`cd`, `put`, `get`, `del`, and so on) can and cannot be used.

When the user enters an allowed command that entails a data transfer, connection setup of the data channel is affected, depending on whether an active or passive FTP connection has been requested on the source computer system (client side).

If a user attempts to use a command for which he lacks usage rights, an error message is displayed, the unauthorized attempt is entered in the logbook of the application gateway and, if specified, sent to Security Management in the form of a spontaneous message.

FILE FILTER

With FTP proxies, restricting the names of files that can be transmitted is usually possible with a file filter. Examples of such file filtering rules are:

- Only files with the name `Input.new` and `Output.new` may be transferred.
- No files with the suffix `.exe` can be transferred.

LOGBOOK

The FTP proxy can routinely write the following protocol entries to the application gateway's logbook:

- IP address and name of the source computer system
- IP address and name of the destination computer system
- Time and date of connection setup
- Name of the user
- Number of bytes transmitted
- Name of the files transmitted
- Commands used
- Time and date of disconnection

USE OF AN FTP PROXY

Using the FTP proxy, the commands used in an FTP session can be precisely specified. If, for example, a software house wants to send an update to a particular server, an employee of the software house is permitted to use the commands `cd` and `put`. These commands are sufficient, enabling him to perform his work.

Reducing the number of permitted commands prevents any unintentional or deliberate damage from occurring as a consequence of this action. For example, an attempt to execute the `del` (delete) command will be detected in the FTP proxy of the application gateway and indicated to the user. The event is entered in the logbook and, if the ruleset so specifies, a spontaneous message is sent to Security Management with the corresponding log data.

HTTP PROXY

The HTTP proxy is responsible for controlled communications using HTTP. It provides appropriate special security-enforcing functions for this service.

A connection is established from the source computer system (client) to port 80 of the application gateway (the port for the HTTP service). The user on the source computer system (client side) now identifies and authenticates himself, informing the HTTP service of the connection destination. Once identification and authentication have been successfully completed, a user profile containing entries that correspond to the following information is activated:

- IP address of the source computer system that wants to establish the connection
- User name used during authentication
- IP address of the destination computer system

The HTTP proxy establishes a second connection from the application gateway to port 80 of the destination computer system. The user can now use the HTTP service of the destination computer system from the source computer system via the application gateway (HTTP proxy) (see Figure 4-23).

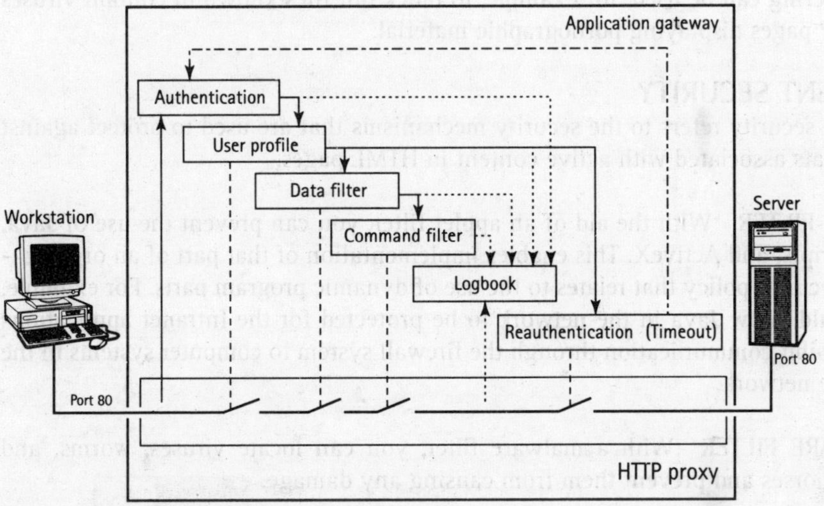

Figure 4-23: HTTP proxy

REAUTHENTICATION

The HTTP protocol does not work in a session-oriented manner. In other words, the HTTP proxy cannot tell when a session is ended on its own. Every time a WWW page is requested, a connection is established through the firewall system, the WWW page is transmitted, and then cleared. On the first occasion, authentication is performed prior to transmission. For this reason, a timer that records the beginning of the session is set. Following expiry of the timer, the HTTP proxy automatically shuts down the associated HTTP session. As soon as any user activity is detected in this session, the timer is restarted. The proxy can be configured so that, if the timer has previously been switched off, identification and authentication must be repeated if communication is resumed.

COMMAND FILTER

The command filter analyzes and checks the methods (FTP, HTTP, NNTP, SMTP) and commands (`put`, `get`, `post`, for example) that are used.

Any attempt to use an invalid method or an illegal command is indicated as such to the user, and a corresponding entry is made in the application gateway logbook. If the ruleset has been so defined, a spontaneous message is also sent to Security Management in such cases, together with the log data.

DATA FILTER

A data filter can be incorporated in the HTTP proxy so that only predefined URLs are allowed, effectively acting as a URL blocker. For example, a data filter can specify that users may only use HTTP servers with the domain `*.de`. The data filter can also be used within the proxy to filter out known, undesirable files or HTTP pages. This filtering can be used, for example, to block out files known to contain viruses or HTTP pages displaying pornographic material.

CONTENT SECURITY

Content security refers to the security mechanisms that are used to protect against the threats associated with active content in HTML pages.

APPLET FILTER With the aid of an applet filter, you can prevent the use of Java, Java scripts, and ActiveX. This enables implementation of that part of an organization's security policy that relates to the use of dynamic program parts. For example, you could allow Java in the network to be protected for the Intranet applications but prohibit communication through the firewall system to computer systems in the insecure network.

MALWARE FILTER With a malware filter, you can locate viruses, worms, and Trojan horses and prevent them from causing any damage.

LOGBOOK

The HTTP proxy can enter the following log data in the application gateway's logbook:

- IP address and name of the source computer system
- IP address and name of the destination computer system
- Time and date of connection setup
- Name of the user
- Number of bytes transmitted
- Name of the file or HTML page (name of the page and IP address of the server/destination computer system) transmitted
- Time and date of disconnection

JAVA PROXY

Java proxies enable Java applets to be used with confidence. Given the continuing discovery of security vulnerabilities in the Java sandbox model establishing protection from Java applets is a necessity in most cases. There is also a bit of a "war" waging between Microsoft and Sun (the original inventor of Java). Microsoft refuses to license the Java run-time from Sun and has instead created its own Java interpreter. Microsoft's Java interpreter is not fully compatible with Sun's implementation of Java. The incompatibilities between Java implementations have lead to security issues due to the necessity to maintain and patch two different Java environments.

BASIC OPERATION

The basic operation of Java is as follows:

- The Java runtime environment used in the enterprise to execute Java applets is standard.
- The technology of the Java runtime environment used has been evaluated and is thus viewed as highly trustworthy.
- Using check mechanisms (special Java applets that are sent by the Java proxy), it is possible to check whether any changes have taken place in the Java runtime environment on the client.

If a user accesses a WWW server from his computer in a network to be protected and an applet is downloaded, the Java relay detects it. Using the Java Policy Manager, the Java relay determines which policy has been specified for which user. If necessary, a Java applet is sent down with check mechanisms to check the trustworthiness of the Java runtime environment. Only when a reply is received to the effect that the Java runtime environment is still trustworthy and has not been manipulated is the real Java applet downloaded from the proxy and securely executed in the trustworthy Java runtime environment. Figure 4-24 illustrates a Java proxy.

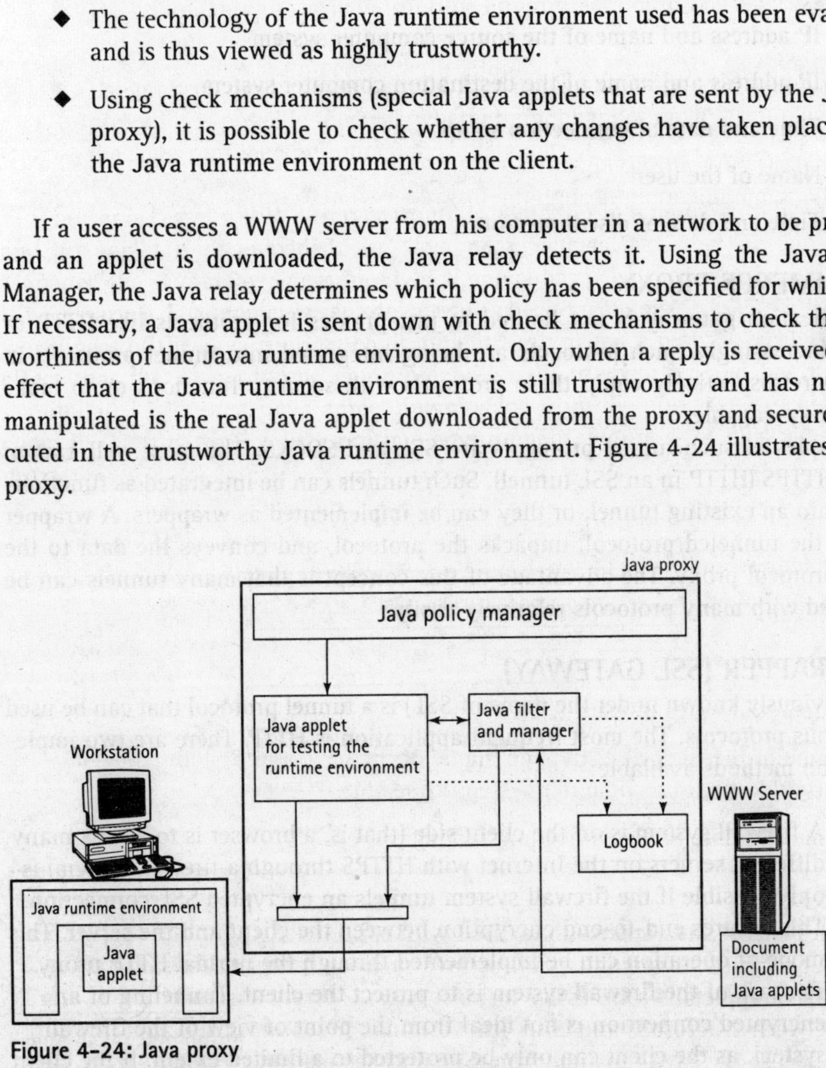

Figure 4-24: Java proxy

JAVA PROXY MANAGER

The Java Proxy Manager is responsible for the security policy for Java applications in the entire organization. Accordingly, definitions are entered here to define which permissions the individual user can implement. The Java Proxy Manager also specifies what Java class operating system access a given user is allowed in the relevant Java runtime class library.

LOGBOOK

The Java proxy can enter the following log data in the application gateway's logbook:

- IP address and name of the source computer system
- IP address and name of the destination computer system
- Time and date of connection setup
- Name of the user
- Time and date of disconnection

E-COMMERCE PROXY

An application gateway is not limited to just proxies for protocols like HTTP or Telnet. Increasingly, such protocols are being integrated into tunnel protocols in order to retrospectively equip these protocols with security functions or to make them proxy-capable.

Examples of such tunnel protocols are SSL and SOCKS. The most well known case is HTTPS (HTTP in an SSL tunnel). Such tunnels can be integrated as functionalities into an existing tunnel, or they can be implemented as wrappers. A wrapper accepts the tunneled protocol, unpacks the protocol, and conveys the data to the actual protocol proxy. The advantage of this concept is that many tunnels can be combined with many protocols relatively easily.

TLS WRAPPER (SSL GATEWAY)

TLS (previously known under the name of SSL) is a tunnel protocol that can be used for various protocols. The most frequent application is HTTP. There are two implementation methods available:

- A firewall system is on the client side (that is, a browser is to access many different servers on the Internet with HTTPS through a firewall system) is only possible if the firewall system tunnels an encrypted SSL connection. This ensures end-to-end encryption between the client and the server. This mode of operation can be implemented through the normal HTTP proxy. The task of the firewall system is to protect the client. Tunneling of an encrypted connection is not ideal from the point of view of the firewall system, as the client can only be protected to a limited extent. If the client demands an end-to-end encrypted connection to the server, the firewall system can only accept or reject it.

◆ If the firewall system is on the server side, it is expected to protect the server. In this case, the firewall system can take over the entire security functionality for the Web site. This entails:

- Secure and logged authentication of the client to the server using a client certificate. This function is optional. A bank might perhaps only grant access to the online banking server to existing customers. An Internet shop, on the other hand, will want to allow access to its product range to all new customers. In this case, client authentication can be omitted.
- Secure and logged authentication of the server to the client using a server certificate.
- Secure storage of the server certificate. If a hacker steals the server certificate, the hacker can assume the identity of the Web site on the Internet and cause extensive damage, as clients will rely on the server certificate to securely authenticate the server. The secure storage can either be on a separate system behind the SSL gateway – a separate authentication server – or it can be realized in a suitable hardware module. The certificate can never leave this module, which operates like that of a smart card.
- Efficient processing of encryption operations, including authentication via asymmetric encryption algorithms and data encryption via symmetric encryption algorithms. This offers an advantage, since many Web sites operate at the limits of their capabilities, and it is often impossible to implement SSL on the Web server itself without experiencing a significant loss of performance.
- Independent logging of attacks. This logging is reasonable, since Web sites are a popular target for attacks on the Internet. The firewall system offers a uniform logging and alarm mechanism, continuously monitored by the administrator. In this case, it makes sense to supplement the firewall system with an intrusion detection system. However, the firewall system can also log information about the authentication process that is not accessible to the intrusion detection system, which operates as an outsider.

NOTE Pure SSL tunnels through a firewall system are a disadvantage from a security standpoint, since they place the responsibility for security on the server, which is usually unable to guarantee it.

IMPLEMENTATION OF AN E-COMMERCE PROXY

An e-commerce proxy is implemented as follows: The client establishes an SSL-encrypted connection to the application gateway. The client assumes that the application gateway is actually the e-commerce Web server. The application gateway performs the mutual authentication and encryption tasks in a secure manner. After the data has been decrypted, the application gateway can filter the data at the protocol (for example, HTTP) and content (for example, viruses and JavaScript) levels. The normal proxy can perform this filtering. Then the application gateway passes the data on in plaintext to the Web server, which is responsible for the content of the Web site itself. This connection occurs in the internal network of the Web site operator. If this network is not sufficiently secure, the segment can be further protected through line encryption (for example, by using a VPN gateway).

An e-commerce proxy in an application gateway guarantees a clear separation of security functionality and Web content (refer to Figure 4-25). Web servers and e-commerce proxies each concentrate on their own core competencies.

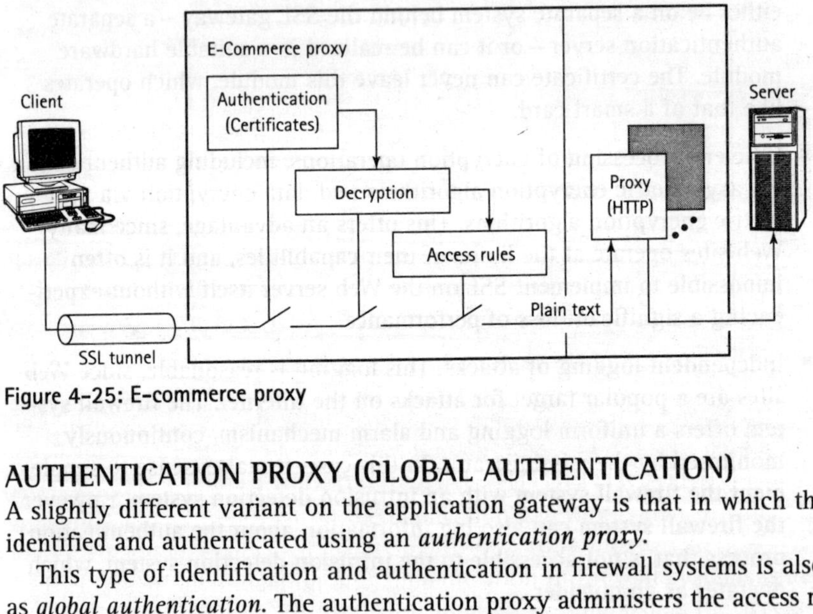

Figure 4-25: E-commerce proxy

AUTHENTICATION PROXY (GLOBAL AUTHENTICATION)

A slightly different variant on the application gateway is that in which the user is identified and authenticated using an *authentication proxy*.

This type of identification and authentication in firewall systems is also known as *global authentication*. The authentication proxy administers the access rights for the different services (for FTP, Telnet, and HTTP, for example); re-authentication is unnecessary if the user wants to switch services. One disadvantage of this method, which particularly affects multi-user systems, is the fact that the connection between service and user is not unique. Moreover, while the connection on the application gateway is in operation and the client is connecting, the service could be used by attackers.

The authentication proxy controls the identification and authentication of a client on a server in the application gateway. The permitted services can then be used under the control of the firewall system (refer to Figure 4-26).

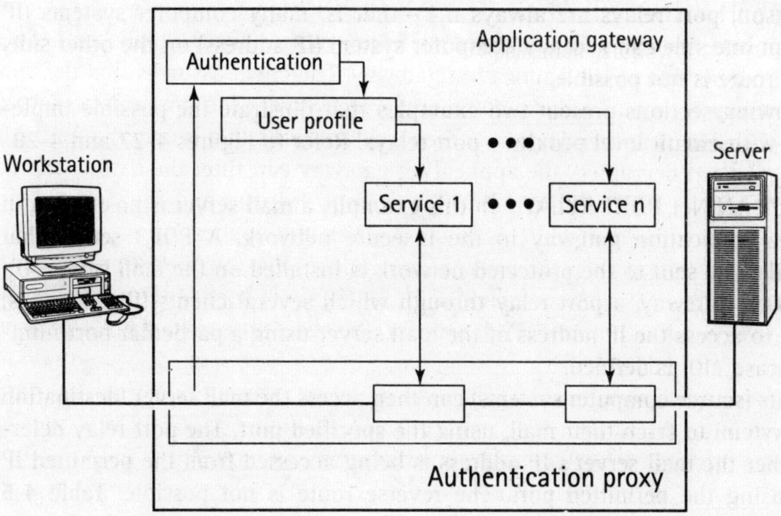

Figure 4-26: Authentication proxy

TRANSPARENT PROXY

Transparent proxies are proxies that can behave as if they are transparent to the client. These proxies ensure, for example, that computer systems in the insecure network can be addressed directly from the network to be protected. The advantage of proxies that behave outwardly in a transparent manner is that the client software does not need to be altered upon integration of a firewall system. Particular applications, such as home banking solutions, which send fixed IP addresses via Java applets, can then also be implemented through firewall systems.

SPECIAL PROXIES

Certain proxies can in turn provide additional security services for particular applications tailored to those services. Again, proxies can be implemented for nonstandard services.

CIRCUIT-LEVEL PROXIES

With application gateways, routing should for security reasons not be possible in the Network layer. For services for which no application level proxy is available, communication through the application gateway can nevertheless still be implemented if circuit level proxies are provided. Circuit level proxies are a kind of generic proxy that can be used for most services with different protocols.

These circuit level proxies, which are also known as *generic proxies*, *port relays*, or *plug gateways*, can generally be used for TCP and UDP applications. With a port relay, it is possible to communicate through the application gateway in a controlled manner with *one* defined IP address using a defined port. As the communication is addressed using the port number of the port relay, the only communication allowed through the application gateway is directed to an IP address from the "other side."

For this reason, port relays are always n:1 – that is, many computer systems (IP addresses) on one side can access a computer system (IP address) on the other side. The reverse route is not possible.

The following sections present two examples that illustrate the possible implementations with circuit level proxies – port relays. Refer to Figures 4-27 and 4-28.

EXAMPLE OF AN N:1 PORT RELAY In this example, a mail server is positioned in front of the application gateway in the insecure network. A POP3 server that enables mail to be sent to the protected network is installed on the mail server. On the application gateway, a port relay through which several clients (IP addresses) are allowed to access the IP address of the mail server using a particular port number (in this case 110) is defined.

The clients (source computer systems) can then access the mail server (destination computer system) to fetch their mail, using the specified port. The port relay determines whether the mail server's IP address is being accessed from the permitted IP addresses, using the permitted port. The reverse route is not possible. Table 4-5 shows a sample firewall rule used to achieve this port relay.

TABLE 4-5 N:1 PORT RELAY

Source IP addresses (n), Network to be Protected	Destination IP Address of the Application Gateway, Network to be Protected	Port Number	Source IP Address of the Application Gateway, Insecure Network	Destination IP address (1), Insecure Network
192.168.1.1, 192.168.1.2, 192.168.1.3, 192.168.1.4	192.168.1.60	110	194.173.3.10	194.173.3.1

n:1 port relays are very rigid and can only be used for certain applications. However, it is possible to configure an n:m port relay out of many n:1 port relays.

EXAMPLE OF AN N:M PORT RELAY This example shows how one can access different computer systems in the network to be protected (for example, an intranet) from the insecure network (the Internet) using different IP addresses of the insecure network. The application gateway can then be addressed from the insecure network using several IP addresses. The IP addresses of the computer systems of the network to be protected should remain concealed.

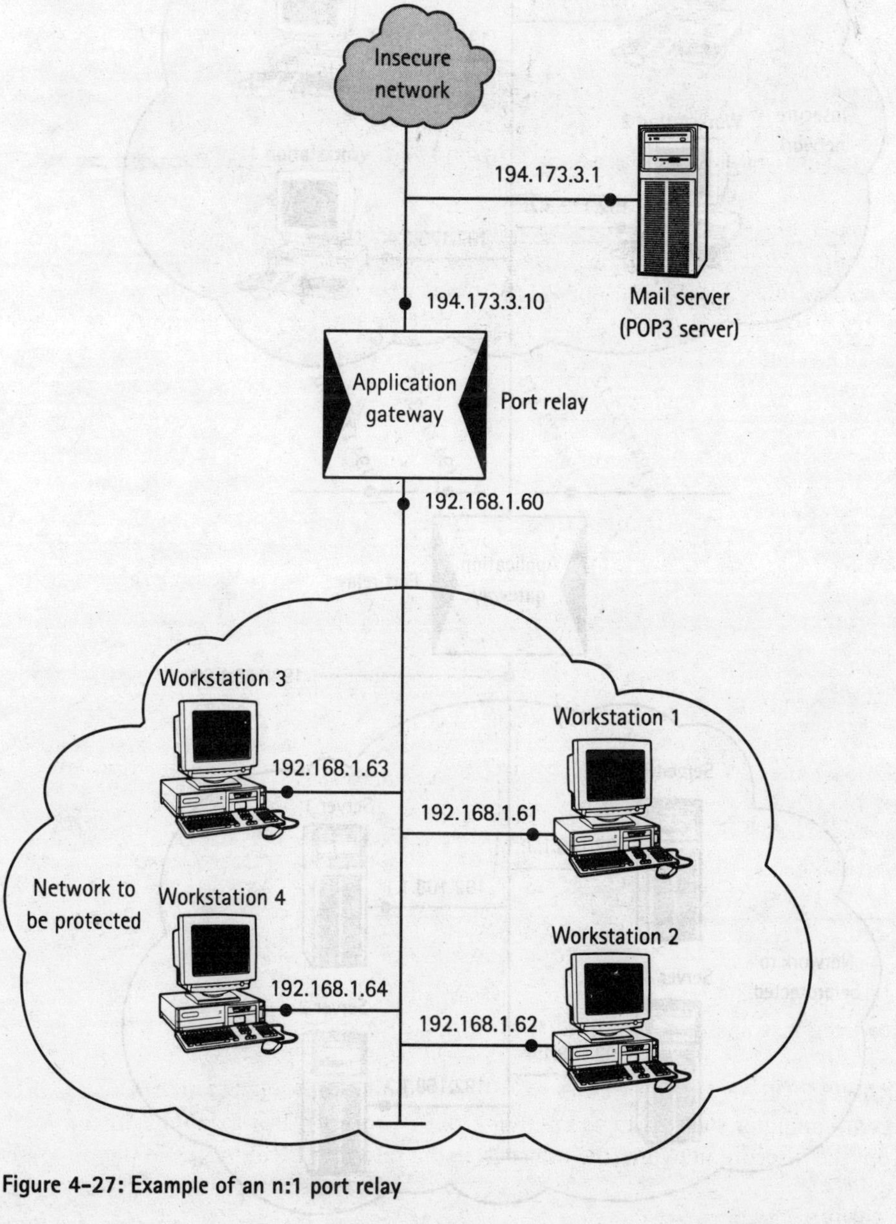

Figure 4-27: Example of an n:1 port relay

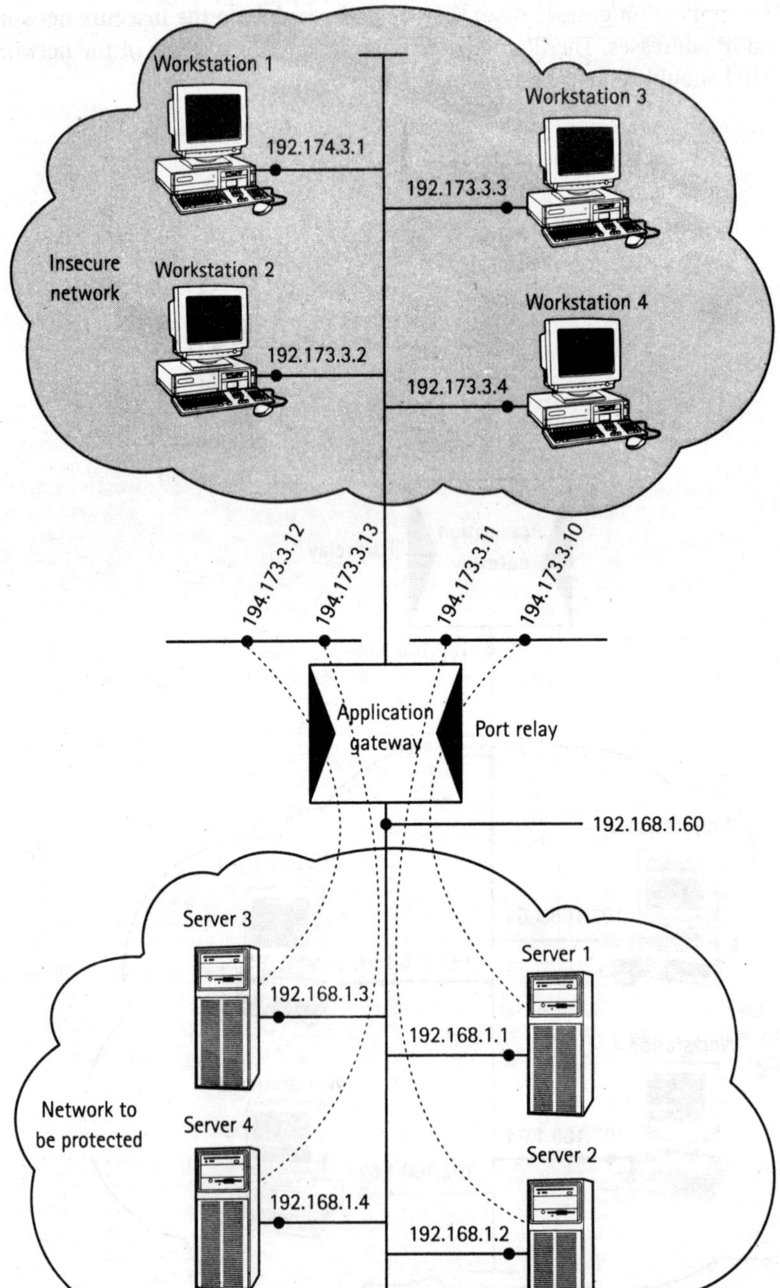

Figure 4-28: Example of an n:m port relay

To this end, an n:1 port relay is defined m times for the different IP addresses that are allowed to access the network to be protected from the insecure network, and the computer systems in the network to be protected that they are allowed to access are specified.

From the point of view of the computer systems in the insecure network, the IP addresses of the servers in the network to be protected appear to be IP addresses of the insecure network.

The port on which this relay is possible is predefined (see Table 4-6, *port 2000*). With an n:m port relay, it is possible to keep the IP addresses of the network to be protected hidden (since they are only the external IP addresses), and limit communication over a given port to defined computer systems in one direction only.

TABLE 4-6 N:M PORT RELAY

Source IP Addresses, Insecure Network	Destination IP Address of the Application Gateway, Insecure Network	Port Number	Source IP Address of the Application Gateway, Network to be Protected	Destination IP Address, Network to be Protected
194.173.3.1, 194.173.3.2, 194.173.3.3, 194.173.3.4	194.173.3.10	2000	192.168.1.60	192.168.1.1
194.173.3.1, 194.173.3.2, 194.173.3.3, 194.173.3.4	194.173.3.11	2000	192.168.1.60	192.168.1.2
194.173.3.1, 194.173.3.2, 194.173.3.3, 194.173.3.4	194.173.3.12	2000	192.168.1.60	192.168.1.3
194.173.3.1, 194.173.3.2, 194.173.3.3, 194.173.3.4	194.173.3.13	2000	192.168.1.60	192.168.1.4

LOGBOOK FOR THE PORT PROXIES The port proxy in the logbook of the application gateway can make the following entries:

- IP address and name of the source computer system
- IP address and name of the destination computer system
- Time and date of connection setup
- Number of bytes that have been transmitted
- Time and date of disconnection

EXAMPLE OF A SPECIAL CIRCUIT LEVEL PROXY A special circuit level proxy, as provided by many application gateways, is illustrated in Figure 4-29.

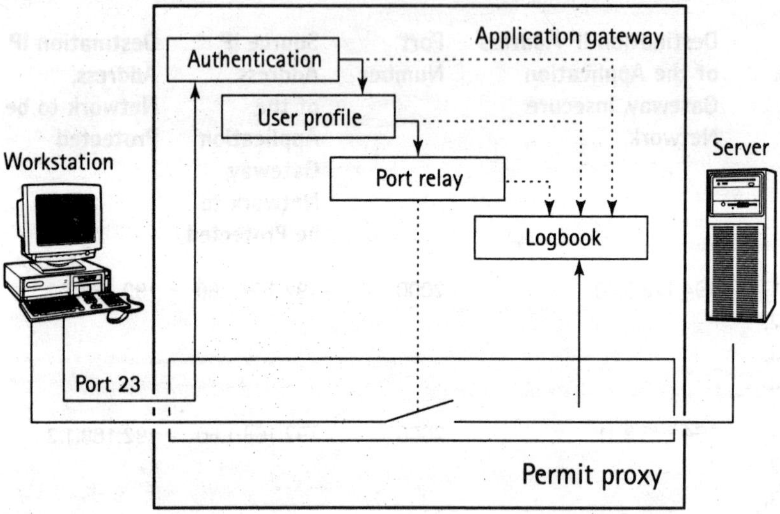

Figure 4-29: Permit proxy

A permit proxy controls access of a client to a server through the application gateway for TCP-based services that do not offer identification and authentication facilities. A good example of such services is NetBios protocols, which are tunneled by IP. No special proxies can be used for such protocols, as there is no login mechanism in the programs on the client side. In such cases, a permit proxy can ensure that access is confined to particular computer systems and users. In this case, the user must first establish a Telnet connection (or an HTTP connection) to the application gateway on an external computer system before he can start his actual application. Following successful identification and authentication, the user can access the real service through a port proxy.

The permit proxy can specify over which port, with which computer systems (IP addresses) from the insecure network, and with which computer system (IP address) in the protected network communication can take place. In this example, other definitions could be negotiated over the Telnet connection with the application gateway, such as specifying the IP address with which communication is to take place (similar to a flexible n:m port relay).

The Telnet session is automatically terminated when the application is closed. If the Telnet program is terminated before the application, the permit proxy suspends the connection to the application.

LOGBOOK The permit proxy can make the following entries in the application gateway's logbook:

- IP address and name of the source computer system
- IP address and name of the destination computer system
- Time and date of connection setup
- Name of the user
- Time and date of disconnection

In principle, the permit proxy is a circuit level proxy with authentication.

LOGBOOKS OF THE APPLICATION GATEWAY A wealth of information can be stored in the application gateway logbooks. Which information should be logged should be specified in an organization's security policy; otherwise the quantity of data can become very large, making extensive demands on administrator time.

SOCKS

SOCKS provides a standard environment for the transparent and secure use of a firewall system. To achieve this, SOCKS is integrated between the Application and Transport layers (refer to Figure 4-30).

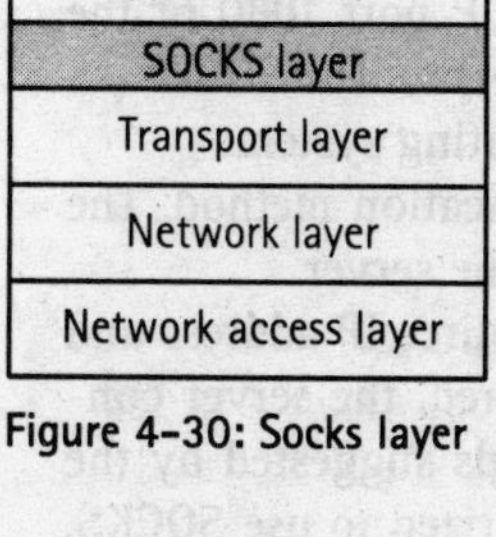

Figure 4-30: Socks layer

In this intermediate layer, SOCKS intercepts the TCP and UDP connection requests for the applications and converts them to the SOCKS protocol. Communication over the SOCKS protocol is confined to the segment between the SOCKS client and the SOCKS server so that the result is a tunnel.

This tunnel has the characteristic that a security context can be defined both for the connection-oriented TCP protocol and for the connectionless UDP protocol. This means that strong authentication, integrity checking, and preservation of confidentiality through encryption are possible (RFC1929). The integration of these capabilities is defined in the SOCKS protocol standard (RFC1928). In the present case, we are interested in the definition of version 5 of the protocol (SOCKS v5).

SOCKS combines the capabilities of a circuit level proxy with those of an application level proxy. However, in order to use SOCKS, one must implement software changes on the client side, since very few applications are available that support SOCKS directly. Figure 4-31 illustrates SOCKS' support for TCP.

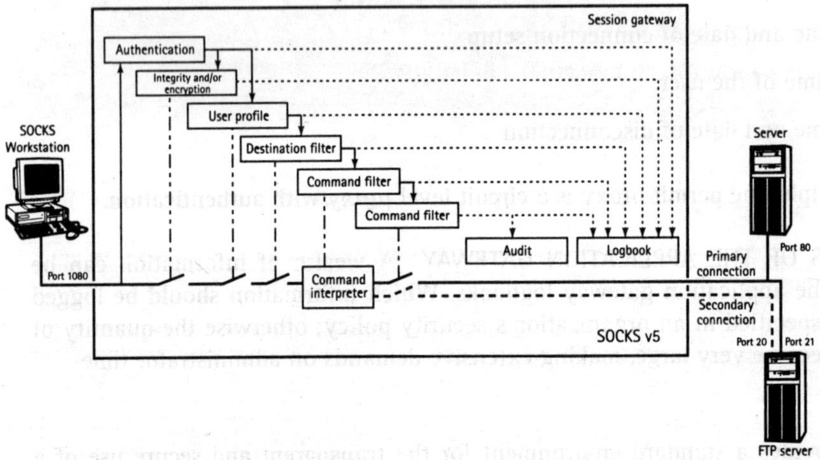

Figure 4-31: SOCKS v5 support for TCP

Connection setup is performed from the client application on the client workstation. It is intercepted by the SOCKS v5 client library and converted to the SOCKS protocol. The endpoint of a standard SOCKS connection is TCP port 1080 of the SOCKS v5 server. In order to affect this interception and conversion the SOCKS v5 client implementation is integrated transparently into the operating system.

Connection setup is followed by negotiation of the authentication method. The SOCKS v5 client transmits a list of the methods it supports to the server.

The SOCKS v5 server selects a method specifically for the source IP address and passes it to the SOCKS v5 client. If no authentication is required, the server confirms the communication setup directly. If none of the methods suggested by the SOCKS v5 client is suitable, or if this workstation is not authorized to use SOCKS, the connection is terminated.

In all other cases, the SOCKS v5 clients and server now go through the authentication steps and additional method-dependent subnegotiations that are necessary.

The methods for preserving the integrity and/or confidentiality of the data follow directly from successful authentication. These are applied once the authentication process is complete. Moreover, a user profile that contains the permitted destinations as well as commands is activated (RFC1961).

Following authentication, the additional connection details are passed to the SOCKS v5 server. The SOCKS v5 server typically checks the connection details passed to it on the basis of the source and destination IP addresses and the command. If the query details match the connection rules derived from the user profile, a connection is established to the server. Connection setup is performed through the command interpreter. The successful completion of connection setup is communicated to the SOCKS v5 client.

The client application is informed that a connection has been successfully established so that data can be exchanged between the application and the server from that point on.

DESTINATION ADDRESS FILTER The destination address filter compares the requested destination transmitted with the requirements contained in the user profile that has been activated. If a discrepancy is evident, the connection is suspended and an appropriate entry is made in the logbook.

Three types of address specifications are available:

- IP v4 address
- IP v6 address
- Domain name

These capabilities enable an *IP v4 to IP v6 address translator* to be established, and vice versa, using a SOCKS server.

COMMAND FILTER The command filter compares the commands transmitted in the SOCKS protocol with the requirements contained in the user profile that has been activated. If a non-permitted command is used, the connection is cut off and an appropriate entry is made in the logbook.

The following commands are possible in protocol version 5:

- `Connect`
- `Bind`
- `UDP Associate`

The `Connect` command is used for the establishment of connections between the client and the server. The `Bind` command enables connections that have been established by the server to be accepted by the client (such as the active FTP data channel that is established from port 20 of the server to the client). `UDP Associate` stands for the establishment of a UDP relay through the SOCKS v5 server (RFC2478).

COMMAND INTERPRETER The command interpreter executes whatever action is associated with the corresponding command. It is also responsible for disconnection.

CONTENT INSPECTION Normally, SOCKS provides facilities that enable the data content to be checked. This implementation-dependent capability can, for example, be used with a plug-in API.

AUDIT The review of the content opens up the possibility of an audit.

LOGBOOK The SOCKS v5 server can routinely make the following entries in the logbook:

- IP address and name of the source computer
- IP address and name of the destination computer
- Time and date of connection setup
- Name of the user and the authentication procedure used
- User profile activated
- SOCKS protocol commands used
- Number of bytes transmitted
- Content information of the tunneled TCP and UDP protocols
- Time and date of disconnection

Figure 4-32 illustrates SOCKS' support for UDP.

The protocol sequence of operations is similar to that described for a TCP connection. Nothing extra is added until the UDP datagrams are forwarded from the SOCKS v5 client library to the SOCKS v5 server.

The UDP client application sends a UDP datagram to the server. This action is intercepted by the SOCKS v5 client library and forwarded to the SOCKS v5 server as a request for connection with the SOCKS command `UDP Associate`. After the authentication process has been successfully completed, all the integrity and/or encryption methods have been considered, a user profile has been activated, and the connection request examined, the command interpreter performs the assessment. If a request has previously been expressed for a `UDP Associate`, the command interpreter replies with the UDP port which the SOCKS v5 client should use to forward the datagram that has been withheld (RFC2078). A UDP relay instance is also generated. It filters all the UDP datagrams that arrive, only forwarding those that have the same source IP address as the TCP control channel.

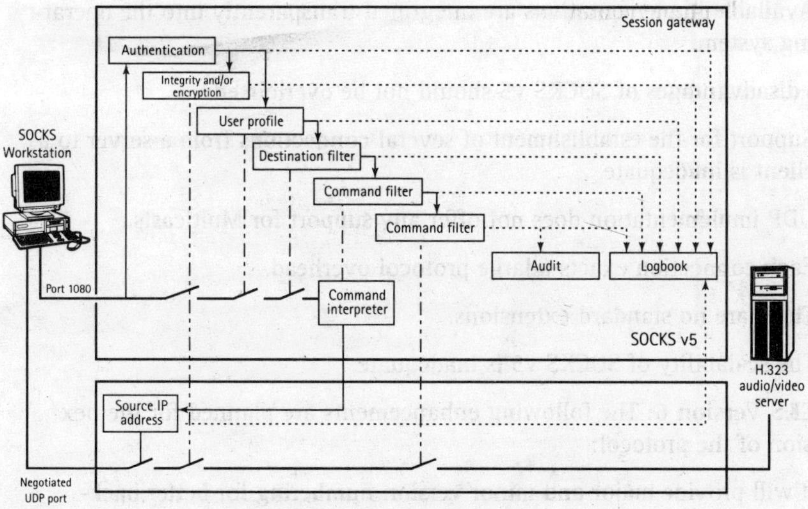

Figure 4-32: Socks v5 support for UDP

The method-dependent criteria regarding confidentiality and integrity are applied on this second connection as well.

Content examination is also possible here, provided that it is supported by the implementation.

SOURCE IP ADDRESS The command interpreter passes on the source IP address of the TCP control channel to the UDP relay instance as a filter value. All datagrams that do not bear this address are rejected.

These datagrams with an incorrect address can be logged in the logbook.

SOCKS VERSIONS The SOCKS protocol has undergone several revisions over its life cycle. The functional differences between SOCKS versions is as follows:

- SOCKS Version 4: The superseded version 4 of the SOCKS protocol did not contain security measures for authentication and preservation of confidentiality and/or integrity. Only the commands `Bind` and `Connect` were supported.
- SOCKS Version 5: The current version 5 contains the following features:
  - It provides standard interfaces for integrating strong authentication mechanisms.
  - It has an extended address scheme to support IP v4, IP v6, and domain names.
  - It supports TCP and UDP.

- Available implementations are integrated transparently into the operating system.

The disadvantages of SOCKS v5 should not be overlooked:

- Support for the establishment of several connections from a server to a client is inadequate.
- UDP implementation does not offer any support for Multicasts.
- Each connection exacts a large protocol overhead.
- There are no standard extensions.
- The scalability of SOCKS v5 is inadequate.

◆ **SOCKS Version 6:** The following enhancements are planned for the next version of the protocol:

- It will provide major and minor version numbering for better backwards compatibility.
- It will include a standard mechanism for negotiating protocol extensions.
- It will use a control channel to reduce the overhead.
- TCP's `bind` command should be enhanced so that it supports several connections to the open port and allows the client to specify a particular port.
- UDP should support Multicast in both Multicast and Multicast-free environments.
- UDP will have an option to choose between sending and receiving datagrams.
- UDP will have optional tunneling of datagrams through a reliable channel.

EXAMPLE ILLUSTRATING THE USE OF THE SOCKS V5 SERVER With the SOCKS v5 server, it is possible to implement services such as H.323 (digital audio and video transmission) and CORBA (IIOP) through a firewall system. When H.323 is supported, protocol extensions from version 6 of the SOCKS protocol must be used.

Person- and session-specific, strong authentication can be implemented over the Internet and can even be extended to include mechanisms for the preservation of confidentiality and/or integrity. In some cases, strong authentication constitutes the only opportunity to use several cascaded firewall systems securely.

For further information, see (IETF1, IETF2, and IETF3).

When to Use Application Gateways

An application gateway is an ideal active firewall element whenever protective measures must be made available to applications. The possibility of logging in the Application layer is also a good reason to consider the application gateway in a firewall concept.

Wherever a connection to the Internet is planned and the computer systems in the network to be protected have a high protection requirement (see also Chapter 3), inclusion of an application gateway in the firewall configuration should be considered.

Organizational units that want to be isolated from other parts of the enterprise network can achieve special protection using an application gateway.

CAPABILITIES, ADVANTAGES, AND SPECIAL ASPECTS OF AN APPLICATION GATEWAY

The use of an application gateway yields several desirable security conditions.

- Secure design concept, since modules are small and straightforward (proxies)
- Concentration on what is essential
- Higher security, since without exception all packets are passed through the proxy
- The communication partner of the computer systems that communicate through the application gateway is the proxy. This means that services can be kept truly separate.
- Connection data and application data can be logged, enabling the actions of users who communicate through/over the application gateway to be recorded.
- Concealment of internal network structure
- Security-enforcing functions are made available to the applications (command filters, file filters, data filters, and so on).
- Network Address Translation takes place

DISADVANTAGES AND LIMITATIONS OF AN APPLICATION GATEWAY

Application gateways have some disadvantages as well as advantages.

- Low flexibility, since a new proxy must be provided for every new service
- Application gateways are generally expensive

- Not transparent, since a different procedure is used during communication over the application gateway
- Some application gateways cannot detect IP spoofing, although this is not a common problem

Adaptive Proxy

Some vendors of security applications attempt to combine the advantages of packet filter and application gateway into an *adaptive proxy.* The adaptive proxy functions like an application proxy during the connection setup phase and acts like a packet filter during the data transfer phase (see Figure 4-33). The advantages of this approach are obvious: a very high level of security is achieved in the first phase, and thereafter, only the rapid packet filter functions are performed. Assuming that all attacks involve the first phase – that is, the establishment of a communications link – a high level of security could be achieved.

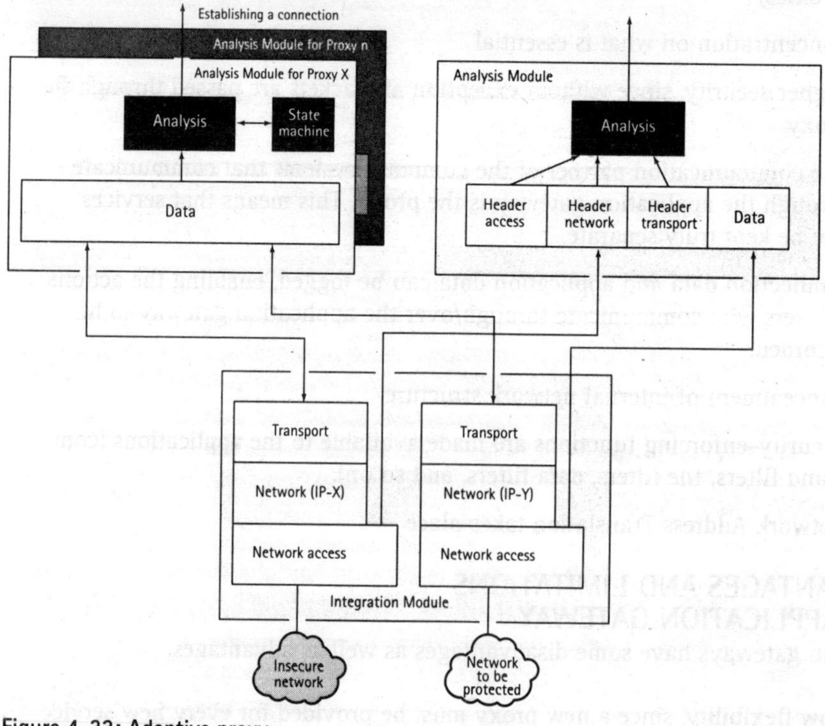

Figure 4-33: Adaptive proxy

Analogy to the Security Guard

In the connection setup phase, the adaptive proxy works like the application proxy: it not only inspects the address of inbound packets, it also opens them and examines their contents. If the "adaptive proxy security guard" has known the supplier for a long time, then he sends the supplier's truck through the gate, allowing the driver to deliver the goods directly. However, if he does not know the supplier, he sends the truck driver away after the delivery is unloaded and arranges for a company driver to take the packet to the receiver in a company vehicle.

Capabilities and Limitations of an Adaptive Proxy

Since an electronic security guard cannot establish and rely on personal, human bonds, the adaptive proxy appears to be more interesting in theory than in practice, as it can scarcely attain the quality of an application proxy. Alternatively, the equivalent of the personal, human bond could be implemented using trustworthy networks and/or encryption systems. However, an accurate analysis of the threats and the operational environment must be performed in that case.

Virtual Private Networks

Virtual Private Networks (VPNs) allow for secure external communications between remote entities and the internal network. As such, they form an important mechanism for firewalling. VPNs function by using encryption to encapsulate packets inside other packets, a process commonly referred to as *tunneling*. This encapsulation allows entities at either end of the "tunnel" to transparently hold private communications across the Internet. VPNs, along with encryption, are covered at length in Chapter 7.

Firewall Elements and the Speed-Versus-Security Tradeoff

Figure 4-34 presents a classification of firewall elements. The relative merits of the various firewall elements with regard to speed and security are presented qualitatively.

NOTE: If several parallel application gateways (with application proxies) are used, then together they can produce a higher capability (throughput)), thereby surmounting the speed penalty shown. (See also Chapter 6.)

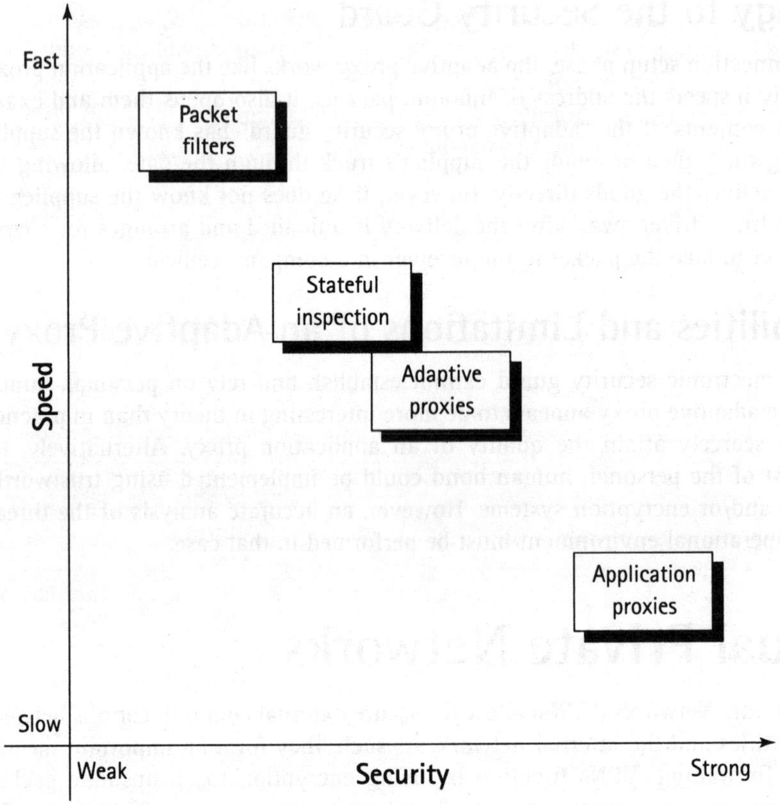

Figure 4-34: The speed-versus-security tradeoff

Security Management for Active Firewall Elements

With a Security Management module, simple, reliable, and verifiable administration of the active firewall elements should be possible.

Because of the special design requirement that active firewall elements be implemented with minimal software, it is essential that Security Management be separated from the active firewall element. A separate Security Management module can, for example, be implemented on a separate computer system, or with the aid of removable hard disks that are only introduced when the ruleset is to be modified.

Requirements for a Security Management Module

The Security Management module must itself be resistant to attack; otherwise, attackers could disable the security functions of the active firewall elements by penetrating the Security Management software. To this end, the Security

Management module itself must offer security mechanisms, such as identification and authentication, role distribution, logging with audit capabilities, and encryption of security-relevant information.

Security Management for active firewall elements should at least fulfill the security services *Ease of use* and *Consistency of rules.*

- **Ease of use:** The Security Management menus should have a reliable design and permit easy navigation around the system. Furthermore, you should not have to enter the same data twice.
- **Consistency of the filter rules:** Input errors in the data entry fields (MAC address, IP address, protocol number, port numbers) should be detected by the validation process. Syntactic validation should be used here.
- **Filter rules should only be configurable for the appropriate protocol layer.** It should not be possible for users to be entered as both active and barred from a service. Multiple entries should be eliminated. The filter rules should also be subjected to semantic validation.

To ensure a high overall security of the entire firewall system, the additional security functions of access control, access rights administration, encryption, and logging must be available as well.

- **Access control in Security Management:** Identification and authentication of users should be performed in order to prevent unauthorized persons from using the Security Management functionality.
- **Access rights management (roles) in Security Management:** To ensure secure operation of the Security Management functions, Security Management should offer the roles of Security Administrator, Operator, Data Entry Operator, Observer, and Auditor.
  - The Security Administrator is responsible, for example, for the personalization of the Security Management, the granting of access rights to the Security Management, and the creation and restoration of backups.
  - The Operator is responsible for inputting the rights of users who are allowed to communicate through the active firewall elements under the security policy of his organization.
  - A Data Entry Operator is responsible for capturing non-security-critical data, such as user names, computer systems, profiles, and so on. He cannot grant or withdraw any rights.
  - The Observer observes the operation of the active firewall element and, if necessary, analyzes any problems. He cannot grant or withdraw any rights.

- The Auditor assumes the task of examining the Security Management logbook data for security-critical actions. He cannot grant or withdraw any rights.

For quite special, security-critical actions within Security Management, a two-person rule can be required, in which two or more persons must simultaneously enter a separate password to initiate a given action.

The security-relevant information, such as passwords or keys for authentication with the active firewall elements, should be stored within the Security Management in an encrypted form to eliminate the possibility of misuse.

The various functions within the Security Management should be logged in separate logbooks. For this purpose, the Security Management should provide the following:

- A function logbook that contains a record of all actions performed using the Security Management (for example, the granting of user rights, the deletion of logbooks, and so on). In this logbook, the actions of the various users of the Security Management module (Security Administrator, Operator, and so on) can be recorded.
- All the logins that are sent to the Security Management must be recorded in a login logbook.
- The error logbook records must detail all errors that are detected in the Security Management.
- The backup logbook is used to log all the backup actions the Security Administrator performs within the Security Management.

Coupling to a Network Management System (NMS)

In general, firewall systems' particularly high availability requirements means that certain spontaneous messages that provide information about the availability of the system must be sent from the firewall elements to the Network Management System (NMS). In larger organizations, the NMS is manned 24 hours a day and can respond quickly in the event of failures. For this purpose, the Security Management module should be able to exchange SNMP traps and simple GET commands with the NMS using an SNMP proxy.

COMMUNICATION PROTECTION FOR SECURITY MANAGEMENT

In many firewall system configurations, it makes sense to isolate the Security Management functionality itself with the aid of a packet filter. If a packet filter with encryption (VPN box) is used, it is also possible to access the Security Management remotely. If there were a number of local Security Managers in the various organizational units, they would be able to access a central Security Management function remotely.

Summary

This chapter covers the functioning of several firewall elements in detail. Understanding how each element works is necessary for proper use of each element. Comprehending what each element can and can't do is necessary to insure proper choice of security elements for fulfilling your organizational security requirements.

Chapter 5

Concepts of Firewall Systems

THIS CHAPTER DISCUSSES firewall system design concepts that are intended to protect data and communications passing between an insecure network and a protected network. The firewall concepts differ in terms of the degree of security they provide and the applications for which they are suited. This chapter covers only conceptual aspects of firewall implementation. Practical application cases are covered in Chapter 9.

The active firewall elements used are security components that are exclusively responsible for providing security services, and comply with the secure design criteria set forth in Chapter 3. Any router functionality provided by routers – rather than packet filters or application gateways – are not expected to play a security-enforcing role. The discussion in this chapter assumes that the active firewall elements are controlled and managed through a dedicated, separate, central, and secure Security Management function.

Packet Filtering

With this firewall concept, a packet filter is the only active firewall element used to provide protection between the insecure network and the protected network. Security Management is located on a separate system in the protected network. By using a packet filter, the following security objectives can be achieved:

- Access control at the Network Access and Network levels. Only logical connections that are allowed can be established. This control is achieved with the following actions:
  - Checking the MAC destination address and the MAC source address (are they allowed/not allowed)
  - Checking the IP destination address and the IP source address (for example, is an IP address belonging to the internal network attempting to come from outside the network)

- **Access rights management.** Access is only possible over protocols and services (port numbers) that are defined and permitted, and only at certain times.

The following packet attributes can be checked with packet filters:

- The options that are permitted with IP (for example, fragmentation, source routing)
- The communication protocols (TCP, UDP or ICMP) that may be used
- The source and destination ports available for TCP
- The source and destination ports available for UDP
- The ICMP commands that are permitted

Additional security objectives include the following:

- **Log analysis.** Security-relevant events are logged and can be analyzed to identify any security breaches.
- **Alarm function.** When they occur, serious security-relevant events are reported spontaneously to Security Management as alarms so that prompt action can be taken in response to the attack.

Evaluation of Packet Filters

A firewall concept that relies solely on the use of a packet filter cannot be used to connect the protected network to the Internet, because the security requirements for most networks requiring protection are too high to be satisfied solely by a packet filter. Using only a packet filter, however, you can achieve controlled communications in an intranet. Combined with encryption, a packet filter is a flexible and inexpensive means of ensuring confidential and controlled communications within this type of network.

Packet filters usually support other protocol families, such as IPX, OSI, DECnet, and SNA.

Use of Packet Filters

Packet filters are very good at discarding broad types of problem traffic. For example, if you want to prevent any Microsoft Networking packets from entering or exiting your protected network, packet filters are a sound choice. Packet filters are best at stopping activity at the protocol level (that is, only http traffic to and from the Web server). If encryption is used with the packet filters, an even higher degree of security can be achieved in the intranet.

Application Gateways

With this firewall concept, the application gateway is the only active firewall element used to provide protection between the insecure network and the protected network. Security Management is located in the protected network.

Typically, the application gateway is configured as a dual-homed host, which means that the application gateway works with two network interfaces and has complete control over the packets that pass between the insecure network and the protected network.

Through the use of an application gateway, you can achieve the following security objectives:

- **Access control at the Network level. Only logical connections that are allowed can be established. This control can be achieved through checking the IP destination address and the IP source address in the relevant networks.**
- **Access control at the user level. All users who want to communicate through the application gateway can be identified and authenticated.**
- **Access rights management. Access is only possible over protocols and services that are defined and permitted, and only at certain times. Only services for which a proxy has been installed on the application gateway and enabled are possible.**
- **Control at the Application level. The user is allowed only those assets that are necessary for his work. This control is achieved for the services concerned through special application filters for commands, application data, and files.**
- **Decoupling of services. Programs that are particularly vulnerable to risk (for example, Sendmail) are only made available to the insecure network through separate auxiliary programs with restricted functionality (proxies).**
- **Securing evidence and log analysis. Connection data and security-relevant events can be logged and analyzed to identify any security breaches and preserve evidence of the actions of users.**
- **Logging and alarming activity. A Security Management *alarm function* causes a spontaneous message to be sent to Security Management whenever a serious security-relevant event is detected. This function enables a quick response to an attack.**
- **Concealed internal network structure. Application gateways conceal the internal structure of the protected network, making it difficult for an attacker from the insecure network to access internal, sensitive systems.**

The following additional objectives can be achieved through the use of an application gateway:

- Accounting (IP- and user-oriented)
- Network Address Translation (NAT)

Evaluation of Application Gateways

An application gateway alone can be used to link a protected network to an insecure network outside of the organization, provided that the protection requirement is low.

Through the use of an application gateway alone, you can achieve a very strong barrier against the relevant types of attack.

Use of Application Gateways

If the insecure network and the protected network have a comparable level of protection and the insecure network is outside the control of the organization, the two networks can only be connected in a controlled manner through an application gateway. For example, this could be the case for two similar, homogeneous organizations that are cooperating. One particular advantage of the use of application gateways is that detailed connection data can be logged.

Combination of Firewall Elements

A skillful combination of individual active firewall elements provides a higher degree of security than the presence of a single active firewall element. This section discusses various combinations.

The use of the application gateway differs in each firewall concept. Two variants of the use of application gateways are presented.

Dual-Homed Application Gateway

A dual-homed application gateway works with two network interfaces. The packets arrive over one network interface (for example, from the insecure network) and leave over the other network interface (for example, into the protected network). In this way, the dual-homed application gateway has complete control over the packets passed between the insecure network and the protected network. There is no way to circumvent the dual-homed application gateway.

Single-Homed Application Gateway

In a single-homed application gateway, the packets come in and go out over the same network interface. As a result, the application gateway itself cannot guarantee that all packets will be analyzed and checked before being sent on. As far as the application gateway is concerned, there is only one network (hence the term *single-homed*).

By combining packet filters and application gateways, you can achieve greater security than either technology can achieve by itself. In the relevant sections, an assessment of the firewall concepts is also provided.

Packet Filter Plus Single-Homed Application Gateway

When a packet filter is combined with a single-homed application gateway, the active firewall packet filter provides most of the security, while the single-homed application gateway optionally makes additional security services available. Refer to Figure 5-1.

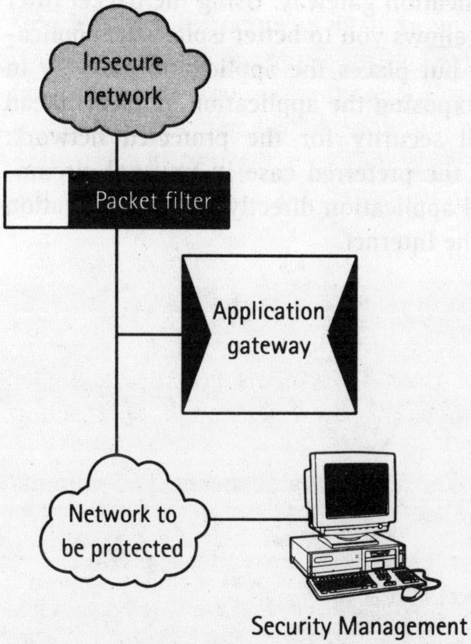

Figure 5-1: Packet filter and single-homed application gateway 1

You can configure the packet filter so that communication from the insecure network is only allowed through the single-homed application gateway by rejecting all packets to destinations other than the gateway. In other words, only the single-homed application gateway is "visible" from the insecure network. All the security services can be provided by the single-homed application gateway. In this firewall concept, the single-homed application gateway is logically located in the protected network. Communication between the computer systems in the protected network and the computer systems in the insecure network is achieved through the application gateway, and checked by the packet filter. If an attacker were to gain access to the single-homed application gateway, he would also be able to access all the computer systems in the protected network, because no other protection is available.

By moving the packet filter behind the application gateway, communication from the protected network can be controlled by the packet filter. Figure 5-2 illustrates connecting the packet filter behind the application gateway. In this scenario, the communication is only permitted through the single-homed application gateway. Only the single-homed application gateway is "visible" from the protected network. All the security services can be provided by the single-homed application gateway. Under this firewall concept, the single-homed application gateway is logically located in the insecure network and must be particularly resistant to attacks from the insecure network. IP masquerade attacks from the insecure network present a serious risk. Communication between the computer systems in the protected network and the computer systems from the insecure network is effected through the packet filter, and controlled by the application gateway. Using the packet filter behind the application gateway only really allows you to better isolate the application gateway from the protected network, but places the application gateway in significantly more danger in the process. Exposing the application gateway ahead of packer filtering results in less overall security for the protected network. Generally, this configuration will only be the preferred case in unusual circumstances such that you need to run a special application directly on the application gateway that requires unfiltered access to the Internet.

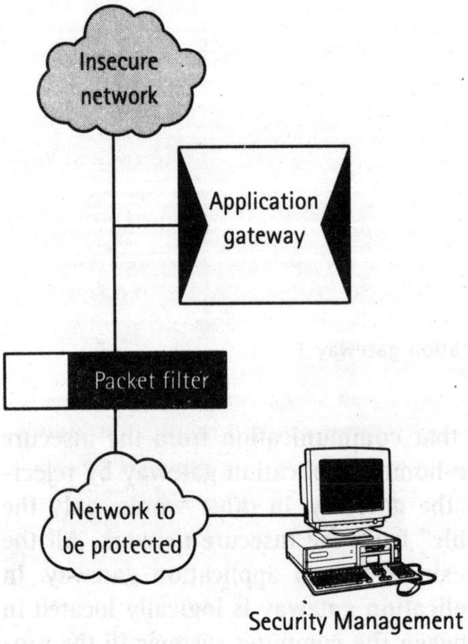

Figure 5-2: Packet filter and single-homed application gateway 2

EVALUATION OF COMBINED PACKET FILTERS AND SINGLE-HOMED APPLICATION GATEWAYS

The combination of packet filter and single-homed application gateway means that certain connections can allow communications only through the packet filter – for services, for example, for which there are no proxies on the single-homed application gateway. This variant makes the firewall concept very flexible because some services can be allowed only through the packet filter, while others must also pass through the single-homed application gateway.

The degree of security provided by this firewall concept depends primarily on the security of the packet filter. Because most networks require a higher level of protection than the security mechanism of a packet filter can offer, this concept is insufficient when a protected network is connected to the Internet.

As far as the protected network is concerned, the solution shown in Figure 5-1 offers a higher degree of security because the packet filter protects the single-homed application gateway.

USE OF COMBINED PACKET FILTERS AND SINGLE-HOMED APPLICATION GATEWAYS

If the insecure network is afforded a low level of protection or its level of protection can't be rated – yet both the insecure network and the protected network are under the control of a single party – combinations of a packet filter and single-homed application gateway can be used. This scenario would apply, for example, to a particularly sensitive organizational unit, such as a human resources department, that is separated from an intranet.

Packet Filter Plus Dual-Homed Application Gateway

This firewall concept entails direct connection of the active firewall elements packet filter and application gateway, as shown in Figure 5-3. With a single-homed application gateway, the possibility exists that an attacker can bypass the application gateway by simply directing network traffic around it. With a dual-homed application gateway, it is physically impossible for the network packets to bypass the application gateway because the gateway is the only physical route that traffic can take. The primary downside to dual-homed gateways as compared to single-homed gateways is the greater performance impact they inflict.

The dual-homed application gateway is protected from the insecure network by the packet filter. Under this firewall concept, the dual-homed application gateway is logically located in the protected network.

The packet filter can also be implemented behind the application gateway, as shown in Figure 5-4.

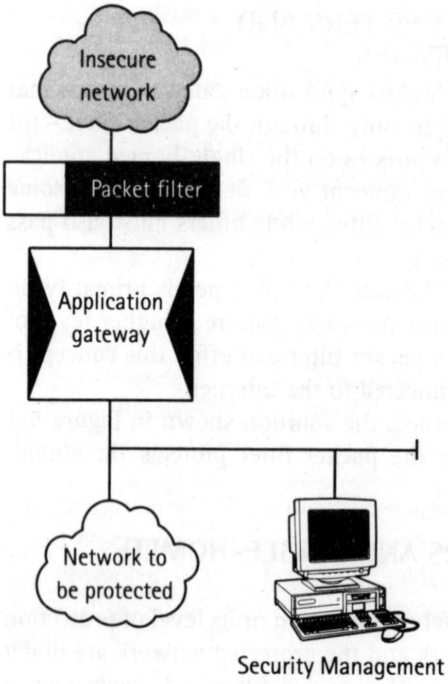

Figure 5-3: Packet filter and dual-homed application gateway 1

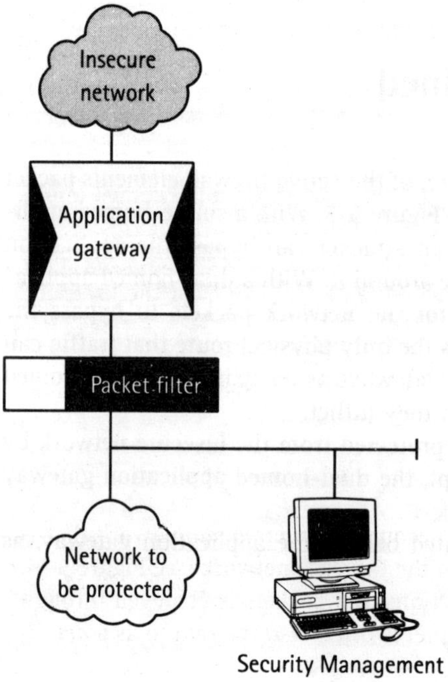

Figure 5-4: Packet filter and dual-homed application gateway 2

From its location in the protected network, the packet filter protects the dual-homed application gateway. Under this firewall concept, the dual-homed application gateway is logically located in the insecure network and must be particularly resistant to attacks from the insecure network.

The decision to place the packet filter behind or in front of a dual-homed application gateway is based on the same factors as a single-homed application gateway. Generally, the placement of the packet filter in front of the application gateway is the more secure option.

EVALUATION OF COMBINED PACKET FILTERS AND DUAL-HOMED APPLICATION GATEWAYS

The packet filter and the dual-homed application gateway control communications between the computers in the protected network and the computers in the insecure network. Under this concept, you cannot circumvent the dual-homed application gateway.

The degree of security offered by this firewall concept depends on the security of the packet filter and the security of the dual-homed application gateway. As both active firewall elements work with different integration and analysis concepts, all the security objectives – and hence a maximum degree of overall security – are achieved with this combination.

The design shown previously in Figure 5-3 is preferable because the packet filter in the insecure network protects the dual-homed application gateway.

The use of both a packet filter and a dual-homed application gateway creates a very strong barrier against most types of attack. Thanks to the upstream packet filter, the effect against attacks on the firewall system itself is strong compared to the use of an application gateway by itself.

USE OF COMBINED PACKET FILTERS AND DUAL-HOMED APPLICATION GATEWAYS

A combination of a packet filter in the insecure network and a dual-homed application gateway in the protected network can be used in the following cases:

- The insecure network is afforded a low level of protection (or the level of protection can't be assessed).
- The protected network does not have a particularly high protection requirement.

The Screened Subnet

The *screened subnet*, or border network, is a decoupled, isolated subnetwork that is interposed between the protected network and the insecure network (see Figure 5-5). In the screened subnet, control of the connections and packets is achieved through the use of two packet filters. The screened subnet is often also referred to as a *demilitarized zone (DMZ)*.

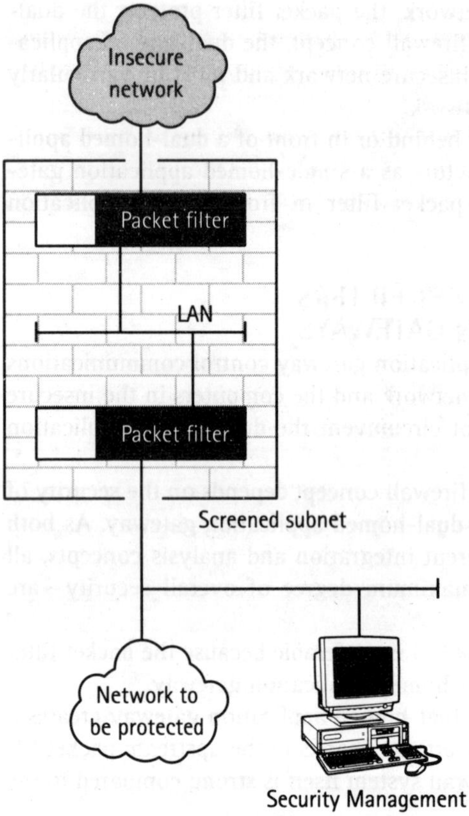

Figure 5-5: Screened subnet

The outer packet filter protects the screened subnet and the protected network from attackers from the insecure network. The outer packet filter is the first hurdle that must be surmounted from the insecure network. It also determines who is allowed access to computer systems that are positioned in the screened subnet.

The inner packet filter is the last hurdle to be overcome. It also allows or denies access between the protected network and computer systems that are positioned in the screened subnet.

All the computer systems positioned within a screened subnet are protected from both sides. Furthermore, the filter rules are easier to define because they can be formulated with both the insecure network and the protected network in mind.

Two Packet Filters as Screened Subnet and Single-Homed Application Gateway

In this firewall concept, security is provided primarily by two packet filters, which constitute a screened subnet. The single-homed application gateway optionally provides additional security services.

You can configure the two packet filters to only permit communication through the single-homed application gateway, which in this case provides all the security services. Communication between the computers in the protected network and the computers in the insecure network is achieved through the two packet filters, controlled through the application gateway. In this firewall concept, the single-homed application gateway is located in the screened subnet and is protected by the two packet filters. Refer to Figure 5-6 for an illustration of this configuration.

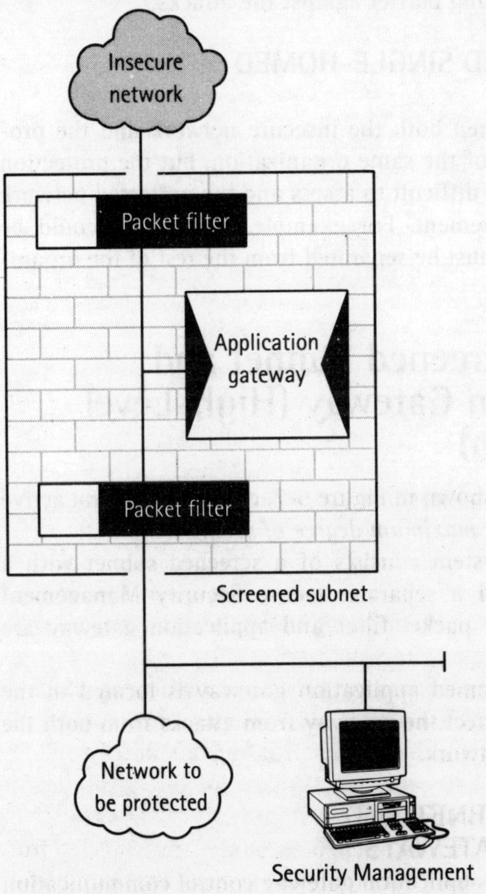

Figure 5-6: Screened subnet and a single-homed application gateway

EVALUATION OF SCREENED SUBNET AND SINGLE-HOMED APPLICATION GATEWAYS

With this configuration, communications on particular connections can be run exclusively through the packet filters – for services, for example, for which there are no proxies on the single-homed application gateway. This makes the firewall concept very flexible. Some services are allowed only through the packet filters, while others must also pass through the single-homed application gateway.

The degree of security provided by this firewall design depends primarily on the security of the packet filters. Because the protection requirement of most networks is higher than that offered by the security mechanisms of a packet filter, this concept is insufficient when a protected network is connected to the Internet.

Using a single-homed application gateway and two packet filters as a screened subnet, you can achieve a weak to strong barrier against the attacks.

USE OF SCREENED SUBNET AND SINGLE-HOMED APPLICATION GATEWAYS

This firewall design is appropriate when both the insecure network and the protected network are under the control of the same organization, but the protection level of the insecure network is low or difficult to assess and the protected network exacts a very high protection requirement. For example, this design could be applied to a management board that must be separated from the rest of the organization in an intranet.

Two Packet Filters as Screened Subnet and Dual-Homed Application Gateway (High-Level Security Firewall System)

A high-level security firewall system, shown in Figure 5-7, comprises several active firewall elements in order to achieve a *maximum degree of security.*

The high-level security firewall system consists of a screened subnet with a dual-homed application gateway and a separate, secure Security Management function. In this firewall system, the packet filter and application gateway are directly connected.

In this firewall design, the dual-homed application gateway is located in the screened subnet. The packet filters protect the gateway from attacks from both the insecure network and the protected network.

EVALUATION OF SCREENED SUBNET AND DUAL-HOMED APPLICATION GATEWAYS

The packet filters and the dual-homed application gateway control communication between computer systems in the protected network and computer systems in the insecure network. In this firewall system, the dual-homed application gateway cannot be circumvented in any way.

The overall high degree of security offered by this firewall system is the sum of the security achieved by both the packet filters and the dual-homed application gateway.

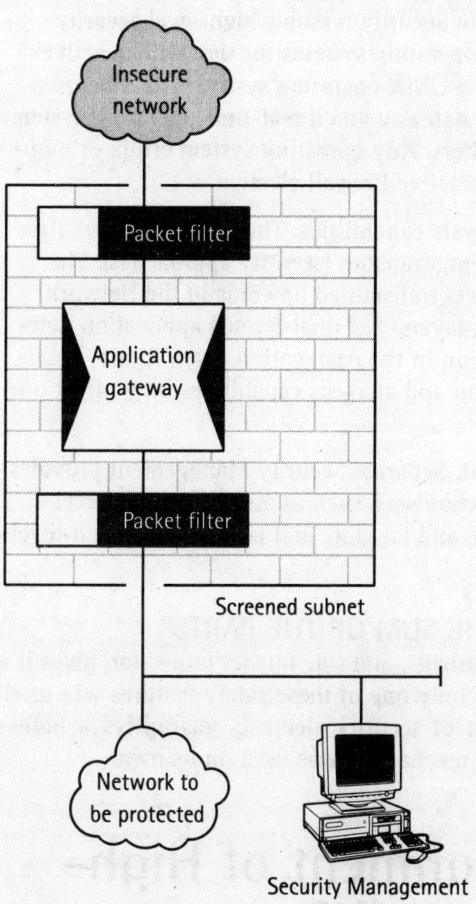

Figure 5-7: High-level security firewall system

The characteristics of a high-level security firewall system include the following:

- **Simple rules.** The arrangement of the packet filter and application gateway enables simple definition of the rules for the individual active firewall elements. As far as the packet filter is concerned, the application gateway alone always communicates with the computer systems of the corresponding networks.
- **Mutual protection.** The packet filters determine who may access the dual-homed application gateway, and protect the dual-homed application gateway itself.

- **Nested security.** Anyone wishing to access a network that is protected through a high-level security firewall system must overcome a number of barriers: a packet filter, then a dual-homed application gateway, and finally another packet filter.
- **Different operating systems.** For security reasons, high-level security firewall solutions use different operating systems for the various active firewall elements. For example, a UNIX operating system would be used for the dual-homed application gateway and a real-time operating system would be used for the packet filters. Any operating system errors or loopholes that occur affect only one active firewall element.
- **Different integration and analysis capabilities.** The different active firewall elements work with different strategies (security approaches). The packet filters interpret the packets transmitted upwards in the Network Access, Network, and Transport layers. The dual-homed application gateway interprets the communication in the Application layer. Again, possible weaknesses in the integration and analysis capabilities only affect one active firewall element.
- **Separate Security Management.** Separate Security Management provides numerous separate security mechanisms, such as access control, access rights management, encryption, and logging, and takes care of high-level security.

"THE WHOLE IS MORE THAN THE SUM OF THE PARTS"

Equipping a vehicle with safety belts, airbags, and side impact protection gives it a much higher level of protection than if only one of these safety features was used. In a similar way, using a combination of security elements guarantees a higher degree of security than if each security mechanism was used on its own.

Operational Environment of High-Level Security Firewall Systems

High-level security firewall systems work in an operational environment in which a secure operating system, secure Security Management, and firewall protection mechanisms are implemented.

In general, the high-level security firewall system is the most effective solution against the wide array of possible attacks.

Whenever you want to connect an insecure network, such as the Internet, to a network with a low level of protection that is outside the responsibility of the organization, you should use a high-level security firewall system. This firewall concept is generally considered the best overall approach for most organizations when implementing an Internet firewall.

In Figure 5-8, a simplified symbol consisting of two packet filters around an application gateway (shown on the right) indicates use of a high-level security firewall system. This symbol stands for a screened subnet with two packet filters and a dual-homed application gateway.

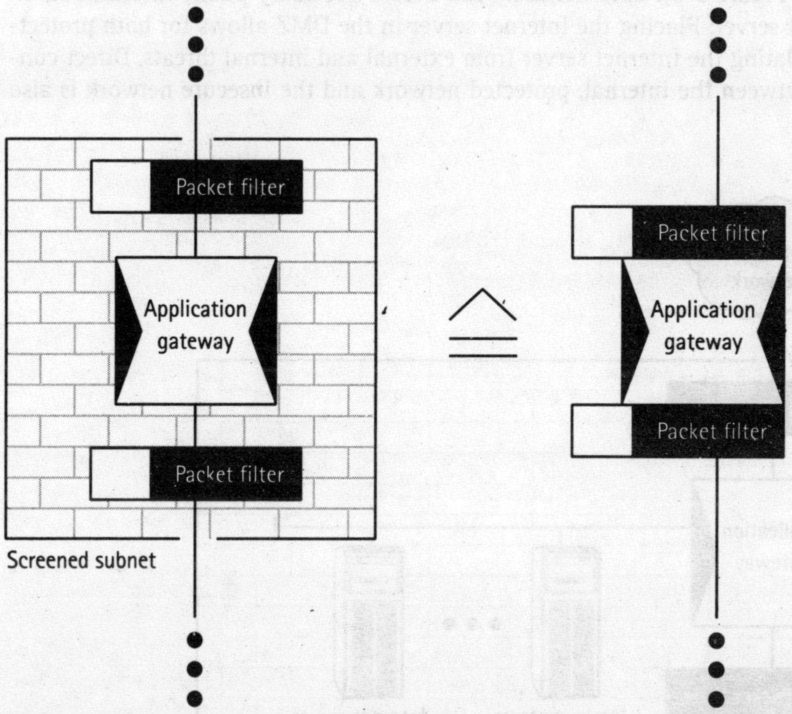

Figure 5-8: Symbol of a high-level security firewall system

Capabilities of a High-Level Security Firewall System

The future development of business processes over communication networks requires that firewall systems be scalable. A few of the basic scalability options that are feasible with a high-level security firewall system are discussed in this section. To differentiate more clearly between them, the area between an inner packet filter and the application gateway is referred to as an *internal screened subnet*, and the area between the application gateway and an outer packet filter is called an *external screened subnet*.

Internet Server

Information that is to be publicly accessed can be made available to the Internet on one or more information servers. An Internet server might be located, for example, behind the outer packet filter and the application gateway in the external screened subnet (see Figure 5-9). External users can access necessary public information on the Internet server. Placing the Internet server in the DMZ allows for both protecting and isolating the Internet server from external and internal threats. Direct connectivity between the internal, protected network and the insecure network is also prevented.

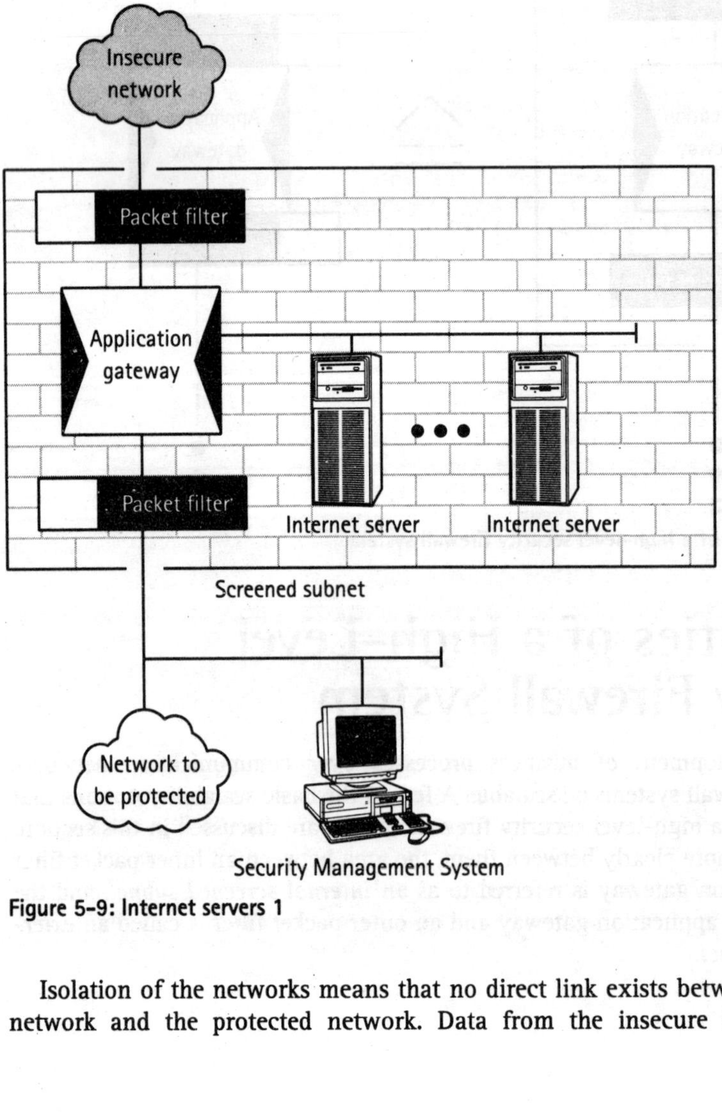

Figure 5-9: Internet servers 1

Isolation of the networks means that no direct link exists between the insecure network and the protected network. Data from the insecure network is only transported as far as the Internet server (or servers) located in front of the application gateway, but it cannot pass through unchecked.

The protected network stores data intended for the public on the Internet servers for retrieval. All users with access to the Internet servers are monitored through the outer packet filter.

If an attacker were to successfully access the Internet server and install his own software on it, enabling him to carry out an attack on the application gateway, he would have already overcome the first barrier – the first packet filter. This potential weakness can be eliminated if attention is paid to the following points:

- The outer packet filter must be configured so that only those services necessary for its operation are allowed. In the case of an Internet server, for example, only the HTTP protocol (port 80) should be enabled.
- Internet servers must be configured so that an attacker from outside cannot access the operating system level of the Internet server and carry out an attack. Adhere to the following guidelines:
  - Configure the operating system and Web server software for maximum security, following the applicable vendor recommendations.
  - Allow only a few select systems staff to have administrative access to the server.
  - Remove all software from the Web server not directly needed for the Web server functionality.
  - Only read access should be allowed on the server systems.

DEDICATED PACKET FILTER FOR THE INTERNET SERVERS

Another way to integrate Internet servers is to use a separate packet filter exclusively for them, as shown in Figure 5-10. This makes a higher level of security possible because the packet filter is independent of the Internet servers' computer systems and a clearer separation of security objectives can be implemented.

THIRD NETWORK INTERFACE AT THE APPLICATION GATEWAY

Using a third network interface at the application gateway is another way to integrate Internet servers (refer to Figure 5-11). This third network interface is also used for integrating anti-virus systems, content filtering, and special URL filters/blockers.

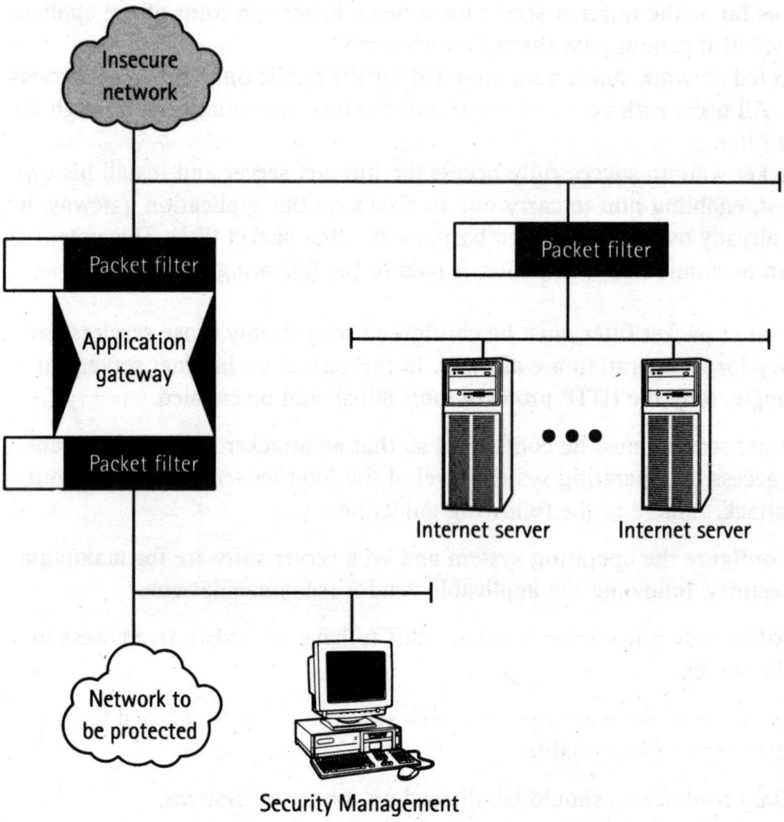

Figure 5-10: Internet servers 2

Intranet Servers

Information for users from the protected network can be made available to the intranet on one or more intranet servers. The intranet server is located between the inner packet filter and the application gateway in the internal screened subnet. This positioning means that users do not need to access the insecure network from inside the protected network.

Isolation of the networks means that no direct link exists between the insecure network and the protected network. Data from the protected network is only transported as far as the intranet server (or servers) located behind the application gateway, as shown in Figure 5-12.

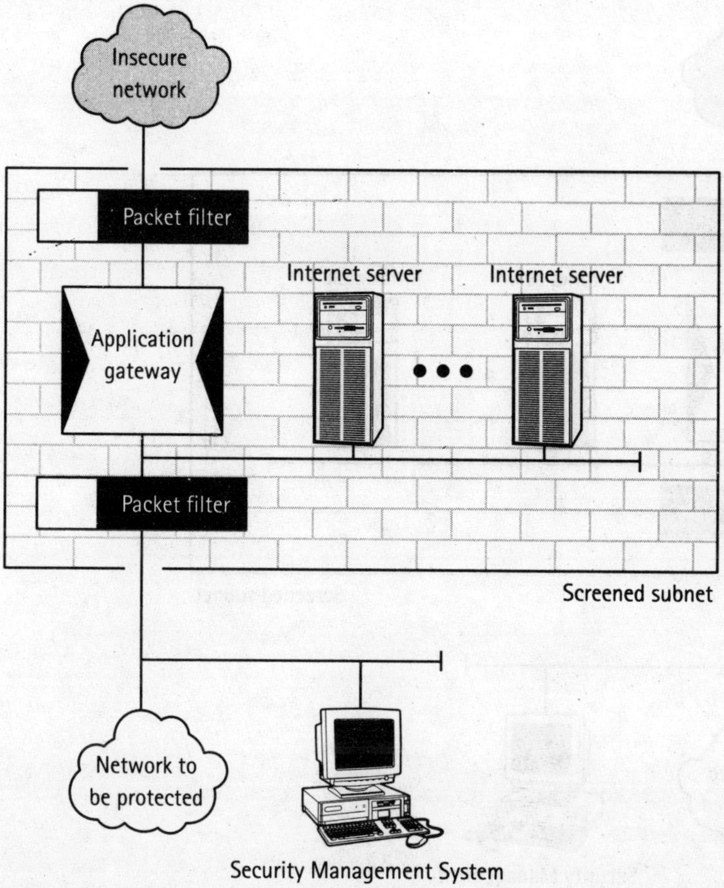

Figure 5-11: Internet servers 3

Data intended for users from the protected network is stored on the intranet server in the internal screened subnet for retrieval. All users with access to the intranet server are controlled through the inner packet filter. Communications between computer systems in the protected network and the intranet servers can also pass through the application gateway. The application gateway operates as a single-homed application gateway, providing security services such as user authentication and logging of user actions.

XREF

Chapter 9 describes other ways intranet servers can be used.

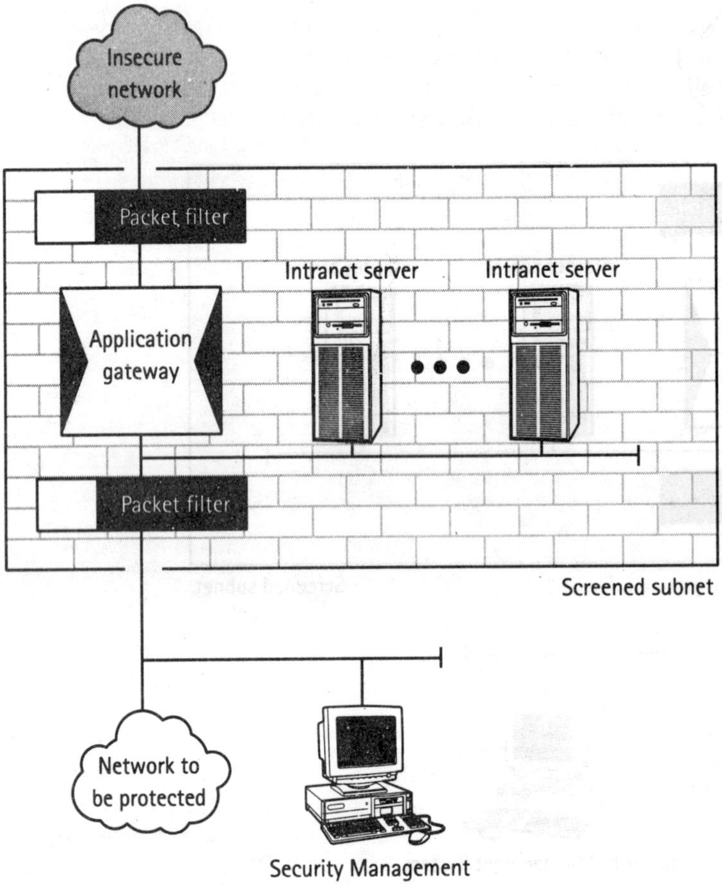

Figure 5-12: Intranet servers

Several Application Gateways in Parallel

In practice, there are applications for which it is appropriate to operate several application gateways in parallel in the screened subnet. This is the case, for example, when performance is to be increased, redundancy is to be achieved, or separation is to be maintained between certain services. These performance or redundancy requirements are used in large organizations to cope with future requirements flexibly and securely.

The implementation of parallel firewalls results in avenues for both redundancy and fail-over. Actually, implementing parallel firewalls presents two challenges when it comes to synchronizing rules and consolidating log information.

Normally, the Security Management function is used to implement parallel rules on the multiple gateways. Proper execution requires routing support as well as firewall configuration. In addition, the use of parallel firewalls necessitates the consolidation of log information from the gateways. Failure to consolidate this information makes detecting malicious activity more difficult in most configurations because an attacker's activity is spread across the parallel systems, effectively reducing the level on each system (note Figure 5-13). This reduced level may cause the attacks to fall below malicious activity thresholds. By consolidating the activity from the parallel gateways, you regain the advantage of analysis.

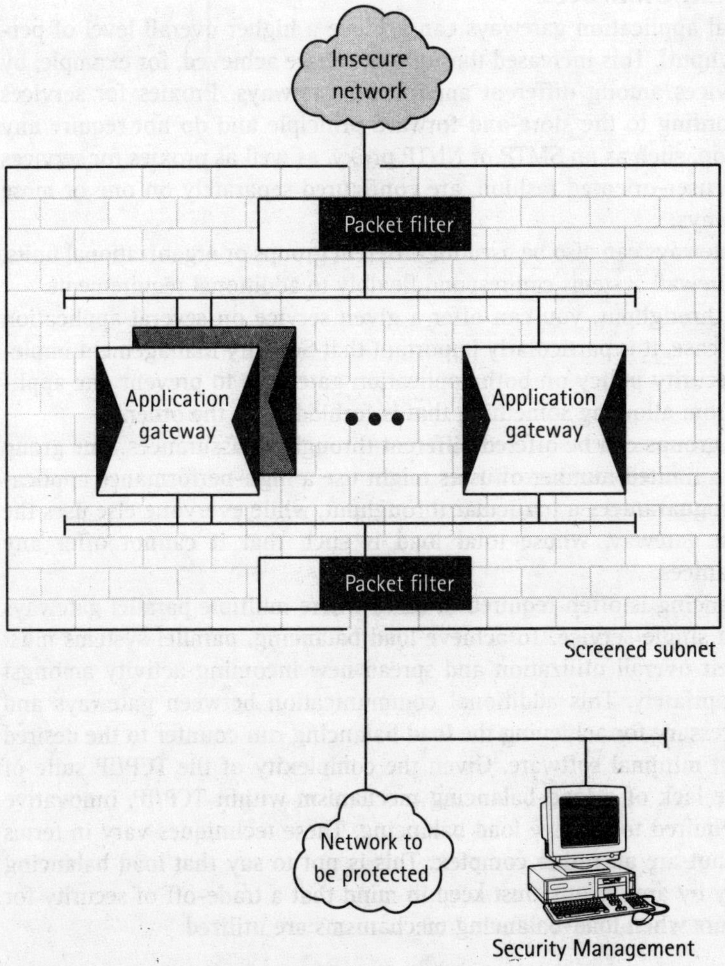

Figure 5-13: Several application gateways operated in parallel

SEPARATION BETWEEN PARTICULAR SERVICES

One application gateway can be responsible for the communications that pass from an insecure network to the protected network, and a second application gateway can be responsible for communications in the opposite direction, from the protected network to the insecure network. With this configuration, you can more clearly define different operating times, security policies, and individuals who are responsible for operations.

Experience shows that large firewall systems benefit from having separate application gateways for applications, such as the e-mail service, in order to ensure an even level of performance.

INCREASED PERFORMANCE

The use of several application gateways can achieve a higher overall level of performance (throughput). This increased throughput can be achieved, for example, by dividing the services among different application gateways. Proxies for services that operate according to the store-and-forward principle and do not require any user authentication, such as an SMTP or NNTP proxy, as well as proxies for services that operate in a user-oriented fashion, are configured separately on one or more application gateways.

Application gateways can also be used for different groups or organizational units. In this case, the firewall systems can respond flexibly to additional requirements.

For a greater throughput, you can offer a given service on several application gateways. In this case, it is particularly important that Security Management implement the same security policy on both application gateways to prevent one application gateway from allowing something that is forbidden by the other.

Different user groups can be offered different throughput assurances. One group comprising only a limited number of users might use a high-performance application gateway that guarantees a particular throughput, while everyone else uses the other application gateway, whose total load is such that it cannot offer any throughput guarantees.

True load balancing is often required in cases where multiple parallel gateways are required on a single service. To achieve load balancing, parallel systems must communicate their overall utilization and spread new incoming activity amongst themselves appropriately. This additional communication between gateways and the protocols necessary for achieving the load balancing run counter to the desired design concept of minimal software. Given the complexity of the TCP/IP suite of protocols and the lack of a load-balancing mechanism within TCP/IP, innovative techniques are required to achieve load balancing. These techniques vary in terms of methodology but are all rather complex. This is not to say that load balancing precludes security by any means. Just keep in mind that a trade-off of security for performance occurs when load-balancing mechanisms are utilized.

CREATING REDUNDANCY

Another reason for operating several application gateways in parallel is high availability. If, for example, the application gateways operate in parallel in hot standby mode, a higher level of availability can be assured.

The Right Firewall Concept for Every Application

Different decision criteria are used when choosing a particular firewall system design. The primary goal is always to achieve a level of security that matches the protection requirement of the secure network.

The comparison shown in Table 5-1 was developed to determine which firewall system best meets the security requirements of different organizations. Table 5-1 rates several factors – trustworthiness of the insecure network, trustworthiness of the communications partner, and attack potential – based on whether the insecure network is inside or outside the organization.

A firewall system is primarily used to reduce the vulnerability of an organization's sensitive data. If the data on a network does not need to be protected, a firewall system isn't necessary. However, if protection is required, the relevant circumstances must be considered and an appropriate firewall system must be selected.

TABLE 5-1 SECURITY REQUIREMENTS MATRIX

Criteria	The Insecure Network is within the Organization	The Insecure Network is Outside of the Organization
Trustworthiness of the Insecure Network	Very high Company is responsible for the insecure network It is checked regularly	Dependent on special factors that are difficult to measure Company itself is not responsible for the insecure network All the risks must be considered
Trustworthiness of the Communications Partner	Very high The communications partners belong to the same organization and the same security policy applies to them One still needs to beware of insiders	Probably very low In principle, no assumptions can be made regarding the trustworthiness of communications partners from outside

Continued

TABLE 5-1 SECURITY REQUIREMENTS MATRIX *(Continued)*

Criteria	The Insecure Network is within the Organization	The Insecure Network is Outside of the Organization
Attack Potential	Very low The communications partners belong to the same organization and the same security policy applies to them One still needs to beware of insiders	Very high The network partners have very different protection requirements (for example, hackers and professional attackers from the Internet)

EVALUATION OF PROTECTION REQUIREMENT

Even when IT systems are used within organizations, ***blind trust*** in employees would be a mistake and would mean that security was only deceptive, as suggested by case histories involving insiders. The 2002 FBI/Computer Security Institute crime survey for 2001 found that 33 percent of respondents suffered an attack from internal employees. Of even greater concern is the fact that insider attacks are almost always more severe (and monetarily more costly) in nature because of the inside information possessed by the attacker.

Table 5-2 presents a decision matrix for, depending on the protection requirement and the scenario, what active firewall element or combination of active firewall elements should be used.

TABLE 5-2 DECISION MATRIX FOR THE FIREWALL SYSTEM

Protection Requirement	Risks	Scenario	Firewall System
Low	Minor infringement of laws	Within the organization	Packet filter
	Limited negative external effect	Outside the organization	Dual-homed application gateway
	Financial loss <$10,000		

Protection Requirement	Risks	Scenario	Firewall System
High	Major infringement of laws Wide negative external effect	Within the organization	Packet filter plus single-homed application gateway or stateful inspection or adaptive proxy
	Financial loss >$10,000 but <$2.5 million	Outside the organization	Packet filter plus dual-homed application gateway
Very High	Fundamental violation of laws Extremely serious negative external effect	Within the organization	Screened subnet with packet filter plus single-homed application gateway
	Financial loss >$2.5 million	Outside the organization	Screened subnet with packet filter plus dual-homed application gateway (high-level firewall system)

If a network requires any type of protection, the firewall system must include a dual-homed application gateway.

Depending on the protection requirement, a dual-homed application gateway should be used either on its own or in combination with a packet filter. A screened subnet should probably be used as well.

If the insecure network is under the control of the organization (for example, an intranet), it is sufficient to use only packet filters or a combination of packet filters with single-homed application gateways, depending on the protection requirement. Alternatively, stateful inspection or adaptive proxy concepts, solutions that also provide security functions at the application level, can be used.

A very high level of security is possible if a dual-homed application gateway is combined with a packet filter or screened subnet.

In addition to the basic strength of the firewall system, which determines how it is used, the following security-relevant aspects also play a role.

- The actual security services offered
- The depth of analysis at the different communication levels
- The firewall solution design concept

- The quality of the implementation
- The demonstrability of security
- Any government restrictions on the firewall solution

If the firewall system is to satisfy security expectations, all of these aspects must be considered. Furthermore, infrastructural, organizational, and personnel-related security mechanisms should be considered to achieve a high degree of overall security.

Moreover, care must be taken to ensure that a secure, controlled interface between two different networks can be implemented with the aid of a firewall system.

Additional information about attacks can be gained with additional security mechanisms, such as intrusion detection software. Intrusion detection software (IDS) can alert you to a wide array of attacks, including attacks that are being carried out against the firewall system itself.

Content security problems can be resolved by integrating anti-virus concepts.

Always consider whether mechanisms not directly connected to the firewall system should be considered in its design.

Mail Security

A number of different methods for providing mail security are possible when a high-level security firewall system is integrated. This section discusses a design in which separate mail servers are positioned in the protected network and in the insecure network (refer to Figure 5-14).

When mail is exchanged between computer systems in the protected network, it can be passed through the internal mail server so that it does not leave this network. Mail sent to computer systems in the insecure network is sent through the firewall system to the external mail server (as any mail handling rules in the firewall), which forwards it to its destination.

Mail sent from the insecure network to the protected network is received and transferred by the firewall system.

The mail server in the insecure network is operated by the organization itself, so the following further restrictions can be implemented:

- In the packet filter before the application gateway, the mail server's MAC address can be checked to ensure that all mail will pass through this upstream mail server.
- Mail is only transmitted at certain times, which means that only a limited window of opportunity is available for communications from the insecure network to the protected network.

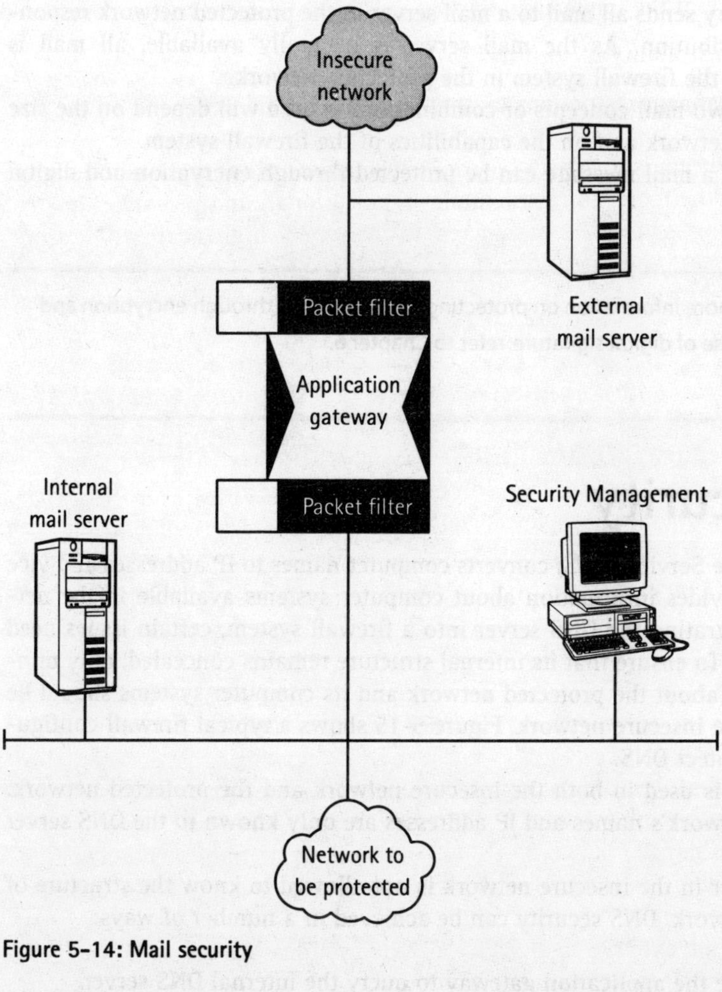

Figure 5-14: Mail security

In many firewall systems, the mail application is the only application for which a connection can be established from the insecure network to the protected network. In all other cases, connections can only be established in the opposite direction.

Configuration in the Protected Network

A Message Transfer Agent (MTA) behind the SMTP proxy is responsible for distributing the mail received from the insecure network in the protected network. To do this, the MTA must be installed on the application gateway. If the computer systems in the protected network are not available, the mail is discarded.

The SMTP proxy sends all mail to a mail server in the protected network responsible for its distribution. As the mail server is generally available, all mail is accepted through the firewall system in the protected network.

Which of the two mail concepts or combinations is used will depend on the size of the protected network and on the capabilities of the firewall system.

The content of a mail message can be protected through encryption and digital signature.

XREF

For more information on protecting mail messages through encryption and the use of digital signature, refer to Chapter 6.

DNS Security

The Domain Name Service (DNS) converts computer names to IP addresses and vice versa. It also provides information about computer systems available in the network. When integrating the DNS server into a firewall system, certain issues need to be considered. To ensure that its internal structure remains concealed, only minimal information about the protected network and its computer systems should be available from the insecure network. Figure 5-15 shows a typical firewall configuration used to protect DNS.

A DNS server is used in both the insecure network and the protected network. The protected network's names and IP addresses are only known to the DNS server in that network.

The DNS server in the insecure network is not allowed to know the structure of the protected network. DNS security can be achieved in a number of ways:

- Configure the application gateway to query the internal DNS server.
- Use split DNS.
- Implement either a dedicated DNS server or DNS proxy.

The Application Gateway Queries the Internal DNS Server

All DNS-related queries are resolved by the application gateway over an internal DNS server. If the internal DNS server cannot perform the necessary resolution, the query is automatically forwarded through the application gateway "transparently" to the external DNS server. The result is sent to the application gateway by the internal DNS server. Communications between the two DNS servers run transparently for the proxies on the application gateway.

The large amount of communication entailed by this DNS approach can result in problems on some DNS implementations. The packet filters are configured so that only the DNS service is allowed between the servers (that is, DNS port 53 is both source and destination port).

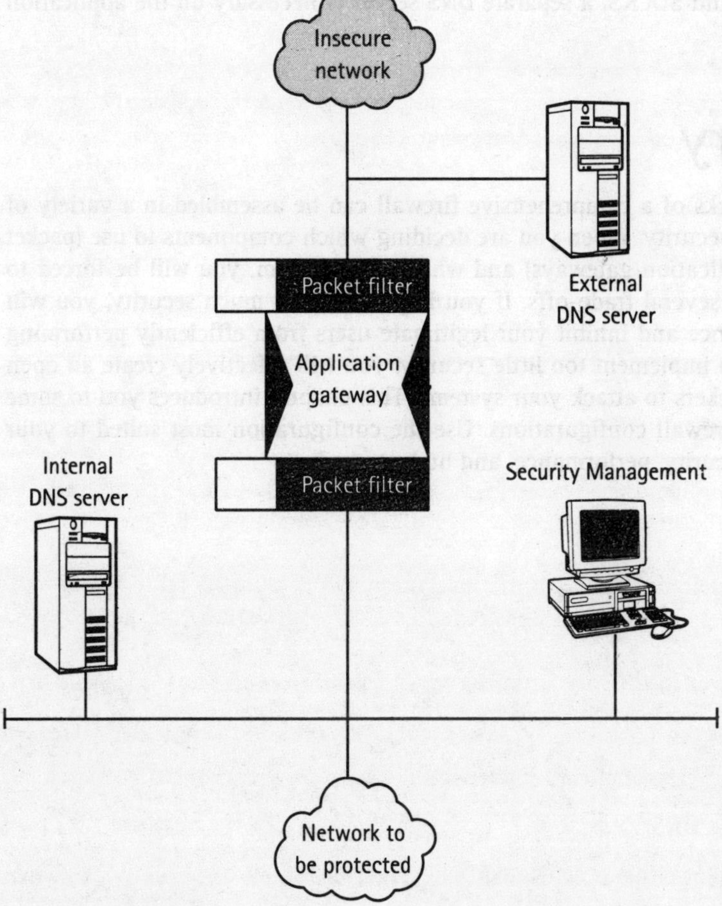

Figure 5-15: DNS security

Split DNS

Under the split DNS concept, the application gateway knows which domain names and IP addresses are in the insecure network and which are in the protected network, and can decide what direction resolution to take. The disadvantage of this solution is that the external IP addresses and names from the insecure network (for example, the Internet) cannot be resolved from the protected network.

Dedicated DNS Server or DNS Proxy

A third possible solution is to implement the DNS server itself in the application gateway and have the IP addresses and names resolved from the internal network via the application gateway. The addresses from the insecure network are resolved from the protected network by the DNS server on the application gateway. For a transport proxy and SOCKS, a separate DNS server is necessary on the application gateway.

Summary

The building blocks of a comprehensive firewall can be assembled in a variety of ways to achieve security. When you are deciding which components to use (packet filtering and application gateways) and where to use them, you will be forced to balance between several trade-offs. If you implement too much security, you will impede performance and inhibit your legitimate users from efficiently performing their work. If you implement too little security, you will effectively create an open invitation for hackers to attack your systems. This chapter introduces you to some of the possible firewall configurations. Use the configuration most suited to your organization's security, performance, and budget needs.

Chapter 6

Firewall Systems and Encryption

YOU CAN ENCRYPT data for TCP/IP communications in a number of ways. For example, you can integrate security functions in the Application layer in an e-mail application. You can also integrate security functions between the Network and Transport layers, as a virtual private network (VPN). Both encryption variants are designed so that firewall functionality can continue to be used. The encryption function is not only used to maintain confidentiality of data, but also to actively rule out residual risks in firewall systems, such as man-in-the-middle attacks. When used together, firewall systems and encryption can achieve a high level of overall security for communications over public networks.

A security component must always be involved in the encrypted communications. This security component must provide for authentication of the source of the encrypted communications. If the encryption is part of a VPN then the system must also provide access control. A common key management function must be organized so that the key used in encryption is the same on both sides. The organization of key management is always simple if the security components are all within the same sphere of responsibility. If this is not the case, a key management system trusted by all of the involved centers of responsibility must be devised. This chapter describes the VPN solution, in which Security Management can be handled by an organization, and discusses encryption in the e-mail application.

The chapter begins with a description of security mechanisms with which encryption can be established.

Security Mechanisms for Encryption and Digital Signatures

This section describes security mechanisms that enable data to be protected in transit over public networks. Security mechanisms are tools with which security services, such as encryption and digital signatures, can be implemented.

Data confidentiality can only be assured if data is transmitted in an encrypted form. Several methods of encryption may be distinguished.

- Private key (symmetric) encryption
- Public key (asymmetric) encryption
- One-way (hash) encryption

Private Key Systems

Encryption systems that use the same key both to encrypt and decrypt data are known as *symmetric*, or *private key*, systems (see Figure 6-1).

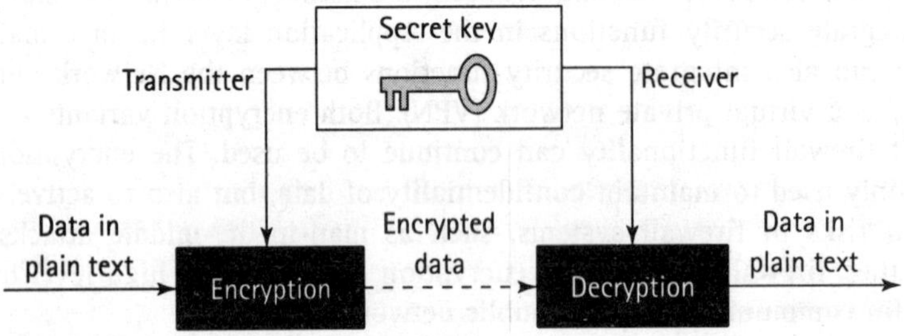

Figure 6-1: Symmetric encryption system

One of the most well-known, widespread, and studied symmetric encryption systems is the *DES algorithm*, standardized in the U.S. in 1978 (ANSI X3.92). DES stands for Data Encryption Standard. Today, the DES algorithm is generally implemented as Triple-DES. The DES algorithm is executed three times, with an effective key length of 112 or 128 bits, using either two (A-B-A) or three (A-B-C) different keys. Other common algorithms include IDEA, RC2, RC4, RC5, Blowfish, Twofish, and Safer.

In a triple pass operation, in which each pass uses a 56-bit key length, the procedure is actually less secure than that of a single encryption procedure using a key length of 168 bits (3 times 56 equals 168). Cryptologists have therefore coined the term effective key length to refer to encryption implementations using keys in such a manner that reduce the security of the key.

The new Advanced Encryption Standard (AES), which uses the Rijndael algorithm, becomes the official replacement for DES on May 26, 2002, for U.S. government entities protecting information that is classified as "secret." The AES standard can use key lengths of 128, 192, or 256 bits. The end result is an algorithm that is both strong and flexible. The Rijndael algorithm was selected for its combination of security, performance, efficiency (low memory use), and easy implementation.

FIPS-197 (Federal Information Processing Standard) specifies the implementation requirements of the new standard for U.S. governmental entities.

The disadvantage of symmetric encryption systems such as Triple-DES is that both communication partners must have the same key. Security depends on nondisclosure of a key that must be sent from one communication partner to the other.

This is an uncertainty factor, whose risk must be minimized by finding a secure method for key management. In an extreme case, for example, this transfer can be affected personally using a courier. The security risk is that the keys that must be kept secret could fall into the wrong hands due to carelessness, intent, or chance.

The advantage of private key systems such as DES is that they are very fast. Certain hardware solutions can encrypt at rates of up to 1 Gb, and certain software solutions can achieve rates up to several Mb.

Public Key Systems

Public key systems, otherwise known as *asymmetric cryptography* (see Figure 6-2), use a mathematically matched key pair for encryption and decryption. One half of the key pair is designated as a public key and disseminated widely. The other key portion is referred to as the secret key and is protected. Asymmetric encryption occurs through the encryption of data using one key and the decryption of data using the other.

Figure 6-2: Asymmetric encryption system

Most asymmetric algorithms support both directions of encryption and decryption. If data is encrypted using the public key, the secret key will decrypt the information. If the secret key is used to encrypt (as in the case of digital signatures), the public key will decrypt the information.

Successful asymmetric encryption is based on the fact that while the keys are mathematically linked, the possession of one key will not compromise or aid in the recovery of the other key. Asymmetric encryption addresses one of the major challenges in cryptography: key distribution. Key distribution is not solved entirely by using asymmetric encryption, because there is still the matter of trusting the key used for encryption. Trust, however, is a much simpler technical challenge than the safe distribution of a symmetric key.

DIGITAL SIGNATURES

One important application of the public key system is the digital signature. Data that has been encrypted with a particular secret key can only be decrypted using the corresponding public key. If someone has digitally signed the data with his secret key, you can use the public key to check the authenticity of that person. If the signature properly decrypts using the public key of the sender then the signature's authenticity is proved.

The *RSA method*, the most well known public key system, permits data to be simultaneously signed and encrypted.

CONFIDENTIALITY OF SECURITY INFORMATION

After information has been encrypted using a specific person's public key, only the person who owns the matching secret key can decrypt that information. This permits the confidential exchange of security-relevant information – that is, the exchange of keys for symmetric procedures such as DES.

DISADVANTAGES OF ASYMMETRIC METHODS

The primary shortcoming of asymmetric encryption is the speed at which encryption and decryption occurs. Public key systems are based on algorithms that are easy to calculate in one direction but nearly impossible to compute in the opposite direction and are highly processor-intensive, rendering them unsuitable for encrypting large volumes of data. The speed achievable with asymmetric encryption is a fraction of that obtainable with symmetric encryption.

One-Way Hash Function

The digital signature is the equivalent of an operation using the public key system and is highly processor-intensive.

To reduce the amount of effort involved in calculations, the public key system is not applied to all of the information in a message. Instead, a "distilled version" of the message is created and digitally signed.

A one-way hash function is applied to a message of variable length, resulting in a fixed-length cryptographic checksum. A special feature of one-way hash functions is that calculating the function value is simple, yet it is virtually impossible to systematically find a second message that produces the same cryptographic checksum. A cryptographic checksum must exhibit a number of other properties such as a low collision rate. A low collision rate means that it is computationally infeasible to take a given output and find an input (source document) that produces the same output. Another property exhibited should be that when any data in the document is changed the resulting hash should change significantly. For example, RIPEMD< MD5, and SHA 1 (all one-way hash functions) algorithms create a "fingerprint" for the document. If any modifications are made to the document, the resulting hash should be different.

Hybrid Encryption Technology

The real-world solution to secure and obtainable data security lies in the combination of all three types of encryption: symmetric, asymmetric, and one-way. By capitalizing on the strengths of each while minimizing their weaknesses, you can find a solution that effectively solves the data security conundrum.

A combination of the three encryption types (asymmetric encryption) is used to distribute the symmetric key. Symmetric encryption is used for the actual data encryption, and one-way functions are used to provide source identification and prevent data modification. Essentially, all of the TCP/IP protocols utilizing data encryption rely on this combination of encryption types. The primary protocol differences involve the types of data being encrypted (for example, HTTP data, IP data, and so on), how the information is exchanged, and the specific mathematical algorithms used to achieve encryption. For example, a person named Bob transmits an encrypted e-mail to a user named Alice. Bob has a public/private key pair (A and B, respectively), as does Alice (Y and Z). Both Bob and Alice possess each other's public keys.

Bob composes the e-mail in his e-mail client, checks the "Encrypt" and "Sign" options in his e-mail program, and then clicks the Send button. "Under the hood," as it were, Bob's computer first chooses a random symmetric key with which to encrypt the e-mail. This randomly chosen key is designated "M." M is used to encrypt the actual e-mail contents. Bob's computer also uses a message digest algorithm (one-way) to compute a message digest (fingerprint) of the message. This digest value is encrypted using Bob's private key, B, resulting in a digital signature. Finally, the random symmetric key is encrypted using Alice's public key. Together, all three of these pieces form the encrypted message that is transmitted to Alice.

Alice's computer begins by using her private key to recover the symmetric key M that is used for encrypting the e-mail. The symmetric key is used to decrypt the e-mail contents. Alice's computer verifies that the message originates from Bob and is intact by using Bob's private key to decrypt the signature and obtain the message digest value computed by Bob's computer. Alice's computer calculates its own message digest using the same algorithm and compares the two digests. If the digests match exactly, Alice knows that the e-mail is indeed from Bob (because, presumably, no one else can access his private key) and that it has not been modified in any way (otherwise, the digest value would be different).

Utilizing all three encryption types in this way maximizes the speed of symmetric encryption, the key distribution capabilities of asymmetric encryption, and the verification aspects of one-way encryption. This combined approach is flexible and efficient for a variety of uses. Had there been multiple recipients in the above scenario, Bob's computer would simply have appended additional symmetric keys encrypted to each of the recipient's public keys. This would have required significantly less space than encrypting the message separately for each recipient.

Certification Systems

Although public key encryption significantly reduces the key distribution problem, it does not solve it entirely. When public keys are used, they must be exchanged in a manner that can be authenticated. An elegant solution for the exchange of public keys in an authenticated manner is to establish a certification system or trust center.

Each user's public key is made available to the system (computer system) in the form of a certificate issued by a trusted third-party entity, known as the *certification authority (CA)*.

> Consider the authentication of persons by means of a personal ID (identity card, passport, and so on). In this case, the authorities (that is, residential registration offices) function as trusted third-party entities. When a person introduces himself to you, you can verify that the stated name is genuine with the aid of an identity card. It is precisely this type of functionality that is needed to implement complex security systems electronically.

CERTIFICATION AUTHORITY

A certification authority (CA), established in a security system, generates a key pair for itself (the CA). The public key for the certification authority is distributed to all users in a manner that can be authenticated – for example, with the use of a smart card.

In a hierarchical trust model of certification authorities (CAs), the uppermost CA is the root CA, which confirms the trustworthiness of the intermediate certification layer certification authority. In practice, a hybrid form that allows CAs to operate in a side-by-side hierarchy is more likely to be established. This form is known as *cross-certification*, under which the adjacent CAs mutually recognize each other but do not necessarily have to operate identical security policies.

The CAs issue keys to the end users or certify the keys generated by the users themselves. Frequently, a registration authority (RA) is also interposed between the user and the CA. Using a separate RA simplifies requests for and distribution of keys, and separates these services from other services provided by the CA.

CERTIFICATE

Each user's public key is made available to the system in the form of a certificate. A certificate is nothing more than a public key distribution mechanism. It is a file format providing compatible key exchange among different applications. The predominant certificate standard is X.509v3.

A certificate contains the following:

- The identity of the certification authority that produced the certificate
- The identity of the user for whom the certificate was created

- The user's public key, and
- The period of validity of the certificate (see Figure 6-3)

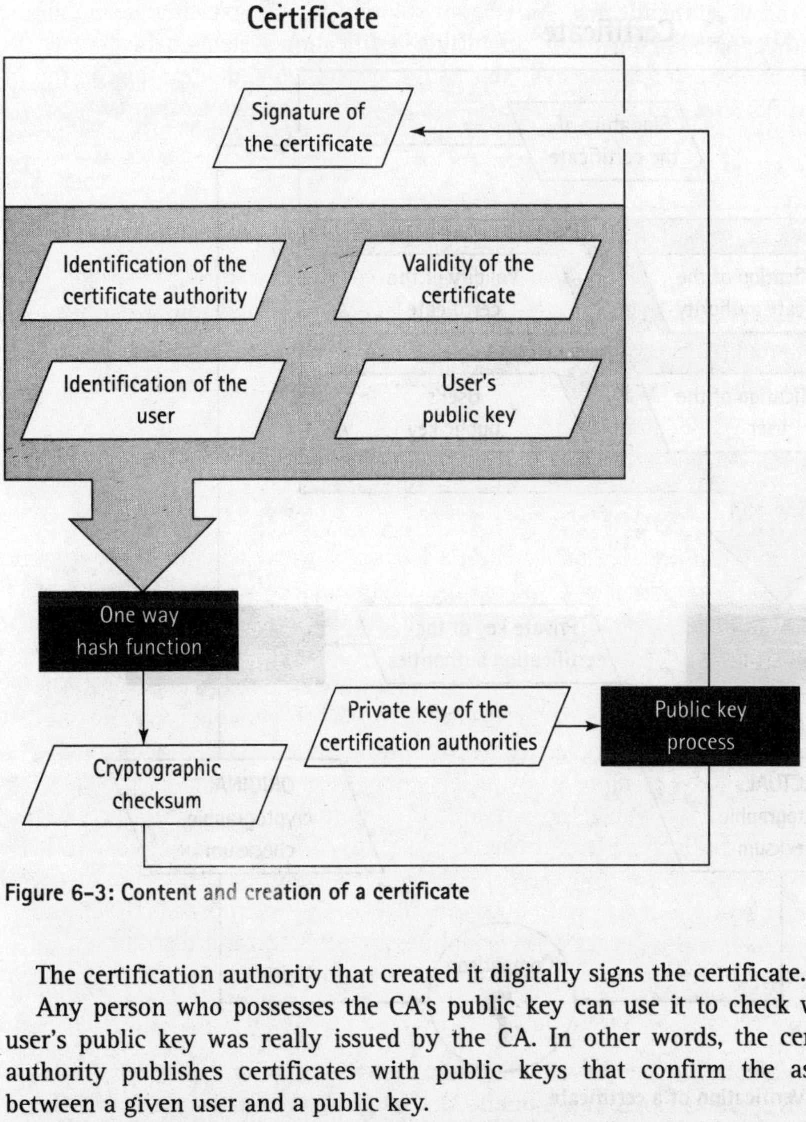

Figure 6-3: Content and creation of a certificate

The certification authority that created it digitally signs the certificate.

Any person who possesses the CA's public key can use it to check whether a user's public key was really issued by the CA. In other words, the certification authority publishes certificates with public keys that confirm the association between a given user and a public key.

After a certificate has been received, the security system calculates the current cryptographic checksum using the content of the certificate. Furthermore, the certificate's signature is taken and, using the public key system, the original cryptographic checksum is worked out using the CA's public key. If the two cryptographic checksums agree, the integrity and authenticity of the public key of the user with whom communication is desired are proven (see Figure 6-4). Integrity is also proven because any modifications of the data would have resulted in the cryptographic checksums differing.

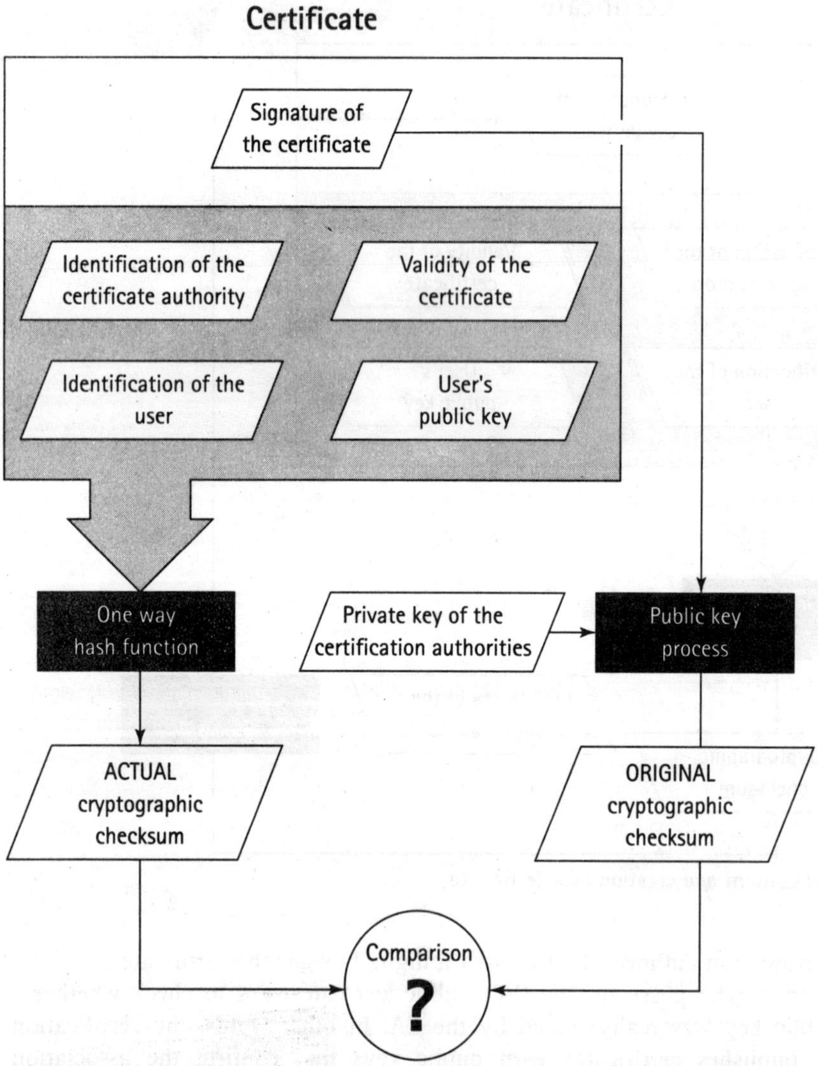

Figure 6-4: Verification of a certificate

The use of certificates requires that all the users of the security system be able to trust the CA, which in turn requires that a CA satisfy certain security requirements, such as the presence of trusted personnel, certified security components, and a secure environment. CAs distributed in parallel or hierarchically can be combined in a global security system.

The hierarchical key distribution procedure is necessary if a complex security system is to be established.

Smart Card

An intelligent chip card, or *smart card*, is a computer system that can provide the following security services to the user:

- Electronic units of value
- Cryptographic applications (digital signatures, and so on)
- Identification and authentication of the user (enabling of the smart card)
- Reading of stored service data
- Secure data storage on the smart card
- Any special computations required by a particular application, such as hashing

In applications such as the security system for the protection of electronic documents, the CA's public key and the secret portion of the key owned by the user are loaded securely onto an intelligent smart card. The smart card is then sent to the user through a trusted transport route.

ACTIVATION OF THE SMART CARD

The smart card is protected with a password. When a user wants to use any security functions on the system, he must first activate the smart card using a personal password. If the user loses his smart card, the person who finds it does not know the user's password and is unable to use the card. In the same way, if a person knows the user's password, he must also possess the smart card to benefit from that knowledge. A user can change his password at any time. Even more secure than a password, however, are biometric identification systems, which identify people uniquely by their physical characteristics. Unlike a password, a physical characteristic cannot be stolen, lost, forgotten, or divulged. Biometric identification uses characteristics such as fingerprints, voice, or facial features for identification purposes.

Successful authentication requires possession of at least two of the following:

- The password
- The smart card
- Biometrics

MULTIFUNCTIONALITY

The smart card is designed for use by several applications. Possible applications include, for example, public telephones, point of sales transactions, digital signing of documents, and access control to buildings.

POSSIBLE SMART CARD SECURITY MECHANISMS

Smart card hardware should provide the following security mechanisms:

- Detection of under- and over-voltages
- Detection of low frequencies
- Scrambled buses
- Sensors for light, temperature, passivating layer, and so on
- Random number generator in the hardware
- Special CPU commands for cryptographic functions
- Memory protection functions
- Passivating layers over bus and memory structures or over the entire CPU

The smart card operating system should provide the following security mechanisms, as defined in ISO 7816-4:

- Controlled access to objects
- State machines that permit commands as a function of identification and authentication mechanisms

Smart cards have the following advantages:

- The cryptographic operations are executed on the smart card. The secret key never leaves the smart card and cannot be read.
- They are the size of credit cards and are easy to carry around.
- They are flexible for functional applications.
- They cost between 3 and 24 dollars (depending on the quantity), making them significantly cheaper than other security modules.

NOTE: Smart cards are designed to use as security components for people. They are designed to provide both a convenient means of transporting identification between places like work and home, as well as provide for significantly better authentication than passwords alone provide.

E-Mail Security

E-mail is the most widely used application on the Internet. Highly sensitive information, such as contracts, is often transmitted in e-mail messages or as attachments to e-mails.

This section describes a suitable means for protecting such valuable information by ensuring at the user level that e-mail communications are trusted.

Today, information is increasingly processed by electronic means. Letters, documents, and transfers no longer exist solely in paper form, but are processed and sent electronically.

How do the security assurances surrounding the transmission of an electronic message compare to the security of an unopened envelope and a handwritten signature? How does an e-mail recipient know that the message is authentic?

Envelope and Signature for E-Mail

To achieve a security system that protects electronic documents, the normal communications system is extended to include a certification authority that issues personalized smart cards to users and provides the system with certificates.

SIGNING A DOCUMENT

A user creates electronic information using an editor (word processing system, browser, e-mail program, and so on). He wants to send this information through a trusted channel.

He invokes the signature function. To do so, he activates the smart card on which the secret RSA key is stored, using his password. Then, using the one-way hash function from the document specified by the user, the signature function calculates a cryptographic checksum (see Figure 6-5).

This cryptographic checksum is digitally signed with the public key system using the secret key stored on the user's smart card. The result is a signature that is appended to the document as accompanying information. The signature function also writes the user's certificate into the accompanying information.

Multiple users can generate signatures for a single document (often a necessity in daily office life). All the signatures to a document are attached to the document itself.

DIGITAL TIME STAMP

Digital documents are generally much easier to reproduce than physical documents. This presents a challenge for some uses of documents, such as in legal proceedings. The evidentiary value of an electronic document often depends on the time it was created. Because altering the time and date functions on commercially available computers and operating systems is relatively easy, these functions cannot be viewed as reliable evidence of the time at which digital signatures were created.

A time stamp requires a digital certificate from a CA. The CA confirms that it certified the document at the time stated by digitally signing the time stamp.

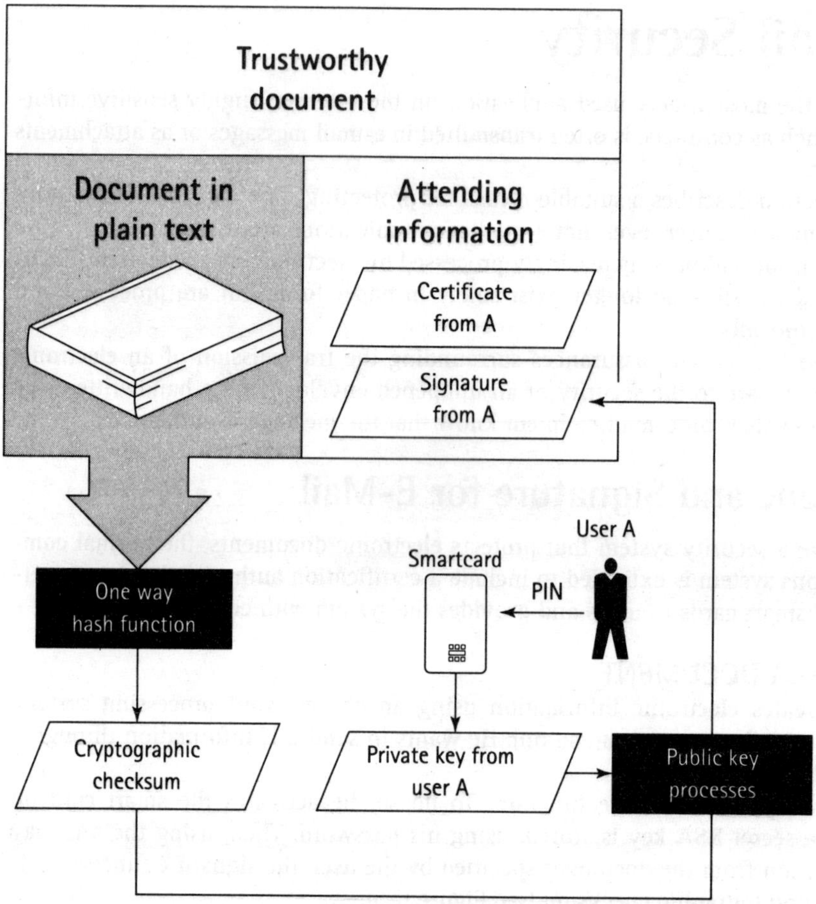

Figure 6-5: The signature function

ENCRYPTING AND SENDING A DOCUMENT

After one or more users have signed the document, it can be encrypted for transmission (see Figure 6-6).

The security system calculates a random number to be the document key. The document is then encrypted with the private key system (for example, Triple-DES) using the document key. The document key is encrypted with the public key system using the receiver's public key and added to the accompanying information. The security system can encrypt the document key for several recipients, in which case the accompanying information will contain several encrypted document keys for the recipients. The confidential document is sent.

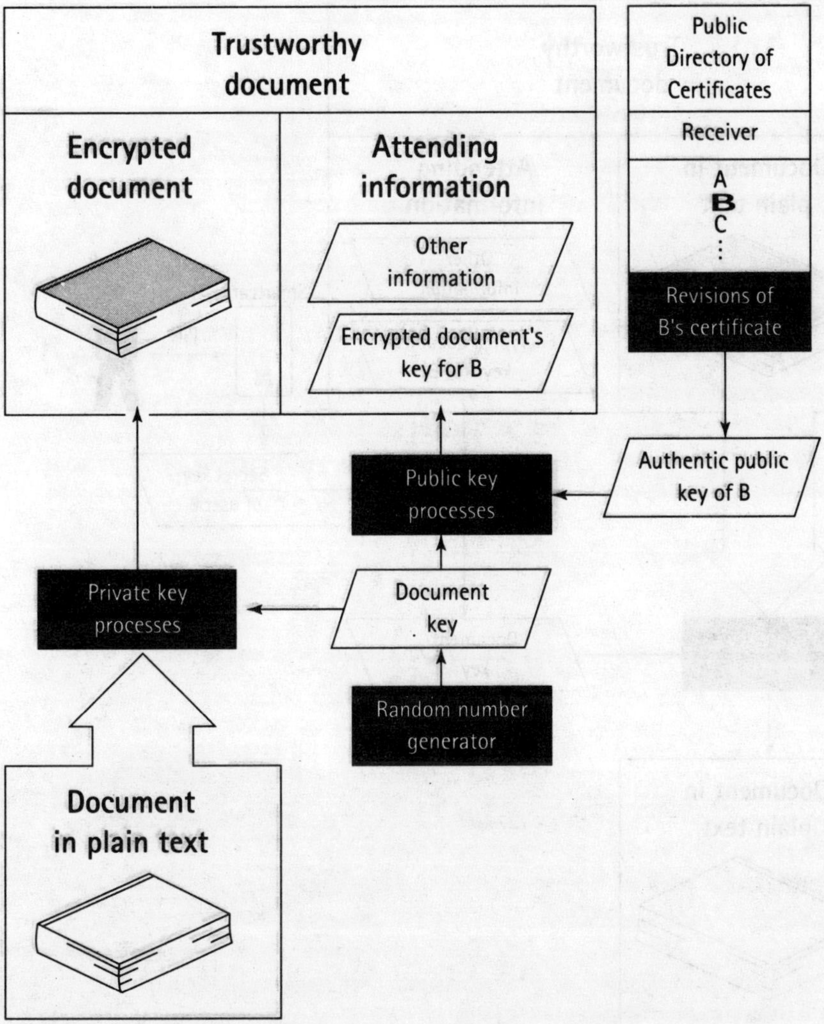

Figure 6-6: Encryption of a document

VERIFYING THE DOCUMENT'S TRUSTWORTHINESS AND DECRYPTING

After the document arrives, the recipient can tell from the accompanying information whether it has been digitally signed and if so, by whom. He can also tell whether the document is encrypted and who is able to decrypt it.

The document can be decrypted with the decryption function and read in plain text (see Figure 6-7).

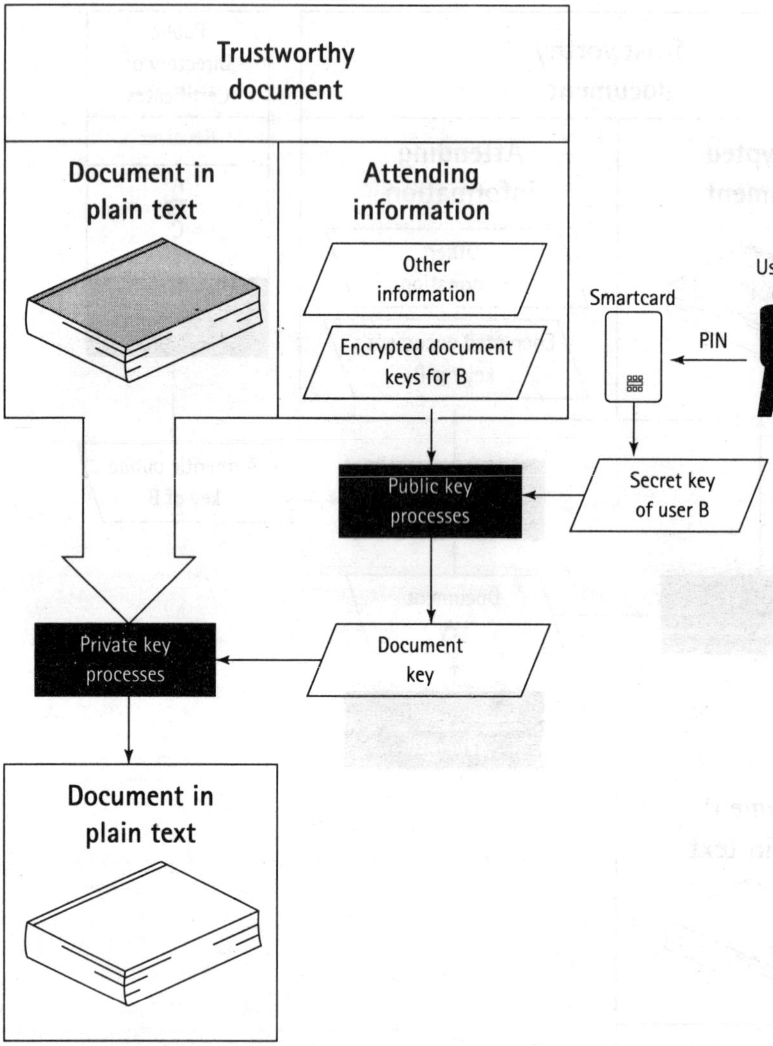

Figure 6-7: Decryption of a document

The recipient is asked to activate the smart card using his password. For the purposes of decryption, the encrypted document key for the recipient is extracted from the accompanying information and decrypted using the secret key on the recipient's smart card with the aid of the public key procedure. The document is then decrypted with the document key using the private key procedure, after which it is available in plain text.

VERIFYING SIGNATURES

If the document is available in plain text, the signature or signatures can be checked using the verification function (see Figure 6-8).

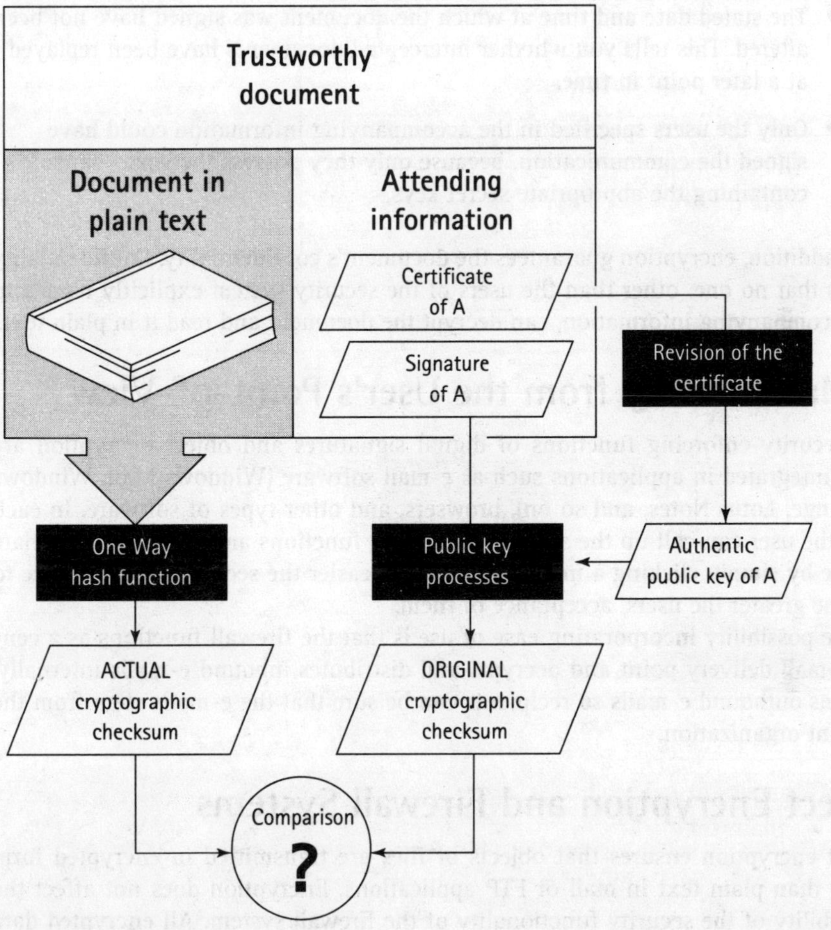

Figure 6-8: Checking of signatures

To check the signature, the one-way hash function calculates the current cryptographic checksum applicable to the document. The signatures are then taken from the accompanying information to obtain the original cryptographic checksum with the aid of the public key procedure, using the relevant user's public key. If the two cryptographic checksums are identical, the received document is intact and the user who signed it is authenticated.

E-Mail Security System Services

After the signature has been successfully verified, you can be sure that the document's integrity has been preserved, meaning the following:

- No one has tampered with the documents.

- The stated date and time at which the document was signed have not been altered. This tells you whether intercepted documents have been replayed at a later point in time.
- Only the users specified in the accompanying information could have signed the communication, because only they possess the smart cards containing the appropriate secret keys.

In addition, encryption guarantees the document's confidentiality. Confidentiality means that no one, other than the users of the security system explicitly named in the accompanying information, can decrypt the document and read it in plain text.

E-Mail Security from the User's Point-of-View

The security-enforcing functions of digital signatures and object encryption are often integrated in applications such as e-mail software (Windows Mail, Windows Exchange, Lotus Notes, and so on), browsers, and other types of software. In each case, the user can call up the security-enforcing functions and use the appropriate service by simply clicking a mouse button. The easier the security functions are to use, the greater the users' acceptance of them.

One possibility incorporating ease of use is that the firewall functions as a central e-mail delivery point and decrypts and distributes inbound e-mails internally, or signs outbound e-mails so recipients can be sure that the e-mails stem from the relevant organization.

Object Encryption and Firewall Systems

Object encryption ensures that objects or files are transmitted in encrypted form rather than plain text in mail or FTP applications. Encryption does not affect the availability of the security functionality of the firewall system. All encrypted data is logged, as is unencrypted data. However, object encryption also makes security services such as data integrity, proof of authorship, and encryption available at the user level over the firewall system.

Electronic Contracts

In addition to the traditional verbal and written contractual forms, the electronic contract is in frequent use, although the detailed supporting legal framework is not yet entirely in place.

The electronic contract presents some obvious differences when compared with traditional verbal and written contracts. Electronic contracts are easier to handle than the traditional types, and they enable the securing of information, ensuring non-reputability of the agreements. After all, you can use encryption functions to prove document integrity and authenticity much easier than you can with traditional verbal and written contracts.

SECURITY ADVANTAGES

Verbal contracts have no security mechanisms available. Written documents have only the written signature for authenticity.

The security advantages of electronic documents are obvious:

- All the information in the document can be secured using encryption.
- The algorithms that underlie encryption are the product of decades of research by experts and are mathematically mature.
- The electronic contract based on digital signatures is technically fully developed.

RISKS OF ELECTRONIC CONTRACTS

Electronic contracts contain certain inherent risks. Depending on the system environment, it may be possible to sign a counterfeit document. Another risk factor is the organizational environment, in which someone may not be aware of the electronic implications of some actions. For example, passing on a smart card with a password is equivalent to giving a general power of attorney.

Other Object-Oriented Security Concepts

Secure Multi-Purpose Internet Mail Extension (S/MIME) and *Pretty Good Privacy (PGP)* are two concepts that can be used to implement object-oriented security. Although both are based on similar cryptographic procedures, S/MIME and PGP take quite different approaches.

Both procedures are based on encryption and the signing of messages prior to transmission over an insecure network, but the key management is different. Because the rights to market PGP were taken over by Network Associates, the key management procedures in the two systems have converged somewhat, but the differences that remain are still large enough to affect purchasing decisions.

COMMON GROUND BETWEEN S/MIME AND PGP

S/MIME and PGP both rely on the use of public keys. Each user initially requires a pair of keys that he generates. One key is the user's public key, which should be published. This enables other users in the network to send encrypted messages to the key holder. The private key must be kept secret. It is used to decrypt encrypted messages and to sign messages created by the key holder.

S/MIME and PGP use the combination of different cryptographic procedures previously described. Integrity and authenticity are achieved by generating a cryptographic checksum from the text and the user signing the checksum with his own secret key. When a message is encrypted, the software generates a random number to serve as a document key valid only for that message. The message is then encrypted with a symmetric encryption algorithm using the document key. The document key itself is then encrypted with the specified receiver's public key and transmitted with the encrypted message. Only the designated receiver can reconstruct the document key with his own secret key and decrypt the message text.

When a message is sent to more than one person, an encrypted version of the document key is generated for each of the designated receivers and sent along with the message. In this way, the message itself does not have to be individually encrypted for each receiver.

To sign and decrypt a message, the user must be able to access his own secret key.

SECURE MIME – S/MIME

S/MIME is an extension of the mail standard MIME, which has virtually supplanted the old UUENCODE/UUDECODE procedure for appending attachments to mail. Within MIME, objects are defined with attributes (for example, text, graphics, audio data, and so on) that require a particular type of processing at the receiver's end (for example, the playback of an audio message). S/MIME specifies the use of various cryptographic algorithms, which the user and/or his software can select as required. The primary algorithms available are Triple-DES, RSA, and SHA-1. The old MD5 hash is still supported for compatibility reasons. It would be no problem to extend S/MIME to include other algorithms. The use of other algorithms assumes that both communications partners have the same solution.

The creation of an S/MIME message entails preparing the S/MIME objects (digital signature, encryption, coding) and embedding them as attachments in an MIME message as transformation steps. The S/MIME objects in the message can be signed, encrypted, or both signed and encrypted. S/MIME offers the possibility of sending signed messages in a clear, signed format in which the digital signature is separate from the message, and the message can also be processed by e-mail programs that do not support S/MIME (but do support MIME). The data structure used by S/MIME can also protect the identity of the transmitter, because the signature and the message can be sent together in an encrypted digital envelope.

KEY MANAGEMENT

S/MIME does not prescribe a particular trust model. Theoretically, a web-of-trust model is possible, however, a central or hierarchical trust model is usually employed. This means that you can establish your own PKI or assign public keys to individuals with the aid of trustworthy third parties. In this case, the user receives a certificate only on request (according to PKCS#12) after he has authenticated himself to a CA following a precisely defined procedure. The trustworthiness of the certificate depends on the security of the procedure used to issue the certificate. Different classes of certificates can be issued depending, for example, on whether only the e-mail address is checked or whether a more official form of identity check is required.

> **NOTE:** The Public Key Cryptography Standard (PKCS) #12 defines the personal information exchange syntax. The PKCS specifications cover various tasks related to the use of public keys and were developed by RSA Inc. to accelerate the general use of public-key cryptography. You can obtain copies of the PKCS specifications at www.rsa.com.

With respect to the use of certificates, S/MIME relies on existing standards. Both S/MIME versions support the X.509 format in versions 1 and 3, which are widely used on the Internet. The validity of the certificates issued by the CA can be checked using CA root certificates, which must be verified once.

S/MIME offers the option of creating a digital fingerprint of the official key so that the CA can publish the fingerprint to allow for verification of the CA's certificates. Because S/MIME is not tied to a particular trust model, the user has more options in choosing the model best suited to his purposes. Security-conscious organizations will choose a central trust model, enabling them to check the organization of the certification themselves.

A hierarchical trust model retains the function of a central trust model while allowing better verification of certificates than that afforded by the company's own CA. A hierarchical model is particularly suited to users who prefer a less rigid model and want to generate signatures that comply with digital signature statutes.

If a relatively low level of certificate trustworthiness is acceptable, a Web-of-trust allows you to avoid involving third parties. Exchanging public keys is easy because the certificate is present in every signed e-mail. If a known CA issues the certificate, it can be checked, and the sender's public key can be stored.

Some S/MIME products also offer the possibility of interrogating certificates using LDAP via public keys.

PRETTY GOOD PRIVACY

In 1991, Phil Zimmermann developed the Pretty Good Privacy (PGP) encryption software in the U.S. Due to American export restrictions, several international versions of PGP use different cryptographic routines than the original version. However, the keys and messages used with the various versions are compatible.

PGP is based on the symmetric Triple-DES, IDEA, and Cast procedures, whereby the symmetric keys are exchanged using either the Diffie-Hellman or the RSA algorithm. SHA-1 and MD5 are used to calculate the hash value.

Like S/MIME, PGP generates a header during the processing of plain text. However, this header, rather than being appended to the end of the text, is copied to the beginning. In the classic PGP, the header is a block and there are no individual sections like with S/MIME. The message and the header are enclosed in boundary lines that are different according to the message type.

A PGP user is identified with freely selectable user identification. The public key, which has to exist prior to verification, is associated through its cryptographic checksum and a unique key identification, serving as a "fingerprint."

KEY MANAGEMENT

PGP is also based on the principle of public key certificates, which in this case are formed from the user identification and the corresponding public key. Certificates are stored in encrypted files known as *key rings* that can be distributed to other users as required. In PGP, the secret key is generally linked with a computer or an e-mail address.

The certification process is not specified within PGP. To check a user's public key, compare it with the fingerprint of the corresponding user that you received by an alternate route (telephone, business card, and so on). Moreover, certain trustworthy individuals (known as *introducers*) accept certificates for the public keys of other users.

On the Internet, public key servers distribute the public keys. Every user can store their own public key here and retrieve the public keys of others using simple commands by e-mail. Individual servers synchronize their local databases with each other at regular intervals.

The public key servers only perform a storage function; they do not check the stored keys. Each user following receipt of a certificate must ascertain the correctness of the certificates. A certificate should only be entered in one's own public key ring if its authenticity is guaranteed.

Both S/MIME and PGP can generate signed and encrypted messages in ASCII format that can then be incorporated in a normal e-mail.

NEW TRENDS IN PGP

Having taken over the commercial rights to market PGP, Network Associates has introduced a number of innovations to make PGP attractive for use in the company networks and other organizations. Network Associates has continued to release a free version as well as a commercial version of PGP. The information provided about PGP applies to the freeware version. The most important innovations to the full version are as follows:

- **PGP compatibility with the certification mechanism of X.509.** PGP clients can accept both classes of certificate, making it possible to establish a hierarchical structure of certificates analogous to S/MIME.
- **Extended capabilities of public key servers.** Public key servers can now also form hierarchies of certificates, which are actually more flexible than X.509. In this way, certificates produced by more than one CA can be verified. The client can choose to accept these signatures when the weighted sum of the certificates exceeds a threshold value. A departmental manager certifies the public keys of his staff, and the divisional manager similarly vouches for the public keys of his departmental managers, and so on. As in conventional correspondence, it is possible, for example, to only accept a document that is signed by the authorized signatory and the responsible section manager.

PGP provides mechanisms for key recovery, enabling secret keys within an organization to be recovered. Organization management can create a mechanism that is embedded in all keys so that secret keys can be decrypted by management as well as the individuals. Keys that have been lost or belong to dismissed staff can be retrieved from company records stored in a safe place so that the associated documents can be decrypted.

The new MIME objects defined in RFC2015 allow PGP to be incorporated into standard MIME e-mail correspondence in a fashion analogous to S/MIME.

FINAL COMPARISON BETWEEN S/MIME AND PGP

The S/MIME and PGP solutions both define security mechanisms that enable any document to be encrypted and signed. The cryptographic algorithms of both methods are equally strong. The messages generated can be edited, incorporated into e-mails, and sent, independent of the underlying transport protocol.

S/MIME and PGP exhibit some fundamental differences in key management procedures. In S/MIME and the commercial version of PGP, CAs sign keys. The hierarchy of CAs enables simple and reliable checking of third-party public keys. Without the infrastructure of the certification authorities, it is not possible to use the procedures sensibly.

Freeware versions of PGP are independent of hierarchies, because the user decides what keys he trusts. He can communicate immediately with other users if he knows their public keys and has established their authenticity.

ASSESSMENT OF S/MIME AND PGP

On the Internet, the S/MIME and PGP applications are not rival products. Each has its own application area.

For small user groups looking for secure communication channels, the freeware versions of PGP offer the possibility of object-oriented encryption. No infrastructure is required – only the mutual trust of the users, without any superior certification authority.

In corporate networks or other large organizations, the commercial version of PGP, with its flexible options, offers the possibility of mapping the organizational structure with its diversity of interpersonal relations to the structure of certification. The possibility of accessing e-mails and other files encrypted by staff, in accordance with the "corporate data belongs to the company" philosophy, is another attraction of the commercial version of PGP.

In a large, complex network with many unknown users, the use of a strongly structured certification system, such as that offered by S/MIME or PGP with X.509, is recommended. After the certification infrastructure is built and established, both products may be viewed as effective tools for the secure transmission of objects over an insecure network such as the Internet. A worldwide functioning infrastructure remains to be established. When you consider the rate at which the number of Internet users is increasing, and the fact that Microsoft (Outlook, Exchange) supports the S/MIME standard, it appears that S/MIME is the solution with the best prospects.

Success Is Determined by the Market

Unfortunately, standardization activities often take too long for the rapidly changing IT market. Experience has shown that applications that function in practice and are affordable are accepted by the market and become established as de facto standards. Microsoft, with its operating systems DOS and Windows, and its Office software package, is a case in point.

Virtual Private Networks

The basic idea behind virtual private networks (VPNs) is to use the advantages of an open communications infrastructure – the shared infrastructure of the Internet, for example, which is both inexpensive and available worldwide – and at the same time counter all threats to information security.

A VPN should ensure that the confidentiality of sensitive data is maintained during transmission over networks (LANs and WANs), so that only those individuals who are authorized to see the sensitive data can access it. To achieve these goals, cryptographic procedures and other security components are employed. The procedure described in this chapter can be handled by an organization's IT department and can provide the means by which different areas of responsibility communicate with each other in ciphertext over a common, public security infrastructure.

Security System as a Transparent Solution

With a security sublayer in the communications stack, it is possible to turn an insecure network service into a secure network service. An appropriate security sublayer is introduced into the communications architecture in the computer system. One way to implement such a security sublayer – particularly well suited in a heterogeneous IT environment – is, for example, to use IPSec in black box security systems.

Black Box Solution

Black box solutions are portable devices that are easy to position between computer systems and networks (LANs, WANs). This makes them independent of the terminal devices and operating systems involved and, due to their simple operation, user-friendly. In the sophisticated and intelligent high-tech black box, all the security-relevant operations take place, invisible to the user and without the user's active involvement.

In this section, black boxes are referred to as *VPN boxes*. VPN boxes are effectively packet filters with encryption.

All black boxes in a security system should be centrally administered via encrypted network communications.

A black box that behaves like a bridge is placed in front of each computer system or subsystem to be protected or through which confidential data will be transmitted. The interfaces are typically (fast) Ethernet on both sides of the black box. The security black boxes perform extended security services for the protected computer system (see Figure 6-9).

Working together with an equivalent security device at the other end of the network connection, the black boxes also provide cryptographic protection for communications over the LAN/WAN.

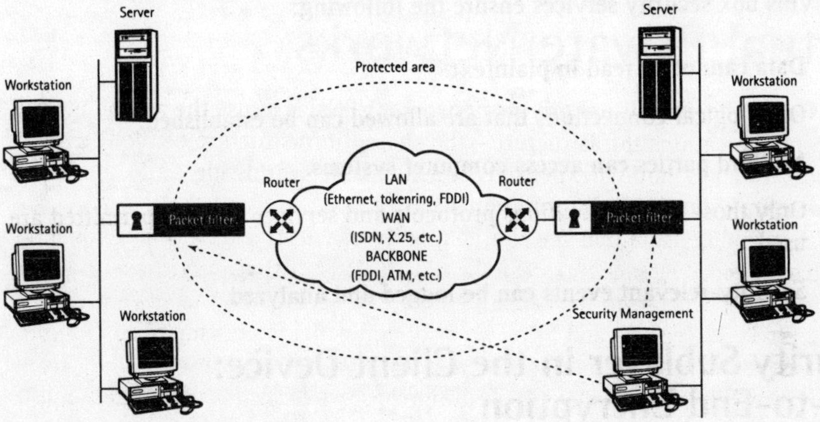

Figure 6-9: Black box solution

ADVANTAGES OF BLACK BOX SOLUTIONS

The black box security device is independent of workstations (PCs, UNIX systems, host computers, and so on) and their operating systems (DOS, WINDOWS 95/98/NT/2000, Solaris, LINUX, and so on). The black box can continue to be used even when terminal devices or workstations are replaced.

The black box solution allows security functions to be installed between end systems for which no security functions could otherwise be integrated (for example, terminals or routers).

The same black box can always be used, even with heterogeneous systems (different hardware, software, and operating system), thereby reducing the associated costs.

Black boxes are easier to implement *securely* than special software solutions in computer systems.

The quality of the security provided by the security devices is not affected by other system components. Security is application-independent.

VPN BOX SECURITY SERVICES

A VPN box can provide a variety of security services, including the following:

- Confidentiality
- Authentication (implicit, using encryption, or explicit)
- Access control (for packets or users)
- Access rights administration of communications protocols and services
- Preservation of evidence
- Log analysis

The VPN box security services ensure the following:

- Data cannot be read in plaintext.
- Only logical connections that are allowed can be established.
- No third parties can access computer systems.
- Only those communications protocols and services that are permitted are used.
- Security-relevant events can be logged and analyzed.

Security Sublayer in the Client Device: End-to-End Encryption

Another way to install the necessary security functions is to integrate a security sublayer into the computer systems. A security sublayer, for example, can be set up on the network service provided by the network device drivers. This security sublayer offers the Transport layer all the services of the network device driver, except that a connection is only provided with the desired security features on demand. From the point of view of the network device driver (Network layer), the security sublayer behaves like a Transport layer; however, from the Transport layer's point of view, it behaves like the network device driver. In this way, the security sublayer is completely transparent to the adjacent layers. The security sublayer thus becomes a security client for the client system.

In practice, the security sublayer software is installed on the computer system as a transparent network device driver. In order to increase security, this solution should be supported by an encryption card on which the secret keys are stored.

Advantages of the security sublayer in the client are as follows:

- Security in the client is cheaper than the black box solution.
- The security client offers end-to-end security. Not only is the connection between different LAN segments isolated from the outside, but also each individual workstation (PC) is isolated from the others.

PC SECURITY COMPONENTS' SECURITY SERVICES

A security client offers various security services, such as the following:

- Confidentiality
- Authentication (implicit, using encryption, or explicit)
- Access control (for packets)

The security client security services ensure the following:

- Data cannot be read in plaintext.
- Only allowed logical connections can be established.
- No third parties can access any computer system.

POSSIBLE APPLICATIONS AND OPERATIONAL VARIANTS

With a VPN box and a security client, security service encryption can be integrated into various application areas. Selected segments, logical areas, or applications can be protected in LANs. Linking LAN segments over public networks with a VPN box means that attackers can be warded off and cryptographically protected logical networks can be formed.

Security in LAN Segments

Security in LAN segments protects selected segments, logical areas in one segment, and selected computer systems or applications within a segment of the LAN, such as a human resources department.

The VPN boxes contain access lists and other security-relevant information. They also provide a logbook to record security-relevant events. In this application example, the communications relationships are determined by the Network Access layer addresses (MAC addresses), and the Type field determines higher protocols.

Depending on the settings, the Network Access layer data can be assigned the following permissions:

- Allowed through in plaintext
- Allowed through in encrypted form
- Blocked

Figure 6-10 shows how communications from Workstation 3 and Workstation 4 to Server 2 can be encrypted and controlled. In the LAN segment, no one can read the transmitted data in plaintext. If Workstation 4 wants to communicate with Server 2, the MAC packet is sent from Workstation 4 to the VPN box. In the VPN box, the access list is referenced to check whether a connection is permitted between Workstation 4 and Server 2 (packet filter).

In this example, encrypted communications are permitted. The contents of the MAC packet are encrypted in the VPN box and transmitted. The VPN box in front of the protected Server 2 reads the MAC packet, determines in its access list that encrypted communications are permitted between Workstation 4 and Server 2, and decrypts the MAC packet accordingly. The VPN box then sends the MAC packet in plaintext to Server 2. For Workstation 4 and Server 2, the security functions are transparent. Control of the VPN box is implemented in a protected form through a central Security Management facility.

If Workstation 4 wants to communicate with Server 1, it transmits a MAC packet to the LAN segment, which is accepted in Workstation 4's VPN box. Here, it is established by referring to the access list that the connection is a permitted plaintext connection. The packet can pass through the VPN box in plaintext and will reach Server 1 over the LAN.

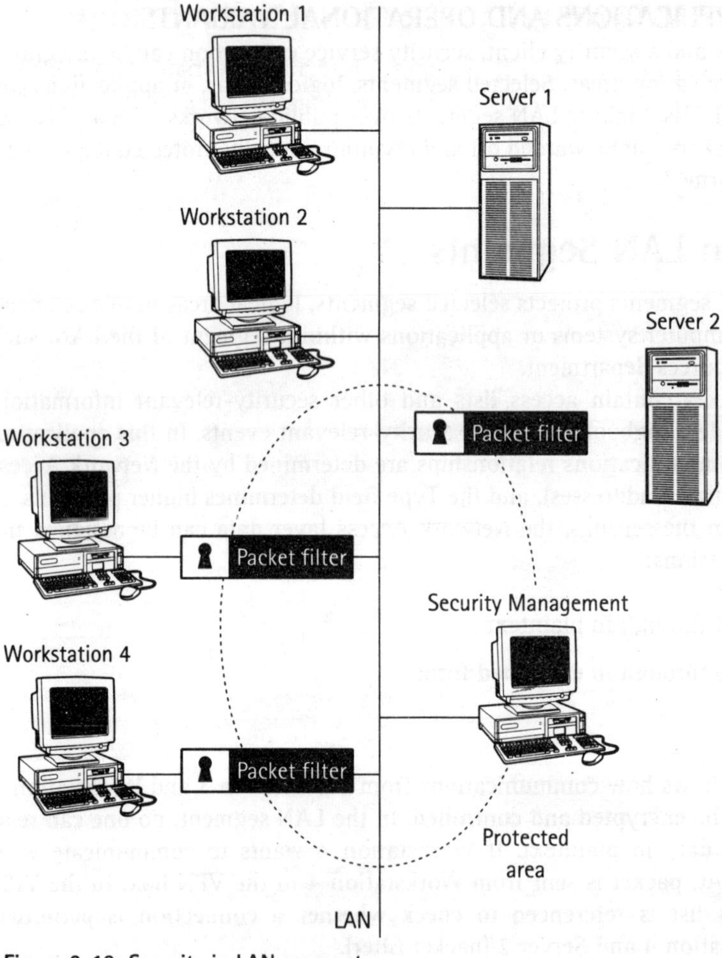

Figure 6-10: Security in LAN segments

If Workstation 2 wants to access Server 2, it sends the MAC packet in plaintext. Server 2's VPN box accepts the packet but establishes that such a connection is not permitted. The packet filter rejects the packet. This security-relevant event is either recorded in the logbook or, if the appropriate configuration settings have been made, Security Management is notified by a "spontaneous message."

Features of MAC encryption include the following:

- MAC encryption is independent of network protocols such as IPX, NLSP, LLC, Netbios, Decnet, SNA, and so on.

- Encryption is independent of the network operating system used.
- The network operating system passwords (for example, NT, 2000, XP, and Netware) are transmitted in encrypted form.

Linking LAN Segments with a Security Bridge

Under the "linking of several LAN segments" integration variant, two LAN segments (twisted pair, fiber optic, and so on) linked together over a publicly accessible area are connected. The cables in the vulnerable building complex B are protected with the VPN box. This is a simple way to guarantee the necessary security (see Figure 6-11).

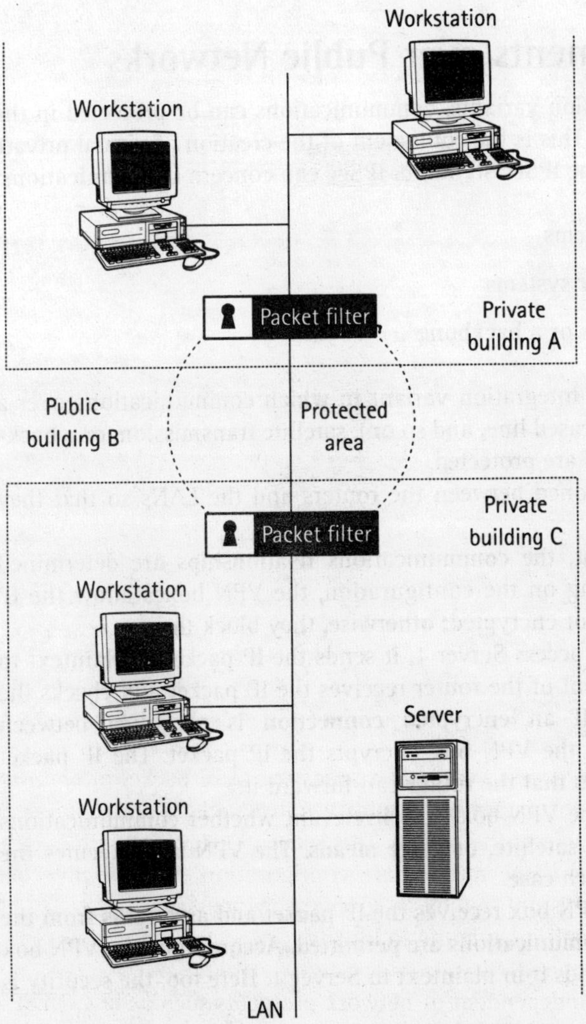

Figure 6-11: Security bridge for several LAN segments

For example, several LAN segments may be linked in the case of an office building and a production facility. The administrative system (server) is located in the offices (building complex C). Stock levels, product serial numbers, shipping manifests, and so on are located in the production facility (building complex A). The workstations in the production facility in building complex A must have access to the administrative system (server) in building complex C.

In this example, the use of VPN boxes is a simple way to ensure the necessary security. In addition to bridging, the VPN boxes guarantee that the data remains confidential through encryption of the MAC packets, and prevent any third parties from accessing the system. Encryption has the effect of imposing authentication, because third parties can't send meaningful packets into the LAN.

In this integration variant, a VPN box can also be operated as a security repeater. All the packets in the VPN box are encrypted and decrypted as MAC packets.

Linking LAN Segments over Public Networks

With the next set of integration variants, communications can be protected in the Network layer (the IP layer). This is the equivalent of the creation of virtual private networks (VPNs) following the IPSec standard. IPSec can concern communications:

- On all computer systems
- On selected computer systems
- Over public networks or a backbone

Figure 6-12 illustrates an integration variant in which communications over a public network (ISDN, DSL, leased line, and so on), satellite transmission, or a backbone (FDDI, ATM, and so on) are protected.

The VPN boxes are positioned between the routers and the LANs so that they protect the networks.

In this integration variant, the communications relationships are determined using IP addresses. Depending on the configuration, the VPN boxes allow the IP packets through in plaintext or encrypted; otherwise, they block them.

If Workstation 1 wants to access Server 1, it sends the IP packet in plaintext to the LAN. The VPN box in front of the router receives the IP packet and checks the rules in the access lists. If an encrypted connection is permitted between Workstation 1 and Server 1, the VPN box encrypts the IP packet. The IP packet header remains in plaintext so that the router can forward it.

From the perspective of the VPN box, it is irrelevant whether communications are accomplished over ISDN, satellite, or other means. The VPN box executes the same security functions in each case.

At the opposite end, the VPN box receives the IP packet and ascertains from the access list that encrypted communications are permitted. Accordingly, the VPN box decrypts the IP packet and sends it in plaintext to Server 1. Here too, the security is transparent to the components involved (workstation, server, router, and so on). A Security Management module effects access rights administration centrally. In such a configuration, you can design the access rights administration in a very simple way – for example, by defining the simple rule "Encrypt all packets that belong to the corresponding LANs" via the subnet addresses of the LANs.

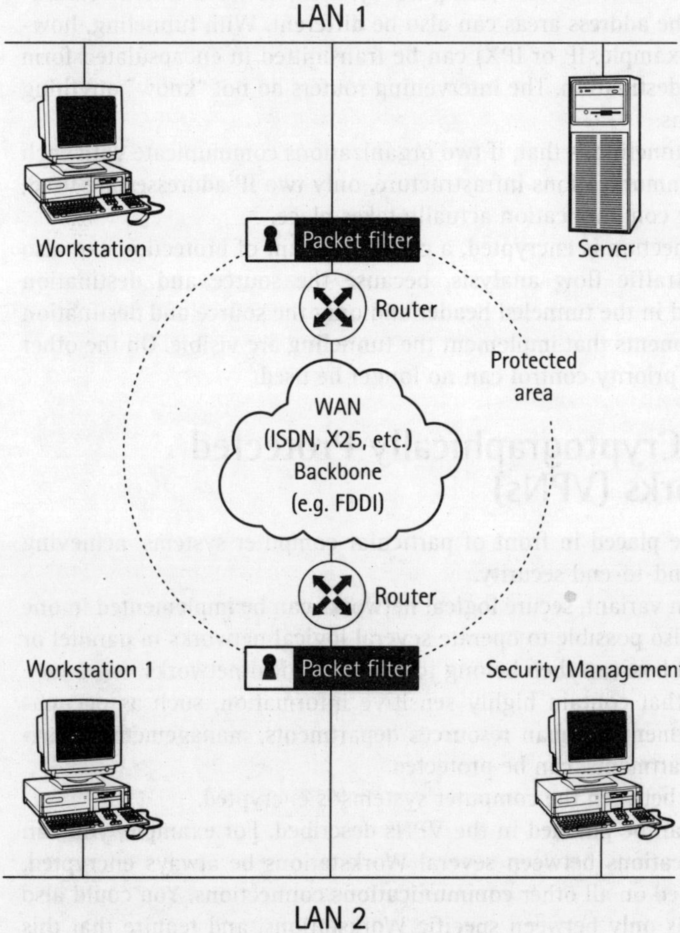

Figure 6-12: Linking LAN segments over networks

One particular advantage of this solution is that it also satisfies the security requirements for backup and flexible bandwidths. Because security is independent of the transmission medium, an equally high degree of security can always be guaranteed, even if a leased line is used for communications in normal operations, with the ISDN network as ~ backup.

TUNNELING

In a process known as tunneling, each packet to be sent is encapsulated in a new packet by adding an additional header. For IP-based networks, for example, an IP header is pre-inserted. Additional information or identifiers are added to the body portion of the packet.

The extra headers specify the endpoints of the tunnel, and the encapsulated headers specify the actual IP addresses (computer systems) between which communication takes place. The address areas can also be different. With tunneling, however, any packet (for example, IP or IPX) can be transmitted in encapsulated form and unwrapped at the destination. The intervening routers do not "know" anything about these mechanisms.

One advantage of tunneling is that, if two organizations communicate with each other over a public communications infrastructure, only two IP addresses are used, irrespective of how the communication actually takes place.

If the tunneled connection is encrypted, a certain amount of protection can also be achieved against traffic flow analysis, because the source and destination addresses are encrypted in the tunneled header and only the source and destination addresses of the components that implement the tunneling are visible. On the other hand, features such as priority control can no longer be used.

Formation of Cryptographically Protected Logical Networks (VPNs)

VPN boxes can also be placed in front of particular computer systems, achieving more "depth" for the end-to-end security.

With this integration variant, secure logical networks can be implemented in one overall network. It is also possible to operate several logical networks in parallel or that are nested. A VPN box can then belong to several logical networks.

In this way, areas that contain highly sensitive information, such as occupational medicine departments, human resources departments, management departments, or research departments, can be protected.

All data exchanged between the computer systems is encrypted.

Various strategies can be pursued in the VPNs described. For example, you can specify that communications between several Workstations be always encrypted, but that plaintext is used on all other communications connections. You could also permit communications only between specific Workstations, and require that this communication be encrypted.

IP encryption is independent of transmission medium and offers a high-investment protection. Data confidentiality is guaranteed in all data and protocols. The encryption at the IP layer keeps all higher layer protocols, such as Telnet, FTP, or rlogin, confidential.

Potential attackers from public networks are prevented from accessing any computer systems. Such a security system can also establish security domains.

NOTE

Because VPN technology works at such a low level of the Network layer, using VPN bridges provides a means of wrapping security around unprotected systems and a means of directly enhancing that security. This is especially useful for legacy systems that may not provide their own encrypted security. By isolating a legacy system behind a VPN, for instance, you can add both enhanced authentication and data transmission confidentiality to the legacy system by requiring users to use the VPN for system access.

Security Client

A security client could be a combination of software and hardware solutions integrated in a computer system. A security sublayer is involved, which provides extended communication security services such as encryption and access control. The use of secure hardware ensures that secret keys are stored securely. With a security client, encryption can be implemented not just between PCs, but also between a PC and a VPN box.

When a workstation communicates with a server without a security client, a packet filter using the required protocols and services can control the communication. Both the security client and VPN boxes can be controlled and administered through Security Management.

Applications

More and more often, computer systems must be remotely connected to an organization's local network. Field personnel must be able to enter orders and access price lists and delivery times directly so that business processes can be carried out effectively and without any need to switch media. Developments in social policy and shortages of skilled staff are making it necessary to offer staff the opportunity to work remotely from home. However, the potential for an attack is particularly high for remote computers and remote access links carry a high risk of abuse.

LINKING MOBILE COMPUTER SYSTEMS (NOTEBOOKS)

Notebooks can be linked to the company network with a modem over the telephone line or with a mobile telephone over the mobile communication network (GSM network). The combination of a security client and a VPN box provides a high level of security.

In Figure 6-13, the IP packets are transmitted from the notebook in encrypted form over the telephone network or the mobile communications network and appropriately decrypted by the VPN box.

The VPN box can determine which user is allowed to access which computer system in order to deliver reports, for example, or to collect new assignments.

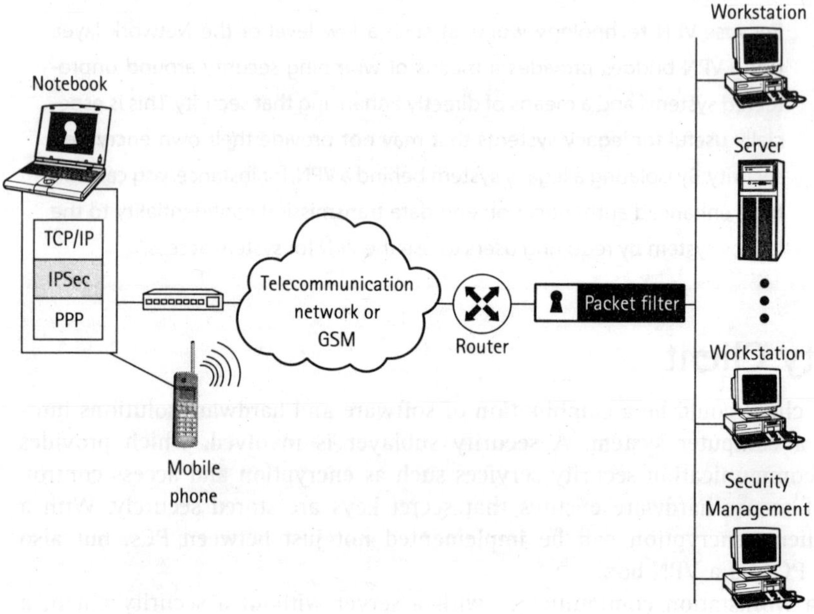

Figure 6-13: Linking mobile computer systems

LINKING TELECOMMUTER WORKSTATIONS

When configuring telecommuter workstations, a faster connection is preferred. Today's options include ISDN, DSL, broadband, and even satellite connectivity.

IP packets are transmitted encrypted and tamper protected due to the digital signature over the network and decrypted at headquarters using the VPN box, as shown in Figure 6-14. The VPN box achieves effective partitioning so that no hacker can access the protected computer systems.

In this way, telecommuter workstations can be protected not only through encryption but also through monitoring and controlled using packet filter functionality.

With the aid of the packet filters on the network side, you can exercise control over which server systems may be accessed by the telecommuter workstations and which protocols may be used. Precise times at which access is permitted can also be specified.

VPN IMPLEMENTATIONS

VPN solutions can be implemented in a number of ways. Some vendors have implemented special security protocols that work with a speed-optimized approach. The advantages of a speed-optimized approach are as follows:

- Absolute transparency
- Extremely low delay times in all phases of communication
- No overhead during communication

- No need for any response on the part of the components that are integrated in the individual networks

This approach is particularly important for real-time-oriented and terminal applications.

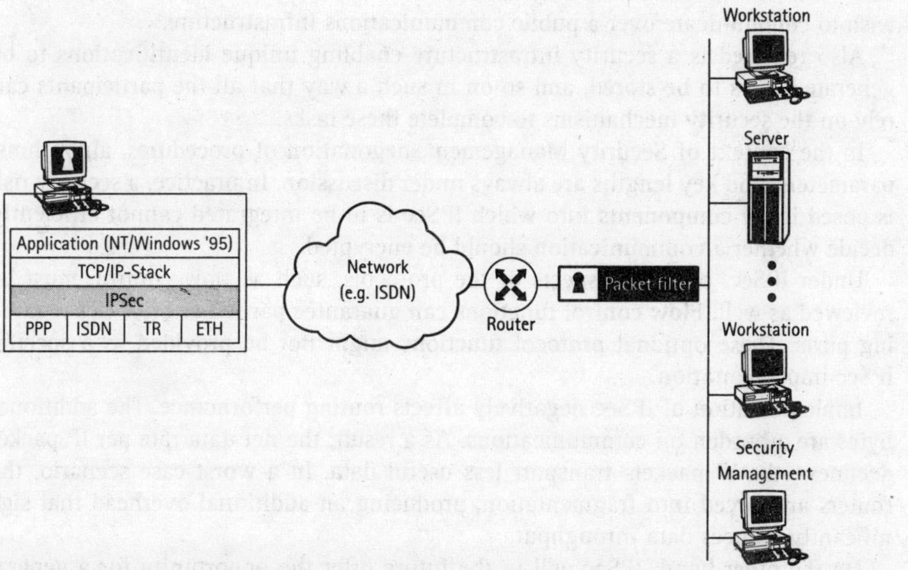

Figure 6-14: Linking telecommuter workstations

IPSEC

The Internet Engineering Task Force (IETF) has defined an Internet security standard known as IPSec. This standard was developed in connection with IP Version 6. However, its security features were soon incorporated into IP Version 4, which is still the market leader.

XREF

Detailed information on the IPSec protocol is found in Appendix A.

IPSec defines mechanisms for building secure VPNs, essentially offering two mechanisms:

- The *authentication header*

- The *encapsulated security payload*

Both mechanisms can be used with or without tunneling. VPNs are generally implemented in the variant with tunneling.

Under IPSec, *ISAKMP-Oakley* is specified as the necessary key management mechanism, but it is also possible to use other procedures, such as SKIP. ISAKMP-Oakley and SKIP are secure key exchange protocols.

Especially important with key management is a common public key infrastructure – that is, a common security infrastructure that can be trusted by users who wish to communicate over a public communications infrastructure.

Also required is a security infrastructure enabling unique identifications to be generated, keys to be stored, and so on in such a way that all the participants can rely on the security mechanisms to complete these tasks.

In the context of Security Management, negotiation of procedures, algorithms, parameters, and key lengths are always under discussion. In practice, a security risk is posed if the components into which IPSec is to be integrated cannot efficiently decide whether a communication should be encrypted.

Under IPSec, optional aspects of the protocols, such as flow control, must be reviewed as well. Flow control functions can guarantee particular priorities regarding ports. These optional protocol functions might not be provided in a specific IPSec implementation.

Implementation of IPSec negatively affects routing performance. The additional bytes are a burden on communications. As a result, the net data rate per IP packet declines – the IP packets transport less useful data. In a worst-case scenario, the routers are forced into fragmentation, producing an additional overhead that significantly reduces data throughput.

On the other hand, IPSec will in the future offer the opportunity for a general security standard, assuming that the corresponding trusted security infrastructures have been created and established.

Two important tasks that a common, secure infrastructure would have to implement are determination of identity and the generation of binding certificates.

A more practical problem that needs to be solved is the compatibility of different IPSec implementations. IPSec is not a rigid ruleset; rather, it offers a wealth of options and variants for communication. IPSec devices produced by the same vendor experience the least number of problems. The combination of two IPSec firewalls produced by different vendors can be a gamble; so thorough testing is needed in advance.

SSH

While not designed primarily as a VPN protocol, the SSH protocol is gaining rapid, widespread acceptance, partly due to its ability to tunnel other application protocols through its own secure connections. When evaluating VPN solutions, consider protocols such as SSH for specific situational solutions. Because SSH was not designed specifically as a VPN solution, SSH is not as convenient for users as most VPNs. In a typical VPN you connect using a small VPN client. With SSH, you have to log in to the SSH server using an interactive session. SSH makes up for small inconveniences like the interactive login by providing more flexibility than most

VPNs. For example, once connected, you can configure SSH to proxy ports and addresses on systems other than the SSH server. This proxy ability allows SSH to be used through firewalls that a typical VPN protocol, such as IPSec, would not work through. SSH does not suffer from compatibility issues from working behind firewalls like most VPN protocols do. This means that a computer station can use SSH from behind a firewall to connect out and establish a secure tunnel to a remote system or network. A full VPN implementation would require a network-to-network-level VPN implementation because of the firewall. The full network-to-network VPN implementation would not be cost-effective if the situation only required a few users to have the necessary connectivity.

Transparent Encryption and Firewall Systems

With transparent encryption, data is transmitted over the communications networks in encrypted form instead of in plaintext.

Decryption must take place before the firewall system so the corresponding firewall element can analyze the communications data above the Network Access and Network layers.

Encryption systems such as IPSec are not integrated simply to promote data confidentiality, but also as a means of positively eliminating design flaws in firewall systems. Design flaws in firewalls can stem from a variety of problems. Typical flaws include bugs in the firewall software itself, improperly configured firewall rules, out-of-date application gateway functionality, or even poor firewall placement in relation to the systems and services being protected. These flaws may include such dangers as the man-in-the-middle attack or the deliberate manipulation of data packets. Firewall systems and encryption are important forms of security; used together, they can achieve a high level of overall security for communications over the Internet.

Comparison of E-Mail Security and VPN Security

VPN solutions are integrated into the communications system in the form of black boxes or security sublayers, together with an intelligent Security Management capability. VPNs should always be considered when the communication to be protected takes place within a single area of responsibility, as is the case with intranet applications and the associated connected organizational units. This area of responsibility is governed by a single security policy that is enforced independent of other requirements. This guarantees the maximum amount of security, especially through the establishment of effective barriers that block other systems.

In the case of e-mail security, allowance is made for special security requirements during communication between partners in different areas of responsibility. In other words, with e-mail security, the two entities communicating will most likely be different organizations subject to different security policies. The common security infrastructure is provided through certification authorities that provide public certificates and through smart card personalization. Personal e-mail communications with banks, tax advisers, doctors, and so on are an example of a communication that needs security but is subject to individual security requirements. Partitioning – that is, operating a controlled interface between an insecure network and a protected network – plays no role in this case and must be implemented through other security components (with firewall systems).

Summary

This chapter explores the use of encryption to satisfy security needs. Encryption can be used to authenticate the source of communication (and also provide non-repudiation). Encryption provides an excellent means of achieving data confidentiality. Finally, the same encryption functions used to provide authentication can ensure data integrity.

Encryption is most widely used to provide VPNs (protected network communications) and e-mail security (protected document communications). Both VPNs and e-mail security use encryption a little differently but provide a vital tool for protecting communications.

Chapter 7

Authentication Procedures

THIS CHAPTER PROVIDES examples of authentication procedures that can be used to check the authenticity of users who want to communicate through a firewall system.

Identification and Authentication

How does a firewall system know that user A, who wants to establish a communications relationship, is in fact user A?

When a user wants to establish a communications link through a firewall system, he must identify and authenticate himself to the firewall system.

An *identification* is the credentials used to demonstrate a user is who he says he is. The most common identification used with computers is the user name and password. Identification must be unique for each user. In large organizations, providing unique identifications requires some planning. Common user name schemes, such as first name and last initial, are bound to be duplicated in a sizable company.

The directory names contained in the International Telegraph Union (ITU) – formerly the International Telephone and Telegraph Consultative Committee (CCITT) – recommendation X.509 and ISO 9594-8 (CCITT, 1997) exemplify the concept of unique, identifying names, or *distinguishing identifiers.*

Authentication refers to a process that checks a person or object for authenticity or authorization. Verifying that the password supplied by a user is correct for the given user name is an example of authentication.

The following parameters can and must be identified and authenticated within a firewall system in order for the firewall system to determine whether to allow traffic to occur.

- **Communications partners** – for example, users, processes, entities
- **Communications media** – for example, workstations, server systems, firewall elements (packet filter, application gateway, proxy, Security Management), and security tokens
- **Messages** – for example, e-mail, files, and Java applets
- **Authorizations** – for example, rights of users (hours/day of week, services, commands, computer systems) and responsibilities (roles within Security Management)

In certain applications, such as electronic money, authenticating users (individuals) is not actually desirable (Chaum, 1987). The term "identification" should be understood as the more general term. In other words, an identification doesn't have to relate to a specific user identity. Bear in mind that even an unnamed person or an alias must still be identified and authenticated. In systems that allow anonymity, you still don't want users to be able to use someone else's account. Identification allows each user to maintain sole access to his account without requiring them to provide information that allows you to know private information such as their name.

General Authentication Procedures

Several different methods of authenticating users to firewall systems are possible.

Password Method

The simplest authentication method is the *password method,* in which the user and the firewall system agree upon a unique password (string). The user proves his identity by transmitting his password to the firewall system during the authentication process – in other words, the user possesses the password and submits it to the firewall system. If the password is wrong, the user is rejected. The strength of this authentication procedure ultimately depends on the secrecy and quality of the password.

If the password is transmitted over the network (for example, the Internet) in plain text during the authentication phase, it can be read by attackers and used for their own malicious purposes. The password method should never be used over networks such as the Internet, except when the communication over the network is encrypted. Only dynamic encryption between user and firewall system can prevent the reading and replay of passwords.

Even if the communication is encrypted, the *quality* of the chosen password critically affects its security. An outsider can easily guess a password that contains all letters, such as the name of the user's wife or girlfriend.

The following list of password rules should be considered a "best practices" for password use:

- Never write down a password.
- Never disclose a password to another person.
- Make the password at least six characters long.
- Never use only first and last names in the password.

- Always include a combination of letters and numbers or special characters.
- Avoid trivial passwords, such as 12345, QWERT, or other combinations of adjacent keyboard keys.
- Change passwords at reasonable intervals, but not too often.
- Don't reuse passwords. (Users should be automatically prevented from reusing an old password out of convenience.)
- Apply the *two-person* rule to important functions or sensitive data. That means two people must each enter a separate password, or they must each enter half of a password.
- The system administrator's password, which is known only to him, should be kept securely somewhere, in case it is necessary for a substitute to take his place. System administrators commonly place their password in a locked safe. In the event access is needed and the administrator is unavailable, the password can be retrieved from the safe by appropriate management and used to gain access.

Attacks on passwords are often automated. For example, an attacker may use a program that cracks passwords by trying every term in the dictionary. With the proper program, however, you can test new passwords at the time they are created to prevent the occurrence of this type of attack.

One-Time Passwords

As its name suggests, a *one-time password* may only be used once. Various methods are available for assigning one-time passwords. Either the firewall system itself determines the one-time password and makes it confidentially available to the user, or both the user and firewall system work out the one-time password following a defined procedure during the authentication process.

If the firewall system determines the one-time password, it is possible to limit the number of login attempts by making only a limited number of one-time passwords available. When the user runs out of one-time passwords, he has to apply for new ones.

One-time passwords overcome the disadvantages of the password procedure. In practice, however, the resources required to support this approach (computational effort plus distribution of the one-time passwords) are high and only acceptable for a few applications.

One-time passwords can be implemented in several ways (using the S/Key system, for example, which is described later in this chapter).

Challenge-Response Procedures

In the *challenge-response procedure*, a user must identify himself cryptographically to the firewall system. The user possesses a secret key with which he must carry out a cryptographic operation to prove that he possesses it. Usually, the firewall system sends the user a random number, the *challenge*, which is then spontaneously cryptographically processed. The result is sent to the firewall system as the *response*. The firewall system checks the response to determine whether the user has performed the cryptographic operation correctly. If he has, the authentication has worked. Otherwise, the authenticity of the user remains unproven and communications are not allowed through the firewall system.

In the challenge-response procedure, neither the challenge, nor response, nor a combination of the two can be used a second time.

For authentication over insecure networks, challenge-response procedures must be used to prevent eavesdropping and improper use of the data used for authentication.

Biometric Authentication

Although still not common, biometric authentication mechanisms continue to make ground as a solution to the authentication challenge. Biometric authentication uses some attribute of an individual for identification. Fingerprint identification is the most prevalent type, but retina, voiceprint, and even facial feature recognition technologies have also been developed.

The primary advantage of biometric authentication lies in its reliance on attributes that can't be lost or forgotten (or easily stolen). The main disadvantage of biometric authentication is cost. Fortunately, this barrier is dropping quickly. Fingerprint scanners are now available for less than 100 dollars per system. Compared to the password method, this technique may still seem to pose a significant cost; however, the cost differential starts to look much more attractive when you consider the significant administrative overhead incurred with the use of passwords.

Extensible Authentication

Given the relatively rapid advances in authentication technology in the last few years, most modern operating systems are adding support for modular and extensible authentication mechanisms. Both Windows NT and Linux, two popular business operating systems, support authentication extensions.

Linux uses a system known as Pluggable Authentication Modules (PAM) for supporting authentication schemes as desired. Microsoft Windows NT supports the addition and substitution of authentication mechanisms through a published API and registry support. Both PAM and Microsoft's extensible authentication architectures allow organizations to tailor their authentication methods to their specific needs. For example, an organization can easily use a combination of biometric and password authentication if desired. Alternatively, a firm may want to eliminate regular passwords and use one-time passwords exclusively. Again, this setup can be achieved using the extensible authentication architectures, even down to the individual system level if necessary.

Authentication Procedure for Firewall Systems

This section presents examples of authentication procedures that work with cryptographic algorithms and can be used in firewall systems.

The firewall system can only carry out authentication if the cryptographic procedure is the same for users seeking access and for the firewall system. Moreover, the users must have unique names (*distinguishing identifiers*) so they can be accurately identified.

S/Key

The one-time password procedure *S/Key*, developed by Bell Communications Research (Bellcore), is based on the one-way hash functions *MD4* and *MD5*. Both server and client implementations are available for almost all operating systems and architectures. In the case of client implementations, the user carries a small physical device called an S/Key calculator. When the user enters the challenge supplied by the server, the S/Key calculator supplies the appropriate response for the user to enter.

The one-time password procedure is standardized in RFC1938.

PROCEDURE

The one-time password mechanism S/Key applies the one-way hash function to a string composed of an initial value *n* and the user's secret password. The result – a cryptographic checksum – is used as the input value on succeeding passes. The cryptographic checksum is then passed through a conversion function that generates a string consisting of six words from a predefined lexicon. This generated string is the one-time password.

The previously calculated cryptographic checksum, which is known as the *seed string*, is stored with the number of remaining passwords (that is, the initial value *n* minus the number of authentications performed so far).

The security of this authentication mechanism depends on the non-reversibility of the one-way hash function and the nondisclosure of the password used during initialization.

Figure 7-1 shows the detailed sequence of steps involved in the S/Key procedure.

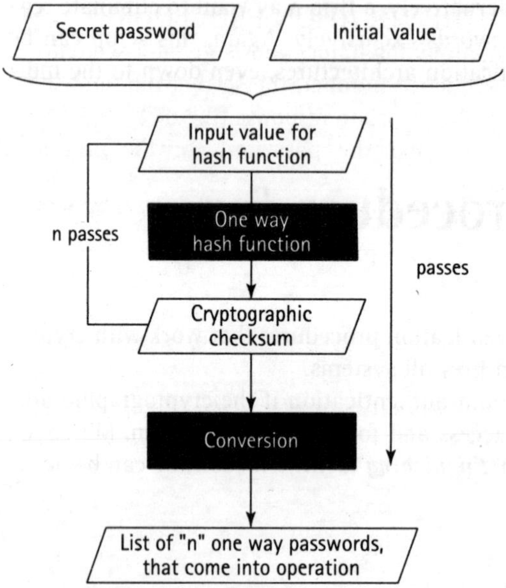

Figure 7-1: S/Key calculation

FUNCTIONAL SEQUENCE

1. The user (S/Key user) either receives a list of all the one-time passwords from the firewall system or generates the one-time password to be used on each occasion with a computational program. Such programs are available for virtually all operating systems.
2. When the user wants to be authenticated, he enters the password that corresponds to the present sequence number, which will be one less than the previous sequence number (in other words, *n*-1 the first time). The password is encrypted with the one-way hash function and compared with the last stored (*n*th) password.
3. If the result is the same as the stored value, the user is authenticated. The firewall system then replaces the stored value with the (*n*-1)th password just entered and decrements the sequence number.
4. After *n* iterations, the supply of one-time passwords is exhausted and the user must be assigned a new series, effectively limiting the number of times he can log on.

The password presented to the user each time he seeks to authenticate is a list of six English words, found by mapping the calculation results to a predefined lexicon containing 2,048 words. The lexicon is given in RFC1938. The assignment is effected using an index.

SEQUENCE OF EVENTS IN THE AUTHENTICATION PROCEDURE

The user connects to the firewall system, enters his name, and is given a sequence number (refer to Figure 7-2). Using the sequence number, the seed string, and the secret password, the user can work out the appropriate response (the new one-time password) or obtain the password by locating the password for the present sequence number on the pre-prepared list.

The entered password is encrypted in the firewall system using the one-way hash function and compared with the stored password. If the values match, the client stores the entered password, the new sequence number, and the old seed string in the user database.

If the sent response and the response calculated by the firewall system do not match, a comparison is carried out internally between the number of failed attempts at authentication and the maximum number of permitted attempts. If the maximum is exceeded, the user is blocked.

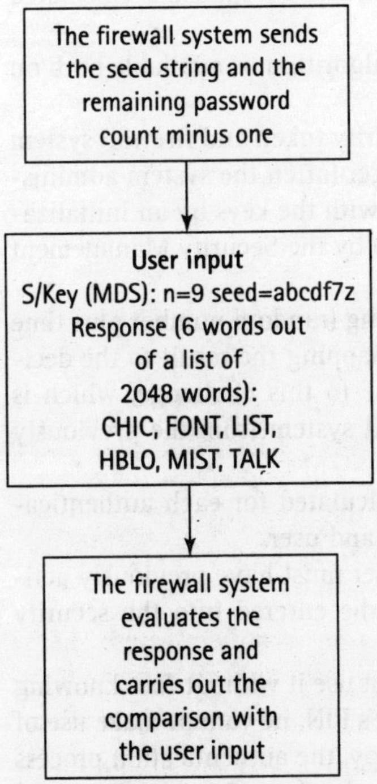

Figure 7-2: S/Key process

The S/Key procedure presents the following advantages:

- The software on the client side is easy to use.
- S/Key is available for many computer systems.

The S/Key procedure presents the following disadvantages:

- Storage of the secret information on the client can be problematic (password) because anyone with physical access to the client can obtain the secret information.
- Entering the required six words is rather cumbersome when the goal is simply to obtain six specific numbers between 1 and 2048.

Authentication Procedure with a Security Token

The Digipass procedure is an example of an authentication procedure with a security token. Digipass is a security token that works with the DES procedure.

PROCEDURE

The Digipass authentication procedure is based on a challenge-response method in which the firewall system issues the challenge and the user's response is calculated with the security token.

The underlying cryptographic algorithm, the DES algorithm, is available both on the security token and on the firewall system.

To arrive at the same result independently, the security token and firewall system must possess the same secret key. The Security Manager (often the system administrator) creates this key. The security token is supplied with the keys by an initialization station. The key is provided to the firewall system by the Security Management module.

The challenge is calculated by taking a random string (random number plus time value), encrypting it with the issued secret key, and mapping the result to the decimal system. The security token calculates a response to this challenge, which is compared with the response calculated in the firewall system from the previously stored challenge.

Like the generated response, the challenge is recalculated for each authentication request and transmitted between firewall system and user.

To use the security token for authentication, the user must have previously activated it using a PIN. In other words, the PIN must be entered into the security token. The user can change the PIN at any time.

An individual who finds a lost security token cannot use it without first knowing the user's PIN. However, if someone discovers the user's PIN, he cannot make use of it unless he also possesses the security token. In this way, the authentication process is protected twice, through knowledge (PIN) and possession (security token).

AUTHENTICATION PROCESS SEQUENCE

Figure 7-3 illustrates authentication using a security token. The user connects to the firewall system and enters his name, after which a challenge is displayed on his screen. The user must activate the security token using his personal PIN. He enters the challenge, and the response is calculated in the security token using the secret key that is stored there. The user enters the response displayed on the security token into his computer system and sends it to the firewall system.

The firewall system compares the response with another response calculated from the previously stored challenge. If the results from the security token and the firewall system differ, the user is asked to recalculate the response. Meanwhile, a comparison is carried out internally between the number of failed attempts at authentication and the maximum number of permitted attempts. If the maximum is exceeded, the user is blocked for a predefined time.

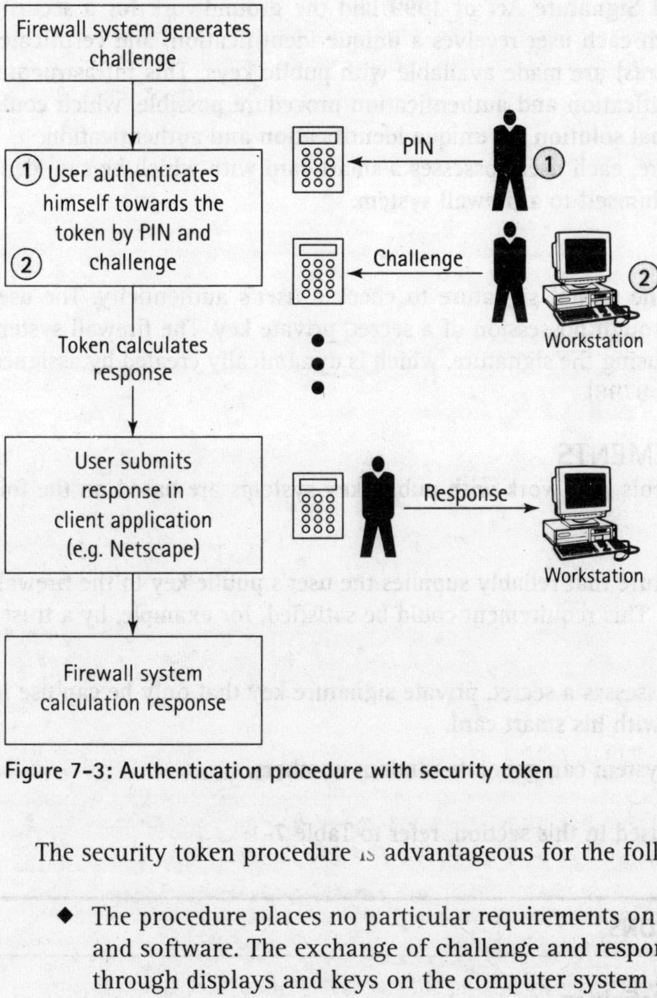

Figure 7-3: Authentication procedure with security token

The security token procedure is advantageous for the following reasons:

- The procedure places no particular requirements on the user's hardware and software. The exchange of challenge and response is implemented through displays and keys on the computer system and security token.
- This procedure is more secure than the one-time password method because the security token is a secure piece of hardware.

The main drawback of the security token procedure is that it is time-consuming for the user, requiring the following several steps:

1. Activation of the security token
2. Input of the challenge
3. Input of the response

Signature Card

In Europe, the Digital Signature Act of 1999 laid the groundwork for a security infrastructure in which each user receives a unique identification, and certificates (electronic *identity cards*) are made available with public keys. This infrastructure makes a unique identification and authentication procedure possible, which could lead the way to a global solution for unique identification and authentication.

In this infrastructure, each user possesses a smart card with which he can identify and authenticate himself to a firewall system.

PROCEDURE

Authentication uses the digital signature to check a user's authenticity. The user proves his identity through possession of a secret, private key. The firewall system checks the secret key using the signature, which is dynamically created by assigned random numbers (ISO 9798).

SPECIAL REQUIREMENTS

Authentication protocols that work with public key systems are based on the following assumptions:

- An infrastructure that reliably supplies the user's public key to the firewall system exists. This requirement could be satisfied, for example, by a trust center.
- Every user possesses a secret, private signature key that only he can use in combination with his smart card.
- The firewall system can generate random numbers.

For abbreviations used in this section, refer to Table 7-1.

TABLE 7-1 ABBREVIATIONS

Abbreviation	Definition
= sSX (Y)	Signed version of data Y using secret key SX
= ePX (Y)	Encrypted version of data Y using public key PX

Abbreviation	Definition
= A // B	Outcome of the concatenation of A and B
= TX	Time stamp of X
= RX	Random number of X
= TVPX	Time-dependent parameter of X

SEQUENCE OF EVENTS IN AUTHENTICATION PROCEDURE – TWO-WAY AUTHENTICATION

With this authentication mechanism, firewall system A is in a position to authenticate user B, as shown in Figure 7-4. The uniqueness and currency of the authentication data is achieved with the aid of a random number.

The following formula shows the structure of TokenBA:

```
TokenBA = RB // A // RA // Text3 // sSB ( RB // A // RA // Text2 )
Text1, Text2 and Text3 are text fields that depend on the specific
application.
```

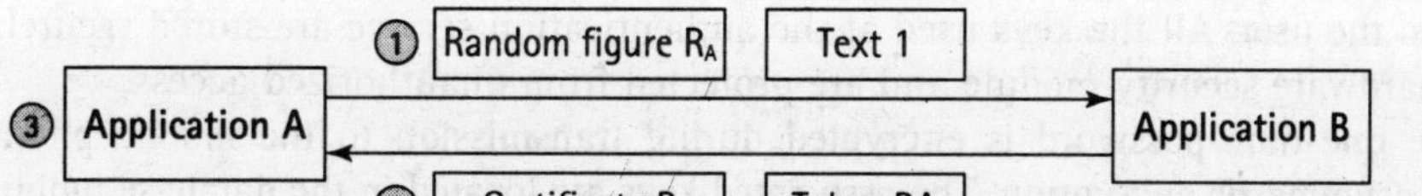

Figure 7-4: Two-way authentication

1. A sends a random number RA and, optionally, a text field Text1 to B.
2. B sends TokenBA and, optionally, its own certificate to A.
3. Following receipt of the message, entity A performs the following actions:
    a. It checks B's certificate or ensures that it possesses a genuine public key for B.
    b. It checks TokenBA's signature.
    c. It checks whether the random number sent in Step 1 agrees with the random number signed with TokenBA.

Firewall system A has authenticated user B when it accepts the checks in Step 3.

This authentication process spares the firewall system the job of authenticating users because an existing infrastructure can be used to guarantee the uniqueness of the names. The certificates of users who want to communicate through the firewall system must be made accessible to the firewall system. One way to implement this is by querying the public certification authorities (trust centers).

Computer systems must currently be fitted with a smart card reader.

Authentication Procedure Using Mobile Phone

One authentication procedure uses Global System for Mobile Communications (GSM) mobile phones as hardware tokens. On request, the authentication service generates a cryptographically secure one-time password with a limited period of validity, which is transmitted to the user over the Short Message Service (SMS) service of the GSM network.

The authentication procedure is based on a central authentication service, consisting of a cryptographically secure database that contains the user information, a hardware security module, and a GSM transmitter. The user information is held in the database and protected with appropriate encryption mechanisms. When a request for authentication is received, a cryptographically secure one-time password is generated with the aid of the corresponding user data record within the hardware security module. It is then sent over the GSM transmitter using the SMS service. A public-key algorithm protects the one-time password during transmission to the user. All the keys used at the authentication service are stored securely in a hardware security module and are protected from unauthorized access.

The one-time password is encrypted during transmission to the mobile phone using asymmetric encryption. The associated keys are located in the database (public key) and on the mobile phone's Subscriber Identity Module (SIM) card (secret key). For the purpose of decryption, the user's SIM card is provided with a PIN-protected additional application that requires a new-generation SIM card. The original SIM cards under early GSM specifications don't support the decryption module. Because the SIM cards are smart cards, upgrading them can be done by the phone vendor.

In a one-off login process, all the necessary data concerning the user, such as user ID, name, mobile phone number, and so on, is entered into the user database. The user is then given an additional application for his SIM card in the mobile phone via data SMS or by exchanging his existing SIM card for a new one.

The authentication service combines mechanisms and communications services from other existing procedures to provide a flexible and secure means of user authentication for firewall systems.

The essential elements of the authentication service follow:

- **Hardware security module.** This unit stores and uses all cryptographic keys.
- **Encrypted user data in a central database.** At the very least, data held in this database includes the user ID plus the public key of the user whose

private portion is held in the mobile telephone (SIM card), fields for the period of validity, telephone number, number of failed attempts, and authorizations.

- **One-time passwords.** The one-time passwords are generated in the authentication service's hardware security module and stored in the encrypted user data record. Once generated, the one-time password is only valid for a limited time.
- **Encrypted transmission of the one-time password.** The SMS service of the GSM network transmits the one-time password to the user's mobile telephone.
- **PIN-protected additional application on the mobile phone's SIM card.** Within this application, following input of a PIN known to the user, the one-time password is decrypted with the user's secret key and displayed in plain text.

SYSTEM OVERVIEW

The complete system using GSM authentication consists of the following components shown in Figure 7-5:

- A computer system connected to the Internet, which interacts with the firewall system
- The central firewall system, which acts as the central access point to the service provider's internal network
- An authentication service for checking access authorization

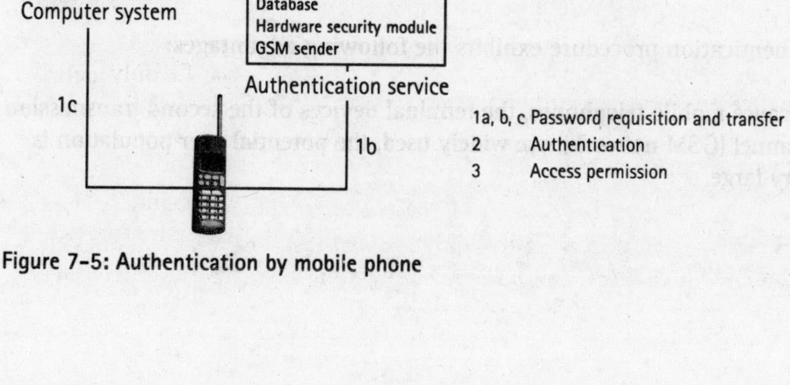

Figure 7-5: Authentication by mobile phone

The following sequence of steps details authenticating using a mobile telephone:

1. The user dials in to the central firewall system from any computer system in the Internet.
2. The user is asked on the login page to enter his user ID.
3. The authentication service searches for the user ID in the database. If it is there, the corresponding data record stored in encrypted form is loaded into the hardware security module and decrypted with the key that it contains.
4. The hardware security module generates and enters a one-time password in the user data record. The user data record is re-encrypted and stored in the authentication service's database.
5. The one-time password is encrypted in the hardware security module with the user's public key, which is part of the user data record, and sent via GSM transmitter to the user's mobile phone.
6. The user receives the encrypted one-time password as an SMS. After entering a secret number, the additional application on the mobile phone begins deciphering the one-time password in the SIM card using the user's secret key.
7. On the login screen, the user enters the one-time password that has been transmitted. Both the user id and one-time password are re-sent over the Internet to the authentication service.
8. The authentication service passes the encrypted user data record from the database to the hardware security module. In the security module, the one-time password, the amount of time already expired, and the number of login attempts are checked; only the result of the check (either valid or invalid) is reported.
9. If the result is positive, the user is granted access to the desired service through the firewall system.

   If the period of validity has been exceeded, or if the maximum number of failed login attempts has been reached, access is denied.

This authentication procedure exhibits the following advantages:

- Because mobile telephones, the terminal devices of the second transmission channel (GSM network), are widely used, the potential user population is very large.

- The user data is always held in a cryptographically protected database that is secure from attack, as only the user-specified ID can be read in plain text.
- Keys used are afforded maximum security because they are stored in a hardware security module.

Implementation of the procedure presented here requires SIM cards with an application for processing the one-time password.

Authentication Procedure Using Kerberos

An understanding of authentication isn't complete without an understanding of the Kerberos protocol. Originally developed at the Massachusetts Institute of Technology (MIT), the Kerberos protocol has gained widespread acceptance as an authentication mechanism. Kerberos is designed to allow for authentication using passwords, both at the user and system levels, without the actual transmission of those passwords over the network.

Kerberos uses a central authentication system known as the *Key Distribution Center (KDC)* and a mechanism termed *tickets* for authentication. To initially authenticate the user's system request, a special ticket from the KDC, known as the *Ticket Granting Ticket (TGT)*, is generated. This ticket is encrypted using a key derived from the user's password. Decryption at the local user's system also occurs using the user password. Without the correct password, the user won't be able to decrypt and use the TGT. This ticket-decrypting process allows for verification of the correct password without actual transmission of the password. After receiving and decrypting the TGT, the user can access systems and services on the network.

When a user wants to access a service, the TGT is sent to the *Ticket Granting Service (TGS)*, which usually runs on the KDC. The TGS verifies that the user has access rights to the service and issues a ticket to the user for that specific service. The user's system transmits the ticket to the service, which grants the desired access.

Kerberos provides a solid authentication mechanism that solves some of the shortcomings of password use. It is readily available, transparent when implemented, and can support virtually any service.

The primary disadvantage of Kerberos is its lack of widespread use. It didn't help matters when Microsoft chose to implement its own variation of the protocol when it incorporated Kerberos into Windows 2000's authentication process. Not much development effort has been placed on implementation tools. As a result, implementation can be complicated due to sketchy documentation and few software tools for implementing Kerberos.

With the inclusion of support for Kerberos in Windows 2000 (albeit a modified version of the protocol), adoption of Kerberos is progressing rapidly. It appears likely that network-based authentication will utilize Kerberos in a majority of networks in the not-too-distant future.

Summary

The process of achieving authentication can occur many different ways. All authentication methods have advantages and disadvantages. Choosing the best authentication depends almost entirely on the needs and configurations of each organization.

Achieving strong authentication can be difficult in some companies, but the result of having dependable user identification is critical. Don't forget that authentication forms the basis of all other security mechanisms. If you can't identify your users properly and users can authenticate as whomever they want, all other security measures will be largely wasted.

Chapter 8

Evaluating Firewall Solutions

FIREWALL SYSTEMS PRODUCED by different vendors vary in how they actually provide different security services, such as spoofing prevention. This chapter discusses and evaluates a number of approaches you can take to implement a firewall solution. Requirements for firewall products security are also discussed.

Public Domain Software or Firewall Product?

Firewall solutions come in three varieties. You can build your own solution using public domain/open source software, or you can buy the solution commercially as either a software product or a turn-key product (hardware/software combination).

Public Domain (and Open Source) Software for the Firewall Application

Some firewall solutions are offered on the Internet as *public domain software*. Public domain software comprises software solutions whose origins are often unclear because different people have developed them. This lack of clear origins (and the corresponding lack of demonstrated validity for techniques used) results in more risk to an organization than the organization would experience using commercial software.

Public domain software is available free of charge; however, no one can estimate or guarantee its effectiveness. It may be most useful to private individuals or institutions – those, for example, who would not suffer appreciable financial damage or ruin if the firewall solution failed.

In the first years of the Internet boom, some organizations used public domain solutions because no firewall products were available. Today, both in business and in public service, it is inadvisable to rely on public domain software; instead, use tested software and hardware solutions from specialist companies that also accept responsibility for their solutions and maintain and refine them.

"Do-it-yourself" solutions are prone to error. Their implementation requires solid experience and know-how in the computer security field. Manufacturers offering firewall products generally invest years (often over ten) in the development of their first version. After that, at least three to five engineers, computer scientists, and mathematicians must test, extend, and maintain the firewall solution to guarantee its reliability. This kind of effort is out of the question with a "do-it-yourself" solution, which means that the degree of security it can afford is inevitably less than that afforded by a commercial firewall product.

The use of public domain software can also be problematic in the following areas:

- **Continued development.** In the rapidly growing TCP/IP market, firewall systems must be rapidly updated so that new services can be used.
- **Performance.** In many cases, the biggest single differentiator between commercial solutions and public domain solutions is the performance level that can be achieved. This is not to say that good performance can't be achieved using public domain software, but, code for code, most commercial software out-performs public domain equivalents.
- **Maintenance.** Maintenance of firewall systems requires an in-depth knowledge of the workings of the security functions in the firewall elements. Without thorough knowledge of the firewall subsystems you increase the likelihood that security-relevant settings will be changed accidentally, which may result in the reduced security of the firewall elements. Such knowledge is difficult to access with public domain software and requires labor-intensive involvement with the particular firewall being used.

An oft-made statement is that "open source leads to better security because more people are examining the code." While this could be true in some cases, the reality lies somewhere shy of the "more secure" result. In other words, most open source software doesn't achieve better security because not that many people are actually examining the code closely for security flaws. In the majority of cases, people examine the open source code only when they see specific problems. In fact, security flaws continue to be discovered in open source software at virtually the same rate they are discovered in commercial proprietary code. The net result is that the single most common argument in favor of open source/public domain software over commercial software (that is, better security) is demonstrably false.

As you may have deduced, using free firewall solutions can be a risky proposition. In the final analysis however, public domain solutions are a viable solution. You can find public domain firewall solutions that address both the need for security and the need for continued development and readily available support. In some cases, in specific intrusion-detection programs, such as Snort, the capabilities of open source software actually exceed those of commercially available solutions. The success of specific open source packages over commercial is the exception rather than the rule, however. The bottom line for open source/public domain versus commercial software is that given sufficient expertise, open source security solutions continue to be an excellent alternative to commercial products.

Firewall Products

Firewall products are developed by experts with extensive experience in the implementation of security solutions in communications systems. The companies guarantee that they will continue to develop their solutions and maintain their firewall products.

Developing security solutions for TCP/IP applications in the Internet and in intranets is a very specialized area. The task of gathering up-to-date information about newly discovered security weaknesses is, in and of itself, time-consuming. The resources necessary for developing security solutions and staying abreast of developments are simply not available in organizations that just want to use the Internet. For this reason, purchasing a firewall product from a specialist company is a sensible, long-term investment.

LINUX AS A SECURE OPERATING SYSTEM FOR FIREWALL SOLUTIONS

None of today's operating systems have undergone evaluation and certification with regard to communications requirements. They have been examined solely in relation to access control and access rights administration.

One solution to this problem is to use an open source operating system, such as Linux, which is appropriately modified to the requirements. These modifications can be evaluated and investigated relatively easily because the operating system source code is readily available.

Given the prevalence of Linux, the National Security Agency (NSA) is involved in an ongoing project to provide security extensions and modifications for the purpose of using Linux as a secure operating system.

The modified Linux has been dubbed, "security-enhanced Linux," by the NSA. Security-enhanced Linux is available at `www.nsa.gov/selinux/`. More information about the research project, including specific details and files needed to create your own implementation of security-enhanced Linux, can also be obtained at that link.

REQUIREMENTS FOR A FIREWALL OPERATING SYSTEM

To adapt the kernel to the requirements of a firewall system, it must first be configured. The kernel should be structured as a monolithic block. This will ensure that individual modules cannot be substituted with modified modules; an attacker would have to replace the entire kernel. Kernel modules and the dynamic loader must be removed from the systems.

During configuration, only necessary drivers, network properties, and kernel options should be selected and compiled in the kernel.

The selected and configured kernel should be checked for any security weaknesses or functional errors, such as buffer overflows or privilege escalation. This procedure ensures that the kernel is "lean" – in other words, reduced to the bare essentials – and that the risk of security loopholes or functional errors is minimal.

The concept of a kernel evaluation must also include the handling of security patches, which can be issued for the evaluated kernel and also for later subversions. Updates affecting the kernel functionality or the supported components/devices must also be considered.

One possible solution here is to port functional or security patches into the existing kernel, avoiding the necessity of upgrading to a new version. When patching is done, the changes must be carefully noted and documented to ensure that the evaluated kernel can continue to be used, and that improvements contained in later versions can be integrated.

The first step in modifying a GNU system is to identify every file on the system. The function served by each file must be analyzed. Redundant files must be deleted, and the permissions of the other files should be examined closely and modified, if necessary.

The removal of dynamically loadable objects, including the loader itself, will result in a higher level of security. Each program should be statically linked to the libraries.

The firewall system can be rearranged so that most of the partitions are read-only. In every case, the system programs and firewall applications should be configured so they are read-only. System management programs should be placed in a separate partition so they can only be loaded under certain conditions, such as when the system is in single-user mode for maintenance functions. The administration programs can be stored on a read-only medium, such as a CD-ROM. The resulting file structure must be monitored by a dedicated process for extra security.

A combination of the measures previously described will produce a secure system.

To ensure the security of a firewall system, the kernel network code should be evaluated by an independent organization. Because Linux is open source, the results of this evaluation can be examined by anyone. Changes discovered during evaluation can be incorporated into the kernel. Use of a third party to evaluate security often uncovers faults and misconfigurations you missed.

In this way, Linux/GNU can be used as an open source operating system for a trustworthy and secure platform for firewall applications.

Software Solution or Turn-Key Solution?

What security aspects must be considered when using a firewall product, especially in regard to choosing between a pure software solution and a turn-key solution?

What Does a Pure Software Solution Offer?

A pure software solution is one in which the firewall product offered by the vendor consists solely of software. Even if a firewall product is purchased from an external company that offers hardware, software, and installation as a package, this still counts as a software solution. A software solution requires independent installation and configuration of hardware and the operating system. In comparison, a turn-key solution uses hardware and operating systems that are incorporated directly into the firewall product.

Certain security aspects, such as vendor capabilities, organizational expertise, support, and underlying operating system must be considered in connection with the use of firewall systems that are pure software solutions.

VENDOR'S CAPABILITIES

Vendors of software solutions that offer firewall products for standard operating systems such as Windows NT, SUN-Solaris, or HP-UX cannot modify the standard operating system during development in order to meet the firewall's requirements. The vendors must program their firewall systems exclusively with supplied operating system resources.

In addition, if the operating system in question has known security flaws, the vendor must program his firewall software to protect against attacks from the insecure network designed to exploit the security flaws in the underlying operating system. This is often not possible at the level of system calls, because communications can bypass the firewall software over internal relays. For example, there is a danger of IP forwarding (kernel functionality) from outside, as shown in Figure 8-1.

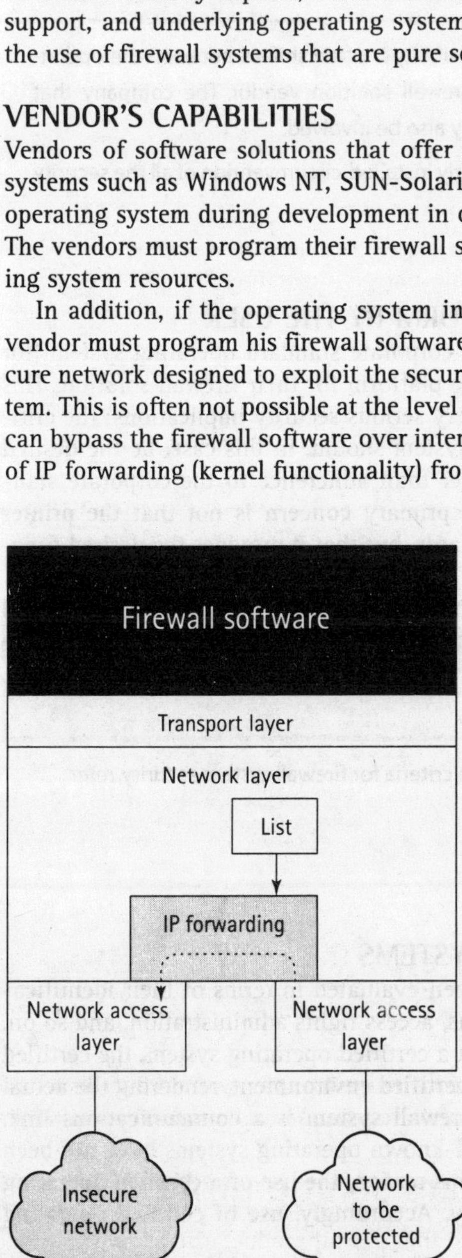

Figure 8-1: Danger of IP forwarding

Many software solutions are problematic because their security mechanisms are not immediately active following the reboot or restart of the firewall system. Therefore, communications are unprotected for a certain amount of time, despite the presence of the firewall system.

With software solutions, responsibility is often shifted between the operating system vendor and the firewall solution vendor. The company that installed the firewall system may also be involved.

If a software solution is incorrectly installed, circumvention of all the security functions may result.

DEFINITION OF FIREWALL PLATFORM BY THE USER

Some organizations like to use only the corporate standard operating system (for example, the NT operating system) as the platform for their firewall solution. This approach is a mistake and can present very serious security implications; the critical criterion in the choice of operating system should, in this case, be the desired degree of communications security rather than adherence to the corporate standard. When a printer is purchased, the primary concern is not that the printer should correspond to the corporate standards, but that it provides the desired functionality in an optimal fashion.

If a firewall solution is to guarantee maximum security, the corporate standard platform must not play any role. Instead, consider design criteria that promote the security of a firewall system.

For more information on design criteria for firewall system security, refer to Chapter 4.

USE OF CERTIFIED OPERATING SYSTEMS

Most certified operating systems have been evaluated in terms of their identification and authentication security functions, access rights administration, and so on. However, if a firewall solution is built on a certified operating system, the certified operating system is being used in a non-certified environment, rendering the actual certification irrelevant. In addition, a firewall system is a communications link, and the communications modules of well-known operating systems have not been evaluated for firewall applications. For this reason, the use of a certified operating system provides only *superficial* security. Accordingly, use of certified operating systems must be critically evaluated.

Considering the importance of using a hardened operating system base for firewall implementations, several groups have produced some excellent references on the proper way to secure an operating system for use as a firewall. Guides for hardening Solaris, Linux, NT, 2000, and XP, for example, can be found at the SANS Web site (www.sans.org).

What Is a Turn-Key Solution?

A turn-key solution is one in which the firewall system offered by the vendor consists not only of software but also of the hardware that goes with it. Such a firewall product is pre-installed and tested. Keep in mind that a turn-key solution is still a turn-key solution even when purchased from an external company, which may also perform the installation.

SECURITY ASPECTS IN A TURN-KEY SOLUTION

There are several inherent advantages in using a turn-key security product.

- **Complete solution.** A turn-key solution provides a complete security product, not just individual modules.
- **Single source of support.** Only one responsible point-of-contact exists for the hardware (packet filter, Security Management, application gateway, and so on), software (operating system, database, and so on), and security functions of the security solution. Responsibility for the product is clearly in the hands of a single company, much as it is when a printer is purchased. In the event that the system is updated, the service engineer will be familiar with the operating environment because all the solutions have an identical design that is not left to the user's discretion.
- **Platform Consistency.** The vendor of the firewall solution is familiar with the technical operational environment. At this level, it is not possible for the user to make mistakes integrating the firewall with the operating system and hardware.
- **No unnecessary components to remove.** With a turn-key solution, the firewall system is pre-installed to ensure its security as soon as it enters service. The turn-key solution is reliable because it is restricted to one operating system (there are no if-then instructions to cover the various operating systems). With turn-key solutions, all the software included is really needed. There are no extra programs to strip out as with hardening an operating system for installing a pure software firewall.
- **Modularity.** Each firewall element is assigned a particular function (Security Management, application gateway, packet filter, and so on).

- **Fully integrated.** The interaction of the security mechanisms is analyzed (for example, for packet filter and application gateway) because the same firewall elements always interact.

The one primary disadvantage to turn-key firewalls is expandability. Because the firewall product is installed completely on proprietary hardware, it is often not possible to upgrade memory or other significant components without replacing the firewall with a bigger model.

OPERATIONAL RELIABILITY IN A TURN-KEY SOLUTION

The advantages to using a turn-key firewall product boil down to a few key points.

- Adapted to the system environment
- System is specifically customized
- Firewall elements are optimally adapted to each other
- All the components integrate fully

If an organization does not have any specialists and/or employees able and willing to take responsibility for the firewall system, then a turn-key solution is probably the most sensible choice.

Criteria for Assessment of the Actual Security Achieved by a Firewall Product

The following are the most important security criteria in the selection of a firewall product:

- Openness and transparency of the security
- Evidence that the claimed security has been verified
- Certainty that governmental restrictions will not hamper the achievement of security

A firewall solution should not only deliver the security services for which it was purchased, it should also prevent any unwanted communications. An organization must have confidence in its firewall solution, just as it trusts its security guard.

Open and Transparent Security

The nature of the security mechanisms used in a firewall solution must be disclosed to allow public review, so the firewall operator gains perspective on the achievable security level.

To achieve security that is demonstrable and transparent, the algorithms used for user authentication in a firewall system, and also in security tokens, should be standard security mechanisms that are generally known and that have been thoroughly researched by experts.

In practice, assume that an algorithm used for encryption or authentication is secure if, five years after its publication, mathematicians worldwide have not been able to crack it.

Experience suggests that algorithms that have not been verified are insecure. The design criteria for the firewall elements should also be presented.

Tested, Demonstrable Security

As with safeguards in other industries (automobile airbags, for example), the security mechanisms used in firewall solutions must be tested – not by users, but by experts. Specific criteria have been developed for firewall-testing procedures.

XREF For more specific information on firewall-testing procedures, refer to Chapter 12.

Security without Governmental Restrictions

If the firewall system is to be truly secure following implementation, the security mechanisms must not be subject to any governmental restrictions. Freedom from governmental restrictions involves having adequate key lengths for cryptographic security mechanisms such as encryption and authentication, and the absence of security loopholes.

The guiding principle should be that it is better to have no security than superficial security. The problem with superficial security is that it imparts a false sense of security, creating actual security that is easily penetrated. Users don't take reasonable precautions because of the false sense of security. When the breach in security occurs, the damages to the organization are more severe because of users' lack of precautions. When users feel there is no security, most will take steps to protect their own information. The users' "self-securing" results in better security than that achieved through superficial means.

Summary

Two fundamental decisions must be made when initially implementing a firewall: whether to use a pure software product or a turn-key product, and how to evaluate specific firewall products.

These early decisions determine the choices available to you when implementing the firewall product in an organization, so consider wisely.

Chapter 9

Practical Use of Firewall Systems

THIS CHAPTER PRESENTS an example of an intranet application that makes use of firewall systems. An intranet uses Internet technology for internal company communications. The term *intranet* is also associated with secure access to public networks (for example, to the Internet) and with the controlled access of external users (for example, workstations telecommuting through Cable or DSL) or subnets of an organization (for example, branch offices).

The advantages of intranet technology are obvious:

- Intranets serve the organization as a common pool of information and a universal communications platform.
- User-friendly browsers provide simple handling and minimize training expenses.
- Scalable information distribution systems can be implemented quickly, economically, and flexibly.
- Documents can be updated dynamically; they can be maintained directly by the author and need only be stored in a single place.
- Intranets facilitate cooperative working (through groupware, workflows, and so on) and support decentralized organizational structures.

In setting up an intranet, an organization aims to reduce costs, speed up work processes, and improve the quality of service. The intranet is also a way to capture and organize a company's knowledge, and make it accessible to every employee.

Intranet technology is also advantageous for the following reasons:

- The use of open standards, such as the Hypertext Transfer Protocol (HTTP), the Hypertext Mark-Up Language (HTML), or TCP/IP, simplifies connecting the intranet to the Internet.
- Standardization enables external and mobile users to conveniently access an organization's internal data.
- Standardization also enables the exchange of information between intranets and business partners via the Internet without complication.

In specific cases, an intranet can be configured so that, in addition to being linked internally to the local network, the various organizational units are linked to each other over the organization's own corporate network. Telecommuter workstations (such as home workstations) or mobile devices (laptops and Notebooks, for example) are connected to the intranet over public networks so that users can access the internal intranet server and retrieve or transmit data (see Figure 9-1).

Secure Connection of the Organization's Intranet to the Internet

A secure connection between the Internet and an organization's intranet is essential if employees are to access information and services from the Internet, such as Web pages, e-mail, databases, or vendor information.

Because connecting to the Internet poses a considerable risk of attack, effective security mechanisms, such as a high-level security firewall system must be used. This type of firewall system constitutes a "Common Point of Trust" for the interface between the Internet and the intranet. In other words, the only communications route from the public network to the intranet runs in a controlled fashion through the high-level security firewall system. The firewall system unequivocally identifies and authenticates users at this checkpoint. Figure 9-2 shows an example of a network configuration using a firewall to link an intranet to the Internet.

Because all organizational units access the services of the Internet through the central firewall system, a uniform security policy can be implemented for the entire organization.

Employ a firewall design that can react flexibly in the event that communications requirements increase.

XREF

For more information on employing a flexible firewall design, refer to Chapter 5.

The access control rights of an organization's employees are flexibly defined with the aid of a central security management function. Employees accessing services on the Internet are identified and authenticated as required by the firewall system, and their actions are logged and evaluated.

To implement the concept of a Common Point of Trust, it is essential that no other connection exist between the organization and the Internet. A single point of trust presupposes additional infrastructural, personnel-related, and organizational security measures.

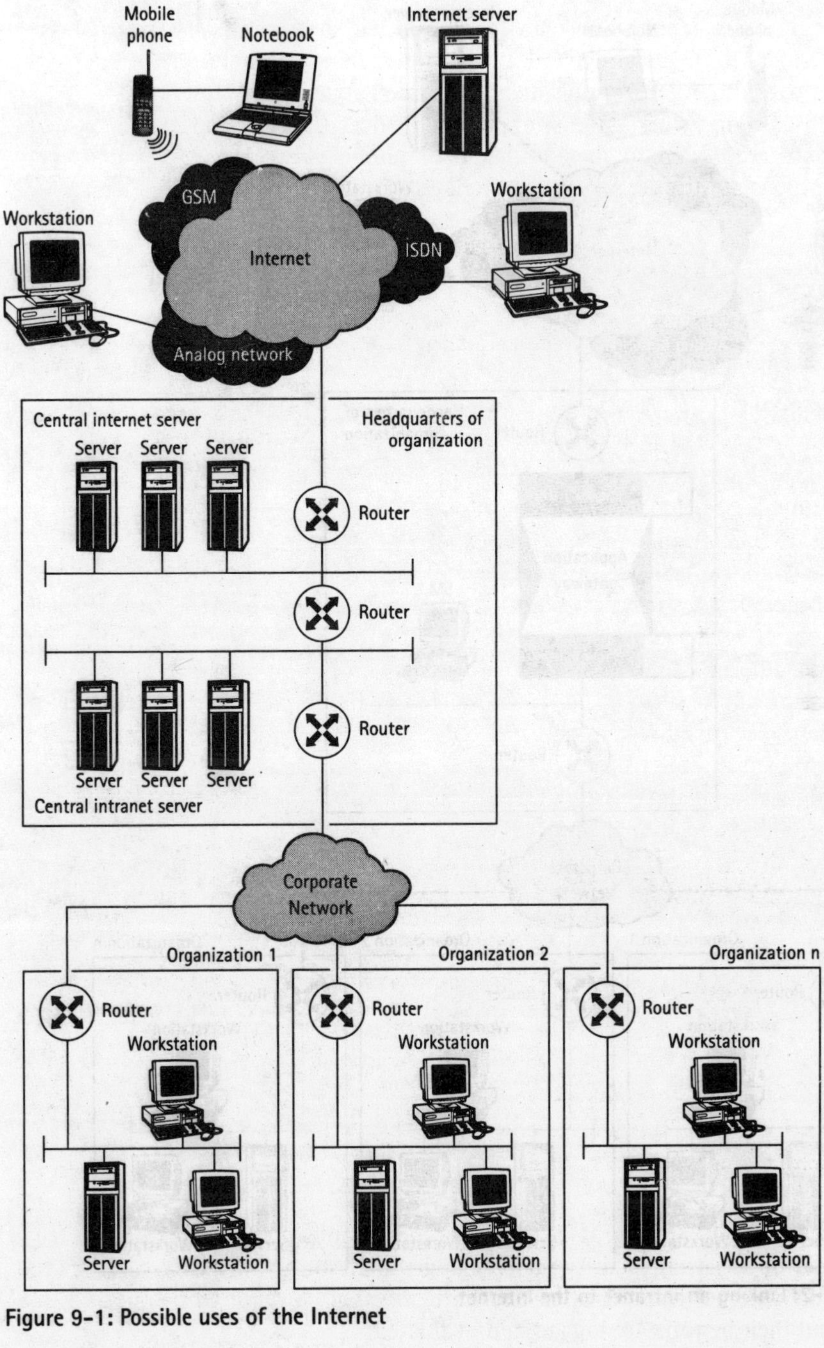

Figure 9-1: Possible uses of the Internet

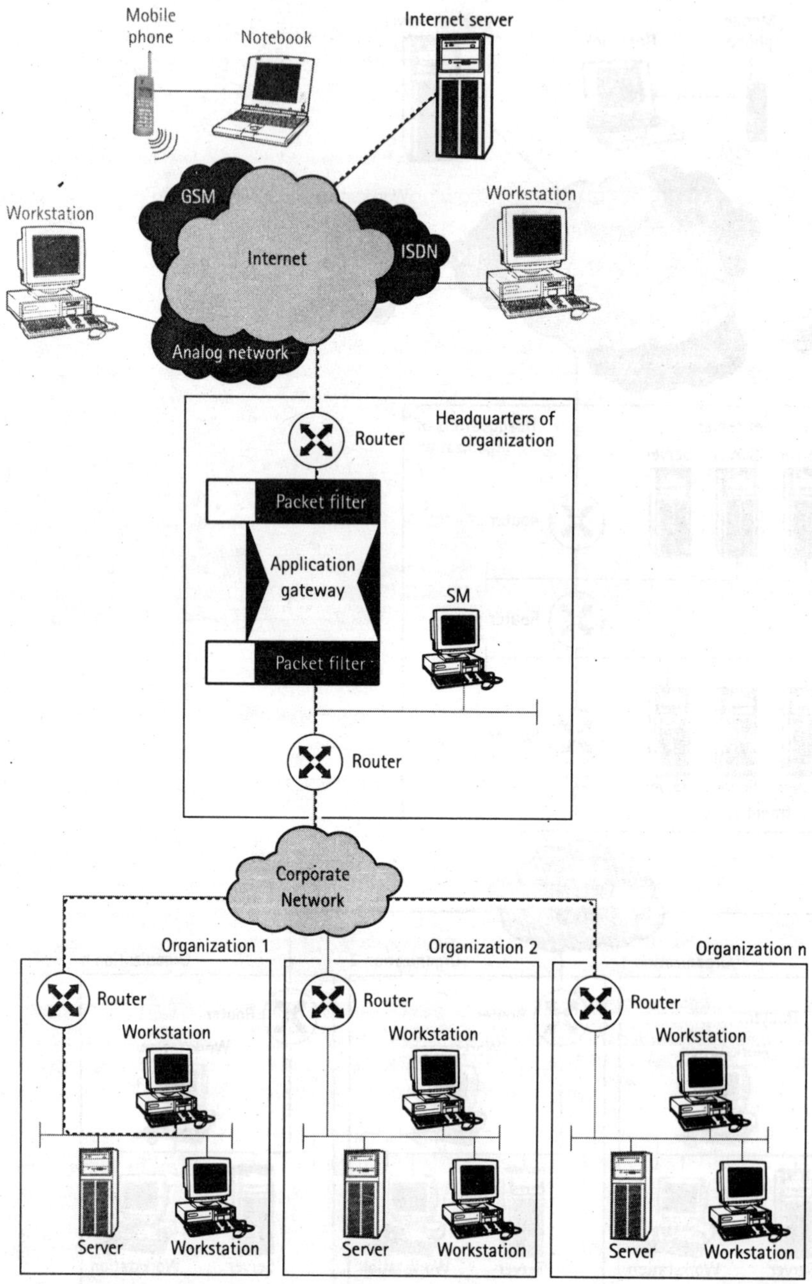

Figure 9-2: Linking an intranet to the Internet

In addition, you must specify the particular authentication procedure to be used in your firewall design – whether, for example, Java may be used on the intranet but not on the Internet.

XREF

For more information on allowing or disallowing Java use on the intranet and Internet, refer to Chapter 11.

When designing the firewall system, a scalable solution should be used so that enhancements can easily be implemented.

Internet Server

Position Internet servers that provide information or services to the public either in front of or close to a high-level security firewall system. This design concept makes it unnecessary for Internet users to access the intranet through the high-level security firewall system because not all the Internet servers reside in the intranet.

Internet servers are connected either within an external screened subnet of the high-level security firewall system or with a separate packet filter (see Figure 9-3). The packet filters restrict access to the services offered on the Internet servers. Attacks on the Internet servers over the packet filters are detected and logged. If the ruleset has been so defined, a spontaneous message is sent to Security Management.

If an organizational unit provides its own Internet servers, the servers can be implemented securely with encrypted communications from the Internet over the corporate network. To this end, packet filters with encryption functions (VPN boxes) are installed both at the organization's central access point and in the organizational unit. Communications over the Internet pass through the VPN boxes at the central access point and run in encrypted form through the corporate network to the appropriate organizational unit. Here, the packets are decrypted by the organizational unit's VPN box, arriving at the Internet server in plain text. In this way, a virtual private network (VPN) is cryptographically implemented.

The individual organizational units' Internet servers have official Internet addresses. To reliably prevent attacks from the Internet, these Internet servers must not be connected to the organizational unit's LAN (an organizational security measure). Organizational unit Internet servers in the corporate network can only be securely linked to the Internet if encryption is used.

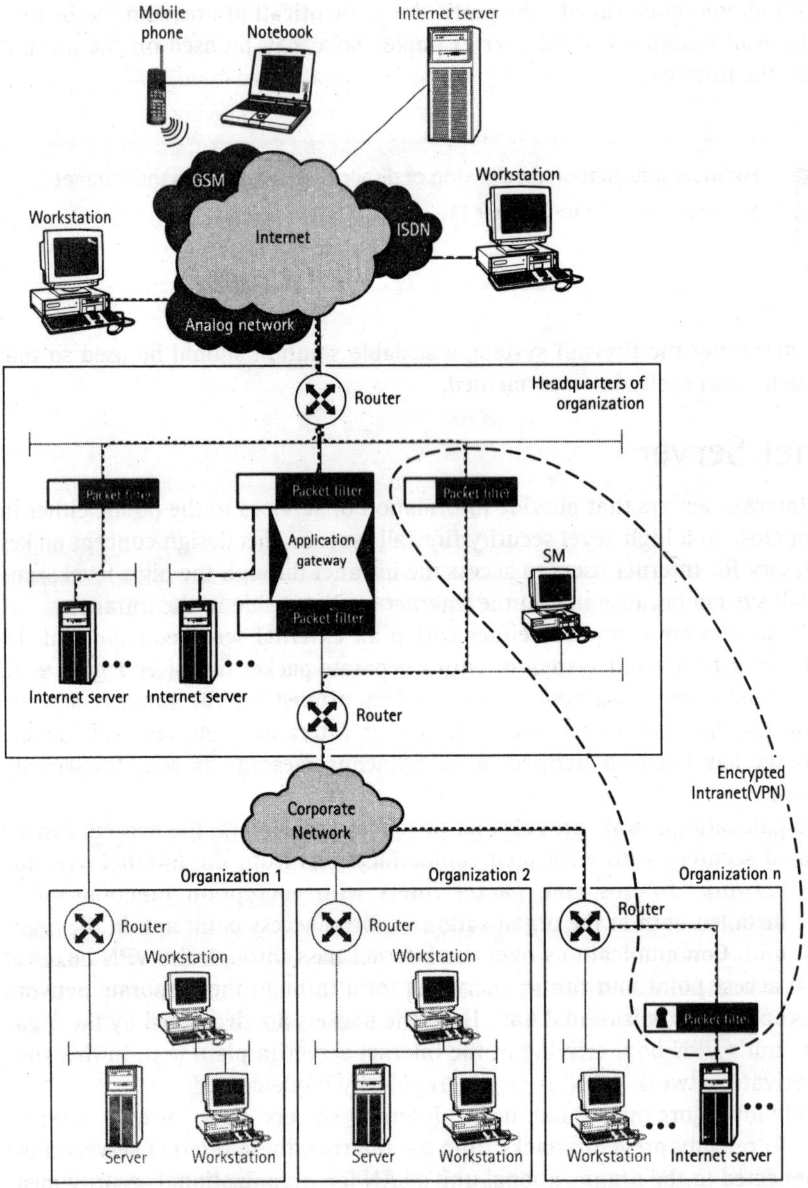

Figure 9-3: Internet servers

> **NOTE:** On the right side of Figure 9-3, the communications flow seems to circumvent the high-level security firewall system, the Common Point of Trust. However, communications take place here at a different logical level because all packets are encrypted. Packet mixing is ruled out cryptographically through encryption.

Intranet Security

After the Internet portion is secured, the intranet subnets can be protected using a combination of encryption with a VPN and access controls in the VPN.

VPN boxes encrypt communications over the corporate network so that no data can be read in plain text. Encryption has the effect of an implicit authentication that prevents certain attacks (for example, man-in-the-middle and masquerade attacks).

In the access rights administration of the VPN box, you can specify which applications (or services) can be used from which computer systems, and at what times.

Security-relevant events are detected by the VPN boxes, recorded in the logbook and, if required, reported to Security Management as a spontaneous message (see Figure 9-4). In this way, security violations can be identified.

In the individual organizational units, the VPN boxes are positioned directly behind the routers. In the headquarters, the intranet servers are connected in the internal screened subnet of the high-level security firewall system, or with a separate VPN box.

For the intranet servers positioned in the internal screened subnet of the high-level security firewall system, communications can also be conducted through the proxies of the application gateway (which function as single-homed application gateways). In this case, additional security services such as user authentication and logging of user actions can be implemented. A separate application gateway can be employed for such expanded security services.

Communications between the organizational units are likewise monitored and protected using VPN boxes.

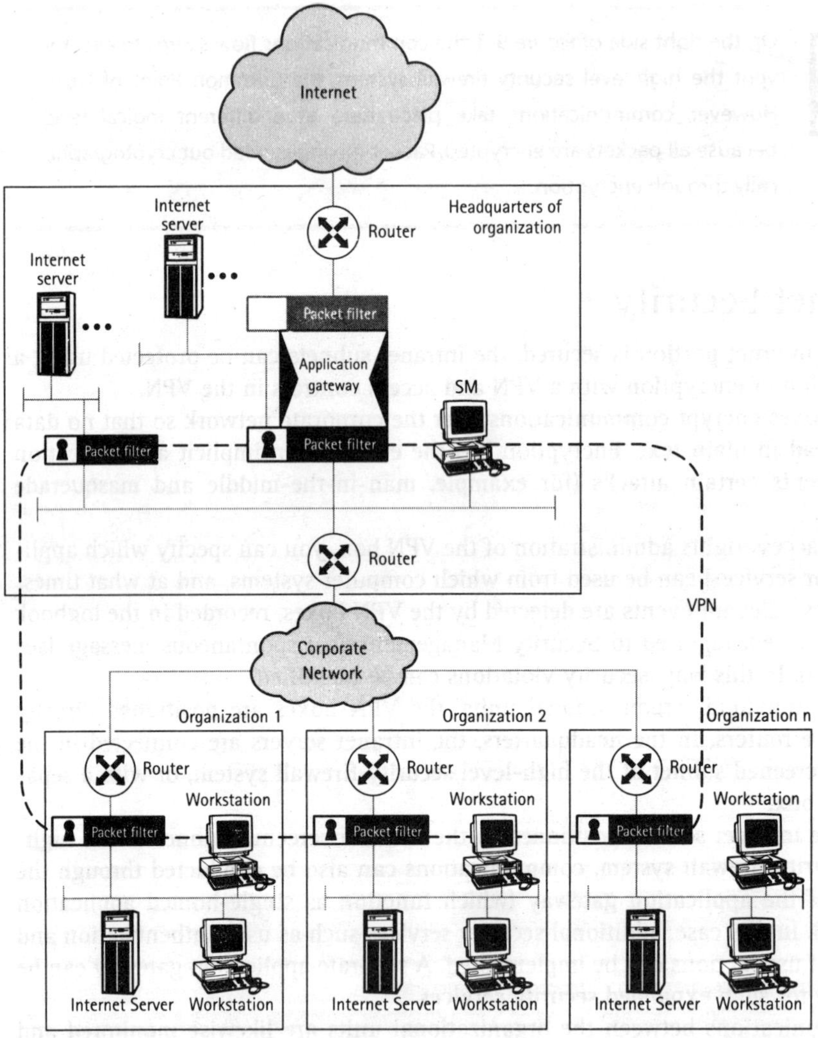

Figure 9-4: Intranet security with VPN boxes

HIGHER END-TO-END SECURITY

Depending on the protection requirement and the number of computer systems in an organizational unit, you may want to employ PC security components in the computer systems so that encryption can be used directly in the computer system. This higher end-to-end security at a deep system level guarantees confidentiality to the LANs of the individual organizational units (see Figure 9-5).

Confidential and controlled communications can also be *locally* implemented in the organizational units themselves with the aid of PC security components and VPN boxes. These security components can be controlled and administered either by the central security management module or by a local security management function.

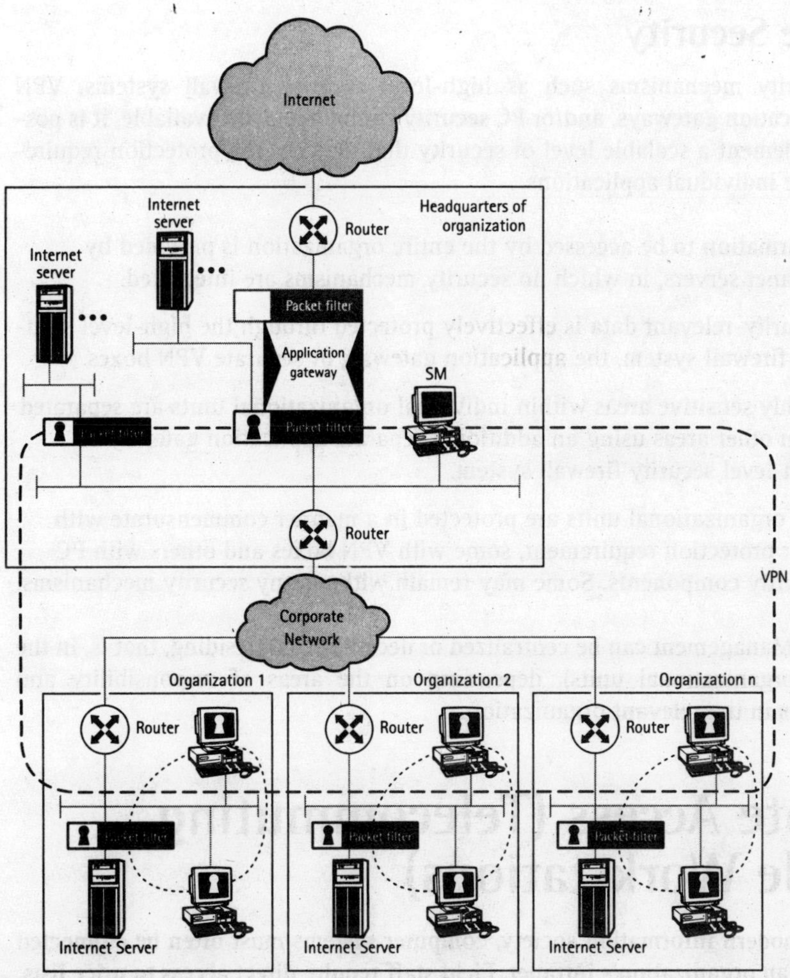

Figure 9-5: Intranet security with PC security components

Partitioning Organizational Units

Organizational units can also segregate themselves from each other through VPN boxes, application gateways, or a high-level security firewall system, depending on the particular protection requirements. Special partitioning is often necessary for organizational units such as central management, human resources, the occupational medicine department, or the research department, because these areas have particularly high protection requirements.

If a separate application gateway or high-level security firewall system is used, the security management can be implemented in the department itself.

Scalable Security

When security mechanisms such as high-level security firewall systems, VPN boxes, application gateways, and/or PC security components are available, it is possible to implement a scalable level of security that matches the protection requirements of the individual applications.

- Information to be accessed by the entire organization is provided by intranet servers, in which no security mechanisms are integrated.
- Security-relevant data is effectively protected through the high-level security firewall system, the application gateway, or separate VPN boxes.
- Highly sensitive areas within individual organizational units are separated from other areas using an additional separate application gateway or high-level security firewall system.
- The organizational units are protected in a manner commensurate with their protection requirement, some with VPN boxes and others with PC security components. Some may remain without any security mechanisms.

Security Management can be centralized or decentralized (residing, that is, in the individual organizational units), depending on the areas of responsibility and requirements in the relevant organization.

Remote Access (Telecommuting, Mobile Workstations)

In today's modern information society, computer systems must often be connected remotely to an organization's intranet. Field staff require direct access to price lists, delivery times, and orders found on the intranet so that business processes can be performed effectively without unnecessarily switching media.

Furthermore, offering home workstations that are remotely linked to the intranet is increasingly necessary. For home workstations, a Cable or DSL link is attractive because it offers high data transfer rates.

Notebooks can be linked to the intranet with a modem over the telephone line or with a mobile telephone over the mobile communication network (GSM network). The attack probability is especially high in the remote computer environment (for example, in hotels).

In the "External connection" security concept, protected remote access to internal intranet servers is possible through the high-level security firewall system, or access can be provided to special Internet servers through VPN boxes. VPN boxes and PC security components enable communication using encryption over public networks, whereby the rights of the party seeking access can be individually specified within the central security management function.

A central access point through a high-level security firewall system that is particularly well-protected guarantees the confidential and controlled connection of external users, such as individuals on home workstations, field staff on remote computers, or customers and suppliers.

Combining VPN boxes and PC security components constitutes a simple concept that delivers the necessary degree of security for communications over insecure networks: IP packets are transmitted in an encrypted form over a Digital Subscriber Line (DSL), Integrated Services Digital Network (ISDN), the telephone network, or the mobile communications network, and decrypted by packet filters with cryptographic functions that serve as central access points.

The use of encryption effectively creates a cryptographic *virtual private network (VPN)* in the insecure network.

If remote access through the high-level security firewall system to the intranet server takes place centrally or locally in the individual organizational units, all the security services available in these units can be used. In addition to encryption, these security services provided by the VPN server include the following:

- User authentication
- Application access rights
- Preservation of evidence regarding user actions

Connection of Special Organizational Units

Undoubtedly, certain organizational units will need to be connected to the intranet through the high-level security firewall system. Doing so achieves a higher level of protection.

With special organizational connections through the Internet, every user from the remote organizational unit must identify and authenticate himself to the high-level security firewall system. In addition, certain services can be restricted and controlled in the Application layer. Certain user actions can be recorded by logging the connection data to retain an audit trail. Confidential and controlled communications over the insecure network are achieved through the VPN boxes.

Organizational units with a lower protection requirement that are connected to other insecure networks can be connected to the intranet in this way. The control and administration of the packet filter in organizational unit Y can be implemented from the central security management module. This measure supports the concept of a Common Point of Trust.

External Modem Connections

For security reasons, modems for accessing external computer systems should only be available centrally within an organization. Position a modem server in front of the firewall system in the insecure area. If an employee of the organization wishes to use the modem, he must first identify and authenticate himself to the high-level security firewall system. He can then access the modem server (for example, using Telnet) and use the modem from his computer system. With a central modem pool that can be reached through the high-level security firewall system, the concept of a Common Point of Trust can be retained. With the aid of Security Management, you can specify which users are allowed to access an external modem for particular periods of time on particular days of the week. The corresponding actions can be logged and evaluated. Note how the modem server in Figure 9-6 is positioned externally to the firewall. Because anyone can call a modem server, they must be considered "untrusted," just as the Internet is.

Modem Connections from the Insecure Network to the Protected Network

A modem server in the protected network can monitor a maintenance company through the high-level security firewall system, when, for example, the company must carry out low-level maintenance for a UNIX system through the serial interface. The requirement to establish a direct, external connection to a critical system device (the UNIX system) significantly restricts your ability to place controls on the connection. This problem can be solved in the following ways:

- A serial interface can be run from the modem server to the computer system that is to be serviced, as shown in Figure 9-7 (Organization 1).
- A modem server can be installed at the headquarters. The modems connected to the modem server can reach their destination by establishing a connection over the internal private branch exchange. A modem is then available for internal communications, as shown in Figure 9-7 (Organization n). With this solution, you cannot access the private branch exchange from outside. Additional security measures must be taken to satisfy this requirement, such as configuring the internal phone system to disallow external calls to the internal modem. The modem server also needs to be protected by establishing access controls in it, restricting who can use the modem server, and how it can be used.

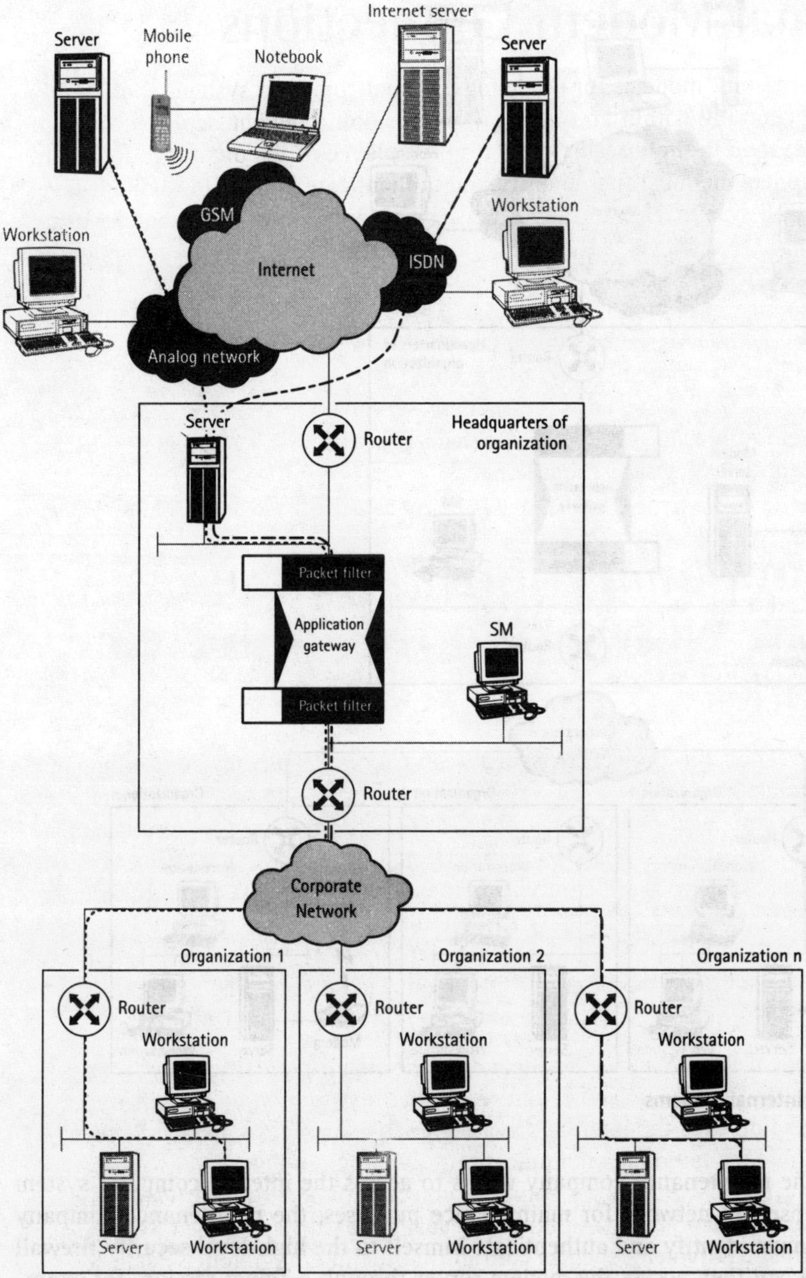

Figure 9-6: External modems

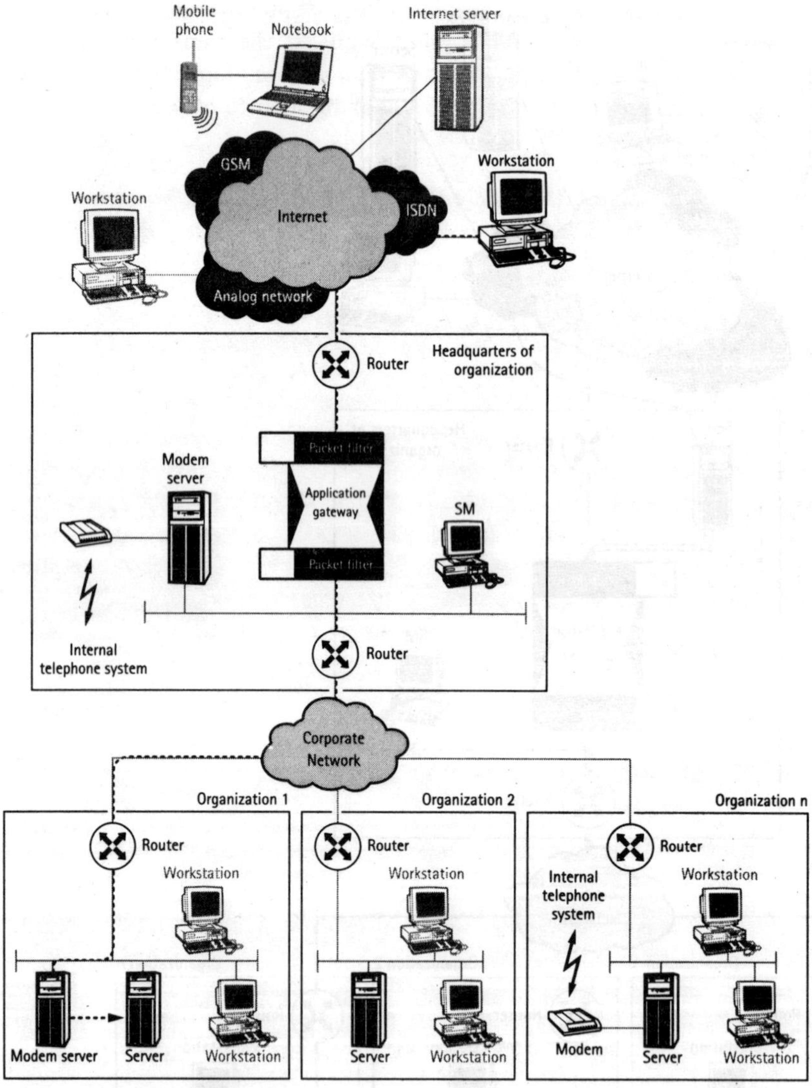

Figure 9-7: Internal modems

When the maintenance company wants to access the internal computer system from the insecure network for maintenance purposes, the maintenance company employee must identify and authenticate himself to the high-level security firewall system. He can then access the modem server through a Telnet session, for example, that is logged in the high-level security firewall system. From there, he can carry out his maintenance work at the lowest level. This procedure ensures the maximum degree of monitoring and logging, while at the same time enabling remote maintenance of the computer system without the use of an external modem. The employee's actions are recorded in the logbook in order to preserve evidence.

Anti-virus and Anti-malware System

When files are exchanged as e-mail attachments or Web documents, there is a risk that these files will contain malware (viruses, worms, Trojan horses, and so on) intended to harm the recipient. For the purpose of this discussion, the term *viruses* will be used to refer to these threats.

Do not underestimate the danger of viruses. Where connection to an insecure network such as the Internet exists, modern viruses can work like dynamite, as they usually propagate quickly using many different mechanisms (e-mail, file infection, direct copying) to replicate. If risks are to be mastered and vulnerability reduced, effective security mechanisms *must* be implemented. Virus scanner programs are available that search for known viruses either centrally or on individual computer systems. If a virus is found in a file, a security-relevant event is displayed.

General Problem Regarding the Detection of Viruses

Given the huge number of viruses that exist, and the fact that new viruses enter circulation every day, it is not surprising that virus scanners can't detect them all. Using anti-virus software doesn't guarantee 100 percent protection. The success rate of such software in detecting viruses during file transmission is even less predictable.

For example, on May 4, 2000, the I Love You virus caused an estimated 30 billion dollars worth of damage in a single day. Even companies that suffered no direct harm were indirectly affected because their providers were down for hours. The anti-virus software vendor Symantec produced a remedy on the same day, but it was already too late.

Compression of Files

Files that are to be transmitted are generally reduced (or *zipped*) using compression algorithms to cut down the number of bytes that must be transmitted. However, virus scanners can generally only detect viruses in uncompressed files. Compressed files must be decompressed before they can be scanned. Virus scanners can only perform the necessary decompression if standardized compression procedures, such as ZIP, are used. If a non-standard compression algorithm is used, the virus scanning programs have no chance of finding a virus. This has the effect of reducing the detection rate for known viruses.

Encryption of Files

When object-encrypted files are transmitted via e-mail or by using FTP, the antivirus software has no chance of detecting any viruses, because only the recipient can decrypt the files.

As the use of file encryption over insecure networks becomes widespread, the detection rate of virus scanners will steadily decline. This does not mean that virus scanners cannot detect viruses in files during transmission, but detection rates may differ widely.

Integration of Virus Scanners at the Common Point of Trust

Various security measures against viruses can be implemented to protect a network's connection to an insecure network. The following section discusses some of the options.

INTEGRATION OF A VIRUS SCANNER IN THE CENTRAL MAIL SERVER

The central mail server can be extended to include a virus scanner (see Figure 9-8). All mail files transmitted by the central mail server from the insecure network into the protected network can then be checked.

Because no additional hardware is required, this solution is inexpensive. With appropriate configuration, the virus scanner can be used centrally so that all inbound mail is checked. However, the disadvantage of this solution is that services such as HTTP and FTP are not used.

CENTRAL VIRUS SCANNER IN THE INTRANET

A virus scanner can be implemented centrally in the intranet as a single-homed solution, as shown in Figure 9-9.

The advantage of this solution is that all the services can be used as long as the virus scanner is so equipped. Virus scanners of this type operate transparently, so that user queries to the firewall system are passed on and the users do not have to learn any new operations.

However, through integration as a single-homed gateway, the IP addresses of the computer systems from the intranet are no longer recognized by the firewall system. The firewall system now sees only the virus scanner's IP address.

The virus scanner functions in a store-and-forward mode – in other words, the scanner takes the whole file, checks it for viruses, and sends it on. This method affects the runtime performance of file transmission as far as the user is concerned.

VIRUS SCANNER AS A SINGLE-HOMED GATEWAY SOLUTION IN THE INTERNAL SCREENED SUBNET

By relocating the virus scanner to a separate screened subnet, as shown in Figure 9-10, you completely prevent external communications from reaching the internal network without first passing through the virus scanner.

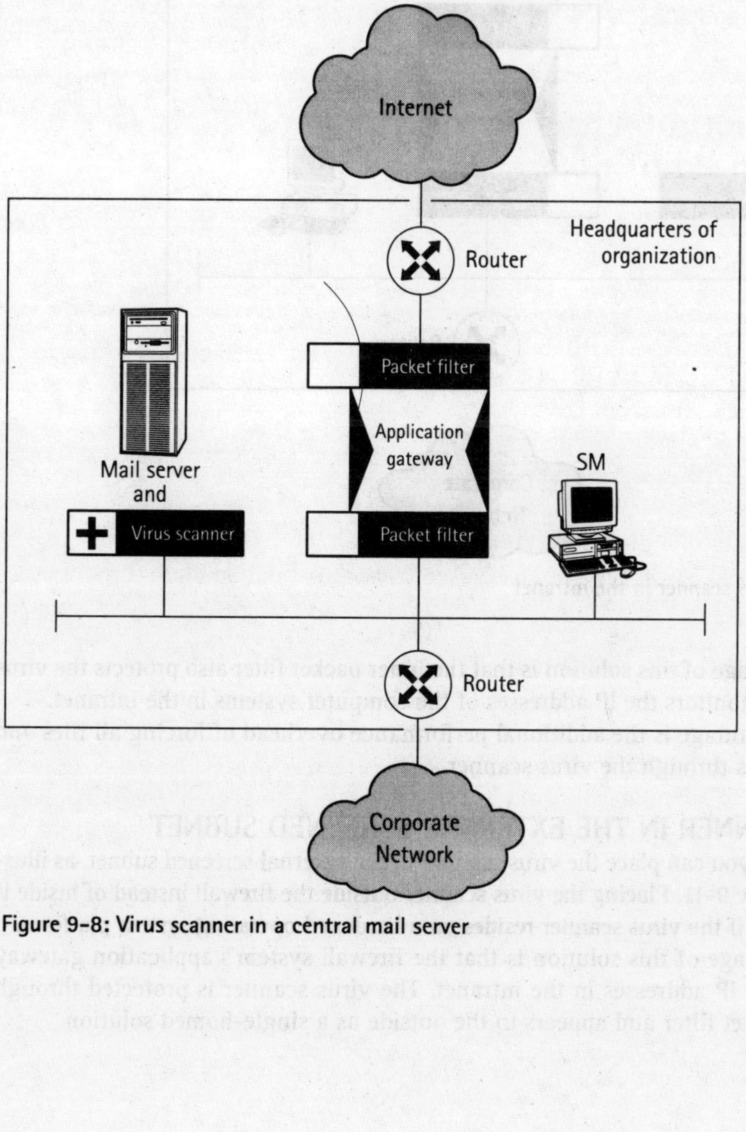

Figure 9-8: Virus scanner in a central mail server

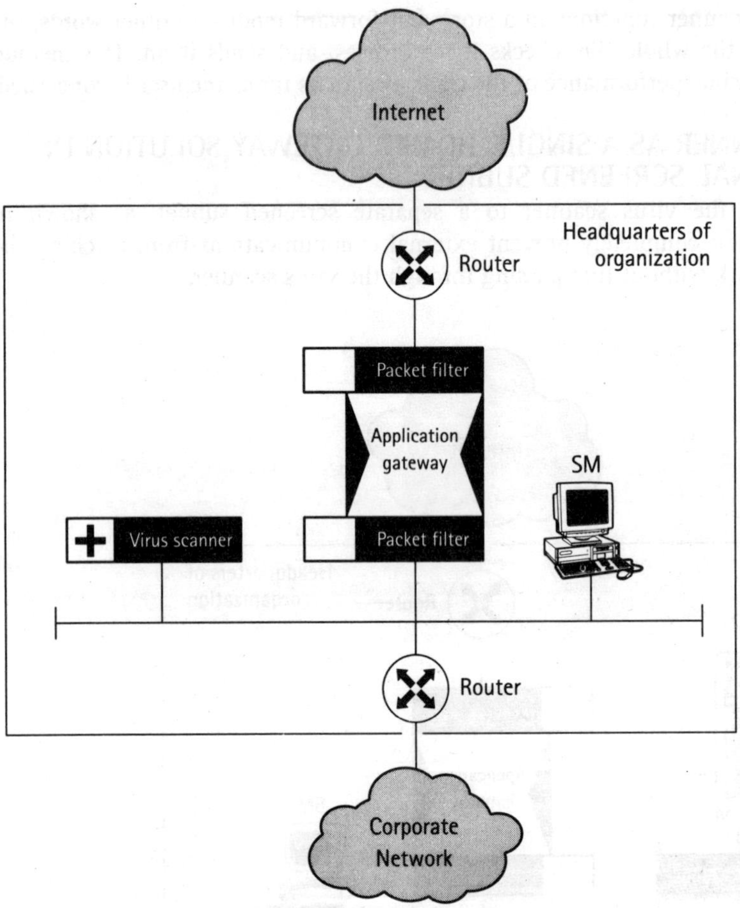

Figure 9-9: Virus scanner in the intranet

The advantage of this solution is that the inner packet filter also protects the virus scanner and monitors the IP addresses of the computer systems in the intranet.

The disadvantage is the additional performance overhead of forcing all files and e-mails to pass through the virus scanner.

VIRUS SCANNER IN THE EXTERNAL SCREENED SUBNET

Alternatively, you can place the virus scanner in the external screened subnet, as illustrated in Figure 9-11. Placing the virus scanner outside the firewall instead of inside is a good option if the virus scanner resides on a hardened operating system platform.

The advantage of this solution is that the firewall system's application gateway can check the IP addresses in the intranet. The virus scanner is protected through the outer packet filter and appears to the outside as a single-homed solution.

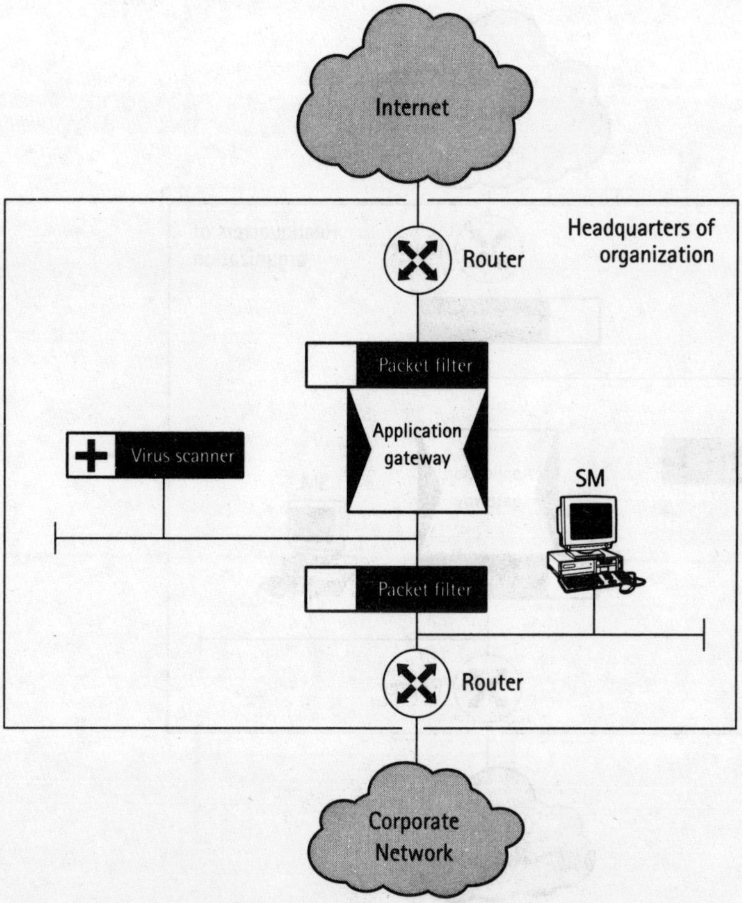

Figure 9-10: Virus scanner in the internal screened subnet

The disadvantage is that the firewall system's application gateway can no longer detect and handle IP addresses from the insecure network. Identification and authentication are limited to the level of user identification and authorization.

INTEGRATION OF MULTIPLE VIRUS SCANNERS

Figure 9-12 illustrates a central virus scanner in the inner, screened subnet as a single-homed solution for the HTTP and FTP services. In addition, a virus scanner is implemented on the central mail server for all e-mail, and several virus scanners are implemented on users' computer systems. The packet filters and application gateways should be configured to protect the virus scanner systems from tampering.

The advantage of this solution is that the central virus scanner is no longer responsible for everything; its tasks are distributed over several systems.

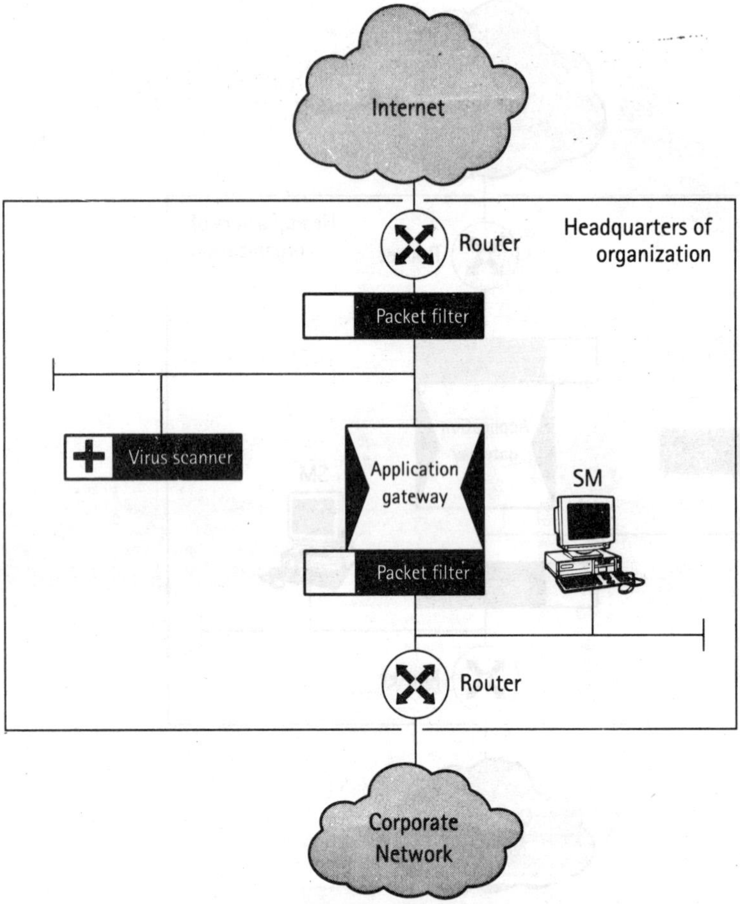

Figure 9-11: Virus scanner in the external screened subnet

Additional Technical, Personnel-related, and Organizational Measures

A single central security component is not sufficient to combat the threat of viruses.

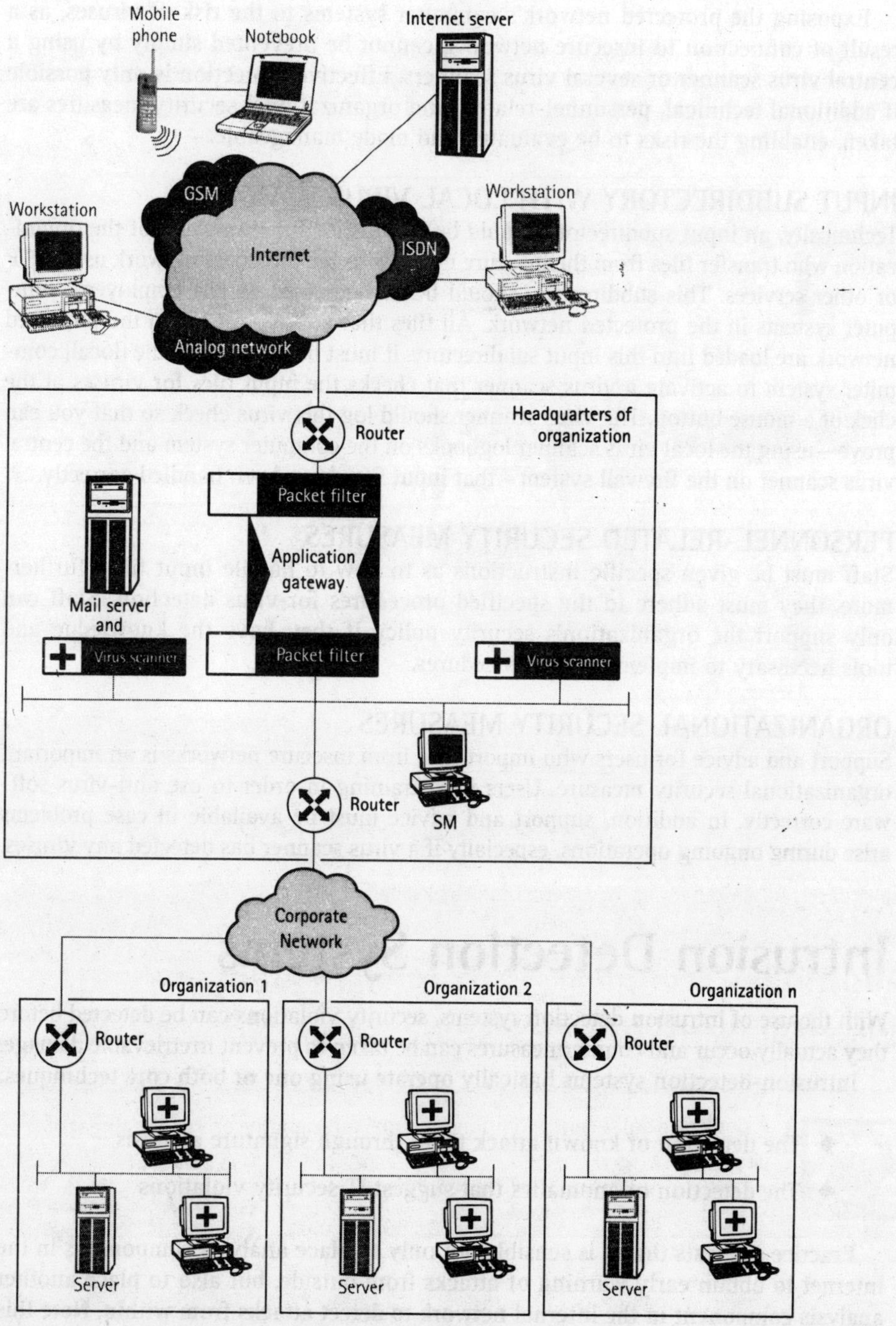

Figure 9-12: Integration of multiple virus scanners

Exposing the protected network's computer systems to the risk of viruses, as a result of connection to insecure networks, cannot be prevented simply by using a central virus scanner or several virus scanners. Effective protection is only possible if additional technical, personnel-related, and organizational security measures are taken, enabling the risks to be evaluated and made manageable.

INPUT SUBDIRECTORY WITH LOCAL VIRUS SCANNER

Technically, an input subdirectory should be established for employees of the organization who transfer files from the insecure network to the protected network using FTP or other services. This subdirectory should be implemented on the employees' computer systems in the protected network. All files that are imported into the protected network are loaded into this input subdirectory. It must be possible on the (local) computer system to activate a virus scanner that checks the input files for viruses at the click of a mouse button. The virus scanner should log this virus check so that you can prove – using the local virus scanner logbooks on the computer system and the central virus scanner on the firewall system – that input files have been handled correctly.

PERSONNEL-RELATED SECURITY MEASURES

Staff must be given specific instructions as to how to handle input files; furthermore, they must adhere to the specified procedures for virus detection. Staff can only support the organization's security policy if they have the knowledge and tools necessary to implement the procedures.

ORGANIZATIONAL SECURITY MEASURES

Support and advice for users who import files from insecure networks is an important organizational security measure. Users need training in order to use anti-virus software correctly. In addition, support and advice must be available in case problems arise during ongoing operations, especially if a virus scanner has detected any viruses.

Intrusion Detection Systems

With the use of intrusion detection systems, security violations can be detected before they actually occur and countermeasures can be taken to prevent irretrievable damage.

Intrusion-detection systems basically operate using one or both core techniques:

- The detection of known attack types through signature analysis
- The detection of anomalies that suggest IT security violations

Practice suggests that it is sensible not only to place analysis components in the Internet to obtain early warning of attacks from outside, but also to place another analysis component in the internal network to detect attacks from within. Note this dual placement illustrated in Figure 9-13.

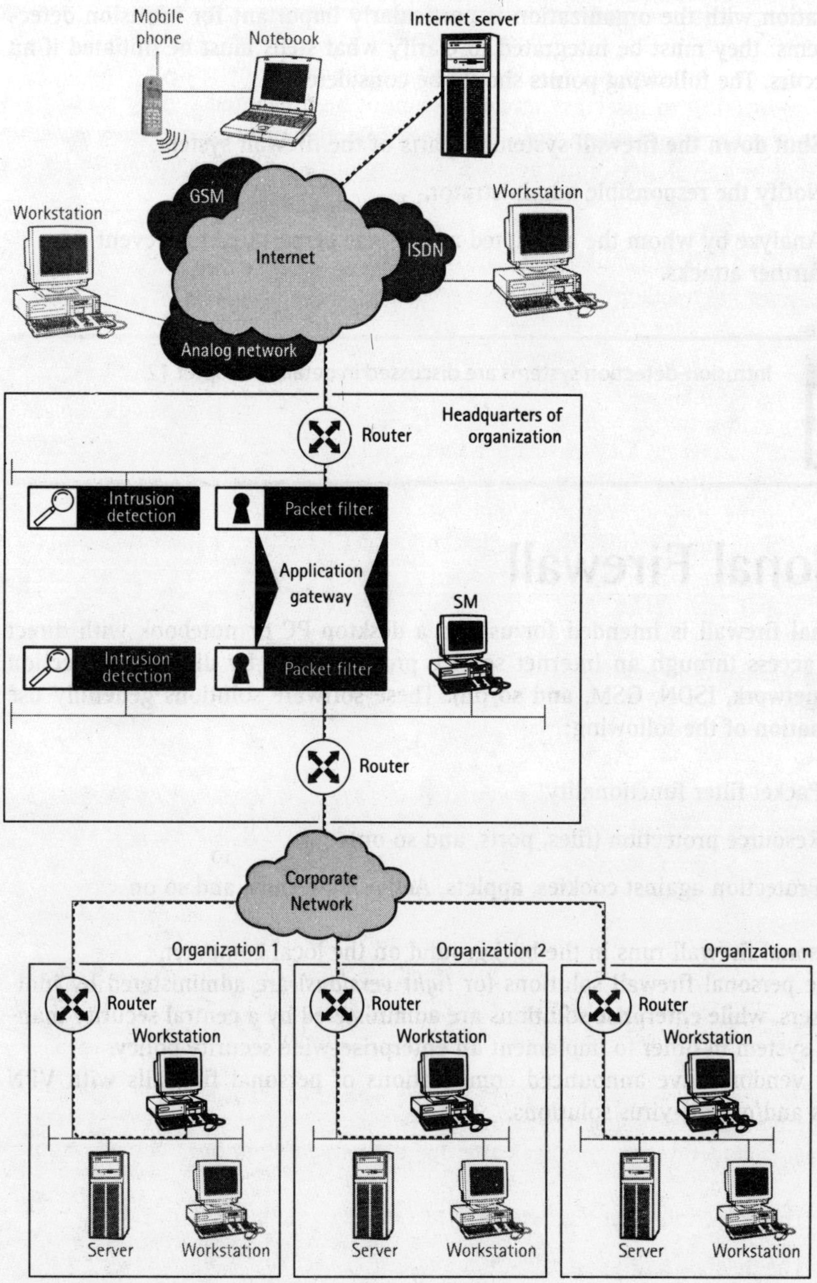

Figure 9-13: Integration of intrusion detection systems

Integration with the organization is particularly important for intrusion detection systems: they must be integrated to clarify what steps must be initiated if an attack occurs. The following points should be considered:

- Shut down the firewall system or parts of the firewall system.
- Notify the responsible administrator.
- Analyze by whom the attempted attack was perpetrated to prevent further attacks.

XREF

Intrusion-detection systems are discussed in detail in Chapter 12.

Personal Firewall

A personal firewall is intended for use on a desktop PC or notebook with direct Internet access through an Internet service provider (ISP) by dial-up connection (analog network, ISDN, GSM, and so on). These software solutions generally use a combination of the following:

- Packet filter functionality
- Resource protection (files, ports, and so on)
- Protection against cookies, applets, ActiveX controls, and so on

A personal firewall runs in the background on the local computer.

Simple personal firewall solutions (or *light versions*) are administered by individual users, while enterprise solutions are administered by a central security management system in order to implement an enterprise-wide security policy.

Many vendors have announced combinations of personal firewalls with VPN solutions and/or anti-virus solutions.

Practical Implementation

You can achieve the maximum amount of security if you equip your computer systems with personal firewalls in addition to operating a central firewall system and other security mechanisms. In this way, comprehensive security is achieved for the organization's resources. The comprehensive security is only achieved if the personal firewalls are installed on all workstations in the organization. This applies to notebooks in mobile workstations, desktop telecommuter workstations, and the workstations inside the organization.

Central Administration

If personal firewalls are managed centrally, organizations can implement their own enterprise-wide security policies simply, cost-effectively, and securely. The administrator can define access rights with reference to specific applications and/or users, and these rights can be monitored with the aid of the personal firewall. All the entries necessary for configuration of the personal firewall in the organization are made centrally and disseminated online to the computer systems.

Personal firewalls help to counteract the increasing vulnerability of electronic assets held on PCs due to the increased use of Internet services. Figure 9-14 illustrates the use of personal firewalls throughout the organization.

XREF

The implementation of personal firewalls is discussed in detail in Chapter 12.

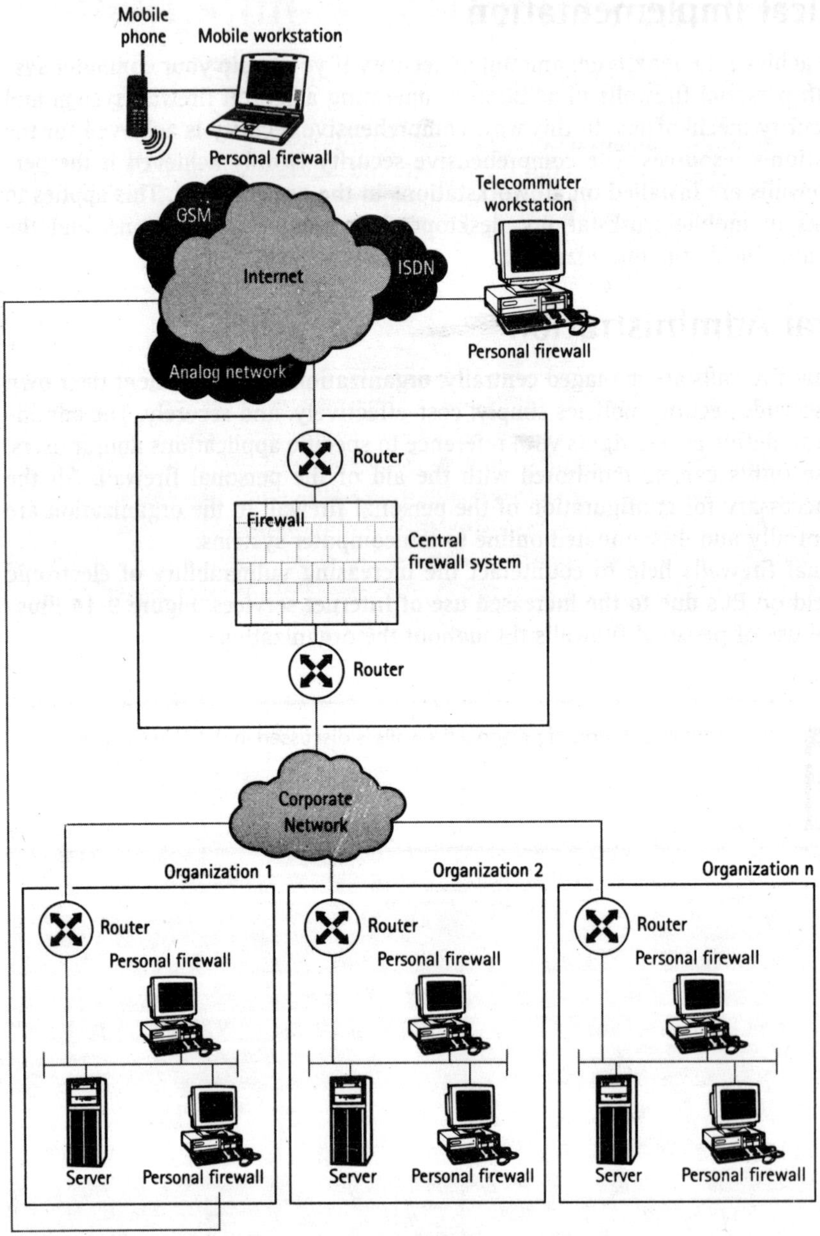

Figure 9-14: Organization with personal firewalls

Application of Firewall Components

The following scenario exemplifies the way firewall components are typically applied in an organization.

ACME Corporation manufactures and sells component parts for automobiles. ACME provides these components directly to the automobile manufacturers, to service repair stations, to third-party installers, and directly to end users. ACME employs salespeople and engineers that travel while selling and working with corporate partners. The sales and engineering personnel must be able to access the corporate network. ACME's vendor relationship requires tight integration between ACME's systems and its vendors and partners. ACME uses a direct order processing system in the form of an extranet that the automobile manufacturers and service organizations can utilize. Authentication is handled with smart cards supplied by ACME. End users can order parts and components from the ACME Web site. Both the ACME Web site and the extranet server access an Oracle server that handles the order processing and inventory status. A Solaris system houses the engineering diagrams accessed by internal engineers, traveling engineers, and engineers from corporate partners such as the automobile manufacturers. The Solaris system contains research and development data and needs to be carefully protected. Figure 9-15 shows the functional components of the ACME network.

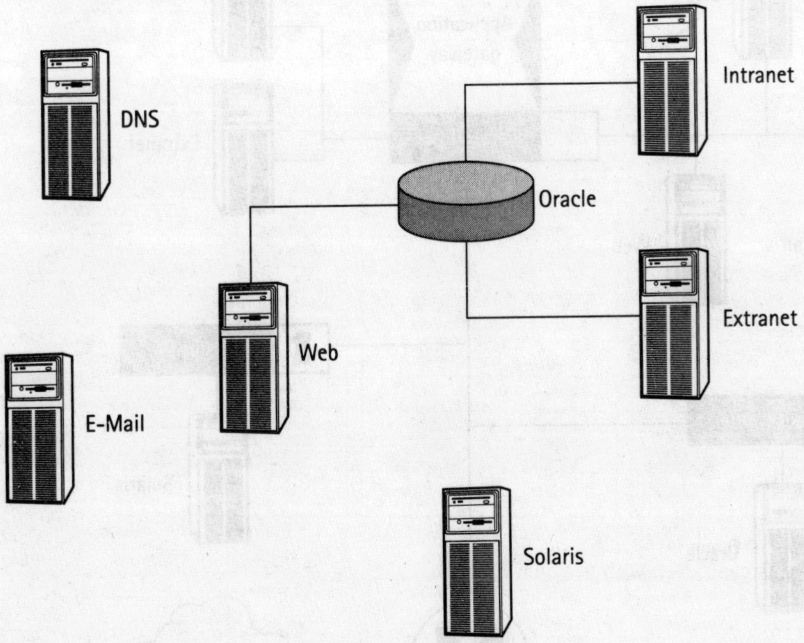

Figure 9-15: Functional components of ACME's network

The first step to achieving security is to provide for access specified as acceptable. Performance is a high priority for the extranet and Internet servers, which need reliable access to the Oracle server. (Remote users, however, should never have direct access to the Oracle server.) The easiest way to prevent direct access is to put the Oracle server on a different network segment and restrict access to Oracle's communications port. Given the high sensitivity of the Solaris server, it should be placed behind a VPN server. The VPN server provides for strong authentication of users accessing the Solaris server. With some of these parameters in place, you can draw up an initial draft of the firewall configuration, shown in Figure 9-16.

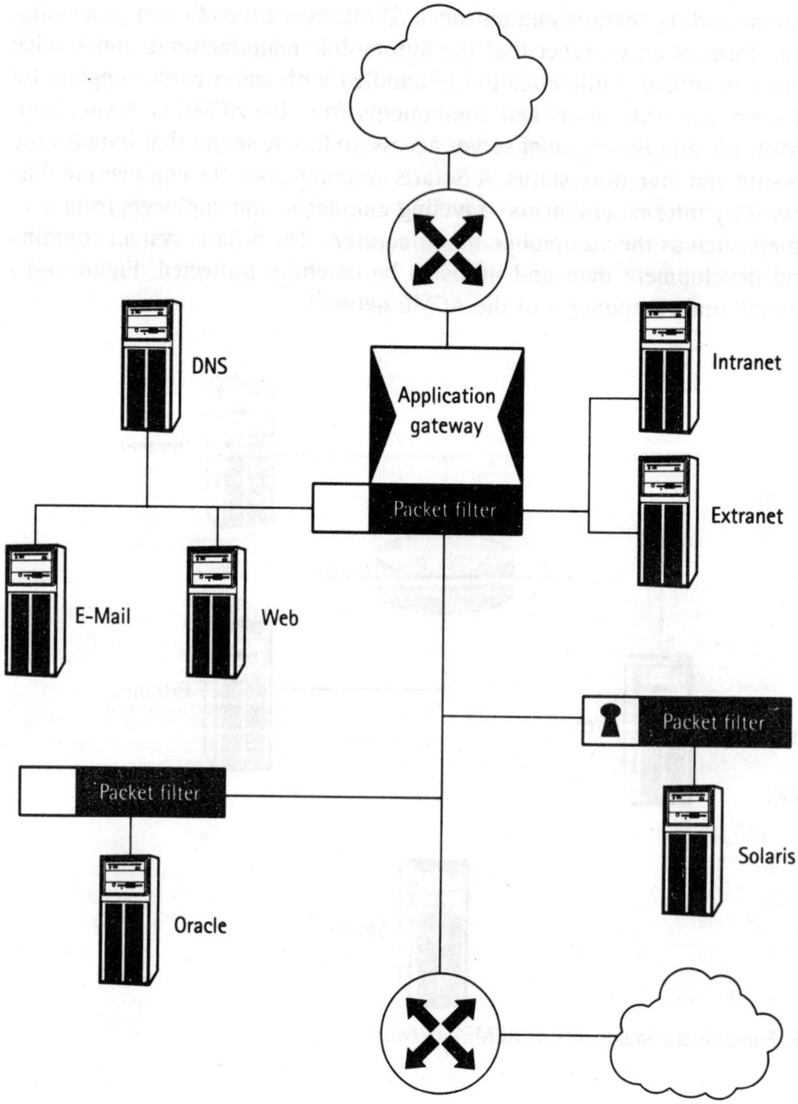

Figure 9-16: Draft of the firewall plan

By documenting and diagramming the configuration, you can more easily spot areas that need additional security measures. An examination of the diagram (Figure 9-16) shows you that it's necessary to put more specific rules in place for the firewall components. Starting at the external router, broad protections such as anti-spoofing and anti-DOS rules can be implemented. Placing the filters at the external router prevents suspect traffic from interfering with the external network's performance or security. Use of broad router filters allows the firewall software rules to be focused on more specific protections, such as application gateways. Distributing the security load helps to maintain performance. It also means that all the protections are not placed in a single failure point. The broad router filter rules would look something like this:

```
DENY SOURCE NET 127.0.0.0 MASK 255.0.0.0
DENY SOURCE NET 10.0.0.0 MASK 255.0.0.0
DENY SOURCE NET 172.16.0.0 MASK 255.224.0.0
DENY SOURCE NET 192.168.0.0 MASK 255.255.0.0
DENY SOURCE NET x.x.x.x MASK 255.255.255.x
DENY SOURCE ADDRESS = DESTINATION ADDRESS
```

NOTE: x.x.x.x and 255.255.255.x are the ARIN IP address ranges assigned to ACME.

The filters apply to external traffic entering the network. Because there is no valid reason for a loopback, reserved internal address, or ACME address to arrive from outside the network, packets with these elements indicate that a router is malfunctioning (spewing internal packets, which is unlikely), or someone is attempting IP spoofing. Neither a broken router nor IP spoofing should be allowed to affect the organization's network.

Several specific rules must be implemented on the firewall system itself:

```
ALLOW UDP 53 (DNS) to DNS HOST
ALLOW SOURCE UDP 53 from DNS HOST
ALLOW TCP 25 (SMTP) to MAIL HOST
ALLOW TCP 110 (POP) to MAIL HOST
ALLOW SOURCE TCP 25 from MAIL HOST
ALLOW SOURCE TCP 100 from MAIL HOST
ALLOW TCP 80 (HTTP) to WEB HOST
ALLOW TCP 443 (SSL) to WEB HOST
ALLOW SOURCE TCP 80 from WEB HOST
```

(continued)

```
ALLOW SOURCE TCP 443 from WEB HOST
ALLOW TCP 1521 (ORACLE) from WEB HOST to ORACLE HOST
ALLOW SOURCE TCP 1521 from ORACLE HOST to WEB HOST
ALLOW IPSEC to VPN HOST
ALLOW SOURCE IPSEC from VPN HOST
ALLOW AUTHENTICATED TCP 80 to INTRANET HOST
ALLOW AUTHENTICATED TCP 443 to INTRANET HOST
ALLOW AUTHENTICATED TCP 80 to EXTRANET HOST
ALLOW AUTHENTICATED TCP 443 to EXTRANET HOST
ALLOW SOURCE TCP 80 from EXTRANET HOST
ALLOW SOURCE TCP 443 from EXTRANET HOST
ALLOW TCP 1521 from EXTRANET HOST to ORACLE HOST
ALLOW SOURCE TCP 1521 from ORACLE HOST to EXTRANET HOST
```

Notice that traffic is being examined in both directions, to and from each host. All possible types of traffic allowed have been covered in the rules. All other network traffic types are discarded.

This ruleset does not allow general Internet connectivity for employees. Because the parameters of the allowable Internet access have not been defined, the Internet access rules can't be implemented yet. Options include implementing a specific ruleset in the central firewall or another route for employee connectivity to the Internet through a separate firewall. Both approaches present certain advantages and disadvantages. Use of a separate firewall allows for separation of rules. Reduced complexity usually yields increased security. Internal employee Internet connectivity can produce large traffic consumption and fluctuations. These variances can make it difficult to balance performance for external users. The primary disadvantage to a separate firewall is cost.

Filters used to control outbound traffic are termed *egress filters*. The main function of egress filters is to complicate an attacker's efforts to extend the scope of hosts that have been partially compromised. Egress filters prevent an attacker that manages to infiltrate the Web server through a CGI attack from transferring tools into the system via FTP or TFTP. Egress filters are a practical necessity due to the probability of an Application-level compromise by a bug in the Web server or another application server.

The rules for the packet filter in front of the Oracle server are straightforward:

```
ALLOW TCP 1521 to ORACLE HOST from WEB HOST
ALLOW TCP 1521 to ORACLE HOST from EXTRANET HOST
ALLOW SOURCE TCP 1521 from ORACLE HOST to WEB HOST
ALLOW SOURCE TCP 1521 from ORACLE HOST to EXTRANET HOST
```

The VPN server is configured to allow only authenticated VPN connections. The Solaris server can then be accessed through the VPN tunnel.

As an additional precaution, all of the systems behind the central firewall except the VPN server are configured to use internal (RFC 1918) addresses. Static network address translation (NAT) is configured for the hosts. Access to the mail server and DNS server – as well as Web, intranet, and extranet servers – is provided by application gateways.

After the rulesets have been configured, several additional steps are required. Authorized users must be added to the central firewall, VPN server, and individual hosts. All of the individual hosts must be locked down at the operating system and application levels. Intrusion detection should be implemented at both the network and host levels. Virus protection should be installed on the mail server and on the central firewall as appropriate. System and application logs should be configured to flow to a central logging system. This central logging system can also be the management station for the central firewall system. If all of these measures are put in place, you will also need to add rules to allow the logging and IDS traffic to flow to the appropriate systems.

The final security diagram is shown in Figure 9-17. Although somewhat complex and difficult to implement, this firewall is sustainable. It also results in a very high degree of security.

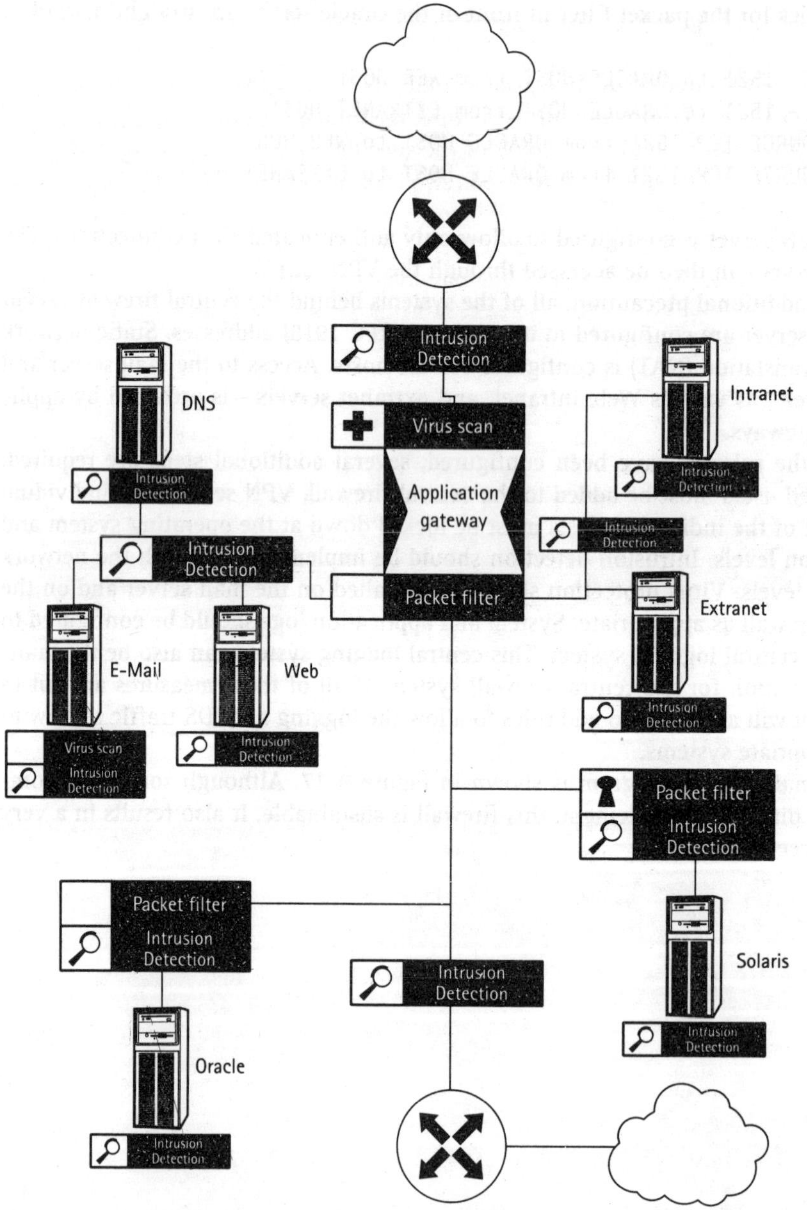

Figure 9-17: Final security diagram

Summary

When you start taking all of the various components possible in a firewall system and building the actual firewall infrastructure, the implementation quickly becomes complex. This chapter addresses many of the specific security challenges that need to be considered when implementing a firewall in an organization. Hopefully, you noticed that most of the solutions to challenges are very modular. All security solutions have trade-offs (performance, security, complexity, and so on). The best security is achieved by using several, smaller layers of protection together (packet filters, application gateways, and so on), rather than placing them all in a single system.

Chapter 10

Firewall Security Policy

A FIREWALL SYSTEM is not a product that automatically guarantees security. A firewall system can only help you achieve the desired level of security if it employs the following guidelines:

- Based on a firewall security policy
- Integrated in the organization's IT security concept
- Correctly installed
- Correctly administered

This chapter uses examples to describe the form a firewall security policy should take and what additional security measures are necessary for the operation of a firewall system. Naturally, security measures related to correct installation or administration cannot be considered, because they depend on the particular product used. Nor is integration of the firewall security policy into an IT security concept covered, because the integration is organization-specific.

Appendix D contains a sample security policy using several of the components from this chapter.

Firewall Security Policy

A firewall security policy is essential to the secure operation of a firewall system. A firewall system does not automatically create security; rather, it provides the opportunity to make the interface between an insecure network and a protected network secure. If a firewall system is installed without a previously developed security concept, a false sense of security may result. Administrators often mistakenly assume that everything is protected after a firewall system has been installed. This assumption is even more erroneous if there is no accurate knowledge of the existing network topology. If the network topology is not known, for example, you can't assume that only one connection to the Internet or to other insecure networks exists.

A company's firewall security policy should be tailored to the protection requirements of the IT systems used and must form part of an existing, organization-wide security policy. The definition of a firewall security policy can affect existing guidelines and provisions in the general security policy, which must also be considered.

The firewall security policy defines the security objectives to be met through the use of the firewall system and describes the resources to be protected. It determines the communications requirements and the services permitted for transmission. The firewall security policy is, like an organization-wide security policy, tailored to the specific organization and business sector (medicine, banking, insurance, energy supply, unions, staff councils, and so on).

Security Objectives

As a first step, you must define the security objectives to be achieved with the use of a firewall system. Use the objectives presented here as guidelines, not hard-and-fast rules.

- **Access control at the Network level.** Only connections with defined subnets, networks, or individual computer systems are allowed. Access (including by attackers) is not possible from non-permitted subnets, networks, or computer systems.
- **Access control at the user level.** All users who want to communicate through the firewall system are identified and authenticated.
- **Access rights administration.** Services and protocols that a user may utilize are specified, including at what times a user may have use of them.
- **Control at the Application layer.** Users are only granted access to the commands related to particular services, such as FTP or HTTP, that are necessary for their specific tasks.
- **Separation of services.** Particularly risky services (for example, *Sendmail*) are only made available to the insecure network in combination with separate auxiliary routines having restricted functionality.
- **Securing evidence and log analysis.** Connection data and security-relevant events are logged and can be analyzed for the purposes of identifying any security violations and preserving evidence of user actions.
- **Alarm function.** The alarm function reports security-relevant events to Security Management for a rapid response, enabling appropriate measures to be initiated.

- **Hiding the internal network structure.** You want to conceal the structure of the protected network from the insecure network. You should not be able to tell from the insecure network how many computer systems are in the protected network (10, 100, 1,000, or 10,000, for example), or what types of computer resources are involved (for example, PCs or mainframes).
- **Message confidentiality.** You should not be able to read plain text messages that are exchanged through distributed firewall systems with a communications partner. The information's confidentiality is ensured through encryption. This encryption also prevents man-in-the-middle attacks.

In addition, a firewall system should accomplish the following:

- Be resistant to attacks
- Perform accounting (IP-and user-oriented)
- Perform network address translation (NAT)

Description of the Resources to Be Protected

Listing the resources to be protected in the firewall security policy serves to document information about all the computer systems and data that need protection so they can be taken into consideration. Resources requiring protection include the following:

- Computer systems
- Communications equipment
- Data
- Printers

Definition of Communications Requirements

The communications requirements determine the manner in which communications should proceed between the insecure and protected networks through the firewall system. At the outset, the following questions should be answered:

- If any files have to be transmitted, are they going from the protected network to the insecure network, or vice versa?
- What information may be exchanged through the firewall system from the insecure network to the protected network, and vice versa?

- What information should the firewall system conceal (for example, the internal network structure and/or the names of the users in the protected network)?
- What authentication procedures are to be used within the protected network or for the firewall system (for example, one-time passwords or security tokens)?
- How are insecure networks to be accessed (for example, internal network → firewall system → Internet Service Provider → Internet; or internal network → firewall system → modem server → analog/ISDN network)?
- How will the internal, protected network be accessed (for example, Internet → Internet Service Provider → firewall system → internal network; or analog/ISDN network → modem server → firewall system → internal network)?
- What throughput is to be expected (for example, 64 Kbps or 2 Mbps or 34 Mbps)?
- What are the availability requirements (for example, continuous or only during particular hours; daily or only Mondays to Fridays)?

Definition of Services and Applications

The communications requirements determine which services or applications should be supported by the firewall system:

- Simple Mail Transport Protocol (SMTP), for sending and receiving e-mail
- File Transfer Protocol (FTP), for transferring files between computer systems
- HyperText Transfer Protocol (HTTP), for the World Wide Web
- Telnet, for access to remote computer systems using terminal emulation
- Network News Transport Protocol (NNTP), for reading and posting in newsgroups

For example, services include access to modems over which remote maintenance can be performed from the workstation in the protected network or that allow external companies maintenance access to systems in the internal network.

A services checklist is used to define which communications direction needs to be supported for the services and applications (refer to Table 10-1).

The following table represents the relevant direction of communications by the distinctions, Outbound Allowed (communications from the protected network to the insecure network) and Inbound Allowed (communications from the insecure network to the protected network), and employs the following symbols:

- Permitted communications are denoted by a plus sign (+).
- Communications that are not permitted are denoted by a minus sign (–).
- A zero (0) denotes communication that is only allowed with logging and strong authentication.

TABLE 10-1 SIMPLE SERVICES CHECKLIST

Service	Outbound Allowed	Inbound Allowed
E-mail	+	+
WWW	+	–
FTP	+	0
Telnet	+	0
News	+	+
Modem	+	0

In addition to permitting services and applications, the security policy can determine when a user is allowed to access certain services or use a particular application. The working hours can be considered when drawing up such filter rules so that non-permitted access outside of working hours can be excluded.

Set the default to disallow all unnecessary services and applications.

INTERNAL USERS

A user on the internal protected network should be able to use only those firewall system services required for his work. The services assigned to a particular user can be specified in communications profiles to significantly reduce the effort of determining the communications requirements of individual users. Table 10-2 shows an expanded service permission checklist with four different permission groups to accommodate a broader range of employee access needs.

Table 10-2 DETAILED SERVICES CHECKLIST

Service	Minimal User Permissions	Standard User Permissions	IT Department Permissions	Maximum User Permissions
E-mail	+	+	+	+
WWW	–	+	–	+
FTP	–	+	–	+
Telnet	–	–	–	+
News	–	+	–	+
Time	7 a.m. to 7 p.m.	7 a.m. to 7 p.m.	24 hours	24 hours
Days	Mon–Fri	Mon–Fri	Mon–Sat	Mon–Sat

In large organizations, a more detailed specification of communications profiles will be necessary.

Essentially, the following principle should apply: Everything that is not explicitly allowed is forbidden!

EXTERNAL USERS

External users are either employees of the organization who need to access current data or read their e-mail while on the road, or service company employees who need to access computer systems located in the protected network for maintenance purposes. The communications requirements from the insecure network must be carefully selected and specified, because every access to the protected network increases the need for protection.

For example, availability and performance requirements may dictate that employees performing maintenance have access to specific services to readily achieve the necessary performance and availability. The necessary work is performed from the insecure network using Telnet or FTP access and is logged.

The firewall security policy should specify further criteria, such as the following:

- Who is responsible for determining the communications profiles?
- Who is responsible for assigning communications profiles or individual services to users?
- Who is responsible for administering and implementing the filter rules?
- What information is logged in the firewall system?

- Who analyzes the logged data and how frequently should this be done?
- What logged data should be analyzed?
- What alarms should be generated and to whom should they be sent?
- What should happen if the firewall system reports an attack? Actions may include the following:
  - Terminating the connection between the insecure and protected networks
  - Deciding whether the attacker should be prosecuted
  - Informing others, such as management, the firewall system vendor, or CERT, of the attack
- How can you ensure that communications between the insecure and protected networks always pass through the firewall system? Solutions may include the following:
  - Organizational instructions to all users
  - Appointment of a person responsible for checking whether any new access routes have been created
- Who checks regularly or sporadically that the security policy is being adhered to?

Additional Security Measures

The actual firewall product consists of software and hardware. Besides the firewall security rules, you must consider additional security measures in the following areas to ensure the secure operation of the firewall system:

- Infrastructural measures
- Organizational measures
- Personnel-related measures

Infrastructural Measures

The following infrastructural measures contribute to the overall security of firewall operation:

- Access-controlled room. All the components of the firewall system should be set up in locked, access-controlled rooms, preventing unauthorized persons from disabling or tampering with the technical security mechanisms.

- **An uninterruptible power supply (UPS)** should be installed to bridge any short-duration power failure, or at least to maintain the power supply long enough to power down any connected computer systems in an orderly manner. The majority of power failures are fixed within five to ten minutes; a bridging time of approximately ten to fifteen minutes would leave a five-minute reserve to allow the connected firewall system to be powered down. Most modern UPS devices offer computer interfaces that can initiate an automatic shutdown after a specified period. The time interval is determined with reference to the actual requirements of the firewall system and the capacity of the UPS. As an alternative to a local UPS, the power supply can be drawn from an existing uninterruptible source – through connection to a central UPS, for example.
- **Protected cable routing.** The electrical leads (to the protected and the insecure networks) should be arranged so that they cannot be physically bridged outside of the restricted access room.
- **Through good documentation and clear identification** of all wiring in the firewall system, wiring errors that would allow someone to bypass the firewall system can be avoided. Documentation is also needed for effective problem correction, successful troubleshooting, and system maintenance. The quality of this documentation depends on its completeness, currency, and readability.
- If the firewall system is coupled to an existing network management system, the management system can retrieve certain information about the firewall system. The firewall system can also report information to the network management system. This includes status messages and alarms triggered when a security-critical event occurs. Because network management systems usually operate continuously – 24 hours a day, 7 days a week – coupling of the firewall system to the network management system increases the availability of the entire IT system.

Organizational Measures

The secure operation of a firewall system depends on the fact that certain organizational security measures are in place. These measures relate to technical implementation, security management, users, and general security:

TECHNICAL IMPLEMENTATION

Some organizational measures can be accomplished by technical means.

- **External access.** Additional, external access to the protected network, through a modem server, for example, should be treated as an access from the insecure network. Position an access server with connected modems on the external side of the firewall system in a configuration that allows access from the modem server to computer systems in the protected network only over specific authorized protocols such as Telnet. The allowed protocols can be logged and secured using an application proxy in the firewall.

Clear guidelines known to all users must specify in detail that no external access that involves bypassing the firewall system may be set up.

- **Secure arrangement of other components near the firewall system.** In addition to the installation and operation of the firewall system, other components that serve communications between the protected and insecure networks must be arranged in a secure manner. These components include the following:
  - Internet and intranet servers for the provision of information to internal or external users
  - Mail servers
  - DNS servers
  - Modem servers
  - Central virus scanners

SECURITY MANAGEMENT

Simply putting technical rules in place is insufficient to sustain good security. Several tasks need to be defined and assigned to specific individuals or groups to make sure that security is maintained in the organization. Also, specify to the users what they should and shouldn't do to maintain security.

ALLOCATION OF RESPONSIBILITIES FOR THE FIREWALL SYSTEM Responsibilities for the firewall system must be clearly defined and separated. In particular, technical and operational responsibilities for firewall use must be specified. The technical manager is responsible for drawing up technical requirements for the firewall system. Technical responsibility normally lies with the IT security management, which prepares a firewall security concept based on the defined firewall security policy. Operational responsibility, on the other hand, covers the secure operation and monitoring of the firewall system. This task is performed by the security administrator, who is responsible for the correct configuration of new users of the Security Management module.

RIGHTS OF ACCESS TO SECURITY MANAGEMENT The technical manager (IT security management) specifies the access rights of users to the Security Management module in the firewall security concept. The access rights determine which of the security management's functions an administrator may use. The operational manager (security administrator) configures the functions assigned to the administrator. Such functions include the roles of operator, auditor, and data entry operator. Only essential access rights – in other words, those access rights that are necessary to execute tasks related to each role – should be granted. The responsible party arranges and documents any changes to access rights. The documentation must specify the following:

- Which functions are granted which access rights, bearing in mind the separation of functions
- Which administrator performs which function
- What access rights an administrator is given
- Whether any conflicts occur in connection with the granting of access rights. Conflicts may arise if, for example, an administrator performs two functions that clash, or because it is not possible to separate certain access rights.

If permitted by security management, the security administrator activates appropriate logging functions for the purposes of creating an audit trail. Activities relevant for an audit trail are successful and failed login and logoff processes, system error messages, and unauthorized attempts at access.

You also need to have a verification process in place to determine employee access rights. Employees will often change roles within an organization and, of course, employees are brought on and leave a company, as well. By establishing a verification procedure, usually with the human resources department in a company, you can avoid an employee falsely claiming he should have access to data or systems he should not.

CHECKING LOGGED DATA Logging security-relevant events is only effective as a security measure if the logged data is also analyzed. Therefore, an auditor must review the logged data at regular intervals. If it is not technically possible to establish the role of an independent auditor for logged data, an administrator can evaluate the logged data. In this case, the activities of the administrator himself will be difficult to monitor and the results of the evaluation should be presented to the IT security officer, the IT officer, or another person appointed as a safeguard.

Regular review and subsequent deletion of logged data also prevents the logs from growing to an inordinate size. As logged data usually contains personal data, take steps to ensure that this data is only used for the purposes of monitoring data protection, data backup, or to safeguard proper operations.

The following evaluation questions can be used to identify possible security flaws, attempts at tampering, and irregularities using logged data:

- Are people logging on and off outside of office hours (suggesting possible tampering attempts)?
- Have many incorrect attempts at login occurred (suggesting possible attempts to guess passwords)?

- Have there been clusters of attempts at unauthorized access (suggesting possible tampering attempts)?
- Are there any strikingly long time intervals during which no logged data has been recorded (suggesting that log records may have been deleted)?
- Is there too much logged data (it is difficult to find irregularities in log files that are excessively long)?
- Are there any strikingly long time intervals during which no apparent logins or logoffs have occurred (suggesting that logging off is not taking place consistently at the end of work)?

Use an analysis tool when regularly analyzing extensive log files. This tool should allow selection of evaluation criteria and highlight particularly critical entries, such as multiple failed attempts at login.

XREF

For more information on logging analysis tools, refer to Chapter 12.

GATHERING INFORMATION ABOUT SECURITY WEAKNESSES IN THE FIREWALL SYSTEM Keep informed of newly discovered security weaknesses. If new security loopholes are publicly disclosed, either the necessary organizational and administrative measures must be taken or additional security hardware or software must be used in order to eliminate the flaws. Good sources of information include the following:

- **Manufacturers or distributors of firewall systems.** These companies inform registered customers of security loopholes that have come to light in their systems and provide corrected variants of the firewall system or patches. This service can be specified in a maintenance contract.
- **Computer Emergency Response Teams (CERTs).** Several groups exist to assist companies in responding to security problems. These groups publish significant amounts of information about current security threats and how to avoid them. The most well known is at Carnegie-Mellon (`www.cert.org`). The Federal Bureau of Investigation (FBI) also maintains a very proactive group through the National Infrastructure Protection Center (NIPC) at `www.nipc.gov`.
- **Internet newsgroups (covering manufacturers, systems, and security).** Almost every major vendor maintains specific Web sites and newsgroups to provide companies with the latest information about security issues in their products. Several independent groups also host discussion groups

specific to security. The two most notable independent security groups are BugTraq (www.securityfocus.com) and SANS (www.sans.org).

- **IT technical journals.** Many companies produce technical journals devoted to security. Tech Republic (www.techrepublic.com) and Computer Security Institute (www.gocsi.com) produce a couple of the better-known technical journals.

REACTION TO VIOLATIONS OF THE SECURITY POLICY Determining in advance how to respond to security policy violations ensures a rapid and effective response in the event of an actual emergency.

The type and origin of the violation must be investigated, appropriate damage-containing measures must be taken, and any lessons for future damage prevention should be formulated. Usually an incident report is created detailing how a violation occurred and what steps are being taken to prevent such violations from occurring again. The specific actions that must be carried out depend both on the type of violation and the responsible party.

Clarify in advance the person or persons responsible for gathering information about known security weaknesses or for disseminating information about security weaknesses that have occurred in other organizations. Make sure that any other offices that are affected are informed as quickly as possible.

THE SECURITY ADMINISTRATOR'S OBLIGATION TO MAKE DATA BACKUPS Because security is never 100 percent effective, violations have to be expected. Backups are one of the most important security measures available because they allow for recovery in the event of various security breaches, such as data being modified or destroyed. Given the importance of backups, the security policy should clearly state the obligation of appropriate staff to maintain the necessary backups. Regular reminders and attempts to motivate staff to carry out data backups of the firewall system should take place.

USERS

Security at an organization will never be achieved without the cooperation of the users. The security policy must spell out users' responsibilities in helping to maintain an organization's security.

NON-DISCLOSURE OF SECURITY TOKENS AND PASSWORDS If security tokens are used for authentication to the firewall system, the security of access rights administration will largely depend on their secure use. Passwords must be kept secret, and security tokens must not be passed to individuals to whom they were not issued. Users must be made aware that they are responsible for their passwords and security tokens and can be held accountable if third parties use them to cause damage.

SUPPORT AND ADVICE FOR USERS WHO COMMUNICATE THROUGH THE FIREWALL SYSTEM The use of a firewall system requires that users be trained in its proper use. In addition to training, support and advice must be available to users to help them during ongoing operations should any problems occur. For example, users may require help learning a new way to use the services over the firewall system.

Larger organizations can benefit from a central office set up to support users who communicate through the firewall system.

GENERAL SECURITY MEASURES

A few miscellaneous items, such as firewall maintenance and employee notification of logging, must also be addressed in the security policy.

PROCEDURES FOR MAINTENANCE AND REPAIR WORK ON THE FIREWALL SYSTEM Implementing proper procedures for performing maintenance work is a particularly important preventative measure to keep the firewall system in working order. Maintenance work should be carried out by trusted personnel or external companies that have passed a stringent background check.

If external parties carry out maintenance and repair work, draw up procedures that cover how the parties will be supervised. In particular, someone with the relevant technical skills should supervise the work. This person will be able to assess whether non-authorized actions have taken place (for example, unauthorized access rights from the external network).

Before and after maintenance and repair work, the following points should be considered:

- The affected staff members should be informed that the work will be taking place.
- Maintenance technicians must identify themselves on demand.
- Maintenance technicians should be granted only access rights necessary for their work, and these rights must be revoked or deleted following completion of the work.
- As a precautionary measure after the maintenance or repair work has been carried out, you may want to change the passwords, depending on the depth to which the maintenance personnel have penetrated the system.
- The maintenance work must be documented (include such data as scope of work, results, time spent, and the name of the maintenance technician).

NOTIFICATION OF MONITORING Logging is a security measure that also allows management to monitor the behavior and performance of users and, therefore, may require the notification of employees.

Personnel-Related Measures

Personnel-related security measures can affect security management as well as users.

SECURITY MANAGEMENT

The individuals responsible for maintaining security in a company also have the greatest ability to bypass security. Because of the higher risk to an organization from the security personnel, extra precautions should be taken. Security staff will also require special authorizations from company management in order to properly respond to security incidents.

PROFILE OF THE SECURITY ADMINISTRATOR The security administrator must possess in-depth knowledge of IT security in general and firewall systems specifically. Furthermore, he must update and extend this knowledge on an ongoing basis. Attendance at training courses on the configuration and secure administration of the firewall system offered by relevant vendors or distributors is recommended. The security administrator must be able to correctly assess error messages and alarms in order to take appropriate countermeasures. Where external personnel have intervened in the firewall system, the administrator must be able to reproduce the work that has been carried out.

SELECTION OF A TRUSTWORTHY ADMINISTRATOR AND DEPUTY A high degree of trust must be placed in the firewall system's administrators and their deputies because they have wide-ranging powers. They are in a position to access all stored data, to change it, and to grant permissions. The potential for taking improper advantage of their privileged position is considerable.

Carefully select the personnel used in these roles, and regularly remind them that their authorizations may only be used for necessary administrative tasks.

DEPUTIZING ARRANGEMENTS Deputizing arrangements are aimed at ensuring that tasks can continue to be performed in the event of either predictable staff absences, such as vacations or business trips, or unpredictable absences, such as illnesses, accidents, or a termination of employment. Draw up arrangements before such events occur, with specifications covering who will stand in for whom, in what capacity, and with what competencies. Deputizing arrangements are particularly important with firewall systems because they require specialized knowledge. It is often difficult on short notice to sufficiently train staff that lacks this specialized knowledge.

Adhere to the following basic conditions in the deputizing arrangements:

- The procedural or project status must be adequately documented.
- The deputy must be trained. The loss of persons who, due to their specialist knowledge, cannot be replaced in the short term signifies a serious risk to normal operations. In this case, deputy training is particularly important.
- Specify the delegation of tasks in case a replacement is required.
- The deputy should be given the necessary access authorization only during the replacement.

- If, in exceptional cases, appointing or training a competent in-house deputy for a particular role is not possible, have a contingency plan to employ external resources.

CONTROLLED PROCEDURES COVERING STAFF LEAVING THE ORGANIZATION If a user terminates his employment with the organization, all the authorizations that give the user access to the firewall system must be revoked or deleted. This rule also applies to external access authorizations through data communications equipment.

USERS

Several security dos and don'ts apply to all users, not just security personnel.

INSTRUCTIONS FOR THE USE OF INTERNET SERVICES Draw up organizational instructions for users who access Internet services. These instructions should address the behavior of users who take part in discussion forums and newsgroups, and the handling of files received from such sources prior to use on their own systems.

A user's personal opinion within a discussion forum may be interpreted as a statement by his company due to the nature of the e-mail address (for example, remarks made by `smith@company-xyz.com` could be viewed as statements issued by the XYZ Corporation). This could result in various problems for the organization, such as legal liability, libel, and tarnished reputation.

Anti-virus scanning must be executed on all downloaded files.

Where WWW browsers are used, users must disable the Java, JavaScript, and ActiveX options because they allow remote servers to execute potentially malicious code on the user's systems.

INFORMATION TO USERS REGARDING THE LOGGING OF FIREWALL DATA Inform users that their connections through the firewall system could be logged. The reason for logging should also be explained, so that it is understood and accepted by the users. Informing the users will also achieve a warning effect that may protect against potential abuse.

RAISING USER AWARENESS OF THE POSSIBLE DANGERS IN USING THE INTERNET Inform users of the risks associated with an Internet connection. Raising user awareness like this can prevent the circumvention of the firewall system. It may also deter users from establishing an unprotected connection to the Internet simply for reasons of convenience.

SECURITY TRAINING The overwhelming majority of damaging incidents arise through carelessness. To counter such incidents, each user must be motivated to use IT assets with care. Training on security measures should cover the following subjects:

- **Sensitization to IT security.** Inform every user that IT security is essential. A suitable first step for introducing staff to the subject is to make them aware that the organization and their job, depends on the smooth functioning of IT systems. In addition, the value of information should be highlighted, especially with regard to confidentiality, integrity, and availability. These awareness-enhancing activities should be repeated periodically and possibly supplemented by practical information – for example, through in-house circulars.
- **User-specific IT security measures.** Communicate the IT security measures that have been devised in a firewall security concept that are to be implemented by individual users. This part of the training effort is very important because many IT security measures can only be applied effectively after adequate training and motivation (for example, a central modem pool).
- **Precautions against social engineering.** Inform users of the dangers of social engineering. Typical attacks that attempt to gain confidential information by targeting individuals should be explained, along with the relevant methods of protection. As social engineering often involves the pretense of a false identity, users should be regularly instructed to check the identity of communications partners and to avoid providing confidential information over the telephone.

Contingency Plans

Despite the best efforts, security incidents will occur. By anticipating and planning for security breaches, an organization is better able to respond quickly to problems. The increased response speed directly translates to helping to mitigate damages and reduce the cost of violations.

SPECIFICATION OF AVAILABILITY REQUIREMENTS

Specify availability requirements for the firewall system and the services provided through the firewall. In the event of the firewall system's failure, an overview plan of the availability requirements will enable those in responsible positions to quickly determine at what point an emergency exists. This forms the basis for investigation and configuration of backup options.

BACKUP OPTIONS

If the availability requirements for particular services are especially high, provide backup facilities that satisfy them. For example, during an emergency, a computer system in the protected network may need direct access from a vendor. Any physical, technical, personnel, or infrastructural requirements for responding to security incidents should be worked out and addressed in the security policy. Having plans for obtaining and connecting necessary spare equipment can save huge amounts of time during a crisis.

Conceptual Limitations of a Central Firewall System

Firewall systems providing security services for communications on the Internet and in intranets exact the implementation of very complex technical security measures. Nevertheless, even elaborate firewall systems cannot guarantee 100 percent security.

This section discusses several factors that must be considered when using firewall systems.

Back Doors

A firewall system protects only the communications links that pass through it. Any backdoor communications interfaces that bypass the central firewall system render the system ineffective. The Common Point of Trust concept is based on the assumption that no other links exist between the insecure network and the protected network. Achieving a common point of trust requires appropriate security measures that relate both to the personnel and technical structure within the company.

Internal Attacks

A central firewall system provides security services aimed at placing a barrier between the insecure network and the protected network, and at controlling the communications traffic between these networks. However, the firewall system itself provides only modest protection against internal attacks. Countering internal attacks requires implementing additional security mechanisms, such as personal firewalls and/or intrusion detection systems.

Attacks at the Data Level

A firewall system per se cannot detect attacks at the data level in the area of permitted communications. Such attacks include the sending of malware, such as e-mail attachments, downloads from the Web, Java applets, and ActiveX controls.

Attacks that are implemented via the contents of application data cannot be warded off solely with the security functions of a firewall system. The complexity of applications such as WWW servers is so great that, even with communications security equipment such as firewall systems, it is not possible to achieve 100 percent security against attacks oriented towards application data.

Correct Security Policy and Implementation

A firewall system can only provide security services that are configured. Develop a security policy that identifies the resources in the protected network that require a high protection requirement (computer systems, communications facilities, data, and so on), and that specifies how they should be protected. The security policy must also define how the security mechanisms for maintaining secure operation of a firewall system are periodically reviewed.

Further questions that illustrate important aspects of a security policy include the following:

- Who is responsible for determining the communications profile?
- Who is responsible for issuing the communications profile or assigning individual services to the users?
- Who is responsible for the administration and implementation of the filter rules?
- What information will be logged on the firewall system?
- Who analyzes the log data? When?
- What should happen when an attack over the firewall system is detected?

The Man-in-the-Middle Attack

Firewall systems are normally security components that are inserted into the communications interfaces and, from there, provide security services independent of other IT systems (computer systems, routers, and so on).

A workstation is allowed controlled access over the insecure network through the firewall system to the server in the protected network. This controlled access requires that the user first pass through a dialog sequence in which he identifies himself to the firewall system and is successfully authenticated. After being authenticated, he can use the services for which he has access rights within the permitted time frame. A possible point of attack exists: an attacker from the insecure network can hijack the user's existing connection and, as a man-in-the-middle, can execute the same actions as the authorized user. Figure 10-1 shows how a man-in-the-middle attack perpetrates a firewall system.

This man-in-the-middle attack can be prevented if communications between the workstation and the firewall system are encrypted. An attacker from the insecure network could still hijack the connection, but he wouldn't be able to perform the encryption procedures (not having access to the secret key) required to process the IP packets in such a way that they could be correctly decrypted by the packet filter.

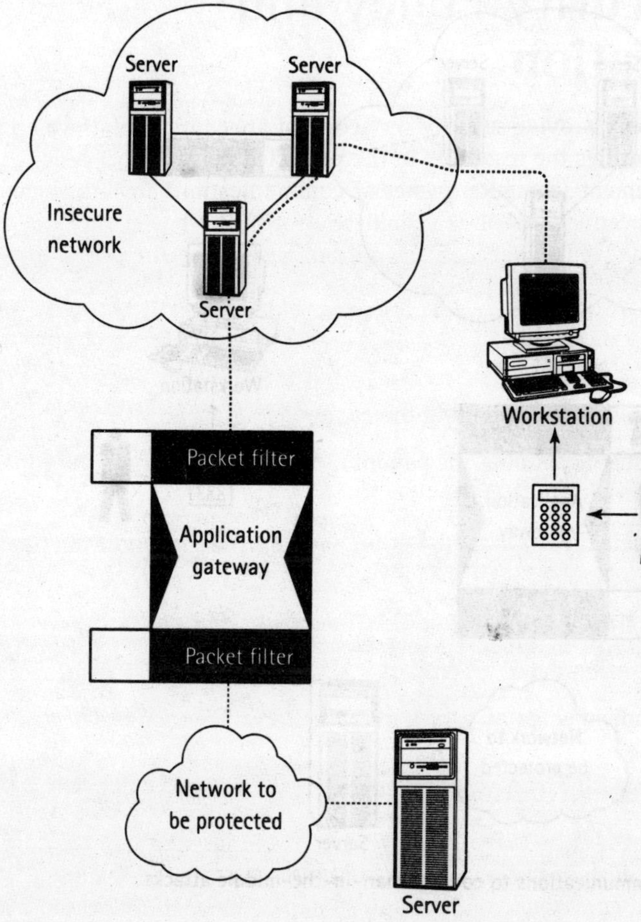

Figure 10-1: Man-in-the-middle attack on a firewall system

The residual risk of a man-in-the-middle attack can be eliminated through encryption of communications over the insecure network, as shown in Figure 10-2.

Internet security is a rapidly evolving field. New attacks are being created every day. A firewall can be very effective against most attacks, in theory, but significantly less than most attacks in practice. The necessities of every organization's users and business requirement always conflict with some of the "best security practices." Never forget that the point of a firewall is to reduce the disruptions to business, not to create more. The best firewall configuration for one company will vary from that of other companies. Equipped with a thorough understanding of an organization's needs, you can combine your knowledge of security into a working plan (hypothesis). Implement this plan and then test it for security weaknesses. Adjusting the security implementation to changing company needs, attack threats, and your understanding of security is a continual cycle.

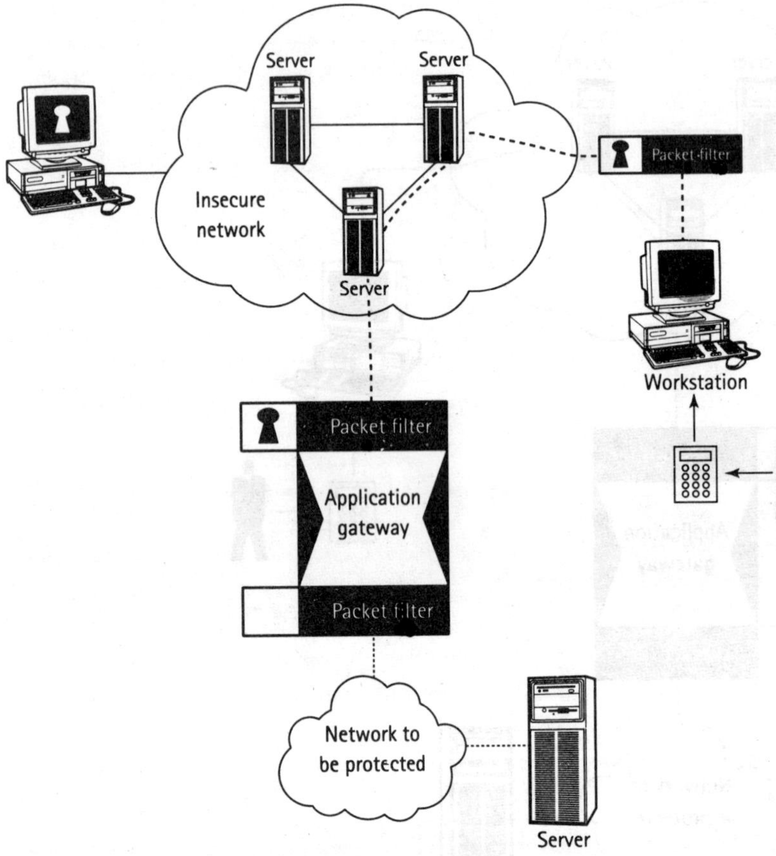

Figure 10-2: Encrypted communications to counter man-in-the-middle attacks

Security versus Connectivity – Risk versus Opportunity

The smaller the number of actions allowed, the lower the risk that damage can occur. Every user and every computer that is allowed to communicate over the firewall system constitutes an additional risk. Even communications partners who are allowed through constitute a risk because they might use unauthorized communications connections. For this reason, make sure that the least possible number of actions is permitted over the firewall system so that the maximum amount of security can be achieved. The relationship between security and number of actions allowed is depicted in Figure 10-3.

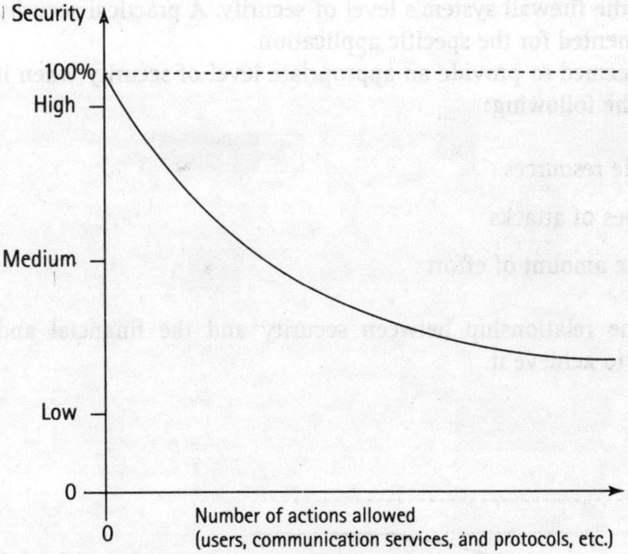

Figure 10-3: Security versus connectivity

The greater the number of permissions, the greater the risk of vulnerability. If nothing is allowed, then no loss or damage can occur over the network. The inherent conflict between security and connectivity becomes clear at this point. Firewall systems should be able to exploit the advantages of communication with the outside world and, at the same time, limit any possible loss or damage arising from these actions.

Users who must communicate in order to perform their tasks should be able to do so employing the communications protocols and services they need for their specific tasks, at the appropriate times – but only to the extent necessary.

Trustworthiness of the Communications Partner and the Received Data

A firewall system can only make and implement its decisions if the communications partner and the received data can be trusted. As these characteristics cannot be entirely ensured through the firewall system's security mechanisms, supplementary security mechanisms, such as encryption (VPN) or digital signatures, must be used.

Practical Security

Even with elaborate firewall elements that have been well planned and are optimally operated, it is still impossible to achieve 100 percent security. However, certain factors can raise the firewall system's level of security. A practical security approach must be implemented for the specific application.

A firewall system is deemed to provide an appropriate level of security when it cannot be overcome by the following:

- With the available resources
- Using known types of attacks
- With a reasonable amount of effort

Figure 10-4 shows the relationship between security and the financial and human resources needed to achieve it.

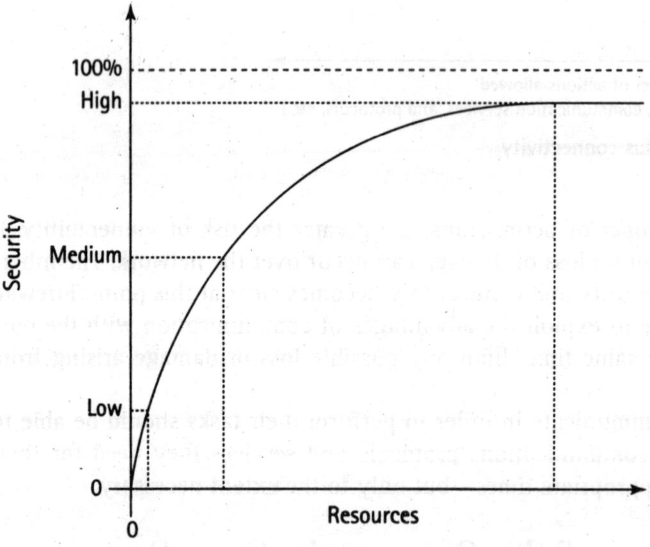

Figure 10-4: The relationship between security and the resources required to achieve it

SECURITY OBJECTIVES OF IMPLEMENTING A FIREWALL SYSTEM

- Completely eliminate all uncertainties with a high degree of probability.
- Counter as many security weaknesses as possible with suitable security mechanisms to reduce the probability of loss or damage as a result of a successful attack to an insignificant level.
- Detect security weaknesses that are unavoidable in order to take appropriate action after an attack, with the objective of minimizing the loss or damage.
- Detect attacks in advance to ensure that no loss or damage can occur.

Summary

Security policies are an essential tool for achieving security. Because the security needs of each organization will vary significantly, there is no "perfect" security policy for all organizations. This chapter lists many of the topics that you should consider addressing in the security policy for your organization.

It is worth noting that you can go too far with a security policy. If you produce a 500-page security policy, almost no one will read it. If no one reads the security policy, no one will adhere to it. An effective security policy requires striking a balance. You can create a much more useable security policy by breaking the policy up into topics. Consider giving various groups within your organization only the sections that apply to them. This sort of "modular" security policy is much easier for users to read and adhere to.

Chapter 11

Special Issues Related to Firewall Systems

CERTAIN ISSUES MUST BE DEALT WITH when integrating firewall systems, such as the conversion of network addresses, the administration of several firewall systems using a Security Management module, communication through several firewall systems, and failure safety.

Network Address Translation

On the Internet, everyone has a unique IP address that is centrally assigned and administered by the Network Information Center (NIC) and its subsidiary organizations. However, because the number of these official IP addresses is limited, a mechanism known as *network address translation* (NAT) enables organizations connected to the Internet to work in their own area with IP addresses that are reserved for private purposes. NAT then converts the private addresses to official IP addresses, and vice versa.

Computer systems in the protected network should be provided with private IP addresses. To ensure that they are unique, only IP addresses that do not occur on the Internet should be used. In fact, *reserved IP addresses*, shown in Table 11-1, are available for use on the protected network.

TABLE 11-1 IP ADDRESSES RESERVED FOR PRIVATE PURPOSES

Address Class	Address Range
1 Class A address	10.0.0.0–10.255.255.255
16 Class B addresses	172.16.0.0–172.31.255.255
256 Class C addresses	192.168.0.0–192.168.255.255

> **NOTE:** The reserved IP address ranges are always contiguous.

As previously stated, these IP addresses are reserved for private purposes and are never granted on the Internet. Furthermore, because they are only used in the protected network, all networks can use the same reserved address ranges internally.

The address range chosen depends on the organization's particular needs. In large protected networks, in which subnet masks do not constitute a problem, the Class A address 10.0.0.0 would probably be used. In a small, protected network, a Class C address (for example, 192.168.1.0) could be utilized.

Additional information can be found in RFC 1918. RFC 1918 is the document that reserves the addresses listed in Table 11-1 for internal use only.

The Internet Assigned Numbers Authority (IANA) assigns external addresses. Major providers, such as Cable and Wireless, obtain addresses from the IANA and re-assign them to subscribers (including ISPs). You can obtain addresses directly from the IANA, but this is normally only done for very large organizations. Due to the lack of available addresses, all external address assignments must be justified closely.

In a small organization with three departments (in which no department has more than 250 computer systems), reserved addresses can be shared in the following way:

- **Department 1:** IP addresses 192.168.1.0–192.168.1.255
- **Department 2:** IP addresses 192.168.2.0–192.168.2.255
- **Department 3:** IP addresses 192.168.3.0–192.168.3.255

This particular address allocation has the following advantages:

- Standard network size (not subnetted)
- A clear separation between individual departments
- The standard network mask can be used in the individual subnets

Big organizations with an extremely large number of computer systems (in which many departments are broken down into sections or sub-departments), address allocation can follow these guidelines:

- The address range 10.0.0.0 should be chosen to allow plenty of room for expansion.
- Each department is given its own Class B network, which can be further subdivided as required – for example, into a Class C subnet or smaller.

- Don't use subnets with the addresses 0 and 255. Doing so may cause ambiguities with broadcasts. The subnets 10.0.xxx.yyy (problem with network addresses 10.0.0.0), 10.255.xxx.yyy (problem with broadcast 10.255.255.255), or 10.1.255.xxx (as in last example) should not be assigned.

Medium-sized organizations can fill their requirements using Class B addresses. In general, however, take the small solution with 192.168.xxx.yyy, or the large solution with the network 10.0.0.0.

Firewall Systems and Network Address Translation

Firewall systems and firewall elements such as application gateways may not perform network address translation in the strict sense of the word, but they achieve the same end by using official Internet IP addresses for the insecure network and reserved IP addresses for the intranet.

When communications occur through a firewall system, an application gateway has a link with the computer system (or workstation) in the protected network and a link with the computer system in the insecure network (or server). In other words, the firewall system is the communications partner for both ends of the connection. The firewall system communicates in the insecure network with the official Internet IP address and in the protected network (intranet) with the reserved IP address. This behavior is similar to network address translation, except that translation tables at the application layer, rather than the network layer achieve it.

The firewall system's IP address, which belongs to the reserved IP address range of the intranet, is always stated as the communications partner within the protected network. The firewall system's official Internet IP address is always given as the communications partner in the insecure network (see Figure 11-1). An attacker can't tell which computer system is hidden behind the firewall system in the protected network.

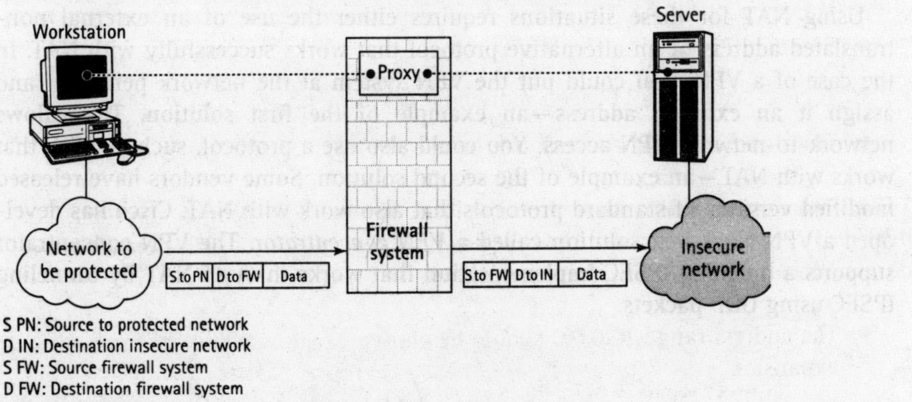

Figure 11-1: Firewall system and network address translation

Problems for Networks That Work with Illegal IP Addresses

Occasionally, a network doesn't use reserved IP addresses, which creates problems when connecting to the Internet. If any IP addresses officially assigned to other organizations are used illegally in the protected network, problems result at the interface because the IP addresses exist both in the insecure and in the protected networks.

There are two possible solutions to resolving the problem of using external addresses internally:

- **Assignment of reserved IP addresses in the intranet.** Replace the illegally used IP addresses with unproblematic reserved IP addresses. Large organizations may experience problems with this approach; the procedure can be time-consuming if a large number of computer systems are involved.
- **IP address mapping.** Map the illegal IP addresses onto reserved addresses. Depending on which illegal addresses are used, this procedure can be implemented using a substitution table, for example, or a simple mapping rule. Some firewall products offer IP address mapping as an additional functionality.

Network Address Translation Problems

The use of network address translation introduces some problems not experienced when using non-translated IP addresses. Ironically, security protocols often don't operate correctly with NAT. The majority of virtual private network (VPN) protocols do not function correctly because of the address translation. Protocols that embed the source client address in the packet generally do not work. When the remote application compares the source address of the packet (the external routable translation address) with the address in the packet (the client's internal IP address) and discovers a mismatch, it disallows communications.

Using NAT for these situations requires either the use of an external non-translated address or an alternative protocol that works successfully with NAT. In the case of a VPN, you could put the VPN system at the network perimeter and assign it an external address – an example of the first solution. This allows network-to-network VPN access. You could also use a protocol, such as SSH, that works with NAT – an example of the second solution. Some vendors have released modified versions of standard protocols that also work with NAT. Cisco has developed a VPN black box solution called a *VPN concentrator.* The VPN concentrator supports a modified IPSEC implementation that works through NAT by tunneling IPSEC using UDP packets.

Domain Names

In general, there is a primary DNS server on the Internet and a primary DNS server in the intranet. In mid-size organizations and larger, these are usually separate physical machines. In smaller companies the two different host groups may be referenced in different zones on the same physical DNS server. The intranet names and IP addresses should only be known to the DNS server in the intranet to keep the assignment of addresses in the Internet unique.

Due to the uniqueness of names throughout the Internet (including an organization's own intranet), the domain names for the intranet should also be adapted to the Internet's name schema. For this purpose, the domain name in the Internet can be appended to the name in the intranet, as follows:

Internet domain: company.com
Intranet domain: intra.company.com

In this way you can implement a simplified procedure for the DNS server and firewall configuration in large intranets.

Administration of Several Firewall Systems via a Security Management Module

Large organizations may require implementing several interfaces for insecure networks. In this case, administering and controlling a number of firewall systems centrally via a Security Management module makes sense.

You can administer several firewall systems from the central Security Management module. This enables an organization with several interfaces to insecure networks to easily implement its security policy. Information is exchanged between Security Management and the firewall systems in a secure way. Other firewall elements in the intranet, such as packet filters and application gateways, can also be administered with the central Security Management).

XREF

For more information on other firewall modules, refer to Chapter 9.

Nested Firewall Configurations

A nested firewall configuration can occur in several applications in an organization. Figure 11-2 depicts a simplified example of such a configuration.

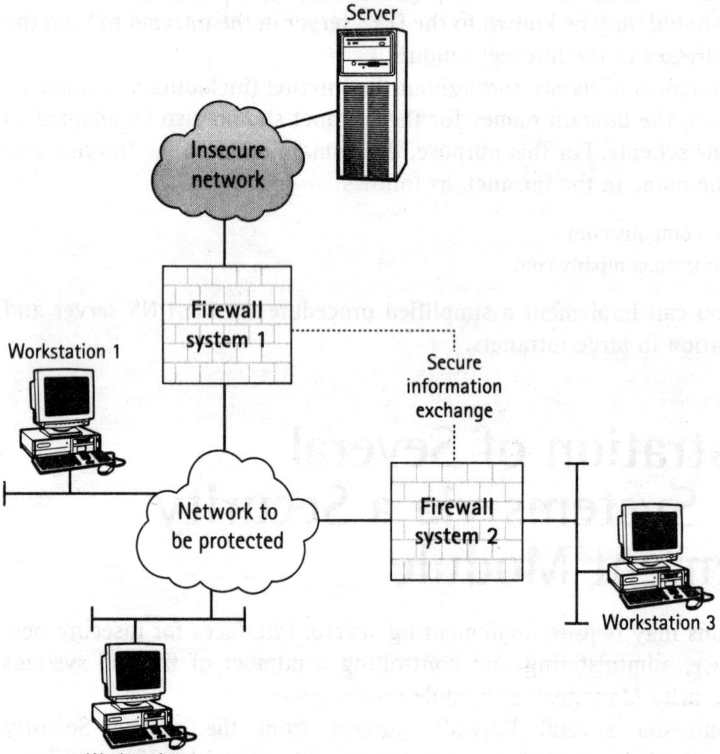

Figure 11-2: Nested firewall configuration

A firewall system is set up between the insecure and protected networks. Another firewall system is installed within the protected network in order to segregate a particularly sensitive organizational unit, such as a board of directors. If a user from Workstation 1 or 2 wants to use the services of a server in the insecure network, Firewall System 1 alone (shown in Figure 11-2) can handle the connection. If, however, a user from Workstation 3 wants to use this server, both firewall systems must process the request.

The configuration illustrated in Figure 11-2 can be implemented either with two independent Security Management modules or with one Security Management module. If one Security Management module is used, special requirements apply. Information about the authentication and destination of the data must be exchanged in a secure form between the two firewall systems.

Availability

Internet users often need continuous and reliable access to the services they use to perform their tasks. This availability requirement affects not only the firewall system components, but also the availability of the network, especially its availability over the Internet. The extent to which organizations can guarantee Quality of Service (QoS) on the Internet depends largely on whether Internet Service Providers (ISPs) can guarantee availability and performance globally in the future. Availability issues must be thoroughly considered before any availability problem occurs. By anticipating where issues can arise, you can implement fail-over and redundant systems for critical infrastructures.

XREF

Chapters 4 and 5 discuss the different components and concepts behind firewalls. These components are the failure points potentially requiring redundancy.

From the user's point of view, minimum requirements in the area of QoS must be guaranteed so that the risk of non-availability can be properly estimated. Redundancy solutions that guarantee a high level of availability must be accessible for firewall systems.

An availability concept for firewall system components must be developed. Accordingly, the most important components of the system must be designed to be redundant. Moreover, load balancing is necessary to achieve the degree of availability that will in turn achieve the QoS rating required for the application. Fortunately, several mechanisms, including the following, can be used to address availability:

- Redundancy
- Hot fail-over
- Clustering

Some firewalls include Quality of Service modules. QoS modules allow you to specify traffic quality of service profiles. For example, you might specify that traffic to and from the corporate Web servers takes precedence over internal employee Web browsing. In the event that traffic has to be discarded, the employee traffic is discarded, preserving maximum availability for the more critical traffic. The firewall then makes decisions about allowing or disallowing traffic based on these policies. QoS policies work by giving you the ability to classify traffic based upon type. Traffic parameters include the following packet characteristics:

- Source or destination
- Time of day
- Specific URLs
- Users
- Applications

Critical business functionality can be classified as priority, and other traffic can be held or disallowed as necessary.

A second option involves *hot fail-over* or clustering systems. Hot fail-over can be as simple as maintaining a redundant system with duplicate rulesets that can be activated quickly in the event of a failure on the primary system. At the other end of the spectrum is *full-system clustering.* Clustering usually involves two or more systems sharing a central drive subsystem. In the event of a system failure, the other system or systems continue transparently. Because of the shared storage system, no data is lost during the switch.

Availability problems may result from more than simple hardware or software failure. Connectivity failure, for example, makes using systems as desired rather difficult. Failures in other services, such as connectivity, require firewall configuration support as well. Having a redundant T1 in place won't do any good if the firewall isn't also configured to use the alternate T1 in the event of a failure of the primary T1.

Denial-of-Service attacks can pose a particular challenge for availability planning. While the problem of DoS attacks is not solved yet by any means, several of the techniques being developed to combat Denial-of-Service attacks look promising. In the interim, planning for redundancies and response plans is your best defense.

Performance

Performance is, in many ways, the other side of the availability coin. Performance considerations often take precedence over security considerations in an organization. Given the importance of performance, a firewall system should be designed and implemented from the beginning with ***maximum*** performance in mind.

Performance is directly impacted by the firewall policies you implement. Packet filtering has the least negative impact on performance, while application gateways produce the most performance degradation. The order in which rules are implemented also affects performance. Putting the most used rules first often results in a measurable, positive performance impact.

The way rules impact both security and performance should also be considered. Traffic rules that have very little impact on security may significantly affect performance. The appropriateness of rules that yield only small security improvements should be carefully evaluated.

Virtually all commercial, firewall software or black box vendors release performance specifications as well as hardware guidelines for optimizing traffic handling in your environment.

Ultimately, performance impact can only be measured by specific environmental testing. Software packages are readily available for stress-testing servers in various capacities. Using a Web server stress suite from outside your firewall can yield useful performance information. You can evaluate specific rule impact by running the same test sequence with different rules enabled or disabled. To perform specific rule testing, run a tool, such as a Web server performance tester, against the Web server while all of the firewall rules are enabled. Then re-run the test while disabling rules in the firewall. Run the test for each rule. Testing in this manner will clearly indicate the performance impact of each rule.

Firewall performance enhancements are also available. These enhancements range in scope from hardware add-ins designed to offload processor-intensive activity such as encryption/decryption to load-balancing tools for balancing system utilization between multiple firewalls and/or computer systems.

Summary

Issues such as NAT, nested firewall configurations, availability, and performance should not be the primary criteria for designing the architecture and configuration of your firewall. That being said, these issues are critical to the success of the firewall. Always bear in mind that firewalls exist to eliminate some of the disruptions to conducting business. If the firewall itself becomes a significant disruption to business, the firewall's primary purpose has failed. Spending the extra planning and time to evaluate criteria, such as performance and availability, enable you to take your firewall to the highest possible level of security and functionality.

Chapter 12

Secondary Issues Related to Firewall Systems

THIS CHAPTER COVERS SEVERAL issues that arise in connection with the operation of firewall systems, including the logging of security-relevant data in logbooks, the security of Java and ActiveX, the necessary cost of purchasing and operating a firewall system, the evaluation and certification of a firewall solution, and the further development of firewall systems.

Logbooks – Burden or Benefit?

Most firewall solutions generate data that is recorded in logbooks and must then be further processed. This section considers whether logging is an unnecessary burden, or whether it brings definite benefits to the operation of a firewall solution. Other topics covered in this section are the alarm function, preservation of evidence, protection of logged data, actions to be taken following detection of a security breach, and data protection.

Purpose of Logging

Logging can be used to achieve different objectives, depending on what information is logged and how it is analyzed.

DETECTING SECURITY VIOLATIONS

A firewall system's logbook holds information about both normal (non-security-relevant) events and unusual (security-relevant) events. Analysis of these events establishes whether a security violation has occurred and what information and computer systems have been affected by it.

In this way, it is possible to detect attacks on the firewall system itself and on computer systems in the network protected by the firewall system, and to initiate responses to these security violations.

PRESERVING EVIDENCE REGARDING USERS' ACTIONS

The recording of events ensures that information about user actions or processes that are executed in users' names is stored. The consequences of such actions can then be attributed to the user, and the user can be held accountable for them. Logging acts as a strong deterrent for users who may be contemplating security-endangering actions.

Logging Events

Firewall elements must provide facilities to record events such as user actions – along with the associated information – so that this data can be used to detect security violations. Logged data that relates to possible events can be generated at different levels. Logging can be a rather tricky proposition, however. As with many security parameters, too much logging can create more problems than it solves. It can impair system performance and resources. It can also create so much data to wade through that the actual events of concern get lost. If you have too little logging, then you risk not capturing the events that concern you in the event of a system security failure.

FAILED AUTHENTICATION PROCESS

Any unsuccessful attempts by users or attackers to authenticate themselves to the firewall system are recorded. A failed authentication may be caused by, for example:

- Use of an invalid user name
- Use of an incorrect cryptographic authentication protocol

VIOLATION OF THE RULESET, IN RELATION TO THE ANALYSIS OF THE COMMUNICATIONS DATA

Here, the aim is to establish whether a violation of the ruleset (security policy) has occurred during analysis of the communications data about the firewall system. Examples of typical violations include the following:

- Attempt to use a non-permitted command (for example, del) on an FTP connection
- Attempt to use a non-permitted service, such as Telnet
- Attempt to use the firewall system at a non-permitted time (for example, at 5 a.m. on a Sunday)

DETECTING ATTEMPTS TO ATTACK THE FIREWALL SYSTEM ITSELF

The firewall system can tell when it has been attacked. The following occurrences are an example of detecting attacks on the firewall:

- Unsuccessful attempt at authentication to the Security Management module (for example, by an attacker)
- Capacity of a logbook exceeded

IDENTIFYING MALFUNCTIONING FIREWALL SOFTWARE AND HARDWARE

The firewall element itself can determine that a malfunction has occurred that is not specified for the normal operation of the firewall. The firewall element may detect, for example:

- Software in an undefined state (state machine of the Analysis Module)
- A fault in the storage medium (hard disk)

STORING ACTIONS THAT HAVE BEEN PERFORMED THROUGH THE FIREWALL SYSTEM

The firewall system records all actions that have been performed during communications through the firewall system, such as:

- Information about a Telnet or FTP connection
- Information about actions within the Security Management module

Another issue that must be considered for the secure operation of a firewall system is the logging of all Security Management activities. This is a particularly sensitive area, since the ruleset can be directly influenced via the Security Management (see Chapter 5). The primary concern is to be able to quantify all administrative activity, specifically, which firewall system administrator has performed what actions when. These actions could include the following:

- Assigning rights to users
- Deleting logbooks

Alarm Function

Not all security events are of equal concern. Some security events warrant immediate staff notification, while others may rate simple logging or even ignoring. Alarming of security-relevant events can be arranged so that it occurs at different levels. Typically, security-relevant events are identified in a firewall element and, depending on the definition contained in the ruleset, either written to a logbook or reported to a higher entity (the Security Management) as a spontaneous message. After a particular predefined procedure, the logbooks are likewise made available to the Security Management at a later time.

With the help of the ruleset, you must specify in the firewall elements which events are particularly security-relevant and should be reported immediately, and which events only need to be entered in a logbook and made available to the Security Management at a later time.

The Security Management can respond in different ways to the spontaneous messages. They can be displayed to the administrator directly with the aid of visual and auditory signals, or they can be analyzed first via an evaluation mechanism and the results – in other words, the conclusion that an attack has taken place – can be displayed accordingly.

It is also possible to make the analysis mechanism first read all the logbooks from the different firewall elements and take these results into account before deciding whether an attack is concealed behind a spontaneous message.

Using the spontaneous messages, security-relevant events and security violations can be detected promptly. You should also be able to send an alarm from a Security Management module to a network management system over standard network management protocols such as SNMP. Defined reactions could then be initiated from network management.

The messages themselves can serve as a source of further alarm indications. Here is an extract of an Apache Web server access log.

```
x.x.x.119 - - [27/Mar/2002:13:40:09 -0500] "HEAD /cgi-bin/cart.pl
HTTP/1.0" 404 0 "http://apache.badsecurity.com/" "Mozilla/5.0 [en]
(Win95; U)"
x.x.x.119 - - [27/Mar/2002:13:40:09 -0500] "HEAD /cgi-
bin/filemail.pl HTTP/1.0" 404 0 "http://apache.badsecurity.com/"
"Mozilla/5.0 [en] (Win95; U)"
x.x.x.119 - - [27/Mar/2002:13:40:12 -0500] "HEAD /cgi-bin/filemail
HTTP/1.0" 404 0 "http://apache.badsecurity.com/" "Mozilla/5.0 [en]
(Win95; U)"
x.x.x.119 - - [27/Mar/2002:13:40:12 -0500] "HEAD /cgi-bin/php.cgi
HTTP/1.0" 404 0 "http://apache.badsecurity.com/" "Mozilla/5.0 [en]
(Win95; U)"
x.x.x.119 - - [27/Mar/2002:13:40:12 -0500] "HEAD /cgi-bin/jj
HTTP/1.0" 404 0 "http://apache.badsecurity.com/" "Mozilla/5.0 [en]
(Win95; U)"
x.x.x.119 - - [27/Mar/2002:13:40:12 -0500] "HEAD /cgi-bin/info2www
HTTP/1.0" 404 0 "http://apache.badsecurity.com/" "Mozilla/5.0 [en]
(Win95; U)"
x.x.x.119 - - [27/Mar/2002:13:40:12 -0500] "HEAD /cgi-bin/nph-pub-
lish HTTP/1.0" 404 0 "http://apache.badsecurity.com/" "Mozilla/5.0
[en] (Win95; U)"
x.x.x.119 - - [27/Mar/2002:13:40:12 -0500] "HEAD /cgi-bin/ax.cgi
HTTP/1.0" 404 0 "http://apache.badsecurity.com/" "Mozilla/5.0 [en]
(Win95; U)"
x.x.x.119 - - [27/Mar/2002:13:40:12 -0500] "HEAD /session/admnlogin
HTTP/1.0" 404 0 "http://apache.badsecurity.com/" "Mozilla/5.0 [en]
(Win95; U)"
x.x.x.119 - - [27/Mar/2002:13:40:12 -0500] "HEAD /cgi-bin/rpm_query
HTTP/1.0" 404 0 "http://apache.badsecurity.com/" "Mozilla/5.0 [en]
(Win95; U)"
x.x.x.119 - - [27/Mar/2002:13:40:12 -0500] "HEAD /cgi-bin/AnyForm2
HTTP/1.0" 404 0 "http://apache.badsecurity.com/" "Mozilla/5.0 [en]
(Win95; U)"
x.x.x.119 - - [27/Mar/2002:13:40:12 -0500] "HEAD /cgi-bin/AnyForm
HTTP/1.0" 404 0 "http://apache.badsecurity.com/" "Mozilla/5.0 [en]
(Win95; U)"
x.x.x.119 - - [27/Mar/2002:13:40:12 -0500] "HEAD /cgi-
bin/textcounter.pl HTTP/1.0" 404 0 "http://apache.badsecurity.com/"
"Mozilla/5.0 [en] (Win95; U)"
```

This extract came from a Web server being scanned for known CGI security problems. A first indicator of an attack would be trying to access numerous Web applications not resident on the Web server. Simple tools such as `grep` can be used to filter logs for access to files outside of our application. For instance, if you create and maintain a file with a list of the files used by your Web server, then the following line will list all accesses to files outside of your Web server.

```
grep -v -f web_file_list access_log.txt
```

Other tools, such as `Logwatch`, assist with the handling of log files.

Preserving Evidence

The purpose of preserving evidence is to record actions that are performed through or using the firewall system so that this data can later be used as evidence. Preservation can only be ensured if the stored log data is protected against tampering. Recording data (or logging) is the first step. Preservation is taking the additional steps to make sure that no one can modify the recorded logs. If you can't demonstrate that given logs are free from tampering, they will have little or, more likely, no value in a court of law should you need them for evidence.

For evidence retention purposes, it is appropriate to record the following events:

- Who had access to the data (logs)?
- Why did they have access to the data?
- What was done to the data (specifically) while in each person's custody?

SERVICE WORK

Service work that is performed remotely from the insecure network on computer systems in the protected network is logged on the firewall system so that the logged data can be used as evidence of the actions performed by the service company employees. You may have a situation, for example, where a service company maintains a computer system in the protected network, accessing it via Telnet. Records are kept on the firewall system regarding which service company employee worked on a particular computer system, on what date, and for how long. If required, the entire Telnet session can be logged.

If the computer system no longer works following completion of the service work, it is possible to establish from the logged data whether a particular service company employee is responsible.

Protecting the Logged Data

Logged data can be used as evidence in criminal and employment law investigations. To be used for such purposes, the data must be stored in a proper manner and its authenticity and integrity should be indisputable.

To this end, attackers should not be able to disable logging, delete the logged data contained in the logbooks, or tamper with their content. This can be achieved through the following security mechanisms:

- Access control and access rights administration functions with the Security Management must ensure that only authorized persons can access the logged data.
- The logged data for all firewall elements should be sent via a trustworthy route to the Security Management, to ensure that it cannot be altered prior to evaluation and final storage.

Reactions to a Security Breach

If a security breach is detected through the security mechanisms in the firewall system, actions must be initiated. This section describes what actions can be performed and in what sequence.

A DECISION MUST BE MADE AS TO WHETHER THE FIREWALL SYSTEM OR ITS COMPONENTS SHOULD BE IMMEDIATELY SHUT DOWN

It must be clearly specified who is authorized to make and execute this decision. An automatic shutdown of the firewall system can be configured, as long as it doesn't impair availability.

Depending on the type of attack, the shutdown can be effected at different levels.

- For example, it is possible to selectively block or reduce the times when communications are permitted through the firewall system for particular users, particular services, particular computer systems, and so on.
- On the other hand, the entire firewall system can be shut down if the risk of a possible attack is too great.

THE ATTACK MUST BE ANALYZED

If a security breach is detected, the relevant data stored in the logbooks is analyzed to see who performed the attack from the insecure network and on which computer system. Further analysis identifies which computer system in the protected network and what information was targeted by the attack. The computer system logbooks help with this analysis.

You must decide whether the attacker will be prosecuted. At the very least, the IP address from which the attack was executed can be determined.

Even if the prospect of carrying out a successful prosecution is slender (because any user can assume any IP address), prosecution should still be considered. Contacting the attacker for possible prosecution lets him know that the log data was analyzed and that he can be detected in the event of a future attempted attack.

The threat of possible prosecution alone will often dissuade the attacker from further attacks.

An attacker may be using another organization as a springboard from which to carry out his attempted attacks. If so, the organization should be informed of its involvement. It can then implement measures to prevent the attacker from using it, in the future, as an unintentional accomplice.

Conducting the analysis can be somewhat tricky. Keep in mind that several different systems will probably have individual pieces of data that must be correlated. The process is analogous to putting together a puzzle. The more data you can assemble to assist in this process, the better. Start by using the source address of attack. If the source address isn't known, start with a known result and trace back from there. It is important to determine as much as possible about what occurred. If the source address is known, you can use it to determine user IDs and processes that may have been used. These user IDs and processes can be used to determine further actions that were taken by the attacker. Once the individual actions are determined, you should assemble them in chronological order. Any missing time segments will be apparent, indicating that further activities may have occurred.

PREVENTING ANOTHER SECURITY BREACH

Once the attack has been analyzed in detail, a strategy must be developed to prevent future security breaches. The firewall system can respond in a number of ways:

- The attack is recorded in the log analysis knowledge base so that if it is repeated, it will be detected more quickly, enabling appropriate action to be taken.
- A check must be performed as to whether such an attack can be prevented in the future with new and/or additional security mechanisms. The attack scenario can be discussed with the firewall system vendor. The vendor should, in any case, be informed of the attack so that he can respond to it and also inform the other users of his firewall systems. Such information is beneficial to all the parties involved.
- You can use a firewall system to restrict access rights so that such an attack can no longer take place. The following restrictions can be considered:
  - User
  - Computer systems
  - Services
  - Times at which communications are permitted through the firewall system
  - Commands offered by applications
  - Authentication attempts

Extra log data can be recorded. If the attack is repeated, more information will be available, either to support a prosecution or to ward off the attack.

Data Protection Issues

If data is not carefully protected, it should be considered suspect for the purposes of evaluation. For instance, any log files directly residing on a compromised system must be thought of as suspect, since they may have been tampered with. Use of protocols such as syslog can allow you to log data to external systems for protection. Printing data to hard copy as it is collected is another good security technique, albeit one that is not very practical for most systems. The technique might be warranted on systems that deserve extra protection mechanisms, but is likely not appropriate in most cases.

Logging and monitoring a company's computer systems is acceptable under the law, but employees should be notified. Logs and monitor data that are collected can be used for a variety of purposes besides security. For example, log activity can be used to evaluate employees and determine information about employees that is usually private, such as employee tastes and interests. Collected data should be used judiciously and its handling restricted to select individuals and specific uses. The handling itself must be subject to monitoring to prevent abuse.

Privileged administrators, such as the operator, should not be given any opportunity to manipulate the logged data. You should be able to prove in every case when the logged data was accessed. If you do not maintain this handling, gathered evidence will not be admissible in court in case prosecution occurs. Consider including specific handling parameters in your corporate security policies as well as your HR policies.

In situations where an agreement on the evaluation of logged data from a firewall system does not already exist, it is generally recommended that one be drawn up together with the staff council. An official agreement provides assurance that logging will not be used in a way that was not intended—for example, to monitor employee behavior or performance. This agreement should state what analysis may be performed on the log files (who may analyze them, how, using what tools, and for what purpose) and how the results will be used.

Java and Its Relations

When it comes to communications over firewall systems, some other innovative IT client concepts are also relevant because they affect security. This section discusses Java, JavaScript and ActiveX. However, only a simplified version of the differences in the concepts and the security problems will be presented.

Basics

When the World Wide Web made its debut a few years ago, it offered the opportunity to present text, graphics, and hyperlinks to related topics in the form of HTML documents. The meteoric growth of the Internet soon imposed limits on the implementation of creative ideas through text-oriented HTML documents. The initial response was to develop various additional modules, known as *plug-ins*. Plug-ins are tailored to each type of browser; they enable, among other things, the transmission of audio and video clips or the presentation of virtual, three-dimensional worlds (Virtual Reality Modeling Language, or VRML) on the Internet. However, due to the proliferation of hardware and software systems, these solutions eventually proved unsatisfactory. A means of transporting individual content or programs to the user's computer that is not affected by the user's particular hardware or software configuration was missing.

The Common Gateway Interface

The *CGI*, or *Common Gateway Interface*, was a first step toward implementing interactive functions, enabling functions by programs written in a wide range of programming languages to be accessed in a special interface. These programs are activated on the user's own computer system when he retrieves a URL or hyperlink; they run on the relevant WWW server. CGI is used above all for searching through extensive databases, storing customer information, and evaluating graphical menus. The user information – captured using special input fields within an HTML document – or the coordinates of a mouse click are transmitted from the user's computer to the CGI program. The results are transmitted to the user following processing.

The disadvantages of CGI are obvious:

- All the data is transmitted from the user's computer system to the server and then processed. The results are sent back to the user. An attacker could intercept or manipulate the information on its way through the network.
- CGI applications are executed on the relevant server and require system resources for their execution. This constitutes a potential security risk and means that the server operator must put a corresponding effort into security measures.
- Transmitting the information between computer system and server places demands on the network infrastructure. Where use is heavy, network overload and delays may occur, turning the server into an information bottleneck. This is especially noticeable when graphical applications or animation are involved, as the large volume of data moves slowly through the network.
- For complex computational processes, the user's computer system is used only slightly or not at all. This system is reminiscent of the old mainframe computers, which were operated from "dumb" terminals (computer systems with little, if any, computing power). But since today's computer systems have their own intelligence, and their capability is growing steadily in line with technical developments, CGI applications are essentially a technological step backwards.

Despite its disadvantages, CGI is not going to go away any time soon, and must be dealt with. The primary security risk represented by CGI is that it provides a mechanism whereby remote users can pass data directly to system processes. This condition requires that all user input be validated extensively. The lack of user input validation is the source of the vast majority of CGI security failures.

Active Server Pages

To resolve some of the problems with CGI, Microsoft developed its own proprietary standard, *Active Server Pages (ASP)*. ASP is server-based (that is, the corresponding resources must be available on the server). However, ASP does have some advantages compared with CGI. A separate process is not started every time the client retrieves a script. Upon starting a process, many resources are consumed – by logging on to the operating system, creating an entry in the process list, assigning memory, and so on. On most CGI applications, this single-process approach is in stark contrast to the few commands with which the user query is handled. ASP handles client queries in the normal process context of the server, for example, through threads.

Additional functions for session management offset the disadvantages of the HTTP protocol (and also of CGI), which are both stateless. Complex access to databases, however, is only efficiently performed with a state machine.

The ASP programming interface is very flexible, with the Perl, VBScript, JavaScript, and ActiveX Script languages all supported.

Despite these advantages, the use of ASP is currently limited mostly to Microsoft environments (that is, Internet Information Server); the WebSite Pro Web server from O'Reilly is the only Web server from an independent supplier to support ASP. Nevertheless, ASP is very widespread on the Internet. ASP pages can be recognized in a browser from the file suffix `*.asp` (compared with the suffixes `*.html` or `*.htm` for normal HTML pages).

The use of ASP in lieu of CGI does not remove all security risks; rather, ASP poses new ones. Because ASP execution is meant solely for the remote Web server, programmers often make assumptions about the security of the ASP source code. These assumptions lead to activity such as embedding user names and passwords in the source code for accessing other systems such as database servers. Unfortunately, numerous techniques have been discovered for tricking the remote server into disclosing the ASP source rather then executing it. This provides the remote user with all sorts of potential internal information, including user names and passwords. Few, if any, current firewall application proxies will protect you against this type of abuse.

PHP

PHP is a scripting language primarily used on the Apache Web server platform. Similar in nature and scope to ASP on Microsoft's Web servers, PHP allows complex Web applications to reside and execute solely at the server level. As an alternative technology to ASP, PHP has the same advantages and disadvantages as ASP with regard to security. PHP is a solid replacement for CGI. If PHP is coupled with good programming habits, then PHP can yield a solid Web application base.

Java

The development of the programming language, Java by Sun, was intended to solve many problems. Originally, Java was developed to enable simple programming of electronic household appliances, such as video recorders, stereo systems, and microwave ovens. However, it was recognized early on that Java had a far more promising future. With Java, it is possible to transport programs and data over the Internet to any connected computer system and have them run there locally, independent of the hardware platforms used. In this way, the work is performed on the user's computer system.

Java consists of three components: the actual programming language, a compiler, and the run-time system. This division has already proved itself with many other computer languages, and it is therefore not surprising that Java is based closely on existing concepts. Compared with C++, around whose syntax Java is oriented, Java is simpler. Its object-oriented design and use of classes or object types makes Java a powerful programming tool that builds on the modern base of software development.

A URL or hyperlink within an HTML document, similar to a CGI program, activates a Java program, also known as an applet. But unlike CGI, the data is not transmitted to the server and evaluated there. Instead, the program that will perform the calculations is transmitted as a byte code from the WWW server to the user's computer. The browser, which must have the appropriate run-time environment, executes this program on the local computer system. This makes it possible to implement resource-intensive programming, which can then be used spontaneously and dynamically. Software distribution is implemented in the application; updates are necessary only centrally on the WWW servers.

The *Java Virtual Machine* (*JVM*, or *VM*) was defined so that Java programs might be handled on any platform. This virtual machine can be regarded as a virtual processor that executes machine commands in a language specially defined for it. In practice, a VM is implemented through an interpreter that is adapted to the relevant computer architecture.

Despite all the early euphoria, a number of security defects in the VM concept and its various implementations have come to light over the years. The Java security concept is based on the assumption that an applet runs in a closed environment, totally isolated from the resources of the computer system. The security mechanisms consist of the following four elements that constitute a "sandbox model":

- The actual VM language was designed to be secure and robust from the beginning. By definition, code modifications, direct access to memory, or direct addressing of computer system resources (for example, reading and writing to the hard disk) are not allowed.

- Before the run-time system executes a Java program, a *Byte Code Verifier* checks the received code for validity of assignments, correct parameters within the byte code instructions, and consistency of the memory (stacks). It also ensures that all registry accesses are permitted.
- Java makes a sharp distinction between local and external code. Local code, for example, classes installed during configuration or applications created by the user, is viewed as trustworthy by the run-time system and executed without access limitations. External code – code received from the network and checked using the Byte Code Verifier – is marked as such and installed using the *class loader*. This ensures that external code cannot be linked with local code or with other, previously installed external code. Name spaces are used by Java as a means of distinguishing and storing the classes. Every external code is kept isolated in its own name space, which prevents a newly received external code from overwriting or adding to an existing code.
- The security manager is part of the run-time system that monitors all the external access of code to system resources and prevents non-permitted access. Examine Figure 12-1 for a diagram of how the components of the sandbox interact.

In principle, the sandbox concept seems well thought-out, but on closer examination, a number of weaknesses become apparent:

- The transmitted byte code is exposed to attack during network transmission and is not protected against modification or manipulation.
- The logical separation between the different security mechanisms does not constitute a set of independent hurdles for an attacker that must be sequentially overcome; instead, the mechanisms build on each other. Only when all four mechanisms work together in a coordinated fashion without errors is a certain degree of security guaranteed.
- Responsibility for the individual security mechanisms lies with different manufacturers. In this way, implementation of the security mechanisms depends on particular corporate decisions.
- It is impossible to preserve evidence in Java.
- The security manager must be started from the run-time system. If this fails due to an installation error or a manipulation, all access is allowed and the attacker can do as he pleases.

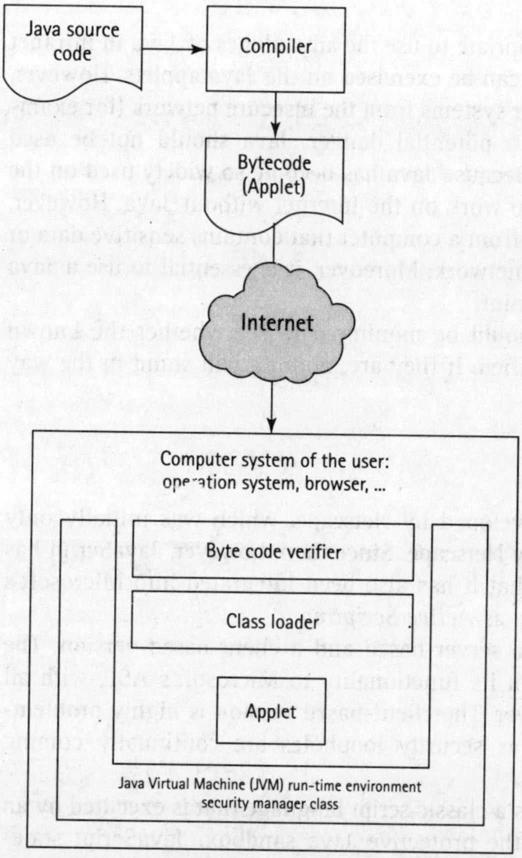

Figure 12-1: The Java security structures "sandbox model"

Much has already been said about implementing security mechanisms. Many institutions and individuals around the world are involved in analyzing such mechanisms. Lists of newly discovered errors and security weaknesses are regularly published on the Internet. Usually, these security weaknesses are based on incorrect manufacturer implementations. A number of these flaws have been eliminated through new versions or software patches, but the probability remains high that further security weaknesses that will only come to light gradually exist.

Another development of Java applets is JavaBeans. Unlike a Java applet, which is often large and is always started from a browser, a JavaBean is a compact, reusable mini-module that can be used by one or more Java applets and also by applications. Despite stronger modularization, JavaBeans retain all the advantages of the virtual machine and the sandbox.

ASSESSMENT

At the present time, it appears appropriate to use the advantages of Java in intranet applications, in which an influence can be exercised on the Java applets. However, when communicating with computer systems from the insecure network (for example, the Internet), there is always a potential danger. Java should not be used unthinkingly in such applications. Because Java has become so widely used on the Internet, it is currently unfeasible to work on the Internet without Java. However, such work should not be performed from a computer that contains sensitive data or is connected to a security-relevant network. Moreover, it is essential to use a Java applet filter at the Internet access point.

Future developments in Java should be monitored to see whether the known security defects are eventually rectified. If they are, nothing will stand in the way of unrestricted use of Java.

JavaScript

JavaScript is a script language developed by Netscape, which was initially only available for products distributed by Netscape. Since then, however, JavaScript has become widespread – so much so that it has also been integrated into Microsoft's Internet Explorer, where it is known as *Active Scripting.*

JavaScript is available in both a server-based and a client-based version. The server-based version corresponds in its functionality to Microsoft's ASP, with all processing taking place on the server. The client-based version is highly problematic from a security perspective, as security loopholes are continually coming to light.

JavaScript in the client version is a classic script language that is executed by an interpreter on the client, without the protective Java sandbox. JavaScript statements can be scattered on the Web server's HTML pages. When a page is viewed, they are automatically loaded onto the client and executed there.

Because the entire security resides in a single component (the interpreter), special caution is urged when dealing with JavaScript. Hackers using properly constructed Web sites can directly exploit every error in the interpreter. Numerous JavaScript attacks are known to date. They range from reading particular files on the hard disk to execution of any program code on the client.

The conclusion is obvious: Keep well away from JavaScript! In every browser, you should set the default so that JavaScript and Active Scripting are deactivated.

Unfortunately, JavaScript is now so widely used that it is far more common than all other comparable products, such as Java or ActiveX. Its popularity is largely due to its programming simplicity, which enables even an unpracticed layperson to program colorful windows containing clever effects. You can find many serious Web sites, such as telephone information sites, based on JavaScript. If you must access the JavaScript-based site, there are two alternatives. Either JavaScript is activated selectively upon accessing the site and then immediately disabled, or a filter is inserted at the Internet access point to ensure that only a few trusted JavaScript programs are allowed through.

ActiveX

In addition to Java and JavaScript, ActiveX, propagated by Microsoft, has also become established on the market. Unlike Java, ActiveX is not a discreet system, but an integral element of the operating system and programs used.

An ActiveX control can be written in any programming language as long as it satisfies the ActiveX interface specifications. As in Java, activation of the relevant program is effected by calling a URL or through a hyperlink from the user's browser. Whereas, originally, only Microsoft Internet Explorer was able to process these controls, different versions or plug-ins are now available for a multitude of other products.

Microsoft's corporate policy enables the programmer of the ActiveX control to access all system resources. The programmer is given the same rights as the user who is currently logged on. In short, there is no security architecture for a computer system with ActiveX applications.

The lack of any security structure inspired Microsoft to develop its own Authenticode technology. This procedure enables the origin of the ActiveX controls to be identified, rather like a digital signature (see Chapter 7). It is silently assumed that the user will automatically be able to tell which providers are serious and which are dishonest.

A provider requests a certificate for a small charge, which allows him to sign his control. The certificate is sent to him, along with a private key. In return, the provider need only declare that he does not intend knowingly or negligently to manufacture malicious code or viruses.

Many attacks against ActiveX are known, most of which attempt to undermine the Authenticode procedure. In one case, an Excel spreadsheet was concealed on a prepared Web page; it started a lethal ActiveX program when the page was viewed. Since Excel is a local program with the highest security level, the Microsoft security check was passed without difficulty.

The potential danger with ActiveX should be regarded as significantly higher than with Java or even JavaScript. This will be apparent from the large number of attacks that are disclosed virtually every week, each of which results in one or more hot fixes from Microsoft. Unfortunately, Microsoft is fully committed to ActiveX – so much so that, for example, it is not possible to carry out a Windows 98 software update over the Internet without ActiveX.

Using ActiveX technologies on commercial systems in networks with public access, such as the Internet, is not advisable. Even when setting up an intranet or closed system, however, this system should only be used if it is protected through additional security measures.

Issues of liability are paramount here. If this liability can be resolved in a manner satisfactory to all parties, it would be conceivable to use ActiveX in conjunction with Authenticode technology. This would allow the user to claim compensation in the event of defective software or software contaminated with viruses.

Microsoft .NET and Web Services

Microsoft is heavily pushing a new model it calls *Web Services*. Web Services is an application infrastructure that allows for distributed applications across the Internet. Web Services is based on a Microsoft initiative called .NET. .Net uses the SOAP (Simple Object Access Protocol) for creating multi-system applications. Web Services applications claim to provide a means for seamless applications that encapsulate lower-level Internet functionality as needed, such as e-mail or Web server functionality, providing a platform that simplifies program use for the end user while allowing different organizations to communicate on a level of integration previously not possible. Since SOAP is the communications protocol used in Web Services, it is the protocol controlled at the firewall. SOAP messages are encapsulated within HTTP protocol communications. Extending current HTTP application gateways offers the quickest short-term means of adding firewall support for SOAP.

Web Services is in a very early stage of development, and as such, has not yet proven to be either a boon or an impediment to secure systems. Given that the goal of Web Services is to allow for tighter integration between companies, Web Services may potentially allow for deeper access to external entities. This access will need appropriate levels of security.

Firewall Systems from a Business Perspective

This section examines firewall systems from a business perspective. Organizations often want to calculate a Return on Investment (ROI) to determine the feasibility or impact to a company for the implementation of a firewall. This section is designed to help with the process of calculating ROI by quantifying expenditures involved with firewall implementation. The amount of expenditure required for a firewall system is spread over three phases:

- The procurement phase
- The installation phase
- Maintenance of operations

The amount of expenditure discussed in this section represents the effort that is required, independent of when work is performed. Effort is rounded to working days, which are assumed to be six hours long. In the expenditure figures provided in Tables 12-1, 12-2, and 12-3, it is assumed that at least 1,000 employees in the organization are allowed to communicate through the firewall system.

Labor is assumed to cost approximately 730 dollars per day. If specialist companies perform the stated services, their fees would probably be higher.

The Procurement Phase

During the procurement phase, the organization must draw up a firewall security policy that will serve as the basis for operating the firewall system. It is particularly important to analyze the protection requirement of the protected network and its component computer systems so that the security requirements can be accurately assessed.

Once the security policy has been defined, the organization can begin the process of selecting a firewall system product – by obtaining quotations, evaluating test installations, and obtaining reference assessments, for example. You must determine in advance the criteria against which products are to be evaluated.

During the procurement phase, it is important to facilitate the next phase by preparing infrastructural, personnel-related, and organizational security measures.

EXPENDITURE IN THE PROCUREMENT PHASE

If the organization has not yet developed a general security policy, the expense of drawing one up should be considered in the procurement phase. It can take between two weeks and three months to draw up a security policy, depending on the size of the organization and the protection requirement.

The amount of effort involved in selecting a firewall product can vary greatly, depending on the product selection procedures adopted – depending on whether, for example, the selection is made purely on the basis of brochures, or whether test installations of several firewall systems are to take place.

Definition and preparation of the infrastructural, personnel-related, and organizational security measures can take between one week and four weeks.

The procurement costs for a firewall product are between approximately 4,900 and 73,000 dollars, depending on the degree of security and trustworthiness which the system is to provide, and its capability.

The Installation Phase

In the installation phase, the costs related to a firewall system can fall into three categories:

- **Installation of the firewall system.** This phase covers all infrastructural security measures that are necessary for the secure operation of a firewall system.
- **Entry into service of the firewall system.** In this phase, it is appropriate to define user profiles for particular groups of employees in accordance with the provisions of the security policy, so that subsequent input of the

ruleset can be expedited. Once the user profiles have been drawn up, the users who are allowed to communicate through the firewall system are entered, with their user rights, in the Security Management module.

- **Other security measures.** In the installation phase, it is important to perform other security measures, such as user training, so that users learn how to work with the firewall system. These measures preclude potential complications during operation.

Tables 12-1, 12-2, and 12-3 show the time periods and financial resources that should be planned for in the procurement and installation phases.

TABLE 12-1 EFFORT AND EXPENSE DURING THE PROCUREMENT PHASE

Procurement Phase	Time Expenditure	Minimal Cost	Maximum Cost
Security policy	Two weeks to three months	$7,200	$43,100
Selection of a product	Two weeks to three months	$7,200	$43,100
Other security measures	One to four weeks	$3,600	$14,400
Product costs		$4,800	$72,000

TABLE 12-2 EFFORT AND EXPENSE DURING THE INSTALLATION PHASE

Installation Phase	Time Expenditure	Minimal Cost	Maximum Cost
Installation of the firewall system	2 to 5 days	$1,430	$3,600
Entry into service of the firewall system	3 to 10 days	$2,200	$7,200
Other security measures	3 weeks to 3 months	$10,800	$43,100

TABLE 12-3 TOTAL COSTS DURING THE PROCUREMENT AND INSTALLATION PHASES

Procurement and Installation Costs	Minimal Cost	Maximum Cost
Total	$37,230	$226,500

The Maintenance Phase

The cost of maintaining the firewall system can be considered in terms of access rights management, analysis of logbook data, configuration of new services, general administration, and secure operation.

ACCESS RIGHTS MANAGEMENT

A firewall system is designed in principle so that after all the access rights have been entered, it is completely independent and can be run without any active intervention on the part of an administrator.

In reality, however, human intervention may become necessary, perhaps to configure new staff members or to change the access rights of staff already entered. Depending on the number of changes to the defined user profiles, the amount of effort required on the part of the administrator for these tasks can vary widely.

It takes an administrator ten minutes on average to enter a new employee or to amend the access rights of an employee who is already entered on the system. If it is assumed that 5 percent of the employees in the organization who are allowed to communicate through the firewall system will change in a given month, then 50 changes will take place per month for every 1,000 employees. Access rights administration will take a total of 500 minutes every month (50 multiplied by 10). That's the equivalent of 9 hours a month, or 18 days a year.

ANALYZING LOGBOOK DATA

Analyzing the logbook data generated by the firewall system is a task performed by the administrator and should be included in the maintenance cost. Here, too, the staffing required to perform the work can vary considerably. With firewall systems that carry out an automatic preliminary evaluation, the effort expended on the part of the administrator is significantly lower than it is with firewall systems in which the administrator must evaluate the logbook data himself.

Analyzing logbook data is a task that usually takes up to three hours per week (two days per month or 24 days per year).

CONFIGURING NEW SERVICES

As TCP/IP technology is regularly subject to change, it must be assumed that one update will be carried out on the firewall system every three to six months to keep up with new requirements. Again, implementing these updates takes a certain amount of time, as they must be tested to guarantee that the operation of the firewall system continues to be secure.

You can assume that each update will take at least two days per update, or an average of six days per year.

GENERAL ADMINISTRATIVE EFFORT RELATED TO THE FIREWALL SYSTEM

For the secure operation of the firewall system, certain administrative tasks, such as backups of the current ruleset and the logbook data and deletions of protocol data on Security Management, must be performed.

General administrative work usually requires 3 hours per week (2 days per month or 24 days per year).

ANALYZING LOGBOOK DATA RELATED TO SECURITY MANAGEMENT ACTIONS

As security management of a firewall system is critical to overall security, all the management security actions taken by administrators must be audited at regular intervals using the logbook data in the Security Management module.

This type of work is assumed to take three hours per month, or six days per year.

SECURE OPERATION OF A FIREWALL SYSTEM

To ensure that communications between the insecure network and the protected network are effectively protected with the aid of a firewall system, the following conditions must be satisfied:

- The firewall system must be integrated into the organization's IT infrastructure.
- Operation of the firewall system must be based on a comprehensive security policy.
- The firewall system must be correctly installed.
- The firewall system must be correctly administered.

Regular checks of the implemented security measures implemented are required. In particular, you should determine whether the various security measures are being correctly adhered to.

This review must include all the security measures – technical, infrastructural, organizational, and personnel-related – that are responsible for the secure operation of the firewall system:

◆ **Technical security measures.**

  ■ Regular tests should be performed to check whether the rules laid down in the security policy are being correctly implemented.

  ■ An integration test of the firewall system that checks whether the firewall system and the ruleset are intact should be initialized.

◆ **Infrastructural security measures.**

  ■ Checks should be made at regular intervals to determine whether the infrastructural security measures (access-controlled rooms, protected cable runs, documentation, and labeling of firewall system labels, for example) are being adhered to.

◆ **Organizational security measures.**

  ■ Checks must be performed at regular intervals to determine whether any new connections that circumvent the Common Point of Trust (the firewall system) have been created.

  ■ The logbook data must be checked regularly to determine whether any attacks have taken place.

◆ **Personnel-related security measures.**

  ■ Measures aimed at raising awareness about security should be initiated at regular intervals. (These measures may take the form of circulars, training, informational events, and so on).

Table 12-4 quantifies the effort involved in maintaining the effectiveness of a firewall.

TABLE 12-4 MAINTAINING THE EFFECTIVENESS OF A FIREWALL SYSTEM

Measure to be Performed	Effort Required
Technical security measures	4 days per year
Infrastructural security measures	4 days per year
Organizational security measures	4 days per year
Personnel-related security measures	12 days per year
Total	24 days per year

Table 12-5 quantifies the effort required to maintain the firewall system itself.

TABLE 12-5 MAINTAINING THE OPERATION OF A FIREWALL SYSTEM

Measure to be Performed	Effort Required
Access rights management	18 days per year
Analysis of logbook data	24 days per year
Configuration of new services	6 days per year
General administrative tasks	24 days per year
Analysis of logbook data relating to Security Management actions	6 days per year
Secure operation of a firewall system	24 days per year
Total	102 days per year

The cost of operating a firewall system serving 1,000 users that is in accord with the assumptions outlined earlier is approximately 73,300 dollars per year, or 73.30 dollars per user per year.

Summary of Costs

The expense incurred with a firewall system comprises the cost of acquisition, which may fall between 36,900 and 226,300 dollars, and the operating cost. If you assume 1,000 users and a large number of changes, this expenditure is estimated at 73,300 dollars per year.

These figures depend to a large degree on the structure and size of the organization. In addition, the following issues must be considered:

- What firewall system will be used?
- How strong is the firewall design?
- How many users will be allowed to communicate through the firewall system?
- How much will the communications profiles change?
- How qualified are the administrators who will be performing security management tasks?
- What operating times will be considered?
- What additional services (modem servers, intranet servers, Internet servers, and so on) will be used?

- Are the user rights subject to change?
- Will there be any changes in the network structure?
- To what depth is the logbook data to be analyzed?
- What authentication procedures will be used? The options include:
  - S/KEY (new passwords must always be made available)
  - Security tokens (only need to be configured once)

Cost-Benefit Analysis of Firewall Systems

This section provides a sample cost-benefit analysis of a firewall system, assuming a bank with approximately 1,000 employees. It is assumed that the probability of a successful attack is very high if no firewall system is used.

BANK'S PROFIT OVER THE LAST YEAR

- 23.9 million dollars

COST OF A FIREWALL SYSTEM

- Acquisition costs: 239,000 dollars (1 percent of profit)
- Operating costs: 76,600 dollars

DESCRIPTION OF A POSSIBLE ATTACK A hacker attacks a bank over the Internet. The hacker takes a copy of the names and account balances of the 500 most important bank customers from the protected network. The names and account balances are then published on the Internet, the story is reported on television and in the press, and, as a result, the bank sustains a serious loss of image.

POSSIBLE DAMAGE AS A RESULT OF THIS ATTACK A serious loss of image causes large numbers of customers to move to another, more trustworthy bank, causing the victimized bank to sustain the following financial loss:

- Immediately: 11.9 million dollars (50 percent of profit)
- In the middle term: 2.39 million dollars

SUMMARY Assuming that the bank's loss might have been prevented had a firewall system been in place, then the investment in a firewall system would have been worthwhile. By investing 1 percent of its annual profits, the bank avoids a loss that would have added up to many times the amount of the investment (in this example, 60 times greater).

Public disclosure of the attack could also result in "free-riders" attempting to imitate the attack. The result is an increased risk of a second attack, and the cost of procuring a firewall system that is suitable to warding off further attacks must be added to the cost of rectifying the damage.

PROBABILITY OF A PARTICULAR PROFIT Figure 12-2 shows how the investment in security mechanisms depends on the protection requirement and the probability of being able to achieve a particular profit.

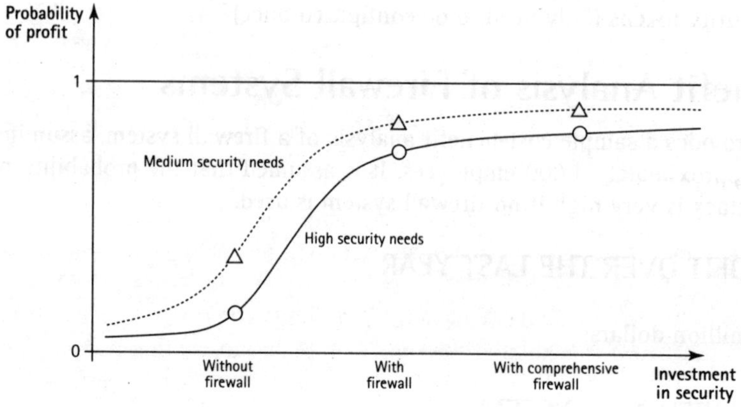

Figure 12-2: Probability of profit

In areas for which the protection requirement is high (for example, in financial institutions), higher investment in security measures is necessary to preserve the same prospect of making a particular profit.

As money is invested in security mechanisms, the probability of achieving a particular profit also increases. In other words, the procurement of security systems such as firewall systems, VPN, intrusion detection, and anti-virus software is an investment in protecting an organization's profits. The more money invested in security mechanisms, the greater the probability of achieving a particular profit. However, these measures alone cannot provide 100 percent certainty of making a profit, as there is always a residual risk.

The probability of achieving a given profit depends also on the protection requirement and, furthermore, on the probability of an attack. The greater the probability, the greater the need for protection against an attack.

If the protection requirement is very high, the probability of achieving a given profit is lower than when the protection requirement is only low.

If the use of security mechanisms is abandoned, this difference is much greater than if extensive use is made of security mechanisms, as the probability of an attack is lower when the protection requirement is low. In the final analysis, the company's management is responsible for the enterprise security, and it must make a decision on the correct cost-benefit ratio.

Management would be well advised to spend a certain percentage of the profit on IT security as a kind of "profit insurance." This percentage will be higher in organizations, such as banks and insurance companies, whose success is based on an image of trustworthiness. In organizations such as transport companies or breweries, IT security has only a minor effect on image.

Evaluation and Certification of Firewall Systems

Before purchasing a firewall system, customers and users must determine what security criteria it satisfies. Vendor marketing claims regarding the product's capabilities are not regulated and often highly suspect. Given the scope and effort involved in a firewall implementation, it is imprudent to move forward based solely upon vendor claims.

The aim of the evaluation is to give the user of the security system confidence that the security mechanisms are effective against the known types of attack and that his assets are appropriately protected.

A customer or user can either evaluate a firewall system himself or have the evaluation performed by a specialist. However, the first option is often not possible due to lack of expertise or the large number of resources required to perform the evaluation properly.

The alternative is to have the evaluation carried out by a competent and independent agency (evaluation laboratory). A certificate granted by experts at the end of an evaluation provides customers and users with a yardstick against which to assess the trustworthiness of different firewall systems. The evaluation is generally performed against defined criteria.

The evaluation and certification of firewall systems can be carried out in a number of ways. The next few sections present some of the most well-known certification procedures, certification according to the ITSEC and ICSA criteria. The depth of assessment that can be achieved using the two methods is also described.

ITSEC Certification

France, the Federal Republic of Germany, the Netherlands, and Great Britain developed *Information Technology Security Evaluation Criteria (ITSEC)* on the basis of existing national IT security criteria. Harmonization of the different criteria was driven on the one hand by the interests of the IT industry, which was faced with different security criteria in different countries, and on the other hand by the desire on the part of participating countries to put their accumulated experience to good use. While ITSEC certification is not directly applicable in the United States, the evaluation criteria and methods used offer some valuable lessons in properly determining firewall security.

The developed criteria constitute the basis for certification by the national certification authorities, which mutually recognize certificates issued on the basis of these criteria.

Certification can be applied for and carried out both by the vendor and by the distributor of a firewall system. When the applicant *is* the vendor, the necessary documentation is already available and does not have to be prepared anew. However, the certification process is very expensive. Certification by a distributor is only worthwhile if the evaluation level to be applied is low, because the relevant sources (for the software, for example) will generally not be available to the distributor.

This section describes, by way of example, what documentation the vendor or developer must provide, and what tests must be carried out to obtain certification to evaluation level E3.

In addition to the vendor or developer and the certification authority, an accredited testing body is also involved in the evaluation. The testing body (test laboratory), which is commissioned by the vendor to perform the necessary technical tests under the supervision of the certification authority, produces the relevant test reports. Finally, the certification authority prepares and publishes a certification report containing all the findings. The certification report contains, for example, a description of the types of attack against which the firewall system provides protection, a list of the security mechanisms implemented, details of the precise technical and organizational operational environment of the firewall system, and residual risks under particular assumptions.

The evaluation is performed against the yardsticks of correctness and effectiveness. The evaluation of correctness examines whether the security-enforcing functions and mechanisms have been correctly implemented. The evaluation of effectiveness assesses whether the security-enforcing functions and security mechanisms of the firewall system actually achieve the stated objectives. In addition, the capability of the security mechanisms to withstand a direct attack is assessed.

The documentation that is required for the assessment of correctness and which must be provided by the manufacturer or distributor includes the following elements:

- Informal description of the firewall system's architecture
- Informal description of the firewall system's detailed design
- Test documentation
- Library of test programs and test tools that were used to test the firewall system
- The source code and/or hardware design drawings for all security-specific and security-relevant components
- Informal description of correspondence, presenting the relationship between source code or hardware design drawings and the detailed design
- Configuration list that uniquely identifies the version of the firewall system
- Information on the configuration control system

- Information on the acceptance procedure
- Information on the security of the development environment
- Description of all the implementation languages used
- User documentation
- System administrator documentation
- Delivery and configuration documentation
- Start-up and operating documentation

The following documentation on the firewall system must be provided in connection with the evaluation of effectiveness:

- Suitability analysis of the security mechanisms
- Binding analysis of the security mechanisms
- Analysis of the strength of the firewall system's security mechanisms
- List of known weaknesses in the design
- Ease of use analysis
- List of known weaknesses that affect operational use of the firewall system

SECURITY GOAL

The firewall's security specifications are a description of the firewall system's security features. The relevant security criteria apply to the security features on three different levels:

- Security objectives. Why is the functionality needed?
- Security-enforcing functions. What functionality is made available to achieve the security objectives?
- Security mechanisms. How is the functionality provided?

The security target must contain the following items:

- A product description (what services are implemented, what security management facilities are available, and so on)
- The type of product used
- The envisaged operational environment (technical and administrative)
- Definition of the security objectives
- The assumed threats the firewall system is to counter

- The security-enforcing functions provided
- The security mechanisms
- The effectiveness of the security mechanisms

The test laboratory checks whether at least one security-enforcing function exists for every possible threat, and whether it effectively combats the threat. The security mechanisms that provide the corresponding functionality are checked for their effectiveness.

ARCHITECTURAL DESIGN

The architectural design describes the general structure of the firewall system and all its external interfaces. The firewall system is broken down into security-enforcing and non-security-enforcing components. Security-enforcing components directly perform security-specific functions or are involved in them. The separation between security-enforcing and non-security-enforcing components is described, and the effectiveness of this separation is reviewed in the architectural design document.

DETAILED DESIGN

The detailed design of the firewall system contains the specification of all the components and their interfaces. All security-enforcing functions must be described and mapped onto the components, and all security mechanisms must be defined and specified. The detailed design must demonstrate that the stated security mechanisms can in no way be circumvented.

TESTS

The correspondence between the security mechanisms and the source code must be explained. In other words, a description must be provided of where and how each security mechanism is implemented. Each individual security mechanism must be demonstrated in tests. For this purpose, the manufacturer's test documentation must include plans, objectives, procedures, and results for the tests used, as well as libraries for all test programs and tools. Additionally, the source code for the firewall system must be available.

The test laboratory checks the source code and test documentation to see whether all security-enforcing functions have been considered and whether all security mechanisms have been tested. To this end, the source code is analyzed to find any possibilities of circumventing the security mechanisms, and the tests are repeated. In addition, penetration testing and error detection tests are performed. Several commercially available tools – for example, SATAN and Internet Security Scanner (ISS) – as well as proprietary, special tools are used to test all security mechanisms individually and thoroughly.

DEVELOPMENT ENVIRONMENT

The development environment comprises the configuration control system, the acceptance procedure, the configuration list, and a description of all the implementation languages used.

In the sections covering the configuration control system, the acceptance procedure and the configuration list, the manufacturer ensures that the firewall system is compliant with the documentation provided, that only authorized changes to it are possible, that the firewall system is complete, and that the stated version is unique.

The test laboratory checks the use of the configuration control system and the acceptance procedure at the manufacturer.

The programming languages used for the implementation, along with all options, must be clearly stated. This is necessary in case there should be a requirement to reconstruct the firewall system.

Using information about the security of his development environment, the manufacturer must show how the protective measures regarding the integrity of the firewall system and the confidentiality of the associated documentation are implemented. All security measures necessary for this must be described. The measures are broken down into:

- **Material measures** – limited access rooms for the computers on which the firewall system is developed, uninterruptible power supplies
- **Organizational measures** – restrictive rights administration for the computers on which the firewall system is developed, control of modem usage
- **Personnel-related security measures** – security-certified firewall system developers and staff

The test laboratory checks the application and adherence to the specified procedures and provisions. In addition, the test laboratory staff searches for any errors that might exist in the procedures that are used.

OPERATIONAL DOCUMENTATION

The firewall system's operational documentation falls into two categories: user documentation and administration documentation.

User documentation must be structured and internally consistent. It must contain guidelines for the secure operation of the firewall system and a description of how the user may operate it in a secure manner.

The administration documentation must also be structured and internally consistent. It must describe how the product is installed, configured, and securely administered. The administration documentation must contain a description of the security parameters and must explain the various types of possible security-relevant events, the procedures relevant to security administration, and the security features and their interaction.

OPERATIONAL ENVIRONMENT

Documentation of the operational environment covers two separate aspects:

- Delivery and configuration
- Start-up and operation

The information on delivery and configuration procedures must describe how the manufacturer maintains the security of the firewall system – for example, through software checksums, seals on the hardware, and so on. If different configurations are possible, their effects on security must be described.

The test laboratory must check that the delivery procedure for the firewall system has been correctly implemented and must search for any possible errors.

The manufacturer must describe how the procedures for start-up and operation are implemented and how they maintain security. To this end, the security-enforcing functions that can be disabled or modified during start-up, operation, or maintenance must be described. Examples of any audit output and example results from diagnostic test procedures that are created during start-up and operation must be presented. The test laboratory checks the audit output and the results from diagnostic test procedures and searches for errors.

SUITABILITY ANALYSIS

The analysis of functionality suitability checks whether the security-enforcing functions and mechanisms of the firewall system actually counter the threats identified in the security target.

BINDING ANALYSIS

The binding analysis reveals the ability of the firewall system's security-enforcing functions and mechanisms to work together in a way that is mutually supportive and that provides an integrated and effective whole. The binding analysis also shows that there are no security-enforcing functions or mechanisms that conflict with or contradict the intent of other security-enforcing functions or mechanisms.

STRENGTH OF MECHANISMS ANALYSIS

The mechanisms analysis assesses the resistance of the security mechanisms to any direct attack based on deficiencies in their underlying algorithms, principles, or properties. The level of resources required to execute a successful direct attack is also considered. Analysis of the algorithms, principles, and properties underlying the security mechanisms must be prepared or referenced. The analysis must show how the claimed rating of minimum strength is satisfied, and must use all information available, including the firewall system source code.

Using all available information, including the source code, the test laboratory checks whether the security mechanisms deliver the claimed minimum strength. In addition, active and aggressive penetration testing is carried out in order to confirm the minimum strength.

EASE OF USE ANALYSIS

The ease of use analysis shows whether any human or other operational error exists that deactivates or disables security-enforcing functions or mechanisms. It also reveals whether a possibility exists to configure or use the firewall system in an insecure way, particularly when an end-user or firewall system administrator would believe it to be reasonably secure. The ease of use analysis must describe any of the firewall system's possible operating modes, including operation following failure or operational error, and the failure or error's consequences for maintaining secure operation.

Within the ease of use analyses and using all available information, including the source code, the test laboratory must check to see if undocumented or unreasonable assumptions about the intended operational environment have been made. Every configuration and installation procedure must be repeated, to check that the firewall system can be configured and used securely.

EFFECTIVENESS OF THE FIREWALL SECURITY MECHANISMS

This section examines firewall security mechanisms from the perspective of efficacy. This examination is based on a vulnerability analysis of the firewall system. In this analysis, every route that would allow an attacker to deactivate, circumvent, alter, disable, directly attack, or otherwise neutralize security-enforcing functions and security mechanisms is investigated. All the information available, including the source code, is used.

STRENGTH OF THE SECURITY MECHANISMS THAT ARE IMPLEMENTED IN THE FIREWALL SYSTEM

Even if a security mechanism cannot be circumvented, neutralized, or corrupted in any other manner, it might still be possible to defeat it in a direct attack, due to defects in the underlying algorithms, principles, or characteristics. For this aspect of effectiveness, the ability of the security mechanisms to withstand such direct attacks must be assessed. This aspect of effectiveness differs from others in that it considers the level of resources an attacker would need in order to carry out a successful direct attack.

EFFECTIVENESS OF SECURITY SYSTEMS

One important criterion regarding the assessment of security systems is whether the security systems that a firewall system offers are also suitable to counter the most critical threats.

It is possible for security services to be inadequate even when their security mechanisms have sufficient strength. If an attack does not target the security services but rather bypasses the services the attack can succeed despite the security mechanisms being strong. An attack that bypasses security mechanisms in this manner is classified as an indirect attack. An indirect attack might be carried out if, for example:

- An attacker can alter the firewall system's access rights management module through the operating system used.
- An attacker can use IP forwarding (kernel functionality) from outside.

The strength of security mechanisms can be given three possible ratings: basic, medium, and high.

One variable that is important to the assessment of security mechanisms is the *minimum strength of the security mechanism (SoMmin)*, which is necessary to successfully counter all security threats.

Examples of circumstances where the security mechanism is not sufficiently thick to stop an attack include the following:

- The depth of analysis does not detect or prevent the attack.
- Security mechanisms can be breached due to security shortcomings in other areas. A typical example of this type of problem can be seen with plain-text passwords. Although a particular service, such as telnet, may be protected with a password, authentication can be achieved by successfully using a sniffer program to collect the passwords while users are logging in legitimately.
- Another service is executed on a well-known port in the packet filter.

Mechanisms employed (algorithms, principles, and characteristics, for example) assure the necessary minimum strength of the security mechanisms so that an attack can be successfully warded off.

The effectiveness of the security mechanism can be increased still further through external measures, with the aim of warding off attacks. Examples of external measures used to increase security effectiveness include the following:

- Assurance of the network
- Assurance of the network prevents the occurrence of a masquerade attack, for example
- Trustworthiness of the communications partner

In the event an attack succeeds, you can trace the attack and implement measures that reduce the amount of damage and future vulnerability. A couple common mitigations to attack include the following:

- Logging security-relevant information for the detection and analysis of attacks
- Evidence retention so that the permitted participant cannot deny having performed certain actions

THE STRENGTH OF SECURITY MECHANISMS IS DEFINED AS FOLLOWS:

- **Basic:** To be rated "basic," the SoMmin must be shown to provide protection against random accidental subversion, although it may still be capable of being defeated by knowledgeable attackers.
- **Medium:** To be rated "medium," the minimum strength of a critical security mechanism must provide protection against attackers with limited opportunity or resources.
- **High:** To be rated "high," the SoMmin must show that only attackers possessing a high level of expertise, opportunity, and resources can defeat it. The requirements for a successful attack are beyond normal practicality. Use of a 1024 bit key for encryption (requiring millions of years to find the key through trying possible combinations) is an example of a high security mechanism.

EXPERTISE, OPPORTUNITY, AND RESOURCES

The term *expertise* refers to the knowledge that a person must possess in order to attack a security system. A *layperson* is defined as a person without any particular expertise, such as a normal Internet user. A *proficient person* is familiar with the internal workings of the security system. An *expert* is familiar with the underlying principles and algorithms of the firewall system. Experts would include, for example, hackers, security experts, or secret services.

Resources are the means by which an attacker successfully attacks the security system. In this discussion, a distinction is made between two types of resources: time and equipment. *Time* refers to the amount of time required to complete an attack, excluding any planning activities. The phrase "within minutes" means that an attack can be successfully carried out in less than ten minutes. "Within days" means that an attack can be successfully carried out in less than one month. "Within months" means that at least one month is required for a successful attack.

Equipment refers to computers, electronic devices, hardware, tools, software, and so on. The phrase "without equipment" means that it is possible to perpetrate an attack without any special resources – using only a browser, for example. "Existing equipment" refers to equipment that is already available in the firewall system's operational environment, is part of the actual firewall system, or can be purchased. "Special equipment" refers to special equipment that is required to perpetrate an attack.

Opportunity refers to factors that are generally outside the control of an attacker: help from another person (collusion), the probability of certain circumstances coinciding (chance), and the probability that the attacker will be identified (discovery). These factors are generally very difficult to assess. However, it is possible to define discrete categories regarding collusion:

- **Alone:** Collusion with another party is not required for an attack.
- **With one user:** To successfully perpetrate an attack, the attacker needs the collusion of a user of the security system who is not rated as particularly trustworthy.
- **With a system administrator:** A successful attack requires the collusion of a user of the firewall system who is held to be highly trustworthy.

The following rules can be used to calculate the strength of the security mechanism:

- If the security mechanism can be defeated within minutes by a layperson alone, then the security mechanism cannot even be rated basic.
- If the security mechanism can only be defeated over a period of months by an expert using specialist equipment, who is also dependent on the collusion of the system administrator, then it is rated high.
- If the security mechanism can only be defeated with the collusion of a user, then it is rated at least medium.
- If the security mechanism can only be defeated with the collusion of a system administrator, then it is rated high.
- If it takes months to successfully defeat the security mechanism, than it is rated at least medium.
- If a successful attack requires months of effort by an expert using special equipment, then the security mechanism is rated high, whether or not the collusion of any other party is needed.
- If it takes days to successfully defeat the security mechanism, then it is rated at least basic.
- If a successful attack can be perpetrated within minutes by anyone other than a layperson, then the mechanism is rated low.
- If a successful attack can only be perpetrated by an expert who needs several days using existing equipment, the security mechanism is rated medium.

With Tables 12-6 and 12-7, it is possible to estimate the strength of security mechanisms. The numbers calculated in the two tables should be added, and the results assessed as shown below.

TABLE 12-6 STRENGTH OF THE SECURITY MECHANISM WHEN FACTORING IN COLLUSION

Time	Alone	With a User	With a System Administrator
Within minutes	0	12	24
Within days	5	12	24
Months or a year	16	16	24

TABLE 12-7 STRENGTH OF THE SECURITY MECHANISM WHEN USING TOOLS OR EQUIPMENT

Expertise	Without Tools	With Existing Equipment	With Special Equipment
Layperson	1	n/a	n/a
Proficient person	4	4	n/a
Expert	6	8	12

The scores from Tables 12-6 and 12-7 should be interpreted as follows:

A. If the resulting score is 1, then the strength is not even sufficient for a rating of basic.

B. If the score is greater than 1 but less than 12, then the strength of the security mechanism is rated basic.

C. If the score is between 12 and 24, then the strength of the security mechanism is rated medium.

D. If the score is greater than 24, then the strength of the security mechanism is rated high.

These tables can only serve as a starting point, since they cannot necessarily be used for every security mechanism and operational environment. For example, they are not suitable for assessing cryptographic security mechanisms.

For firewall systems that are used to protect Internet access, the minimum strength must be high, as you will find large numbers of experts equipped with special equipment and unlimited time and money on the Internet.

CORRECTNESS OF THE FIREWALL SECURITY MECHANISMS *Correctness* refers to the correct implementation of security mechanisms and to the degree of assurance provided by the implemented firewall solution.

ITSEC defines seven hierarchical evaluation levels (E0 to E6) for assessing the correctness aspects of assurance. E0 is not actually a level. E1 corresponds to the lowest level, and E6 corresponds to the highest.

Each higher level includes the cumulative requirements of all levels below it. The major requirements that make up the difference between a given level and the level immediately above it are defined in Table 12-8.

TABLE 12-8 THE DIFFERENT EVALUATION LEVELS

Evaluation Level	Description
E0	This level represents inadequate assurance.
E1	At this level, there must be a security target and an informal description of the architectural design of the firewall system. Functional testing must indicate that the firewall system satisfies the security target.
E2	In addition to the requirements for level E1, there must be an informal description of the detailed design. Evidence of functional testing must be evaluated. You must have a configuration control system and an approved distribution procedure.
E3	In addition to the requirements for level E2, the source code and/or hardware drawings corresponding to the security mechanisms must be evaluated. Evidence of testing of those security mechanisms must be evaluated.
E4	In addition to the requirements for level E3, there must be an underlying formal model of security policy supporting the security target. The security-enforcing functions, the architectural design, and the detailed design must be specified in a semi-formal style.
E5	In addition to the requirements for level E4, there must be a close correspondence between the detailed design and the source code and/or hardware drawings.
E6	In addition to the requirements for level E5, the security-enforcing functions and the architectural design must be specified in a formal style, consistent with the specified underlying formal model of security policy.

ICSA Certification

The International Computer Security Association (ICSA, previously NCSA) is an organization founded by various users and hardware and software manufacturers, including firewall manufacturers. Its aim is to help users increase the level of IT security, preserve the integrity of their information, and reduce the number of threats from computer viruses (see also `www.icsa.net`).

NCSA has become well known on account of numerous publications in the area of computer security and the creation of its own set of criteria for firewall systems.

This section summarizes the ICSA criteria for firewall systems, which are subdivided into functional and security requirements.

FUNCTIONAL REQUIREMENTS

Functional requirements specify which services must be available to users of the protected internal network, to users of the unprotected external network, and to firewall system management.

- **Services for internal users**
  - Telnet through the firewall system to external networks
  - FTP through the firewall system to external networks
  - HTTP through the firewall system to external networks
  - SSL and/or SHTTP through the firewall system to external networks
  - SMTP through the firewall system to external networks
  - External DNS information must be made available
- **Services for external users**
  - FTP access to a server on the internal network or a service network
  - HTTP access to a server on the internal network or a service network
  - SSL and/or SHTTP access to a server on the internal network
  - It must be possible for SMTP mail to be delivered to the users of the internal network
  - DNS
- **Requirements regarding management of the firewall system**
  - Access to the firewall system console must be protected through password authentication.
  - If management is to be performed remotely via *external* networks, then one-time passwords or other secure authentication mechanisms must be used, in addition to an encrypted connection mechanism.

- If management is to be performed remotely via *internal* networks, the IP address must not be the only mechanism used to authenticate the security administrator.

SECURITY REQUIREMENTS

The functions necessary to satisfy the security requirements are tested. For this process, the known details of the test configuration and the individual components are used. Attacks are performed both from the external and from the internal network. The following underlying criteria are used:

- The attacker must not be able to overcome control mechanisms of the firewall system or of the underlying operating system through an attack.
- Only those protocols or data content described above in connection with the firewall system may be allowed into the internal network.
- Denial-of-service: It must not be possible for the firewall system to be rendered inoperable through simple network-based attacks. The following exceptions apply:
  - The firewall system has a documented, self-protecting mechanism enabling switching to a condition without firewall services.
  - If it is detected that an attack with the objective of paralyzing the system will be successful, the product must send a logged alarm before switching itself off.

In the test phase, both the protected network and the area outside the firewall system are monitored. For this purpose, the latest version of the ISS Security Scanner is used, including all the data of the firewall system and the system to be protected.

The ISS Security Scanner includes tests for numerous reproducible threats known at the time of the version release. As part of the ongoing tests, the NCSA carries out regular updates of the ISS Security Scanner, always using the latest version of the product.

The tests with the ISS Security Scanner are carried out against the firewall system both from a non-trusted, nearby subnet (external scan) and from the trustworthy subnet (internal scan).

Additionally, the firewall system is tested with a port-scanning tool in order to check whether the system fulfills the functional requirements. These scans are also carried out both from a non-trusted nearby subnet and from the trustworthy subnet.

DISCUSSION OF ITSEC AND ICSA CRITERIA

The ITSEC evaluation criteria and the ICSA evaluation criteria differ in several respects. Table 12-9 highlights some of these differences.

TABLE 12-9 DIFFERENCES IN THE PROCEDURES FOR THE CERTIFICATION OF FIREWALL SYSTEMS

ITSEC	ICSA
The strength of the security mechanisms is stated. This is possible on the basis of the detailed analysis.	No statement is made regarding the strength of the security mechanisms. It must therefore be assumed that the level is low.
The source code is available. A check is performed to determine whether security mechanisms have been correctly implemented and cannot be circumvented.	The source code is not available. It is not possible to check the correct implementation of the mechanisms, and any existing errors or trapdoors are not detected.
The development process and the environment of the firewall system are considered.	The development process and the environment of the firewall system are not considered.
A statement is made about the security level achieved.	A certificate is either issued or withheld.
Which security mechanism implements which security-enforcing function, and which threat is countered thereby, is investigated in detail.	Individual specific and currently known attacks are warded off. Otherwise, no statements are made.
The administration of the firewall system by a firewall management function in different operating modes is analyzed for control and operating errors.	The only requirements placed on firewall management are requirements relating to access control and remote management.
The technical and administrative operating environment must be declared. It is checked, and any remaining weaknesses are identified.	No statements are made on the administrative operating environment or on any weaknesses that may remain.

In conclusion, the NCSA criteria are the equivalent of the ITSEC criteria for evaluation level E1. At this level, functional tests only demonstrate that the firewall system satisfies the required security objectives. No statement is made regarding the strength of the security mechanisms. Since the tests, however, are carried out with a freely available tool, only a mechanism strength of "low" can be assigned.

Further Development of Comprehensive Firewall Systems

Firewall systems, as well as the communications applications themselves, will continue to develop. This section describes selected aspects of firewall system developments.

Increasing Innovations

New means by which firewall systems can be adapted securely, rapidly, and dynamically to new requirements without loss of security should be explored as new innovations come to light in the area of Internet applications.

Integrative, Central Security Management of All Security Mechanisms

In the future, it will be important to integrate the different security mechanisms into a common security system to assure the highest possible degree of security.

Ever Greater Speed Combined with an Ever Higher Protection Requirement

As business processes are increasingly transacted over communications systems such as the Internet, and as the amount of information exchanged increases steadily, higher bandwidths will be necessary for today's communications systems. Depending on usage, the bandwidths will develop differently. For public connections, you will see bandwidths around 34 or 155 Mbps, rising to 622 Mbps and more; in the local area with Fast Ethernet, 100 Mbps; and with the gigabit Ethernet, up to 1 Gbps. This means that in the near future, firewall systems must deliver corresponding speed in order to handle a high data throughput securely.

This development will mean that more high-value information with a high to very high protection requirement is processed and stored.

The future requirements for speed and protection can only be implemented if guidelines are developed regarding how, for example, proxies can be optimized and securely implemented in hardware so that a high level of security can be achieved at a high speed.

New Proxies for New Services

The meteoric development of TCP/IP technology is expected to result in future innovations that bring new services. For such services, if they become established, proxies must be provided on firewall systems so that the services can be implemented on the firewall systems while ensuring optimal protection.

Universal Identification and Authentication Procedures

Passwords as a means of authentication present numerous problems. For example, the sheer number of passwords a user must recall is often daunting. Given the current reliance on passwords and the availability of other authentication mechanisms, it stands to reason that superior authentication mechanisms will increase in use and support.

Uniform Representation of Attacks and Security Services and Mechanisms

Since, in practice, no qualitative and comparable statements can be made about the effectiveness of firewall systems against defined attacks, a set of uniform security criteria for firewall systems must be drawn up by the vendors for the benefit of users, enabling them to judge the security and trustworthiness of firewall systems. This process could be implemented, for example, by defining a firewall system *protection profile* along the lines of the Common Criteria.

Log Analysis

Analysis of logged data enables security violations to be found and evidence of the firewall users' actions to be retained. To ensure that these valuable security functions are used in the future, new procedures enabling automatic detection of protection violations and efficient administration of logged data must be developed specifically for the purpose of evidence preservation. This can result in reduced operating costs.

Security Audits

Due to its position as a bastion against a network that is classified as insecure, a firewall system plays a particularly important role in relation to IT security. Safeguarding the firewall functionality is, therefore, an important element of the operation and maintenance of networks. Unfortunately, IT system security is often not taken seriously enough, so it is important to regularly check the correct operation of the firewall system. The reasons for checking the correct operation of the firewall are obvious:

- No complex system is completely error-free. The operating system of the firewall computer and the firewall software itself must therefore be maintained at regular intervals and updated to the latest versions. These errors could stem from either technological or human errors in the form of configuration settings.

- The attack possibilities from outside are so diverse and capable of transformation that a system that counts as secure today could easily exhibit serious security weaknesses tomorrow.
- New services are constantly being implemented on the Internet. If they are to be used in an organization, they necessitate configuration changes to the firewall system.

Whenever the security of firewall systems is under consideration, it must be borne in mind that, from a statistical viewpoint, most attacks on computer networks are perpetrated from *inside* an organization, usually by an organization's own staff. Therefore, in a network that is administered in a responsible fashion, you must widen the security checks to cover the entire IT infrastructure. The procedures and tools described in this chapter may be aimed primarily at the control of firewall systems, but they can be adapted so that they can also be used for checking extensive parts of the network infrastructure through the entire network.

Security Audits

You won't find a fixed definition of the term *security audit*, as every service provider or vendor of relevant tools interprets the term to comprise that which he offers. Nevertheless, there are some framework conditions and criteria that belong to every security audit. The heart of a security audit is the discovery of security defects of any kind, from vulnerability to e-mail bombing through unfettered access to the computer room containing the firewall system. Compared with a security check that simply identifies and documents any defects that are found, a security audit includes a review of a company's internal security policy. To ensure that an audit can be carried out, it is therefore necessary that a security policy exists and is set down in writing, along with in-house security guidelines derived from it. In many companies, these guidelines do not exist, so that when the guidelines aren't provided, it is only possible to carry out the less effective security checks.

AIM OF A SECURITY AUDIT

The aim of a security audit goes far beyond merely discovering weaknesses and security loopholes. It is used to ensure permanent consistency between the security guidelines and their practical implementation. For this reason, a security audit is not confined to the discovery of technological problems, such as non-current versions of operating systems and applications. It is equally important to include data that could reveal organizational or personnel-related deficiencies.

PRACTICAL PROCEDURE

Starting from the security guidelines on the installation and operation of the firewall system, a security audit collects data about security deficiencies using the tools discussed in this chapter. This data is compiled into a report and then – and this is a critical point – put in the form of feedback on the security guidelines and/or their practical implementation. In most cases, deficiencies in the practical implementation of the guidelines are identified as part of the report, but the report can also lead to modification and/or redefinition of guidelines or even of the security policy.

A firewall system generally constitutes only a small subset of a company's internal network infrastructure. However, to collect the data, information sources from the entire network area must be used. Before commencing the audit, plans and inventory lists must be available so that the sequence of actions to be taken in the security audit can be determined. Interviews and site visits are then carried out, in the course of which any organizational, staff-related, and building-related defects are identified. Only then can visibility be gained through technical measurements of any problems in the firewall system itself and/or in its connection to the external and internal networks. A range of commercial products is available for this purpose, including *toolboxes* with freeware and shareware.

REPETITION OF THE SECURITY AUDIT

As the security of firewall systems is never static, an audit must be repeated at regular intervals, even if no defects were found on one particular occasion. As a rule of thumb, you should schedule the audit every six months to a year, unless major changes take place in the interim, such as:

- Upgrade of the operating system or.firewall software
- Release of new services
- Extensive changes in the protected network by the firewall system or organizational changes (relocation, mergers, takeovers of other companies, and so on)
- Building-related or organizational changes that affect the system
- Discovery of new classes of attacks

In these or similar cases, an audit should be carried out after the necessary measures have been taken.

Components of a Security Audit

DETERMINING THE SCOPE OF WORK

Even though the audit is limited to a single firewall system, any number of different approaches can be taken, depending on the particular problem and initial situation. For example, where a new e-mail system is introduced, it is advisable to carry out a security audit that is oriented to that service. In most cases, however, the audit will relate to the firewall system as a whole, with all the services and protocols that are available on it. Systems that are directly connected to firewall systems can also be included in the investigations if required.

OBTAINING THE BACKGROUND MATERIAL

The report produced at the completion of a security audit can only be as good as the material on which the collected data is based. The background material that exists prior to beginning work is of central importance. This material should include:

- The written versions of the security policy and security guidelines. These constitute the "spectacles" through which all the research and analyses should be viewed.
- The results of previous audits, so that progress or even a decline in the quality of security can be documented.
- Inventory lists for hardware and software, so that the currency and completeness of the system installation can be checked.
- Building plans on which the location of computer rooms and cabling, as well as possible access routes, are marked.
- Plans of the network topology, enabling equipment connections to be checked.
- A list of contact persons in case any further information is needed.

Depending on the size and structure of the organization, it can take longer to obtain this material than to collect the rest of the data and/or to analyze it. The quality of the feedback of the audit depends on the completeness of the initial data. For this reason, despite the existence of security guidelines, only pure security checks without feedback are usually carried out because they are easier to perform. However, such results are often more difficult to implement, as they are not properly integrated into an overall design.

AREAS OF FOCUS

After the starting material has been examined, the objectives of the audit should be set out in writing. Areas of focus could, for example, include the following:

- Review of the firewall system's physical security – to check, for example, whether a third party could access the system, log in on the firewall system console, or tamper with network connections.
- Review of the software's currency – to check, for example, whether the versions of software being used agree with details provided by the vendor as to the most up-to-date release statuses, including hot fixes and patches.
- Review of the installation and configuration of the system, checking for known security problems. In this connection, don't assume that older security weaknesses have been taken care of.

- Review of the firewall system ruleset. Apart from the permitted services, it is important that the blocked ports, protocols, and user groups are subjected to in-depth tests.
- Simulation of attacks with the tools used by hackers.

The work identified from the background material and problems must then be split into the three components of the audit: site visits, interviews, and technical measurements.

DATA ACQUISITION

To analyze the IT system as completely as possible, during the actual data acquisition, material must be combined from quite different sources.

- Data on the organizational structure provides an overview of how the IT system has been integrated in the organization and of those staff who provide support for the IT system.
- Personnel data is used to check the reliability of the IT support team.
- Data about the buildings provides information about possible unauthorized routes of access to the network and/or computer room.
- Finally, technical data documents the sensitivity and/or resistance of the IT system to attacks.

The schedule for work performed on the IT system must be carefully coordinated with the work schedule of those users who will be affected by it; this will help prevent expenses incurred from downtime. A "successful" denial-of-service attack in particular can paralyze the communications system or even damage the firewall computer.

PREPARING THE REPORT

The final report summarizes the starting material and the findings obtained to date, and sets them in perspective with regard to the security policy and security guidelines. In practice, the following approaches to the preparation of reports have been shown to work well:

- The report should not simply criticize all the deficiencies that are discovered, but should also bring out the positive aspects of the security measures that are in place.
- In the introduction, the audit strategy and the most important findings should be summarized in a comprehensible form.
- The rest of the analysis should proceed top-down. In other words, it should flow from the general to the specific. Site plans and examples of collected data should go in annexes.

- Most importantly, the summary should contain suggestions for improvements and feedback on the security strategy and security guidelines.
- A CD-ROM (or diskettes) that contains the collected data should be archived together with the report.

PRESENTING THE RESULTS OF THE SECURITY AUDIT

Depending on the scope and impðrtance of the security audit, it is a good idea to make a presentation of the findings. The presentation must be entirely objective, as the errors and weaknesses found generally fall within the areas of responsibility of the people attending the presentation. No attempt to assign blame should be made. Positive points must be mentioned. A presentation should focus on future aspects of IT security and on related tasks and problems.

Data Collection Tools

In the audit's initial phase, data is prımarily collected with paper and pencil. In subsequent analyses, however, separate computers are necessary to uncover security weaknesses and to simulate attacks. There is no one standard on hardware and software, and, depending on the particular problem, a small *toolbox* with several complementary components is usually necessary.

MEASUREMENT COMPUTER

The requirements on the *measurement computer* – the computer that is used to uncover technical security problems – are derived from the configuration of the firewall system and its integration into the rest of the network. Three possible variations can be used. These will be explained with reference to the example of a firewall system with a separate network for mail and FTP servers.

The first two variants work with two measurement computers. All possible problem situations are examined singly. In the first measurement, the router is examined and an attack from outside is simulated. If no filter functions are activated in the router, this measurement can be omitted. In the second and third steps, transmission through the firewall system is checked.

The second variant considers the firewall system as a black box, and examines only the interfaces to the outside.

A single measurement computer can deal with the last variant. For this purpose, additional logging software that records inbound packets for later analysis is installed on the firewall system. The audit information in the firewall system is used. Two measurements are sufficient (a measurement PC is also possible between the router and firewall system in the first measurement).

Measurements that simulate an attack from the screened subnet are normally unnecessary. They can be carried out if the consequence of an "enemy takeover" of the mail server or FTP server from the Internet is desired.

AUDIT TOOLS

You can find numerous software tools available on the market to support the security audit. The tools range from commercial programs to those that can be downloaded free of charge from the Internet. Your selection will depend on the security guidelines and the cost. Keep in mind that the quality of the audit results does not necessarily correlate with the cost of the tools, although extraction of the data is naturally more convenient with one of the commercial programs. Whichever candidate software packages one chooses, the following functionality must always be provided:

- A LAN analyzer, preferably with a graphical user interface. With this functionality, statistical data on network traffic can be collected, and individual, particularly interesting packets can be filtered out and their headers and/or data examined.
- An IP port scanner, with which the services available on the firewall system can be examined.
- A tool to examine the quality of the passwords for all accounts on the firewall system.
- A network scanner, with which the firewall system can be examined for known security loopholes.
- A collection of the attack tools commonly used by hackers, which can be downloaded from the Internet.

PRODUCT OVERVIEW

The summary of products provided in this section is not exhaustive. From this pool of commercial and freely available tools, you can assemble a customized instrument able to analyze the technical weaknesses of firewall systems to any required depth.

LAN ANALYZERS

- EtherPeek from Wild Packets (`www.wildpackets.com/`)
- TCPDump (`www.tcpdump.org/`), included with most UNIX and Linux distributions
- Ethereal (`www.ethereal.com/`), a traffic analyzer for UNIX/Linux
- Observer from Network Instruments (`www.netinst.com/`)
- Protocol sniffers from Radcom (`www.radcom-inc.com/`), combinations of hardware and software
- Sniffer from Network Associates (`www.sniffer.com/`)

NETWORK SCANNERS

- Internet Security Systems ISS (www.iss.net/) provides both free of charge and commercial scanners. The commercial scanner is very convenient and, like CyberCop, is extremely suitable for firewall systems. This product is particularly recommended for Windows NT networks.
- Cybercop (www.pgp.com/products/cybercop-scanner/default.asp) is a commercial tool scanner from network associates. Cybercop is extensible, allowing you to add your own tests.
- The Intrusion Security Analyst (www.intrusion.com/) is one of the few scanners that also run under Novell.
- Nessus (www.nessus.org/) is a freeware tool that is significantly more up-to-date than SATAN.
- The Cisco Secure Scanner (formerly Cisco NetSonar Security Scanner) has a particularly clear graphical representation of the results. It can be found at: www.cisco.com/univercd/cc/td/doc/pcat/nssq.htm.
- Retina (www.eeye.com/) is a commercial vulnerability scanner.
- SAINT (www.wwdsi.com/) is a commercial development of the SATAN scanner. It covers current security loopholes.
- SATAN (ftp://ftp.porcupine.org/pub/security) is a scanner that is available free of charge, but is already showing signs of aging and should therefore only be used in combination with other products.

OTHER TOOLS (FREEWARE)

- NMAP (www.insecure.org/nmap/), the standard for port scanners.
- Whisker (www.wiretrip.net/rfp/p/doc.asp?id=21&iface=2), an extensible CGI vulnerability scanner.
- COPS (ftp://ftp.cert.org/pub/tools/cops) analyzes file authorizations and attributes on UNIX systems.
- Crack (www.users.dircon.co.uk/~crypto/), the standard password cracker under UNIX.
- L0phtcrack (www.l0pht.com/research/lc3/index.html), the standard password cracker for NT.
- Lsof (ftp://vic.cc.purdue.edu/pub/tools/unix/lsof) shows all open file handles on UNIX systems.

- Merlin (ftp://ciac.llnl.gov/pub/ciac/sectools/unix/merlin/merlin.tar.gz) is an interface for data analysis.
- Tiger (ftp://net.tamu.edu/pub/security/TAMU/) is similar in its functionality to COPS.

Additional Sources of Information

A responsible administrator must keep up-to-date with the latest developments in security. It is not sufficient to rely on the developers of network scanners. Fortunately, a number of institutions publish security news concerning firewall systems on Internet sites, as well as mailing lists free of charge. A summary of the most important international addresses is provided in the next few sections.

INFORMATION ON FIREWALL SECURITY ON THE INTERNET

- SANS (System, Administration, Networking and Security Institute; www.sans.org) is an organization aimed at providing a central clearinghouse for security research and information.
- The CERT Coordination Center (Computer Emergency Response Team; www.cert.org) in Pittsburgh, Pennsylvania, has concerned itself since its foundation in 1984 with security issues on the Internet. The CERT site contains an abundance of information, including many documents on security loopholes in computer networks.
- AUSCERT (www.auscert.org.au) is the Australian version of CERT and often acts more quickly than its American cousin.
- FIRST (Forum of Incident Response and Security Teams; www.first.org) is an umbrella organization whose members include a large number of national and international institutions interested in firewalls.
- CIAC (Computer Incident Advisory Capability; http://ciac.llnl.gov) was founded in 1989, and probably holds the most extensive collection of security documents.
- ICSA (International Computer Security Association; www.icsa.net) is an amalgamation of firewall system manufacturers and other institutions.
- The Bugtraq archive (www.securityfocus.com) is an independent communications forum on the subject of security loopholes. Errors are often discussed here long before they reach the "official" bodies.
- The NT Bugtraq archive (www.ntbugtraq.com) deals exclusively with the subject of NT.
- Microsoft maintains its own security Web pages (www.microsoft.com/security).

GENERAL MAILING LISTS

- To register with CERT, you should send an e-mail to `cert-advisory-request@cert.org`, with *SUBSCRIBE <your e-mail address>* as the Subject.
- The extensive Bugtraq archive list can be ordered using a form found at `www.securityfocus.com`.
- To subscribe to NT Bugtraq, send an e-mail to `listserv@listserv.ntbugtraq.com` containing the text *subscribe ntbugtraq <firstname> <lastname>*.
- Internet Security Systems (ISS) offers an alarm function that is not tied to any particular manufacturer. To subscribe, send an e-mail to `request-alert@iss.net` containing the text *subscribe alert*.
- To obtain a list produced by Internet Security Systems (ISS) on the subject of NT security, you should send an e-mail to `request-ntsecurity@iss.net` containing the text *subscribe ntsecurity*. This list is very extensive.

MANUFACTURER-SPECIFIC MAILING LISTS

- One can get onto a Hewlett-Packard mailing list by contacting one of the two Internet service centers (`http://us-support.external.hp.com`). After logging on, select "Support Information Digests."
- To subscribe to IBM's AIX mailing lists, visit `http://rs6000.ibm.com/resource/maillist.html` or send an e-mail to `aixserv@austin.ibm.com` with the subject *subscribe Security*.
- Microsoft maintains its own mailing list, with registration at `microsoft_security-subscribe-request@announce.microsoft.com`.
- Redhat offers a mailing list on the subject of Linux security. To register, send an e-mail to:

  `linux-security-request@redhat.com`,
  `linux-security-digest-request@redhat.com` or
  `linux-alert-request@redhat.com`

  The e-mail should contain the text *subscribe*.
- To subscribe to Silicon Graphics' mailing list "wiretap", send an e-mail to `wiretap-request@sgi.com`, containing the text:

```
subscribe wiretap <your e-mail address>
end
```

- To obtain news on Sun's Customer Warning System (CWS), send an e-mail to `security-alert@sun.com` with the subject *subscribe cws <your e-mail address>*.
- SuSE linux has a security mailing list as well (`www.suse.com/us/support/mailinglists/index.html`).
- Silicon Graphics offers a security mailing list for SGI(`www.sgi.com/support/security/wiretap.html`).

Intrusion Detection/ Response Systems

As firewall systems can only react to events that are already known and included in their rulesets, supplementary security mechanisms are necessary so that new, unfamiliar events can be responded to. The possibilities for tampering with computer systems and/or their data from outside (via the Internet) or even from inside (via the intranet) are practically limitless and there is too great a development potential for tampering. Chapter 3 discussed the fact that large organizations simply cannot afford to shut down their IT operations simply because someone feels like doing a little hacking – for these organizations, the availability of the IT infrastructure is a top priority.

Active defense mechanisms such as intrusion detection and intrusion response systems are therefore becoming increasingly important so that attacks can be appropriately responded to – by *partially* closing down the firewall system, for example. Moreover, with intrusion detection systems it is also possible to detect internal attacks.

Intrusion detection systems are positioning themselves on the market as systems that may not offer any protection to e-mail, network-, and computer system-based attacks and anomalies, but do nevertheless detect, analyze, and report attempts so promptly that the attack can be thwarted before any tampering actually takes place.

Analogy to Video Surveillance

With video surveillance systems, it is possible to monitor outdoor installations or other parts of an organization so that attacks can be detected promptly. If, for example, intruders climb the perimeter fence, plant security or the police are immediately called. In addition, it is possible to retain evidence by making video recordings. Video surveillance is very similar in aim and capability to what can currently be accomplished with ID technology.

Difference between Intrusion Detection and Intrusion Response

The two types of intrusion reaction mechanisms are intrusion detection and intrusion response. Intrusion detection systems are those that only detect attempts at intrusion for the sake of analysis. Intrusion response mechanisms are those that detect attempted intrusions and make a response of some sort, such as sending a denial-of-service against the source of the attack. Theoretically, a clear-cut distinction can be made between intrusion detection and the more extensive intrusion response. However, the distinction is rather fuzzy because most intrusion detection systems respond after non-permitted actions have been detected in the network, whether through an e-mail or by a shutdown of the firewall. The response on the part of the intrusion detection system would technically make it an intrusion response system.

For practical purposes, however, a distinction between intrusion detection and intrusion response can be made. The primary objective of *intrusion detection* is to detect attacks and prevent the affected systems from sustaining damage. This can be achieved through alarms, reconfiguration of systems, or – if there is no other alternative – by shutting down systems (firewall systems).

The objectives of *intrusion response,* on the other hand, are more extensive, and include tracking down the attacker. Intrusion response systems to date have met with extremely limited success. Automated tracking tools such as *traceroute* or *DNS interrogation* have value, but a skilled hacker will be well camouflaged through spoofing. The administrator must almost always take action, such as contacting a CERT organization or the police. The legally problematic counter-attacks, which generally affect the wrong person, also fall within the scope of intrusion response. Normally, a hacker will use IP spoofing to conceal his identity, so that a denial-of-service attack on the hacker's IP address only affects the university at which he logged on. Paralyzing "innocent" systems creates bad feelings among system administrators and will hardly make them more willing to help search for the guilty party.

Conversely, the intrusion response mechanisms can also be used against an organization to execute a denial-of-service. Use of a denial-of-service response is quite risky, however. If an attacker determines that automated responses attack addresses exhibiting an attack, the attacker can then spoof attacks from sources they want to impair communications with. For instance, if an attacker wants to prevent AOL users from accessing your site and you are using traffic-blocking intrusion response mechanisms, the attacker could spoof a variety of attacks from across the AOL address range, causing your communications with all AOL users to be severed.

In conclusion, most security professionals consider the automated computer response a poor idea. The risk of harming someone other than the true attacker is significant. Hopefully, continued research on this front will eventually yield better results.

An important goal for intrusion response systems is to improve flexibility (or a *flexible response*). If a large company's remote access gateway detects a particular attack scenario, shutting off access across the board will deny availability to all. Ideally, only a particular service would be disabled or a particular address blocked.

Integration into Firewall Systems

The intrusion detection system supplements the active firewall elements and monitors the data traffic on either side of the firewall. Intrusion detection systems can be either network-based or computer system–based.

NETWORK-BASED INTRUSION DETECTION SYSTEMS

The data stream is examined in real-time on the network for familiar attack patterns (signatures). All relevant audit files in the firewall system are monitored and analyzed.

COMPUTER SYSTEM–BASED INTRUSION DETECTION SYSTEMS

Computer system–based attacks can also be detected through additional detectors (agents) in the connected computer systems. Other system-relevant data (log files, CPU loading, and so on) are also monitored. If an attack is detected, alarms are sent out once again.

Primary Task of the Intrusion Detection System

The objective of an intrusion detection system is to detect security breaches and respond rapidly and appropriately to them. More specifically, it provides:

- **Detection of misuse at the network level**

  Detection of attacks (denial-of-service, SYN flooding, PING flooding), pre-attack probes seeking information about the network, attacks using PortScan methods (half port, stealth scans, attacks using World Wide Web services (Active X, Java, and so on).

- **Computer-based attack detection**

  All important audit files on the system are monitored and analyzed. In the event that an attack is detected, an alarm is triggered.

- **Detection of anomalies**

  Detection of atypical system and user behavior.

- **Intrusion response**

  In the event of an attack, various countermeasures, such as e-mail alarm, SMS or pager alerts, suspension of connection, and logging of the attack, are initiated.

- **Event reporting**

  All event reports can be displayed, sorted by priority (high, medium, or low).

- **Logging/reporting**

  Log files are maintained. These are evaluated according to different criteria (with graphical presentation of results).

Design and Operation of Intrusion Detection Systems

Intrusion detection systems frequently consist of three main components: a network engine (detector), an agent, and a management component. Together, these components enable abuse or anomalies to be extensively detected at the network and computer level. Such architecture is explained below as a means of illustrating real implementations.

NETWORK ENGINE

The *network engine (detector)* monitors the data packets in real time, sends alarm messages, and initiates countermeasures automatically (response). It consists of five main elements.

- **Network adapter.** The network adapters are operated in *promiscuous mode.* It is also possible to run the network engine in *transparent mode* (no TCP/IP protocol stacks).
- **Packet Capture Module.** The Packet Capture Module organizes the transport of data packets from the network to the analysis module of the network engine.
- **Filter Module.** In the Network and Transport layers – layers 3 and 4 in the OSI model – protocols such as TCP, UDP, and ICMP can be filtered. Depending on the settings in the security policies, source IP addresses, source IP ports, destination IP addresses, and destination IP ports are filtered. One practical application is the parallel operation of two network engines, resulting in load distribution.
- **Assault Detector Module.** The Assault Detector Module examines the data stream for familiar attack patterns. This involves comparing the data packets with existing attack patterns held in the signature database, which contains pattern details for all known attacks. In addition, certain system states can be defined as attacks.
- **Response Module.** In the event that an attack pattern is recognized, different active countermeasures (responses), such as the following, can be initiated:

- Monitoring of active sessions
- Storage of session data
- Maintenance of log files
- Sending an alarm
- Blocking of connections (TCP reset)

Figure 12-3 shows the relationship between the intrusion detection modules and the host computer system and network.

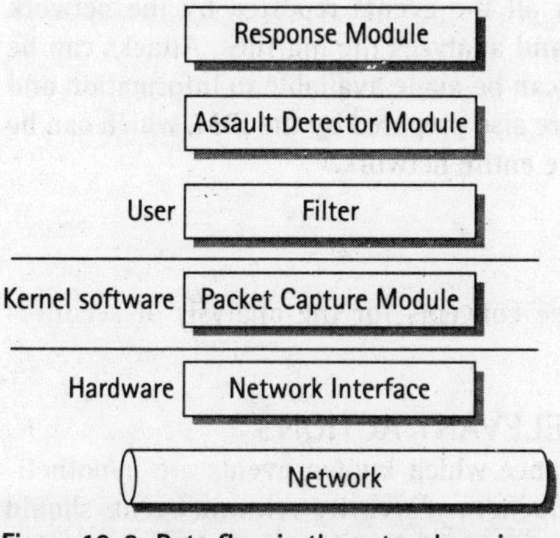

Figure 12-3: Data flow in the network engine

For the alarm function, various services are available:

- Alarm message to the management console
- e-mail
- SMS or pager alerts (with script) or execution of user-defined programs
- SNMP trap (for example, with Tivoli monitoring system)

AGENT

The agent monitors all the system activities of a computer system in the network. All the audit data generated by the operating system or by individual applications is examined for possible attacks and for signs of any abnormal events. All system-relevant data, such as log files, CPU loading, and so on, can also be monitored. If any attacks are discovered, alarm messages are sent out once again.

All user logons and logoffs can be monitored. In this way, unauthorized access can be prevented. All the administrator's activities can be monitored, as well as key system files. This prevents the manipulation of important files and the installation of Trojan horses. Parameters such as CPU loading or the number of active network connections are analyzed.

The detection of anomalies is intended as a means of detecting the direct consequences of an attack. In this way, the system can also be protected from unknown types of attack.

MANAGEMENT

The IDS Management (IDM) component administers and configures the network engines and the agent. It also carries out updates. Communications between the network engine and IDM are encrypted (symmetric encryption up to 128 bits or asymmetric encryption up to 1024 bits).

The IDM forms a collecting point for all the events reported by the network engine and agent. The IDM also fetches and analyzes the log files. Attacks can be logged so that information about attacks can be made available to information and risk management. Reports and statistics are also prepared by the IDM, which can be used to modify security policies across the entire network.

Analysis Concepts

This section presents and compares three concepts for the analysis of security-relevant events.

DETECTING KNOWN SECURITY-RELEVANT ACTIONS

This analysis concept determines in advance which known events are hypothetically relevant to security, or which consequences of security-relevant events should be treated as security breaches. An expert system then searches through the log data in the log files looking for those known events or sequences of events stored in the knowledge base.

The most common example of known security exploit detection is called *signature-based intrusion detection*. Signature-based ID is so-called because it uses a series of attack "signatures," or byte sequences, to indicate the occurrence of an attack. It works in much the same way as virus detection.

In order to process the security-relevant actions, the intrusion detection system uses several sources of information.

SECURITY-RELEVANT ATTACKS

The following incidents may be classified as security-relevant events:

- An incorrect authentication of a user to the firewall system occurs.
- Someone uses the `debug` command (SMTP proxy).
- Someone attempts a hopping attack (Telnet proxy).
- Someone uses the `del` command, although it has been prohibited (FTP proxy).

- An application gateway port that has not been initialized is addressed, even though this is defined in the packet filter as non-permitted (application gateway in a high-level security configuration).
- Someone illegally attempts to establish a connection with a computer system in the protected network.

DETERMINATION OF THE SECURITY-RELEVANT EVENTS AND EVENT SEQUENCES THAT ARE REGARDED AS ATTACKS

Using this method of detecting security breaches, it can be difficult to decide when a given sequence of events constitutes an attack.

A POSSIBLE STRATEGY During authentication of a user to the firewall system or during monitoring of the commands exchanged over FTP, errors may occur. The following rules could, for example, be created to deal with such security-relevant events:

- A single error on the part of the user is treated as an oversight and is ignored.
- Two successive incorrect actions on the part of the user are treated as an unfortunate coincidence, and are also ignored.
- If the user performs the same incorrect action three times within a defined period, however, this sequence of events is viewed as an attack and appropriate steps are initiated.

DETECTING ANOMALIES

With this analysis concept, security breaches are discovered by detecting anomalies – deviations from that which is "normal." This concept is based on the assumption that security breaches can be detected from marked deviations in behavior. Such behavioral deviations are detected in relation to individual users, individual programs, particular services, or communications sequences.

Anomaly detection is based on descriptions contained in reference profiles as to what constitutes normality. These reference profiles are templates of behavioral characteristics specified in terms of characteristics that can be checked. These characteristics can then be selected either with the aid of statistics about normal everyday behavior or on the basis of individual empirical values.

Anomalies in the use of firewalls may include:

- Above average error rate during identification and authentication
- Use of services outside of the normal scope of usage
- Abnormally long period during which users are working through the firewall system

- Unusual times during which communications are passed through the firewall system
- Abnormally frequent occurrence of security-relevant events
- Violation of the ruleset
- Attempted attacks on the firewall system
- Misbehavior of the firewall software and hardware

In this analysis concept, the log data contained in the logbooks is analyzed and processed so that it can be compared with the reference profiles. If the deviation is too great, it is assumed that a security breach has occurred and the necessary steps are initiated.

The reference profiles should not only contain the specific features that constitute typical behaviors, they should also specify how much deviation can be tolerated, how much (weighted) importance deviations relating to individual characteristics should have for the overall results, and how many of these deviations should be registered in what combinations before it can be assumed that a security breach has occurred.

The following behavioral patterns would suggest that a massive attempted attack is taking place or has already taken place:

- Within a defined period of time, an abnormal number of unsuccessful attempts at authentication by different users are detected.
- An abnormally high amount of activity is observed at an unusual time (for example, on Sundays between 3 a.m. and 6 a.m.).
- An abnormally high number of attempts to establish a connection with non-permitted computer systems has been detected and registered.

With this kind of detection system, fine-tuning is often problematic. Highly sensitive software may produce too many false alarms. However, if the tolerance deviations permitted are too generous, the probability that security breaches will be discovered through anomalies is reduced.

Some intrusion detection systems that detect anomalies work with *neural networks*, which are fed with system and network activities as input parameters. In a learning phase – one that is, ideally, uninterrupted – user and computer profiles are built which can then be checked during regular operations.

COMPARING THE ANALYSIS CONCEPTS

Using an analysis concept in which known security-relevant actions are detected provides clear-cut information regarding which security breaches occurred and were detected. Defined reactions can be initiated in response to such findings.

There is a major advantage to using an analysis concept in which anomalies are detected: due to the way log data is analyzed, it is possible to detect security breaches that have not been seen before. They could not be classified as breaches by a method that relied on direct recognition of defined attacks. This offers a way to detect new and unclassified attacks that have not been added to the signature database yet. One disadvantage of this analysis concept is that false alarms can also be generated.

Figure 12-4 shows that more security-threatening actions are detected when both analysis concepts are used simultaneously. The extent to which anomalous actions that do not constitute any security risk but that trigger false alarms are detected is also shown in Figure 12-4.

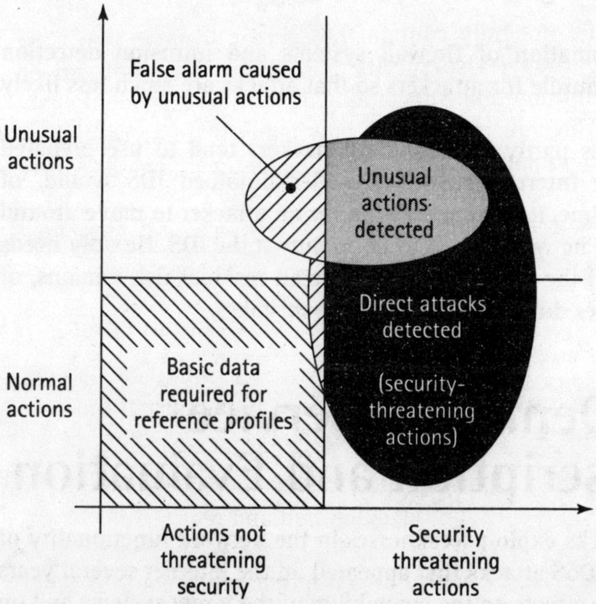

Figure 12-4: Detection of anomalies

Limitations of IDS

Unfortunately, there is no such thing as 100 percent security, even with intrusion detection systems. Sophisticated attack scenarios that cannot be detected by the IDS are conceivable (at least theoretically) with every procedure. If the hacker knows the type of IDS, he has a real chance of bringing off an attack. Even if the attacker does not know the IDS system in use, he can always attempt to paralyze the IDS itself with a denial-of-service attack, and then roam around in the network with impunity. Other attack possibilities include the following:

- Attacks that go undetected compared to the statistical background noise, such as the *slow-scan*, a PortScan that stretches out over weeks or months.
- Accompanying the attack by the addition of manipulated network packets. These packets interfere with pattern recognition by the IDS and may be rejected by the target system under attack, providing a cover for the actual attack.
- Manipulation of anomaly detection by slowly shifting the profiles. The self-learning mechanism of many IDS (neuronal networks) supports this eventuality. For example, bookkeeper Smith could slowly shift his user profile into the evening hours, and then after several weeks, initiate his critical attack on the wages server without triggering the IDS alarm.

In every case, the combination of firewall systems and intrusion detection systems constitutes a major hurdle for attackers so that attacks are much less likely to go undetected.

The increased detection is partly because most hackers tend to use prepared attacks – obtained from the Internet – which a well-maintained IDS would, of course, detect. At the same time, it is more difficult for an attacker to move around in an unfamiliar network, as he would need to do to outwit the IDS. He only needs to make a small mistake and the alarm goes off. A small residual risk remains, of course, but only in the movies do hackers never make mistakes.

Distributed Denial-of-Service Attacks – Description and Evaluation

Denial-of-service (DoS) attacks exploit weaknesses in the network functionality of different operating systems. DoS attacks first appeared on the Internet several years ago. The occasionally drastic effects on the availability of the target systems and on access to the corresponding tools forced local administrators and operating system vendors to react quickly. The countermeasures, which are still effective today, entail loading appropriate patches and activating or installing packet filters on IT security components connected in series.

Distributed Denial-of-Service (DDoS) attacks appeared in 1999. Due to their distributed mode of operation using a small number of masters and a large number of so-called agents – which combine several conventional DoS attack variants, thereby achieving a multiplication of the damage – DDoS attacks can be extremely dangerous. Only through close coordination between those responsible for prevention and reaction can this potential threat be effectively countered.

General Mode of Operation of DDoS Attacks

The sequence of events involved in a DDoS attack involves two distinct phases. In phase 1, an attempt is made, using automated tools, to install DDoS agents in complete network areas. In phase 2, the DDoS agents that have been successfully installed and are actively running in the background are directly instructed by a central master to attack a common target system.

PHASE 1

The attacker begins with a subnet scan of a network area, combined with analysis and identification of the operating system variants that are used, plus an analysis of the versions of activated service programs. At this point, he can effectively conceal the system he is using (which may be a workstation plus several relay systems). Using *exploits*, programs that exploit an existing weakness on a target system to improperly obtain privileged rights, he now attempts to install the above-mentioned DDoS agents (see Figure 13-19). Failure to rectify weaknesses or to install a firewall system, or incorrect configuration of a firewall system – enabling easy, unauthenticated contact with internal network areas – are the main reasons for the frequent success in this phase. At the conclusion of phase 1, the DDoS agents register with one or more master systems – again, automatically (that is, without direct interaction on the part of the attacker). In addition, the attacker can install *root kits*, which remove traces of penetration and conceal the existence of the DDoS agent process from system administrators. One consequence of this procedure is that you may see a relatively long grace period between the end of phase 1 and the start of the attack in phase 2. During this time interval, however, it is possible to track down these improperly installed DDoS agents using specific signatures and to administratively terminate them.

A more straightforward procedure for installing DDoS agents is to program and send Trojan horses (by e-mail, for example). It is imperative, at this point, that the IT security concept provide for organizational precautions, combined with effective staff training programs, if the improper execution of unknown programs is to be prevented. Another means of installing a DDoS agent is to exploit implementation weaknesses with regard to the interpretation and execution of active content on a PC workstation.

Personal firewalls can be used, for example, to prevent this attack variant.

PHASE 2

Once the DDoS agents have been registered in phase 1, a distributed attack can be initiated on a common target system. The attacker sends a particular command to all the masters, which then send out corresponding command sequences to all the DDoS agents. These agents, in turn, send out the actual DoS packets on the attacker's behalf.

In addition to the DoS attack methods mentioned above, there are variants that can cause the target system or series-connected network infrastructure to be inundated by the assembly of random UDP, TCP, and ICMP data packets.

Communications between the master and the DDoS agents increasingly tends to take place over protocols, which are used even if a filter system is present. An example here might be the use of ICMP echo replies, which are frequently interpreted by packet filters as normal replies to corresponding queries and are forwarded to an internal network. A restrictive configuration of this kind of filter component can be effective at preventing communications between master and DDoS agent.

FURTHER DEVELOPMENT OF DDOS TOOLS

It is increasingly observed that simple, and (usually) symmetrical, encryption algorithms are used not only for communications between master and DDoS agent but also for communications between attacker and master. Another trend is the use of alternative protocols for communications between attacker, master, and agents. This makes it more difficult for an intrusion detection system to perform a signature analysis.

The latest DDoS tools allow updates to be controlled centrally and largely automatically.

CONCLUSIONS

Effective, on-site reactive measures at the time of a DDoS attack are possible under the following conditions:

- The attack is correctly recognized as a DDoS attack.
- The DDoS attack is based on protocols that are not directly required for actual operation and can be effectively blocked through the interposition of filter components.
- Blocking of DDoS attacks based on protocols that are essential for actual operations is only possible if the variance of the originating addresses is not too large. Unfortunately, this is not the case with TCP-ACK flooding with forged and randomly set sender IP addresses, which means that this attack may cause an extremely large amount of damage (especially with the new DDoS tool `mstream`).
- In cooperation with the relevant Internet provider, inbound DDoS packets are blocked as early as possible using interposed filter components (often using IP router functionality). Often, the relevant computing capacity and line bandwidths are only available to the Internet providers.
- Preventive operating system patches have been installed in advance (to protect against SYN flooding, for example).
- The administrators are aware of the problems of IT security and, in the event of an attack, can implement countermeasures that have previously been defined jointly with the Internet providers.

INFORMATION GAPS

You can only perform a detailed analysis of attacks if you know the specific effects of an attack and the countermeasures that were taken locally. Answers are therefore needed to the following questions:

- What network components and/or computer systems were most heavily affected locally? What components failed?
- How long was it before the attack was detected?
- What tools were available to detect the attack (for example, IDS/IRS)?
- How long was it before the attack was correctly classified?
- What countermeasures had already been taken in advance as a precaution (for example, the establishment of packet filters in cooperation with the Internet provider)?
- What additional countermeasures were implemented on what system components after the attack was detected?
- How long after activation of the countermeasures did the attack continue to run?
- Was the attack successfully warded off?
- What organizations were involved in dealing with the attack?
- What traces of the attacks were saved for later technical and legal analysis?
- Over what period of time did preparation for the attack take place?
- How many DoS agents were involved in the actual attack?
- How were the DoS agents disseminated? Which organizations and network areas were affected? Where was the attack concentrated (for example, companies, official bodies, universities, private users)?

Personal Firewall

The Internet offers many attractions. However, security issues associated with Internet usage constitute a major drawback. In particular, the following risks should be considered:

- **Attack on an organization's valuable information.** The link to the Internet is not a one-way street. In principle, everyone connected to the Internet can directly or indirectly access the connected computer system and the resources stored on it.

- **Receipt of malware (malicious code, harmful programs).** An attacker who wants to harm an organization sends malware (viruses, Trojan horses, worms, and so on). As a result, the organization suffers a reduction in its assets' value due to damage through acts such as file destruction. It is also possible for such malware to be sent via permitted communications through the central firewall system. Typically, the malware is sent to computer systems in an e-mail attachment or within a WWW document (Java applet, ActiveX control, or other executable). ActiveX controls have, for example, unlimited functionality. They can shut down a PC, delete files, or execute many other functions that cause harm.

- **Cookies and Cache.** When a user visits certain Web sites, cookies are stored on his hard disk. The cookies trace the user's activities and in the long-term, optimize the service offered to the user by the Web site. This confidential, private information can, however, also be retrieved by operators of other Web sites through Java or ActiveX. In a worst-case scenario, knowledge about the user's behavior could be used for criminal purposes.

  HTML files are automatically downloaded upon accessing a Web site and stored on the user's computer in disk caches. Quite apart from the wasted hard disk space, the HTML files can be misused as a means of monitoring user behavior.

Despite the many dangers implicit with Internet use, companies should exploit the opportunities presented by an Internet connection. If you were, for example, confronted by a rampant flu epidemic, you could either remain protected in your home, venture outside and expose yourself unprotected to the risk of infection, or lay in a supply of vitamin C as a way to strengthen your defenses. The last option seems like the most common-sense approach: it gives you the freedom to go where you wish, while reducing the risk of infection. Like vitamin C, the personal firewall is a protective shield for the PC. It constitutes a sensible addition to the armory of security mechanisms available to companies and organizations. Typically, organizations protect themselves both with the security mechanisms of a central firewall system and with anti-virus software.

Central Firewall System

A central firewall system is an extremely effective security mechanism for protecting networks. The central firewall system analyzes communications data and monitors communications relationships and partners alike. In addition, the security services of a central firewall system regiment communications in accordance with an organization-specific security policy, monitor all security-relevant events, and alert the security administrator to any security violations. A firewall system constitutes a Common Point of Trust between different networks. A central firewall system is based on the idea that only one path is permitted from the protected network to the unprotected network and vice versa, and that this access route is reliably and effectively controlled.

However, the use of a central firewall system presents certain conceptual limitations that need to be countered using other technical and non-technical security mechanisms. It cannot protect, for example, against:

- **Backdoors.** The main conceptual limitation of a central firewall system is a *backdoor.* As the firewall system only protects communications links going through it, this protection naturally will not work if communications can bypass the firewall system. In Figure 12-5, a user bypasses the central firewall system using the private branch exchange and an Internet provider to gain Internet access.
- **Internal attacks.** A central firewall system provides security services by placing a shield between the insecure network and the protected network, and by controlling the communications traffic between these networks. The central firewall system cannot protect against internal attacks on its own.
- **Malware attacks at the data level.** A central firewall system per se cannot detect attacks at the data level in permitted communications. Such attacks include the sending of malware as e-mail attachments, downloads from the Web, Java applets, and ActiveX controls.

VIRUS SCANNER

To detect viruses, virus scanner programs that search for known viruses either centrally or on individual computer systems are available. If a virus has been detected in a file, this security-relevant event will be displayed. Virus scanners are also subject to certain conceptual limitations:

- Virus scanners can only find viruses they already know about. The general problem with virus detection is that the programs quickly become out-of-date. Virtually every day, new viruses that virus scanners cannot detect are created. As a result, 100 percent protection against viruses is a myth. The problem increases when data is transferred. In this case, the virus detection rate is even lower.
- If a central virus scanner is used, compressed data must be decompressed in order to be checked. Encrypted data cannot be checked at all.
- A virus scanner cannot "try out" a file to see whether it contains a harmful virus.

Aim of a Personal Firewall

The use of personal firewalls is appropriate when you need to counter the design limitations of a central firewall system – their inability, for example, to protect against backdoors, internal attacks, and malware attacks at the data level.

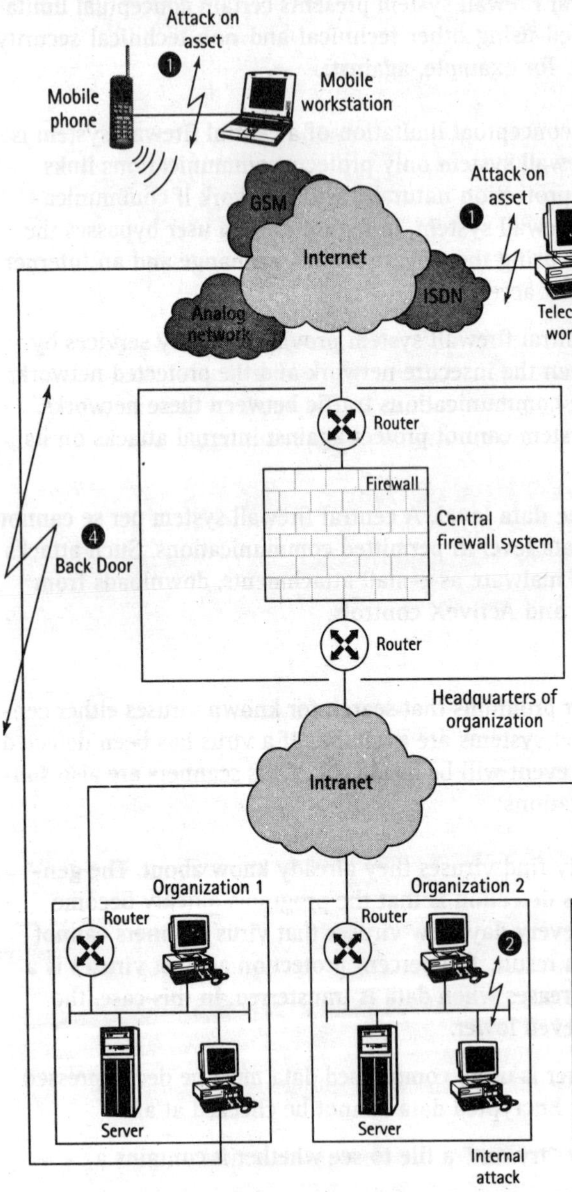

Figure 12-5: Risks of an Internet connection

The aim of a personal firewall is to close any loopholes that remain in central firewall systems and in known virus scanners in order to provide full protection to the electronic assets on a PC. For telecommuting and mobile workstations, the personal firewall acts as the primary firewall system when the machine is connected to the Internet.

The personal firewall (also known as a desktop firewall, local firewall, or distributed firewall) is installed on the PC, protecting it against attacks from the network and against threats that can arise in the context of permitted communications through malicious content. This is achieved not only by strictly regimenting communications on the PC, but also by implementing a secure environment on the sandbox model to isolate every application that runs within the operating system. All valuable system resources and files can be shielded against undesirable access through local applications or against malware penetrating the system.

The architecture of a personal firewall is designed so that the security mechanisms can restrict access to valuable resources within the application and user context. The security mechanisms are integrated into the operating system in a transparent manner and use their programs, DLLs, and kernel device drivers. In this way, it is possible to monitor all events and achieve the maximum possible operational security and compatibility.

Personal Firewall Components

The *agent* is the user interface to the personal firewall, displaying status information to the user. It monitors particular attacks on the computer environment and resources. The *user mode security mechanism* provides higher-level protective measures and protects the runtime environment in a user-oriented fashion. The *kernel mode security mechanism* provides extended lower-level protective measures and protects the runtime environment. Integration into the kernel level enables maximum control. The *remote control module* enables an organization's security policy to be implemented easily via a central Security Management function. These personal firewall components are illustrated in Figure 12-6.

In the Management Module, events are analyzed and logged, and statistics are calculated. Cache and cookie management functions that enable usage to be directed and controlled are also typically implemented in the Management Module. In the Applet Database, references to known malicious applets are stored. With these references, it is possible to output additional warnings about incoming active content and to block these applets automatically.

A personal firewall can be configured offline or online. If configuration is offline, the personal firewall is configured directly on the PC; if online, configuration is controlled centrally.

Personal Firewall Security Components

FIREWALL COMPONENT

The packet filter firewall component interprets the packets and checks whether the data in the corresponding headers of the communications layers complies with the defined rule base. The rules are defined so that only necessary communications are allowed and settings known to pose a security risk are avoided.

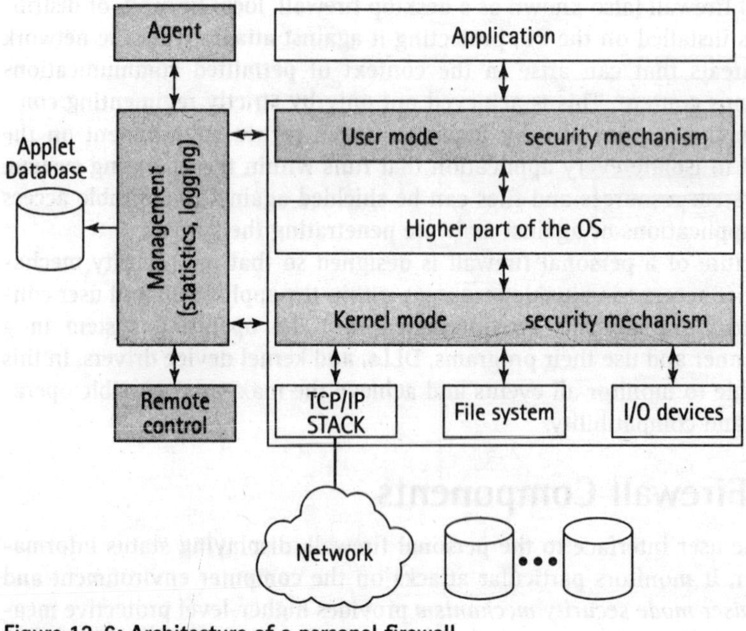

Figure 12-6: Architecture of a personal firewall

COOKIE MANAGEMENT

With cookie management, it is possible to design one's own data protection program. You can specify what should happen with what cookies – which ones are loaded, which ones are not, should the cookies be deleted immediately, or deleted when the firewall system is shut down, the aim of cookie management being to avoid potentially data-damaging attacks.

SANDBOX MODEL

You can place an explosive in a sandbox so that it detonates in a controlled fashion, avoiding any damage. Hence the term *sandbox* model. This model, which is also defined in Java, is a concept for executing a program (Java applets, ActiveX controls, and other executables in a controlled fashion and in an isolated area in which the program can run its course without influencing the rest of the system (see Figure 12-7).

Because of the sandbox, a potentially malicious application can only access the protected system (including the system and network files, resources, and connected devices) if allowed by the personal firewall. All the system resources are protected against untrusted, unknown, or malicious applications in an application- and user-defined environment. With the help of access rights management, it is possible, for example, to specify with which rights browsers may access files or directories. With a sandbox concept, it is also possible for resources to be protected against unknown threats.

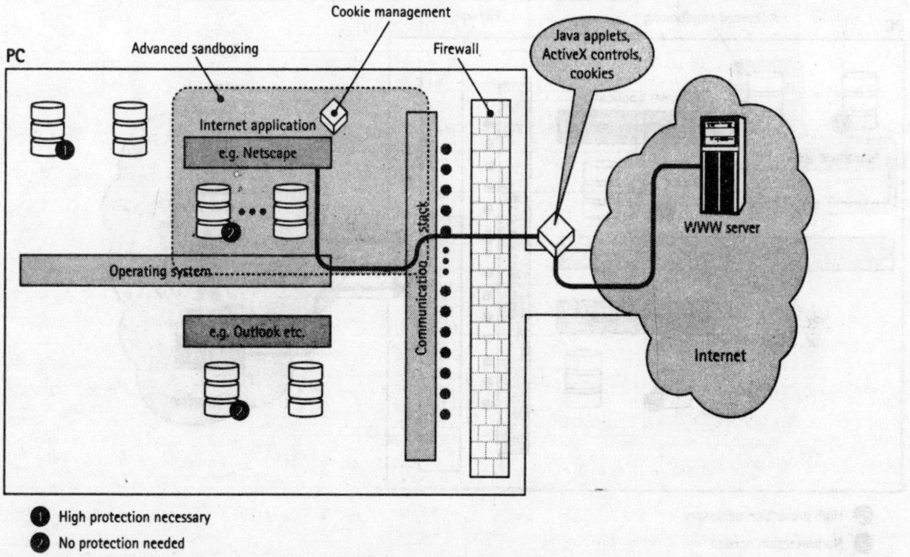

Figure 12-7: Protection of data with advanced sandboxing

EXAMPLE: SANDBOX PROTECTION AGAINST THE I LOVE YOU VIRUS In May 2000, the I Love You virus caused an estimated 30 billion dollars worth of damage worldwide within the space of only 24 hours. The large anti-virus companies only developed a remedy a day later. Nevertheless, systems protected by personal firewalls implementing sandboxes were spared.

The personal firewall stops viruses by intercepting the questionable actions and seeking confirmation of the actions from the user. If the user receives an e-mail with the I Love You virus as an attachment and seeks to execute this attachment, he is prompted by the firewall whether he really wants to delete some graphics files and to send an e-mail to everyone in his address book (the virus pursues the objective of spreading itself as far and as rapidly as possible). In this way, the personal firewall gives the user the opportunity to actively intervene before serious harm results.

Secure Environment for Digital Signatures

Another personal firewall security option is the protection of a signature function. Digital signature legislation that has been passed in different countries specifies that a digital signature must be executed in a secure environment, with no possibility of attack from outside. With the personal firewall, it is possible to ensure that during signing, the firewall shuts out all communications so that no attack can occur. No other processes may access the data being signed, resulting in optimum protection and a secure environment for the signature operation (see Figure 12-8).

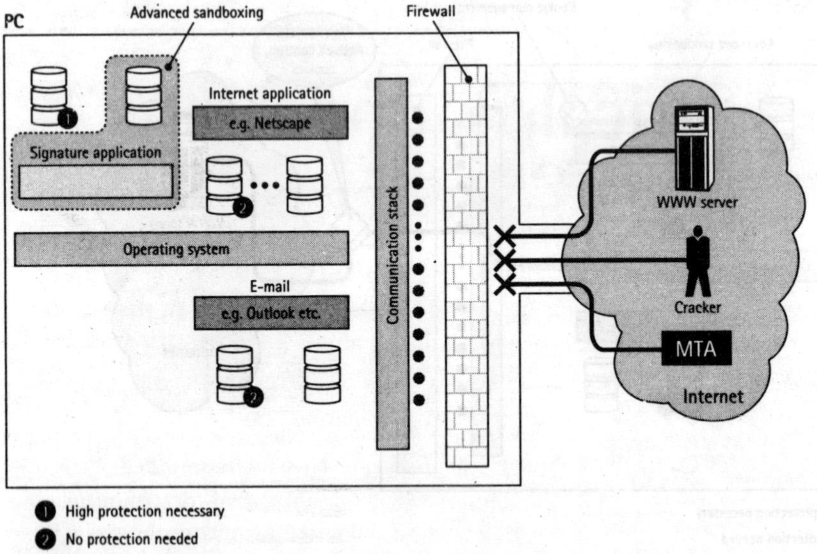

Figure 12-8: Protection of signature function with advanced sandboxing

Display, Logging, and Statistics about Security-Relevant Events

The user is informed when active content (Java applets, ActiveX controls, and so on) is installed and/or started up on the computer system. All suspicious activities are recorded in a logbook so that statistical information can be analyzed.

Summary

This chapter focuses on the issues you need to understand and address when implementing a firewall in most organizations. Although the topics in this chapter aren't part of the firewall system itself, they directly relate to the firewall's ability to protect an organization's network. If the topics in this chapter aren't a significant concern when you initially design your firewall, they almost certainly will be over the life of the firewall. Understanding and anticipating some of these subjects can save you significant time and expense over the life of your firewall implementation.

Chapter 13

Theoretical Foundations of Firewall Systems

THIS CHAPTER STARTS by presenting a limited model by which it is possible to derive and classify standard criteria for assessing the capabilities and limitations of firewall systems in relation to the degree of security and trustworthiness they can provide.

Although some models have been developed in the area of access control, such as the Bell-LaPadula model (see Abrams et al., 1991), they shouldn't be applied to firewall systems because they don't consider the security of communications. For this reason, a limited model has been created in order to deduce and discuss the factors that affect security and trustworthiness.

The Communications Model

Electronic communication entails the interaction of communications systems with the objective of achieving a common task, each communications system processing data in a manner specific to this task. Furthermore, their interaction requires the observance of rules that are laid down in a set of standards (Tannenbaum, 1998). A communications system consists of logical layers. The TCP/IP protocol architecture is made up of four logical layers, as shown in Figure 13-1.

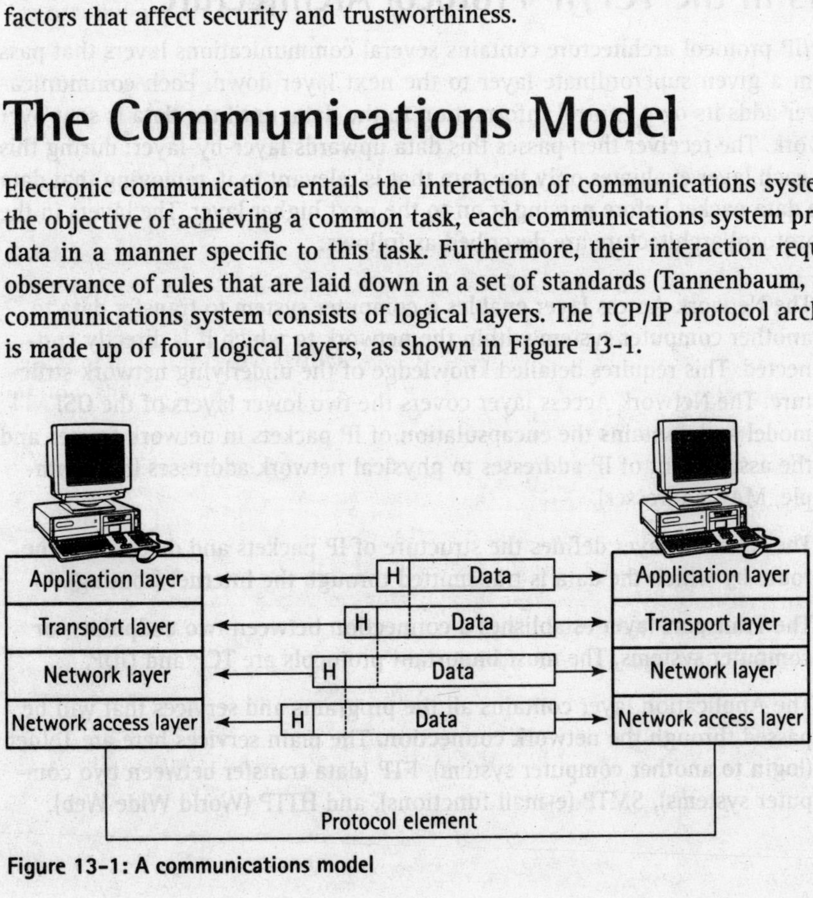

Figure 13-1: A communications model

- In a given layer N, entities (or peers) communicate with each other.
- Protocol elements (x_i) are exchanged between the entities.
- Protocol elements consist of headers and/or useful data.
- Headers contain control information such as addresses, serial numbers, counters, information about the transmission route, and information on the use of the data. The header information can be of a fixed length, but it can also be variable.

  Every layer has its own header, which can also be empty.
- The sequence in which the protocol elements are exchanged is laid down in the communications protocol.
- The vendor is responsible for the implementation of the communications protocol and is not fixed.

Layers in the TCP/IP Protocol Architecture

The TCP/IP protocol architecture contains several communications layers that pass data from a given superordinate layer to the next layer down. Each communications layer adds its own control information to the data, until the data is sent over the network. The receiver then passes this data upwards layer-by-layer; during this process, each layer evaluates only the data that is relevant to it, removing that data from the data packet before passing it on to the next higher layer. The layers in the TCP/IP protocol architecture are described as follows:

- The Network Access layer enables a computer system to transfer data to another computer system within the network to which it is directly connected. This requires detailed knowledge of the underlying network structure. The Network Access layer covers the two lower layers of the OSI model and contains the encapsulation of IP packets in network frames and the assignment of IP addresses to physical network addresses (for example, MAC addresses).
- The Network layer defines the structure of IP packets and determines the route by which the data is transmitted through the Internet (routing).
- The Transport layer establishes a connection between two endpoints, or computer systems. The most important protocols are TCP and UDP.
- The Application layer contains all the programs and services that will be passed through the network connection. The main services here are Telnet (login to another computer system), FTP (data transfer between two computer systems), SMTP (e-mail functions), and HTTP (World Wide Web).

Simplified Logical Communications Model

The simplified logical communications model, shown in Figure 13-2, illustrates the basic principle of a communications sequence. Each layer has its own *protocol state machine*, which corresponds to the communications protocol for that layer.

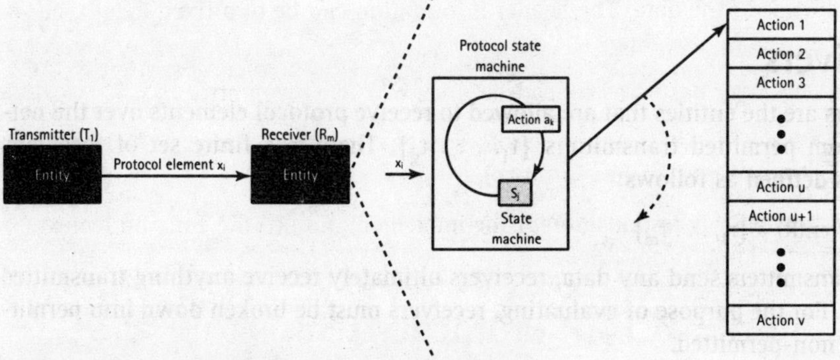

Figure 13-2: A simplified logical communications model

To accomplish the specific task of the entities in a particular layer, the protocol state machine executes a defined action ak as a function of the protocol element xi received, the current state s_f, and other events such as timeouts, status messages, and so on. The header information is usually critical to these actions. Normally, the layers are independent of each other, and they are significantly different in the scope of their task and functioning. Several layers can be involved with one physical protocol element.

Transmitters

Transmitters are the entities that send the protocol elements over the network to the receiver. There is a finite set of transmitters, which is defined as follows:

Transmitter (T) = $\{t_1, \ldots t_l\}$

Transmitters can transmit any legal TCP/IP packet data. At the broadest level, the transmitters break down into permitted and non-permitted.

- **Permitted transmitters $\{t_1, \ldots t_g\}$ – Within the meaning of the communication, permitted transmitters are transmitters that are allowed to initiate actions at the receiver's end. Permitted transmitters constitute a calculable risk with respect to the vulnerability of the assets.**

- **Non-permitted transmitters** $\{t_g+1, \ldots t_l\}$ – Non-permitted transmitters are transmitters that are not allowed to initiate actions at the receiver's end. Non-permitted transmitters (attackers, external parties, unauthorized persons, and so on) constitute a very high risk with respect to the vulnerability of assets.

The security policy specifies which transmitters are permitted and which are not.

Receivers

Receivers are the entities that are allowed to receive protocol elements over the network from permitted transmitters $\{t_1, \ldots t_g\}$. There is a finite set of receivers, which is defined as follows:

Receiver (R) = $\{r_1, \ldots r_m\}$

As transmitters send any data, receivers ultimately receive anything transmitted to them. For the purpose of evaluating, receivers must be broken down into permitted and non-permitted.

- **Permitted receivers** $\{r_1, \ldots r_h\}$ – Within the meaning of the communications model, permitted receivers are receivers at whose end permitted transmitters are allowed to initiate permitted actions over the network. Permitted receivers constitute a calculable risk with respect to the vulnerability of the assets.
- **Non-permitted receivers** $\{r_h+1, \ldots r_m\}$ – A non-permitted receiver (unauthorized person) is one at whose end no actions are allowed to be initiated.

The security policy specifies which receivers are permitted and which are not.

Protocol Elements

The protocol elements that are exchanged between transmitter and receiver can be defined as follows: sum of all protocol element $\Sigma = 2^n$

Protocol elements X = $\{x_1, \ldots x_t, x_t+1, \ldots x_u, x_u+1, \ldots x_v, x_v+1, \ldots x_n\}$

Refer to Figure 13-3 for protocol elements definitions.

The security policy specifies which protocol elements are permitted and which are not.

When considering the security of protocol elements $\{x_1, \ldots x_n\}$, the following additional points must be considered:

- Not all the fields in the protocol elements (for example, sequence numbers, random values, and so on), are security-relevant in relation to the capabilities of a firewall system which has the effect of sharply reducing the number of protocol elements that need to be considered in practice.

- Certain protocol elements are either permitted or not permitted, depending on the state of the communications protocol. Protocol elements can be permitted in a particular state, yet not be permitted in another state.
- The possibility of transferring information over concealed channels is not considered in this model.
- Permitted protocol elements $\{x_1, \ldots x_t\}$ can only be exchanged between permitted transmitters $\{t_1, \ldots t_g\}$ and receivers $\{r_1, \ldots r_h\}$ at permitted times.

$\{ x_1, \ldots x_n \}$ Possible			Set of protocol elements which are possible (possible coding of bits and bytes).	
	$\{ x_1, \ldots x_u \}$ Standardized		Set of protocol elements which are defined in the standard (ISO, RFC etc).	
		$\{ x_1, \ldots x_t \}$ Standardized and permitted	Set of protocol elements from the standard which are necessary for a particular task and hence are permitted, for example the commands >>cdir<< (change directory) or >>put<< (transmit), in order to send a file from the transmitter with the aid of FTP and store it at the receiver's end.	Per-mit-ted
		$\{ x_{t+1}, \ldots x_u \}$ Standardized and not permitted	Set of protocol elements from the standard which are not necessary for the particular task and are therefore not permitted, for example, the command >>del<< (delete files) in FTP.	
	$\{ x_{u+1}, \ldots x_n \}$ Not standardized		Set of protocol elements which are not defined in the standard, not necessary for the actual task and hence are generally not permitted.	
		$\{ x_{u+1}, \ldots x_v \}$ Vendor-defined	Set of protocol elements which are not defined in the standard but offer additional services. In connection with implementing the communication protocols or services, vendors have defined additional proprietary protocol elements in order, for example, to carry out the following tasks: • Error analysis (state of the state machine, state of the operating system etc.) These additional services are offered by the vendors to enable error analysis or other maintenance work to be performed remotely. • Trapdoors, which can be used to perpetrate attacks and to carry out actions that are not defined or permitted at the receiver's end unauthorized. These protocol elements are generally not permitted for security reasons.	Not Per-mit-ted
		$\{ x_{v+1}, \ldots x_n \}$ Not defined	Set of protocol elements which are neither defined in the standard nor by the vendor and hence are not permitted. Normally such protocol elements are recognized by the implementation as errors and treated accordingly. However implementations are constantly coming to light which, on receiving non-defined protocol elements, carry out a flawed action that could be used for an attack.	

t<=u
u<=n (if u=n, then v=n, then there are no undefined protocol elements)
v<=n (if v=n, then there are no undefined protocol elements)
n is the number of bits which are considered in the protocol elements

Figure 13-3: Definition of Protocol Element

Actions

Actions at the receiver's end are defined as follows:

Action (A) = $\{a_1, \ldots a_f\}$

An action consists of a defined number of subactions. The writing of a file to the receiver's hard disk using FTP is one example of an action. Subactions include, for example, selecting the subdirectory, receiving data subsets, and saving data. These actions can all be categorized as either permitted or non-permitted for the purpose of evaluation.

- **Permitted actions $\{a_1, \ldots a_t\}$** – Permitted actions are actions that are necessary for permitted applications (tasks). Allowing permitted applications to access defined assets constitutes a calculable risk regarding the vulnerability of the assets. The range of permitted actions also includes error handling in connection with undefined states and events.
- **Non-permitted actions $\{a_t+1, \ldots a_f\}$** – Non-permitted actions are actions that, although they enable implementation of a communications protocol or service at the receiver's end, are not necessary for the actual task of the host system and therefore are not permitted in the interest of preventing intentional or unintentional damage. For example, a Web server does not also need to provide TFTP services to perform its function as a Web server. TFTP action requests would usually be designated as non-permitted.

The security policy specifies which actions are permitted and which are not.

Permitted actions $\{a_t+1, \ldots a_f\}$ can only be initiated through permitted protocol elements $\{x_1, \ldots x_t\}$, which are exchanged between permitted transmitters $\{t_1, \ldots t_g\}$ and receivers $\{r_1, \ldots r_h\}$ at permitted times.

Communication Sequences

The transmitter sends protocol elements over the network to the receiver. The receiver interprets the received protocol elements as external events and starts its protocol state machine with this and other information (for example, status messages).

The receiver's action can be summarized using the following formula.

a_k = protocol-state-machine(x_i, s_j)
where
a_k equals action in a layer that is executed as a function of the received protocol element x_i and the current state s_j
x_i equals a protocol element
s_j equals the current state

The protocol is viewed as a state machine in which state s_j can change as a function of the received protocol elements and other events, such as timeouts and state messages.

Sequence of Actions at the Receiver's End

With the aid of actions (a_k) that are executed as a function of the received protocol element (x_i) and other events and the current status (s_j), permitted information (assets) is processed or resources (assets: printer, calculations, and so on) are used at the receiver's end.

The information or other resources that may be used with a defined action is generally specified via the access rights management functions of the operating system (Windows, UNIX, MVS) and of the applications (database, SAP).

From the perspective of the communications model, it does not make any difference which computer systems or operating systems the transmitter (T) or receiver (R) uses. All that is necessary is that these computer systems should implement the relevant communications protocols and services in accordance with the defined standards (RFCs).

Attacks from the Network

This section defines and describes the underlying potential attacks that were considered further in this book. A firewall system should provide security mechanisms that effectively counter and minimize the risk of attack.

MOTIVATIONS BEHIND AN ATTACK

An attacker attempts to influence the receiver in a targeted and deliberate fashion in order to:

- Gain access to confidential information (assets)
- Trigger reactions that he is not authorized to trigger
- Use resources (assets) that he is not permitted to use

The attacker does the following:

- To make money with the information (development data)
- With no material gain in mind

Attackers who aren t motivated by material gain generally fall into the category of the "disturbed personality." They might, for example, desire simply to harm the (random) victim – a motivation similar to that which underlies vandalism or arson. They might be motivated by pure boredom, by not having enough work or insufficiently demanding work at their place of employment (as was the case, for example, with the Bulgarian programmers who wrote virus programs). Some attackers may suffer from an inferiority complex. They may engage in their illicit activities to compensate for a lack of self-confidence, lack of recognition, or unrequited love. They may be hunting for the ultimate hacking experience, trying to create a virus program that will make the headlines. They are often motivated simply by youthful high spirits, adapting "proven" hacks (this type of attacker is known as the *script kiddie*).

The following sections describe the different types of attacks (playback, data modification, denial-of-service, masquerade, and so on).

THIRD-PARTY ATTACKS

In this type of attack protocol, elements are repeated, altered, deleted, or inserted actively by a third party. Figure 13-4 illustrates these third party attacks and Table 13-1 defines them.

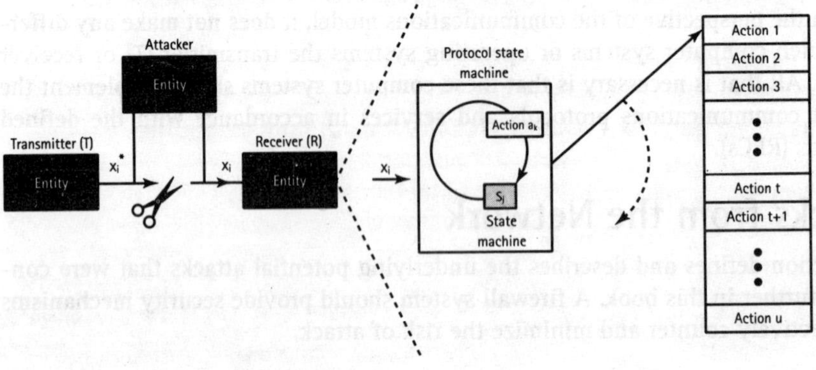

Figure 13-4: Attacks by third parties

TABLE 13-1 THIRD-PARTY ATTACKS

Type of Attack	Attack Objective	Example
Playing back or delaying one or more protocol element(s)	Through replay or delay of one or more protocol element(s), the receiver can become irritated and induced to take the wrong action.	Multiple transfers of a sum of money or replay of an intercepted login.
Inserting or deleting particular data in the protocol elements	To manipulate the receiver, an attacker inserts certain data into the protocol element or deletes it. The receiver can be induced to behave in an inappropriate manner as a result of the suppression of critical information or receipt of additional information.	In a protocol element of an e-mail that contains the words `DO NOT BUY THIS SHARE`, the words `DO NOT` are deleted during transmission so that the receiver receives the instruction `BUY THIS SHARE`.

Type of Attack	Attack Objective	Example
Modifying data in the protocol elements	Modification of the data means that the receiver does not detect changes in the data. By changing the data during transmission, an attacker can induce the receiver to take in appropriate action.	A change in the account number related to a money transfer causes the money to be sent to someone other than the intended account holder.
Boycotting the receiver	If the extent of data inserted or suppressed is too big, or if real-time data is withheld for too long, the receiver may find himself the subject of a boycott.	By being permanently connected to the receiver, the attacker can effectively block him and cause him to become isolated. Instances of distributed denial-of-service (DDoS) attacks have shown that it is possible to deny service on the Internet very effectively, causing enormous damage.
Man-in-the-middle-attack	An attacker from the insecure network can hijack the user's existing connection and, as a man-in-the-middle, can then execute the same actions as the authorized user.	After successful authentication of a home banking customer, the attacker hijacks the connection in order to enrich himself.
Sending malware (viruses, worms, Trojan horses, and so on)	The attacker sends malware to harm the receiver. Typically, the malware is sent to the receiver as an e-mail attachment or inside a WWW document.	Sending viruses, such as the I Love You virus that destroy data belonging to the receiver.

ATTACKS BY THE COMMUNICATIONS PARTNER

In this type of attack, the actual communications partner is the attacker who actively poses a threat. Notice the difference in attack portrayal in Figure 13-5 as compared to 13-4. Table 13-2 characterizes the specific attacks possible by the communications partner.

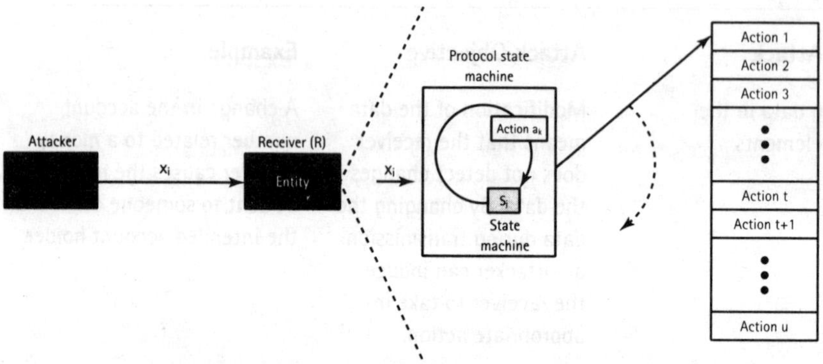

Figure 13-5: Attacks by the communications partner

TABLE 13-2 ATTACKS BY THE COMMUNICATIONS PARTNER

Type of Attack	Attack Objective	Example
Unauthorized establishment and use of communications connections	An attacker uses an existing communications connection to obtain advantage or to harm the receiver.	An attacker uses an existing connection to steal development data from the protected network, to which he should not have access.
Unauthorized use of communications protocols and services	An attacker uses the basic opportunity of effecting a communication in order to gain advantage or to harm the receiver.	The attacker uses the Telnet service to tamper with a computer system.
Taking on someone else's identity (masquerade attack)	If the communications partner pretends to be a different person, he can obtain confidential information under false pretences, use resources (assets) to which he has no entitlement, or trigger reactions that only a different communications partner has the right to initiate.	A communications partner obtains unauthorized access to a database.

Type of Attack	Attack Objective	Example
Use of the communications connection to the receiver for targeted attacks	The attacker uses the communications connection established by the receiver to obtain advantage or to harm the receiver.	The user (receiver) establishes a connection to a Web server and uses this, for example, to steal or delete information via Java applets.
Use of an incorrect configuration	For every service that is to be enabled over the network, there exists a daemon. This can be incorrectly configured or installed so that on the receiver's computer system, any privileged commands (one or more protocol elements) with which an attack could be carried out can be executed.	The attacker exploits the fact that the computer has been configured incorrectly in order, for example, to gain access to the root user rights on the receiver's system, which then targets. For example, the attacker might compromise a WWW server with root privileges and faulty CGI scripts.
Exploiting implementation errors	The attacker takes advantage of implementation errors in the communications protocols or services of the receiver in order to execute non-permitted actions.	Complex applications such as Sendmail have been shown in the past to exhibit implementation and design errors, which enable any privileged commands to be executed on the receiver's computer system. These commands could be used to carry out attacks.
Repudiating communications relationship	The growing use of data communications to process contractually relevant processes requires that neither communications partner can deny having sent a message (one or more protocol elements) or having received a message, as appropriate.	Ordering goods over the Internet from a merchant or concluding a contract over the Internet. Remote maintenance performance works over the network.

PRE-ATTACK ACTIVITIES

The attacker uses this type of attack to subsequently put himself in a better position to perpetrate attacks. Table 13-3 defines some of the actions an attacker might perform when preparing for a full system attack.

TABLE 13-3 PREPARATION FOR ATTACKS

Type of Attack	Attack Objective	Example
Social engineering	The attacker uses his social skills (eloquence, confident demeanor, and so on) to persuade someone to disclose a password to him or to undertake certain operations for him. To this end, the attacker collects information about people's lifestyles, such as their normal working hours, the names of those close to them, and their hobbies.	The attacker pretends to be a superior, a colleague, or a system administrator on the telephone. Usually, he creates an artificial urgency. He might say, for example, "I'm with a potential major customer and I need to show him the system" in order to persuade his victim to spontaneously disclose his password.
Analysis with scanner programs	Using a scanner program, an attacker can determine the structure of the protected network: IP addresses, operating systems (computer systems), users, and services.	Computer systems: A network's active IP addresses can be analyzed, for example, using the `ping` command. An attacker sends the `ping` command to all the possible IP addresses in an address range. In a class C network, this means that a `ping` command is sent to IP addresses A.B.C.1 through A.B.C. 254. From the answers received, it is possible to determine which IP addresses represent a connected computer system.

Type of Attack	Attack Objective	Example
		Active users: With the finger command, an attacker can determine which users are active on a given computer system at a particular time, whether they have already read the e-mails they have received, and so on.
		Active services: By addressing the individual ports, an attacker can analyze for which services a daemon process is installed on the corresponding computer system.
		Vulnerability analysis on individual computer systems: With additional tools such as ISS or SATAN, the attacker can perform a targeted vulnerability analysis, which allows you to check whether, for example, an attack on the computer system is possible due to errors in configuring the daemon processes of the active services or through the use of old software versions that contain errors.

Table 13-4 characterizes the types of attacks that can be perpetrated from inside an organization.

TABLE 13-4 INTERNAL ATTACKS

Type of Attack	Attack Objective	Example
Internal attacks	To sell information (development data, customer data, and so on) for money; to harm the organization; or due to the attacker's own personality disorder, such as an inferiority complex.	The employees of the organization access co-workers' computer systems from inside the company in order to obtain sensitive information.

Firewall Elements

A firewall system consists first of firewall elements that actively intervene in communications between the protected network and the insecure network, and second, of a Security Management module, which is responsible for managing the active firewall element.

A firewall system is a separate communications security system. It generally has no direct connection with the security functions of operating systems and computer systems. A firewall system does not affect the communications protocols and services (extension and amendment of standards) used by the receiver and transmitter. A firewall system is managed by the organization that operates it, and in principle, is kept separate from all other parts of the organization.

The basic structure of the active firewall elements that are inserted into the communications interface between the insecure network and the protected network is illustrated in Figure 13-6. A firewall element thus outlined can comprise a packet filter, stateful inspection, application gateway, proxies, and adaptive proxies.

In a firewall element, the protocol element may be modified before it is forwarded.

Integration and Enforcement Module

The Integration and Enforcement module integrates the active firewall element within the communications system and enforces the security policy defined in the ruleset.

Integration into the communications system must be implemented in such a way that the communications data cannot flow past the Integration module without passing through the Analysis and Decision modules. For this reason, integration is particularly sensitive. The protocol element used determines where in the protocol architecture the Integration module is integrated.

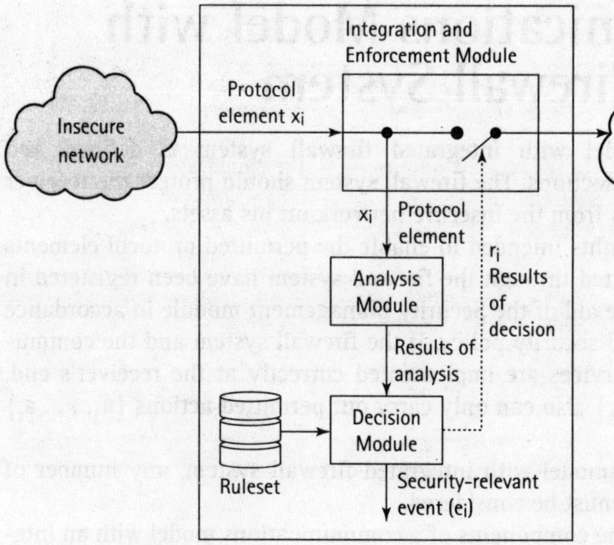

Figure 13-6: Firewall element

Analysis Module→analysis(x_i)

In the Analysis module, the communications data of protocol element (x_i) is analyzed in terms of the capabilities of the active firewall element. The results of the analysis are passed to the Decision module. In the Analysis module, communications status information (connection setup, transfer state, or disconnection) can be captured with the aid of state machines.

Decision Module

In the Decision module, the results of the analysis are evaluated and compared with the security policy definitions laid down in the ruleset. Access lists are checked to see whether the incoming protocol element (x_i) is allowed to pass or not (r_i = result of the decision). If it is, then the Integration module allows it through. If not, the protocol element (x_i) is not allowed through; the event (e_i) is rated as security-relevant and processed further as appropriate.

Ruleset→Security-Management (rules)

The ruleset is the technical implementation of the security policy and is drawn up with the aid of a Security Management module.

The ruleset contains all the information (rules, keys, access lists, attributes, and so on) related to users, authentication procedures, communications connections, communications protocols, and services that are necessary to make a decision in favor of or against transmission of the protocol element (x_i) through the active firewall element. It also defines what to do about security-relevant events (e_i).

The Communications Model with Integrated Firewall System

The communications model with integrated firewall system is defined and described in the following sections. The firewall system should protect the receiver $\{r_1, \ldots r_m\}$ against attacks from the insecure network on his assets.

It is assumed that the rights intended to enable the permitted protocol elements $\{x_1, \ldots x_t\}$ to be transmitted through the firewall system have been registered in the firewall system with the aid of the Security Management module in accordance with the previously defined security policy. If the firewall system and the communications protocols and services are implemented correctly at the receiver's end, then the receiver $\{r_1, \ldots r_h\}$ also can only carry out permitted actions $\{a_1, \ldots a_t\}$ at the permitted times.

In the communications model with integrated firewall system, any number of transmitters and receivers must be considered.

Figure 13-7 illustrates the components of a communications model with an integrated firewall system.

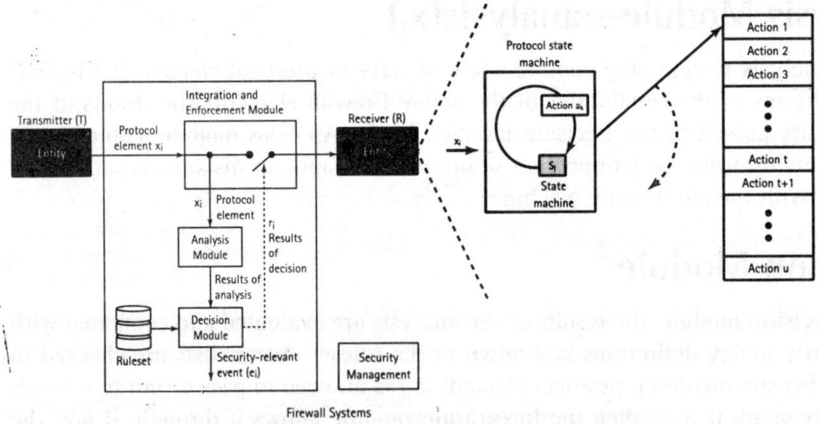

Figure 13-7: Communications model with integrated firewall system

Possible factors influencing the selection and implementation of actions at the receiver's end are used to derive criteria that allow a statement to be made about the capabilities and limitations of the communications model with the integrated firewall system in relation to the degree of security and trustworthiness it can provide.

Functions for Action Selection at the Receiver's End for r_n

The functions for action selection by the receiver can be defined using the following formula:

a_k = action-select(protocol-state-machine(x_i, s_j),
authenticity(x_i, t_l),
result-of-decision(analysis(x_i), security-management(rules)),
functionality-of-the-firewall-system())

Action-select is a function that determines the choice of action depending on the authenticity of the received protocol element x_i and the transmitter t_l, and also on the verification of rights and the existing and trustworthy security services in the firewall system and in the state machine at the receiver's end. Table 13-5 defines the other functions.

TABLE 13-5 FUNCTION DEFINITIONS

Function	Function Definition
a_k	Action in a layer that is executed as a function of the received protocol element x_i and the current state s_j
x_i	Protocol element that arrives at the receiver's end
s_j	Current state (actual state)
t_l	Transmitter that transmits protocol element x_i
Rules	Ruleset: technical implementation of the security policy

NOTE: There are usually other receivers $\{r_1, \ldots r_g\}$ to be considered in addition to r_n.

The elements of the action selection function must also be defined. The protocol state machine can be defined using the following formula:

a_i = protocol-state-machine(x_i, s_j)

A protocol-state-machine is a machine that performs an action a_i on the receiver's side in response to an event (protocol element x_i, timeouts, status messages, and so on) in state s_j.

Authenticity is defined using this formula:

y_i = authenticity(x_i, t_l)

Authenticity is a function that verifies the authenticity of protocol element x_i and transmitter t_l in the firewall system.

y_i = True
Protocol element x_i and transmitter t_l are genuine.
y_i = False
Protocol element x_i and transmitter t_l are not genuine.

The result of the decision is defined with the following formula:

r_i = result-of-decision (analysis (x_i), security management (rules))

Result-of-decision is a function that determines whether the analyzed protocol element x_i agrees with the rules defined in the firewall system.

r_i = True
Protocol element x_i is passed on and, if appropriate, recorded in a log file so that evidence of the action is retained.
r_i = False
Protocol element x_i is not passed on, and a security-relevant event e_i is generated.

Analysis is used to generate events and can be stated with the following formula:

e^* = analysis (x_i)

Analysis is a function that analyzes protocol element x_i. The function produces a defined event, e^*, depending on prior analyses and other states of the firewall system.

Security management serves as the determining element for which other elements can traverse the firewall and when.

e^{**} = security-management (rules)

Security-management is a function that, depending on the communications partner, checks which protocol elements x_i or consequences of protocol elements may be transmitted through the firewall system at particular times.

Finally, the functionality of the firewall is derived from the following formula:

z_i = functionality-of-the-firewall-system()

All the standard security services are implemented in the *functionality-of-the-firewall-system* function.

z_i = True
All the functionality that has been defined is present and trusted.
z_i = False
Not all the functionality that has been defined is present and trusted.

Attacks on the Firewall System

This section discusses additional attacks, described in Table 13-6, that are associated with the implementation of a firewall system.

TABLE 13-6 ATTACKS ON THE FIREWALL SYSTEM

Type of Attack	Attack Objective	Example
Manipulating the firewall system	An attacker manipulates the firewall system to allow a non-permitted action, which he then carries out.	he attacker alters the Tfirewall system's ruleset so he can, for example, access protected computer systems.
Installing a trapdoor	The firewall system vendor has built into the system the means of defeating the firewall system – for example, through self-defined protocol elements, special sequences of protocol elements, or specific data patterns.	The attacker can access the protected computer systems from outside as he pleases.
Exploiting an incorrect configuration of the firewall system	For every service that will be enabled via network access, there exists a daemon, which can be incorrectly configured or installed so that any privileged commands that would enable an attack to be carried out can be executed.	The attacker exploits the fact that the computer has been configured incorrectly in order, for example, to acquire root user rights for the firewall system as a way to achieve his objectives.
Exploiting implementation errors in the firewall system	The attacker takes advantage of implementation errors in the communications protocols or services of the firewall system so that he can carry out non-permitted actions.	The attacker exploits an implementation or design error in order, for example, to alter the access rights in the firewall system.

Basic Factors That Affect the Selection and Execution of Actions at the Receiver's End

This section describes the functions and the factors of those functions that play a role in the communications model with integrated firewall system. Factors that may cause communications sequences to follow an incorrect pattern despite the integrated firewall system are identified and explained.

Defects That Arise from Network Attacks

Authenticity (x_i, t_l) function communications sequences can only follow their correct course if the transmitter (t_l) is authentic and genuine. The protocol element x_i must also be authentic and genuine and must be intact after transmission.

The factors that influence authenticity are as follows:

- Trustworthiness of the network
- Trustworthiness of the communications partner

and/or

- Assurance of authentication of the communications partner
- Assurance of authentication of the data's origin

Sources of Defects in the Communications Solution in Use at the Receiver's End

Defects can originate with either the vendor or the users of the systems.

THE USER'S RESPONSIBILITY

The factor affecting the protocol state machine function (x_i, s_j) follows:

- **Configuration at the receiver's end** – The configuration of the communications protocol or service contains errors, with the result that, although the protocol elements (x_i) are permitted, a non-permitted action is carried out at the receiver's end.

THE COMMUNICATIONS SOLUTION VENDOR'S RESPONSIBILITY

The protocol state machine function (x_i, s_j) is affected by the following variable:

- **Implementation at the receiver's end** – The implementation of the communications protocol or service contains errors with the result that, although the protocol elements (x_i) are permitted, a non-permitted action is carried out at the receiver's end.

Sources of Defects in the Firewall System

Defects stem from both users and vendors.

THE USER'S RESPONSIBILITY

The following are security-management (rules) influencing factors:

- The specific contents of the security policy are a factor themselves.

- The security policy does not restrict individual users to the minimum functionality necessary to do their work.
- The firewall system behaves strangely because the rules have inadvertently been entered incorrectly.
- Incorrect rules have been entered deliberately with the aim of circumventing the firewall system.
- The constraints on the protocol elements may be inadequate, due perhaps to ignorance or incorrect specification.
- New methods of attack cannot be prevented by explicit restrictions, as the person responsible for the firewall system does not know them.

THE FIREWALL SYSTEM VENDOR'S RESPONSIBILITY

The quality of the analysis (x_i) is in direct correlation to the following:

- **Depth of analysis** – The analysis of the protocol elements may not produce sufficiently detailed information, causing the imposition of inadequate restrictions on actions. It could result in too narrow a definition of the decision criteria, so that they are reduced to a choice between allowing through and blocking. Important and/or new decision criteria could fail to be considered in the analysis of the protocol elements. When it comes to synthesizing the criteria into decisions, decision rules that have not been fully developed could be implemented or, alternatively, the decision rules could fail to be implemented in their entirety. This point goes hand-in-hand with the complexity of possible restrictions.

Decision results in result-of-decision (analysis(x_i) and security management(rules)) functions are wholly dependent upon the trustworthiness of the implementation.

Specific attributes that might indicate an untrustworthy implementation include the following:

- The quality of a firewall system implementation is such that in certain situations, it behaves incorrectly.
- The following components must be considered:
  - Operating system on which the firewall application runs
  - Firewall application, security management
  - Hardware of the firewall elements and security management
  - Communications partners' authentication components

A Firewall System's Security Services

Table 13-7 describes the standard security services provided by a firewall system. For each service, the table shows what service is controlled by firewall systems, what stipulations are made, what measures are taken, what is checked, and what effect this service has on the security and trustworthiness of firewall systems.

TABLE 13-7 A FIREWALL SYSTEM'S STANDARD SECURITY SERVICES

Security Service	Checks/Stipulations/ Measures	What Is Checked?	Effect on Security and Trustworthiness
Access control at the network level	What computer systems (transmitters, receivers) may communicate with the firewall system?	IP addresses of the computer systems involved Time at which an action is permitted	Trustworthy implementation Trustworthiness of the each other through network Trustworthiness of the communication partner Security policy
Access control at the user level	What users may establish a connection through the firewall system?	Identity of the user Authentication of the user Time at which an action is permitted	Trustworthy implementation Assurance of the communication partner Security policy
Access control at the data level	Can a specified user's data be transmitted over the firewall system?	Identity of the originator of the data Authentication of the originator of the data Integrity of the data Time at which an action is permitted	Trustworthy implementation Assurance of authentication of the origin of the data Security policy
Access rights management	What times may communications take place over the firewall system and which protocols and services may be used?	Header information inthe various layers Time at which an action is permitted Depth of analysis	Trustworthy implementation Assurance of data integrity Security policy
Control at the application level	Review whether commands are used or data content is transmitted that does not belong to the application's defined scope	Commands and data content related to the different applications Time at which an action is permitted	Trustworthy implementation Assurance of data integrity Depth of analysis Security policy

Security Service	Checks/Stipulations/ Measures	What Is Checked?	Effect on Security and Trustworthiness
Decoupling of services	Isolation of services prevents implementation errors, weaknesses, and design errors in the services from providing opportunities for attack.	Commands Time at which an action is permitted	Trustworthy implementation Concept of isolation
Securing evidence and log analysis	Connection data and security-relevant events are logged and can be analyzed so that evidence of user actions can be retained and security violations detected.	Actions and security-relevant events Time at which an action is permitted	Trustworthy implementation Security policy Concept of evidence retention and log analysis
Alarm function	Especially security-relevant events are passed to security management in order to permit a rapid response to any security breaches.	Time at which an action is permitted	Trustworthy implementation Trustworthiness of the network Security policy

Factors Influencing the Security and Trustworthiness of Firewall Systems

This section identifies factors that impact the security and trustworthiness of firewall systems, taking into account the conclusions drawn from the discussion of the communications model with an integrated firewall system.

The following influence firewall systems:

- Security services and security mechanisms of the actual firewall system
- The operational environment of the firewall system
- The evaluation and certification of the firewall system
- Factors influencing the organization

The way influencing factors work against the various types of attack is covered later in this chapter under the heading Attacks and the effectiveness of different security mechanisms.

The structural interrelationships between defined attacks and the effect of the various influencing factors, such as security services, security mechanisms, and security-enforcing functions, are analyzed and summarized in the Figures that follow (13-8 and 13-9). Table 13-8 provides a key to the symbols used in Figures 13-8 through 13-14.

TABLE 13-8 DEFINITION OF SYMBOLS

Symbol Description	Definition
Very strong effect	The security mechanism in question is so effective against the defined attack that, in practice, no damage can occur. Strength of the security mechanism = High
Strong effect	The security mechanism in question is so effective against the defined attack that, normally, no damage can occur. Strength of the security mechanism = Medium to High
Effect	The security mechanism in question is so effective against the defined attack that, normally, no damage can occur. Strength of the security mechanism = Medium
Weak effect	The security mechanism in question is only moderately effective against the defined attack. Damage cannot occur unless the breach is deliberate. Strength of the security mechanism = Basic
No effect	The security mechanism in question has no effect against the defined attack, which means that damage may occur.
Prerequisite for effectiveness	The security mechanism in question is essential if the firewall system is to be effective against attacks.

XREF

For definitions of Basic, Medium, and High strength, refer to Chapter 12 under Firewall Certification.

Effectiveness of Security Services

Figure 13-8 shows the full effect of the individual security services against the defined attacks.

Type of attack	Security enforcing functions	Access control at the network level	Access control at the user level	Access control at the data level	Access rights management	Control at the application level	Isolation of services	Evidence retention & log analysis	Alarm function	Hiding the internal network structure
Third-party attacks	Playing-back or delaying protocol elements	◔	◕	◕	◕	◕	○	◔	◔	○
	Inserting or deleting data in the protocol elements	○	○	●	◕	◕	○	◔	◔	○
	Modifying data in the protocol elements	○	○	●	◕	◕	○	◔	◔	○
	Boycotting the receiver	○	○	○	○	○	○	◔	◔	◕
	Man-in-the-middle attack	◔	○	●	○	○	○	○	○	○
	Sending malware (viruses, worms, Trojan horses etc)	○	○	○	○	○	○	◔	◔	○
Transmitter attacks	Setting up and using communication connections	◔	◔	◔	◕	◕	○	◑	◔	○
	Using communication protocols and services	○	○	○	●	●	○	◑	◔	○
	Taking on someone else's identity (masquerade attack)	◔	●	●	○	○	○	○	○	○
	Java, ActiveX etc. attacks	○	○	○	○	◕	○	◔	◔	○
	Incorrect configuration / implementation errors	○	○	○	○	○	◕	◑	◔	○
	Repudiating communication relationship	○	○	○	○	○	○	◕	○	○
Preparation for attacks	Social engineering	○	○	○	○	○	○	○	○	○
	Analysis by means of scanner programs	○	○	○	○	○	○	◔	◔	●
Attacks on the firewall system	Manipulating the firewall system	○	○	○	○	○	○	○	○	○
	Installing a trapdoor	○	○	○	○	○	○	○	○	○
	Exploiting an incorrect configuration in the firewall system	○	○	○	○	○	○	○	○	○
	Exploiting implementation errors in the firewall system	○	○	○	○	○	○	○	○	○
	internal attacks	○	○	○	○	○	○	○	○	○

● Very strong effect ◕ Strong effect ◑ Effect
◔ Weak effect ○ No effect ✦ Prerequisite for effectiveness

Figure 13-8: Effectiveness of security services

The Effect of the Operational Environment

Figure 13-9 shows the effect of the operational environment on attacks.

A firewall system's operational environment also determines to what degree the security mechanisms themselves will be effective, and greatly influences the security of the firewall systems.

Type of attack	Operational environment	Communication system: Trustworthiness of the network	Communication system: Trustworthiness of the communication partner		Firewall system: Secure security management	Firewall system: Secure operating system	Firewall system: Mechanisms for the protection of the firewall
Third-party attacks	Playing-back or delaying protocol elements	◕	○		◑	○	○
	Inserting or deleting data in the protocol elements	◕	○		◑	○	○
	Modifying data in the protocol elements	◕	○		◑	○	○
	Boycotting the receiver	◕	○		◑	○	○
	Man-in-the-middle attack	◕	○		◑	○	○
	Sending malware (viruses, worms, Trojan horses etc)	◕	○		◑	○	○
Transmitter attacks	Setting up and using communication connections	○	◕		◑	○	○
	Using communication protocols and services	○	◕		◑	○	○
	Taking on someone else's identity (masquerade attack)	○	◕		◑	○	○
	Java, ActiveX etc. attacks	○	◕		◑	○	○
	Incorrect configuration / implementation errors	○	◕		◑	◑	○
	Repudiating communication relationship	○	◕		◑	○	○
Preparation for attacks	Social engineering	○	○		○	○	○
	Analysis by means of scanner programs	◕	○		○	◑	○
Attacks on the firewall system	Manipulating the firewall system	◑	◑		◑	◕	○
	Installing a trapdoor	◑	◑		○	○	○
	Exploiting an incorrect configuration in the firewall system	◑	◑		◑	◕	◕
	Exploiting implementation errors in the firewall system	◑	◑		◑	◕	◕
	internal attacks	○	○		○	○	○

● Very strong effect ◕ Strong effect ◑ Effect
◔ Weak effect ○ No effect ✦ Prerequisite for effectiveness

Figure 13-9: Effect of the operational environment

If, for example, a firewall system is used in the internal organization and it can be assumed that the internal staff are not potential attackers, a higher level of security exists than in a situation where the firewall system is employed in the Internet – a network in which everyone must be viewed as a potential attacker.

These are important boundary conditions for the secure and trustworthy use of firewall systems.

The Effect of a Trustworthy Implementation of a Firewall System

The trustworthy implementation of a given firewall system, combined with the fact that it has been evaluated and certified, increases one's confidence in it; one can, for example, be assured that the security-enforcing functions and mechanisms will counter the known security threats and appropriately protect one's assets. The organization's own firewall protection mechanisms are also a factor in the trustworthiness of the implementation.

Checking for a built-in trapdoor plays a special role in the overall security of the organization.

The trustworthy implementation of a firewall system is a prerequisite for the effectiveness of all its security-enforcing functions. Figure 13-10 shows the effect of a trustworthy firewall system implementation on security threats.

Type of attack		Trustworthiness: Effectiveness	Trustworthiness: Correctness
Third-party attacks	Playing-back or delaying protocol elements	✦	✦
	Inserting or deleting data in the protocol elements	✦	✦
	Modifying data in the protocol elements	✦	✦
	Boycotting the receiver	✦	✦
	Man-in-the-middle attack	✦	✦
	Sending malware (viruses, worms, Trojan horses etc)	✦	✦
Transmitter attacks	Setting up and using communication connections	✦	✦
	Using communication protocols and services	✦	✦
	Taking on someone else's identity (masquerade attack)	✦	✦
	Java, ActiveX etc. attacks	✦	✦
	Incorrect configuration / implementation errors	✦	✦
	Repudiating communication relationship	✦	✦
Preparation for attacks	Social engineering	○	○
	Analysis by means of scanner programs	✦	✦
Attacks on the firewall system	Manipulating the firewall system	✦	✦
	Installing a trapdoor	○	●
	Exploiting an incorrect configuration in the firewall system	○	○
	Exploiting implementation errors in the firewall system	○	✦
	Internal attacks	○	○

● Very strong effect ◕ Strong effect ◑ Effect
◔ Weak effect ○ No effect ✦ Prerequisite for effectiveness

Figure 13-10: Effect of a trustworthy firewall implementation

The Effect of Influencing Factors within the Organization

Figure 13-11 shows the effect of influencing factors within the organization on attacks.

It is clear that the influencing factors within the organization itself have a strong effect on the security of firewall systems. In particular, it is possible to achieve a very strong effect against social engineering attacks.

Type of attack	Influencing factors within the organization	Non-technical security measures: Infrastructural	Organizational	Personnel-related	Contingency	Security policy	Secure operation
Third-party attacks	Playing-back or delaying protocol elements	○	○	○	○	✦	✦
	Inserting or deleting data in the protocol elements	○	○	○	○	✦	✦
	Modifying data in the protocol elements	○	○	○	○	✦	✦
	Boycotting the receiver	◕	○	○	◕	✦	✦
	Free-rider	○	○	○	○	✦	✦
	Sending malware (viruses, worms, Trojan horses etc)	○	○	◕	○	✦	✦
Transmitter attacks	Setting up and using communication connections	○	○	○	○	✦	✦
	Using communication protocols and services	○	○	○	○	✦	✦
	Taking on someone else's identity (masquerade attack)	○	○	○	○	✦	✦
	Java, ActiveX etc. attacks	○	○	◕	○	✦	✦
	Incorrect configuration / implementation errors	○	○	○	○	✦	✦
	Repudiating communication relationship	○	○	◕	○	✦	✦
Preparation for attacks	Social engineering	○	◕	●	○	✦	✦
	Analysis by means of scanner programs	○	○	○	○	✦	✦
Attacks on the firewall system	Manipulating the firewall system	◕	◕	◕	○	✦	✦
	Installing a trapdoor	○	○	○	○	○	○
	Exploiting an incorrect configuration in the firewall system	○	◕	○	○	✦	✦
	Exploiting implementation errors in the firewall system	○	◕	○	○	✦	✦
	internal attacks	○	◕	◕	○	✦	✦

● Very strong effect ◕ Strong effect ◑ Effect
◔ Weak effect ○ No effect ✦ Prerequisite for effectiveness

Figure 13-11: Effect of influencing factors within the organization

The Effectiveness of Different Firewall Design Concepts

Figure 13-12 shows how effective the various firewall design concepts are against attacks. It is assumed that the high-level-security firewall system has a secure operating system, secure security management functionality, and firewall protection mechanisms.

Type of attack	Firewall concepts	Packet filter	Dual-homed application gateway	Packet filter + single-homed application gateway	Packet filter + dual-homed application gateway	Two packet filters as screened subnet + single-homed	High-level security firewall system
Third-party attacks	Playing-back or delaying protocol elements	◔	◕	◔	◕	◔	◕
	Inserting or deleting data in the protocol elements	◔	◕	◑	◕	◑	◕
	Modifying data in the protocol elements	○	◕	◑	◕	◑	◕
	Boycotting the receiver	◔	◑	◔	◑	◔	◕
	Man-in-the-middle attack	◔	◑	◔	◑	◔	◑
	Sending malware (viruses, worms, Trojan horses etc.)	◔	◕	◑	◕	◑	◕
Transmitter attacks	Setting up and using communication connections	◔	◕	◕	◕	◕	●
	Using communication protocols and services	◔	◕	◑	◕	◑	●
	Taking on someone else's identity (masquerade attack)	◔	●	◕	●	◕	●
	Java, ActiveX etc. attacks	○	◕	◑	◕	◑	◕
	Incorrect configuration / implementation errors	◔	◕	◑	◕	◑	●
	Repudiating communication relations	○	◑	◔	◑	◔	◑
Preparation for attacks	Social engineering	○	○	○	○	○	○
	Analysis by means of scanner programs	○	●	◑	●	◑	●
Attacks on the firewall system	Manipulating the firewall system	○	○	◔	◕	◑	●
	Installing a trapdoor	○	○	○	○	○	○
	Exploiting an incorrect configuration in the firewall system	○	◔	◔	◕	◑	●
	Exploiting implementation errors in the firewall system	○	◔	◔	◕	◑	●
	Internal attacks	○	○	○	○	○	○

● Very strong effect ◕ Strong effect ◑ Effect

◔ Weak effect ○ No effect ✦ Prerequisite for effectiveness

Figure 13-12: Effectiveness of different firewall designs

The Effect of Additional Security Mechanisms

Figure 13-13 shows the effect of additional security mechanisms used to create a comprehensive firewall system on attacks.

Type of attack	Additional security mechanisms	Encryption	Anti-malware system	Intrusion detection	Personal firewall	Audits
Third-party attacks	Playing-back or delaying protocol elements	◕	○	○	◔	✦
	Inserting or deleting data in the protocol elements	●	○	○	◔	✦
	Modifying data in the protocol elements	●	○	○	○	✦
	Boycotting the receiver	○	○	◑	◔	✦
	Man-in-the-middle attack	●	○	○	◔	✦
	Sending malware (viruses, worms, Trojan horses etc.)	○	●	○	●	✦
Transmitter attacks	Setting up and using communication connections	○	○	◑	◔	✦
	Using communication protocols and services	○	○	◑	◔	✦
	Taking on someone else's identity (masquerade attack)	○	○	◑	◔	✦
	Java, ActiveX etc. attacks	○	○	◑	●	✦
	Incorrect configuration / implementation errors	○	○	○	◔	✦
	Repudiating communication relationship	○	○	○	○	✦
Preparation for attacks	Social engineering	○	○	○	○	✦
	Analysis by means of scanner programs	○	○	◑	○	✦
Attacks on the firewall system	Manipulating the firewall system	○	○	◑	○	●
	Installing a trapdoor	○	○	◔	○	○
	Exploiting an incorrect configuration in the firewall system	○	○	◑	○	●
	Exploiting implementation errors in the firewall system	○	○	◑	○	●
	Internal attacks	○	○	○	●	◔

● Very strong effect ◕ Strong effect ◑ Effect
◔ Weak effect ○ No effect ✦ Prerequisite for effectiveness

Figure 13-13: The effect of additional security mechanisms

Summary of the Effect of a Comprehensive Firewall System

Based on all of the results of considering the various factors (Figures 13-9 through 13-14), the effectiveness of a comprehensive firewall system against defined attacks in their entirety is presented in Figure 13-14 and in the summaries.

Type of attack	Security aspects of a comprehensive firewall system	High-level security firewall system	Encryption	Anti-malware system	Intrusion detection systems	Personal firewall	Non-technical security measures	Trustworthiness	Audits	Security policy	Secure operation
Third-party attacks	Repetition or delay of protocol elements	◕	◕	○	○	◔	○	✦	✦	✦	✦
	Inserting or deleting data in the protocol elements	◕	●	○	○	◔	○	✦	✦	✦	✦
	Modifying data in the protocol elements	◕	●	○	○	○	○	✦	✦	✦	✦
	Boycotting the receiver	◕	○	○	◑	◔	◕	✦	✦	✦	✦
	Man-in-the-middle attack	◑	●	○	○	◔	○	✦	✦	✦	✦
	Sending of malware (viruses, worms, Trojan horses etc.)	◕	○	◕	○	●	◕	✦	✦	✦	✦
Transmitter attacks	Setting up and using communication connections	●	○	○	◑	◔	○	✦	✦	✦	✦
	Using communication protocols and services	●	○	○	◑	◔	○	✦	✦	✦	✦
	Taking on someone else's identity (masquerade attack)	●	○	○	◑	◔	○	✦	✦	✦	✦
	Java, ActiveX etc. attacks	◕	○	○	◑	●	◕	✦	✦	✦	✦
	Incorrect configuration / implementation errors	○	○	○	○	◔	○	✦	✦	✦	✦
	Repudiating communication relationship	◑	○	○	○	○	◕	✦	✦	✦	✦
Preparation for attacks	Social engineering	○	○	○	○	○	●	○	✦	✦	✦
	Analysis by means of scanner programs	●	○	○	◑	○	○	✦	✦	✦	✦
Attacks on the firewall system	Manipulating the firewall system	●	○	○	◑	○	◕	✦	●	✦	✦
	Installing a trapdoor	○	○	○	◔	○	○	○	○	○	○
	Exploiting an incorrect configuration in the firewall system	●	○	○	◑	○	◕	○	●	✦	✦
	Exploiting implementation errors in the firewall system	●	○	○	◑	○	◕	✦	●	✦	✦
	Internal attacks	○	○	○	◕	●	◕	○	◔	✦	✦

● Very strong effect ◕ Strong effect ◑ Effect

◔ Weak effect ○ No effect ✦ Prerequisite for effectiveness

Figure 13-14: Summary of the effect of a comprehensive firewall system

Security Mechanisms and Their Effectiveness

This section summarizes the various security mechanisms and outlines the manner in which they qualitatively counter the defined attacks.

High-Level Security Firewall Systems

High-level security firewall systems display a strong to very strong effect against most types of attack. If any other firewall design concepts are used, then the effects of individual security functions become less critical accordingly (see Chapter 4). One particular aspect of central firewall systems is the fact that all the "background" computer systems are protected – all the clients (Microsoft Windows 95/98/2000/NT/ME, Mac, LINUX), servers (Lotus Notes, Novell, UNIX), host systems, and other IT components (printers, MTAs).

Encryption

Encryption significantly increases the protective effect against attacks by third parties. In addition to protections against the defined attacks each service protects against, the addition of encryption renders a security service confidential. Encryption has a particularly strong effect against man-in-the-middle attacks.

Anti-Malware Systems

Anti-malware systems help achieve a strong effect against viruses, worms, and Trojan horses, and prevent any damage caused by these attacks. In particular, the installation of a central anti-malware system is very important if all the computer systems, from the host or UNIX systems through the Windows PCs, are to be protected.

Intrusion Detection Systems

Intrusion detection systems exhibit a strong effect against internal attacks. They enable the detection of irregularities so that a prompt and targeted response is possible. The advantages of early detection for damage prevention (for example, detection of DDoS attacks) and correct follow-up in the sense of damage minimization are especially important after a security breach. Data obtained from intrusion detection systems can be used to optimize configuration of comprehensive firewall systems and to analyze real attack potential.

Personal Firewalls

Valuable system resources and files can be locally shielded against undesirable access through local applications or malware penetrating the system. Personal firewalls have a very strong effect against the infiltration of malware and against attacks with active content (Java, ActiveX, viruses, and so on). They also have a very strong effect against internal attacks. Due to lack of product availability, it is not possible at present for personal firewalls to be used on all computer systems. In addition to the effects already mentioned, a personal firewall also provides pure firewall functionality for telecommuter and mobile workstations. The effectiveness of the firewall functionality depends on the quality of the implementation, the integration into the operating system, and the configuration of the operating system. In this regard, at the very least, the firewall functionality will have a weak effect.

Non-Technical Security Measures

Non-technical security measures exhibit a strong effect against some types of attack and are particularly important when countering social engineering.

Trustworthiness, Audits, Security Policy, and Secure Operation

Trustworthiness achieved through evaluation and certification, the performance of audits, the drawing up of an unflawed security policy, and the secure operation of a comprehensive firewall system are essential to the secure use of a firewall system. Trustworthiness is the only security aspect that can reasonably counter a built-in trapdoor.

Attacks and the Effectiveness of Different Security Mechanisms

This section summarizes the defined attacks and explains which security mechanisms have which qualitative effects.

Trustworthiness (that is, determined effectiveness), audits, the implementation of a security policy, and secure operation are essential to the effectiveness of the individual security mechanisms against all of the following attacks. Rather than list these with each, you may consider them additional factors for all of the attacks.

- Playing back or delaying protocol elements
  - The use of encryption and access rights management in high-level security firewall systems helps achieve a strong effect.
  - The personal firewall offers basic protection to computer systems.
- Inserting or deleting data in the protocol elements
  - The use of access rights management in high-level security firewall systems achieves a strong effect against this kind of attack.
  - Encryption exhibits a very strong effect against this type of attack.

  - The personal firewall offers basic protection to computer systems.
  - Modifying Data in the Protocol Elements
  - The use of access rights management in high-level security firewall systems achieves a strong effect against this kind of attack.
  - Encryption has a very strong effect against this type of attack.
- Boycotting the receiver
  - The dual-homed application gateway mechanism has a strong effect in high-level security firewall systems.
  - Use of intrusion detection systems can enable early detection of this type of attack so that countermeasures can be taken quickly, perhaps with the aid of other organizations such as CERT.
  - The personal firewall offers basic protection to computer systems.
  - The discussion of DDoS attacks shows that global cooperation is sensible and effective. From the operator's perspective, this is an organizational security measure that, for example, can be supported by organizations such as CERT.
  - Contingency security measures, such as providing backup facilities, and infrastructural security measures, such as an uninterruptible power supply, achieve a strong effect.
- Man-in-the-middle attacks
  - This type of attack must be viewed in conjunction with the masquerade attack, where strong authentication plays an important role (high-level security firewall).
  - Encryption is particularly effective.
  - The personal firewall offers basic protection to computer systems.
- Sending malware (viruses, worms, Trojan horses)
  - To counter these types of attack, a central virus scanner – separately integrated into the comprehensive firewall system or contained in the firewall system itself – is recommended. A strong effect can be achieved centrally for all computer systems.
  - The use of personal firewalls can eliminate the possibility of local harm, achieving a very strong effect against this type of attack.
  - Personnel-related security measures (making staff aware of security issues and providing training, for example) have a strong effect.

- Setting up and using communications connections
  - Using access rights management with strict rules controlling system-to-system communications in a high-level security firewall system has a very strong effect against this type of attack.
  - The intrusion detection system can detect irregularities and reduce the amount of loss or damage in advance.
  - The personal firewall offers basic protection to computer systems.
- Using communications protocols and services
  - Using access rights management in a high-level security firewall system has a very strong effect against this type of attack.
  - The intrusion detection system can detect irregularities and reduce the amount of loss or damage in advance.
  - The personal firewall offers basic protection to computer systems.
- Taking on someone else's identity (masquerade attack)
  - A strong authentication mechanism in a high-level security firewall system has a very strong effect. This type of attack must be analyzed in conjunction with the man-in-the-middle attack, against which encryption plays a major role.
  - The intrusion detection system can detect irregularities and reduce the amount of loss or damage in advance.
  - The personal firewall offers basic protection to computer systems.
- Java and ActiveX attacks
  - It is possible to achieve a strong effect centrally against this type of attack with the aid of appropriate security mechanisms, such as applet filters or Java proxy, in a high-level security firewall system.
  - The intrusion detection system can detect irregularities and reduce the amount of loss or damage in advance.
  - The use of personal firewalls can eliminate the possibility of damage to local computer systems, achieving a very strong effect against this type of attack.
  - Personnel-related security measures have a strong effect.
- Incorrect configuration/implementation errors
  - The use of a high-level security firewall system, especially the integration of several different firewall elements such as packet filters and dual-homed application gateways, can achieve a very strong effect.
  - The personal firewall offers basic protection to computer systems.

- Repudiating communications relationship
  - Logging plays an important role with this type of attack. An effect can be achieved if communications occur between known communications partners.
  - In the area of external services, the retention of evidence through logging can even be incorporated into the service contract as an organizational security measure.
- Social engineering
  - Non-technical security mechanisms such as employee training have a very strong effect against this type of attack.
  - Personnel-related security measures have a strong effect.
- Analysis by means of scanner programs
  - The use of the dual-homed application gateway in a high-level security firewall system can achieve a very strong effect against this type of attack.
  - The use of intrusion detection systems enables the detection of this type of attack so that appropriate countermeasures can be taken.
- Manipulating the firewall system
  - Use of a secure design concept, the company's own protection mechanisms, a separate and central security management function, and different firewall elements in a high-level-security firewall system can have a very strong effect in preventing this type of attack.
  - The use of intrusion detection systems enables this type of attack to be detected.
  - Through infrastructural security measures such as access-controlled rooms and organizational security measures such as the specification of access rights for security management, it is possible to achieve a strong effect against this type of attack.
  - Loss or damage can be prevented through regular audits.
- Installing a trapdoor
  - The use of intrusion detection systems may enable detection of this type of attack.
  - This type of attack can only be effectively countered through evaluation and certification.

- Exploiting an incorrect firewall system configuration
  - Use of a secure design concept, the company's own protection mechanisms, a separate and central security management function, and different firewall elements in a high-level security firewall system can have a very strong effect against this type of attack.
  - The use of intrusion detection systems may enable this type of attack to be detected.
  - Organizational security measures, such as clearly defining security administrator responsibilities, can be very effective here.
  - This type of attack can be prevented through regular audits.
- Exploiting implementation errors in the firewall system
  - Use of a secure design concept, the company's own protection mechanisms, separate and central security management functionality, and different firewall elements in a high-level security firewall system can have a very strong effect against this type of attack.
  - The use of intrusion detection systems may enable this type of attack to be detected.
  - Organizational security measures, such as clearly defining security administrator responsibilities, can have a strong effect against this type of attack.
  - This type of attack can be prevented through regular audits.
- Internal attacks
  - Intrusion detection systems can help detect this type of attack in advance before any loss or damage has occurred.
  - Personal firewalls can achieve a very strong effect against this type of attack, as they can be integrated into the system (for example, into Microsoft Windows operating systems).
  - Personnel-related security measures have a strong effect against this type of attack.
  - Internal attacks can be detected and proven through audits.

Summary

The development and discussion of the communications model with integrated firewall system has shown the factors influencing the security and assurance achieved with firewall systems.

Figures have been used throughout the chapter to illustrate the structural relations of attacks and the effect of a wide range of security services, mechanisms, and functions.

With this knowledge gained from this chapter, you can design network interfaces to insecure networks, such as the Internet, so that they are secure and trustworthy.

With the correct configuration of firewall elements, a clear and higher level of security can be achieved. An appropriate combination of firewall elements ensures a higher degree of security than any individual firewall element alone can.

A firewall system with the correct combination of elements can, depending on the protection requirement and the application, clearly improve security.

If additional security mechanisms are added, such as intrusion detection systems, anti-malware systems, personal firewalls, and encryption and audits, other sources of insecurity can be eliminated, reducing still further the residual risk.

Appendix A
Security Standards

A NUMBER OF PROJECTS under the auspices of various groups such as CERT (Computer Emergency Response Team) are currently underway to establish security standards in connection with TCP/IP technology.

- E-mail security solutions, such as PGP and S/Mime, that enable the secure transfer of e-mail or messages between users. These solutions work in the Application layer of the TCP/IP stack.
- Client/server security solutions, such as SSL and SSH, that permit session-oriented encryption above the TCP Transport layer (Session or Presentation layer in the OSI model).
- Security at the Network level, which enables encryption at the IP level (Network layer).

In addition to the specification of the object exchange formats, key management plays a special role in security standards. Key management must be designed to be trustworthy for all involved. This difficult task can only be accomplished if, in addition to the implementation of reliable technologies, support is provided by appropriate legislation.

In a closed user group with its own security policy, key management is often more concerned with technical than with organizational issues. However, in organizations where you find different spheres of responsibility that want to exchange data securely with each other, the implementation of a common key management system is a central and complicated task.

Security standards on the Internet will only be widely used if a secure infrastructure is created for the distribution of authentic public keys, and if cryptographic algorithms with a high guarantee of security are employed in the products.

Cryptography concerns itself with the trustworthiness of data, computer systems, and communications structures. The correct and secure implementation of the cryptographic algorithms is especially important. Firewall systems should not only function simply, they should also guarantee security. Recently, flaws have come to light in the implementation, design, and integration of supposed security standards on which companies had relied – standards they had used in many application areas. A good example of this is the SSH (Secure Shell) version 1 protocol. Early implementations of version 1 had a then unknown buffer overflow condition. Many organizations switched to SSH for its ability to provide secure remote connectivity to UNIX/Linux servers. Several notable security Web sites were compromised through the protocol by hackers exploiting the buffer overflow. SSH was quickly fixed but the vulnerability significantly slowed its adoption rate for quite awhile.

The next few sections present and discuss a selection of security standards, including S-HTTP, Secure Sockets Layer (SSL), SKIP, and IPSec. A brief introduction to the successor of the IP protocol standard IPv4, known as IPv6 or Ipng, is also included.

SSL

Netscape Communications Corporation developed the SSL protocol. The more recent versions of the SSL standard go by the name *TLS*. SSL relies on a security mechanism between computer systems that is situated between the transport protocol (TCP) and the Application layer in the TCP/IP layer model. The application programmer can execute HTTP transactions as usual, which will be protected by the underlying SSL protocol. SSL provides the security functions of server authentication and (optionally) client authentication, as well as message confidentiality and integrity. SSL is transparent to the application.

SSL-capable browsers on the Internet are protected when they access URLs that contain the protocol designator `https`, such as the following:

```
https://www.whitehouse.gov/first-lady-wardrobe.html
```

Because the entire SSL-protected communication is encapsulated in the SSL Record Protocol, which also contains formatted headers and data fields, Web servers that communicate with HTTP over SSL receive messages from users on other network ports than those servers that only communicate over HTTP. A purely HTTP communication normally takes place on port 80; whereas HTTP combined with SSL uses TCP port 443 (SSL-supported SMTP is conducted on TCP port 464 and SSL-supported NNTP on port 563). If both protected and open Internet transactions are executed on one system, it is best to use several servers.

If a user connects to a server with SSL, an SSL handshake sequence occurs first, consisting of the following parts:

```
Negotiation of algorithm for encryption and digital signature
Exchange of a secret session key
Optional authentication of the server
Optional authentication of the client
```

During the first sequence, which serves to determine the encryption or signature, the procedure used to exchange the session key for subsequent symmetric encryption is negotiated. Options available include RSA and Diffie-Hellman (for communications without security certificates). If either party wants to employ digital signatures, this is established in this first stage of negotiations.

For the subsequently negotiated encryption, available options include the following:

```
No encryption.
RC4: stream encryption with 128-bit key.
RC4 export: with 128-bit key. Due to American export restrictions,
however, only 40 bits of
this are secret: during negotiation of the session key 40 bits are
transmitted encrypted
and 88 bits in plaintext.
RC2: block encryption in CBC mode with 128-bit key.
IDEA: block encryption in CBC mode with 128-bit key.
DES: block encryption in CBC mode with 56-bit key.
Triple-DES: in CBC mode with 168-bit key (effectively 112 bits).
```

Subsequent negotiations on the Message Authentication Code (MAC) can produce one of the following variants:

```
No message digest
MD5 with 128-bit hash
SHA 160-bit hash for the Digital Signature Standard (DSS)
```

Digital signatures are generated with the MD5 hash algorithm and the RSA signature algorithm. The public key certificates comply with the X.509 signature standard.

In the second stage of connection setup, the session key is transmitted. The server then confirms its authenticity to the client. Client authentication, which is optional, is seldom practiced. Checking the authenticity of the computers is achieved by using security certificates from generally recognized certification authorities (CAs).

While most SSL components reside directly above the TCP level, certain SSL functions work higher in the TCP/IP stack. They are used for connection setup and for the exchange of error messages between client and server during the session.

Assessment

SSL/TLS is a security sublayer that is integrated above the Transport layer and below the Application layer. By definition, both TCP and UDP services can be protected with SSL, but until now, only TCP implementations have been available. An advantage of SSL/TLS is the security mechanisms' independence from the application, so that services such as Telnet or e-mail could theoretically also use SSL. However, the SSL connection must go through a firewall system. In other words, an encrypted communication is tunneled through the firewall system. From the firewall system's perspective, this is a security risk because its data and communication filters cannot work. The extent to which such an uncontrollable communications link can be permitted from a computer system in the protected network to a server in the insecure network must be determined with reference to the protection requirement.

Conceptually, decryption should be performed in the firewall system so that monitoring of the application data and logging, in particular, can be carried out on the firewall system in a service-specific manner.

SSL Key Management

SSL key management is currently designed so that the client is responsible for encryption. The public keys used to verify certificates are distributed by the software (browser). This procedure is not secure for security-relevant applications, in which the authenticity of the public keys plays a particularly important role as a guarantee of a legally binding communication. It may offer a certain amount of protection against interception of communications from the Internet, but it does not protect against professional attacks. The existence of demonstration certificates, issued by many certification authorities following the sending of an e-mail address, can undermine the SSL mechanism. For effective protection, a certification hierarchy that organizes distribution of the public keys would need to be implemented. To make key management really secure, corresponding trustworthy entities must be used. A trustworthy entity could, for example, be the infrastructure established in connection with a digital signature law.

Secure Shell

The *Secure Shell (SSH) protocol* is designed for secure remote login and network services over an insecure network. SSH can effectively replace the telnet, rsh, rcmd, and rlogin protocols. SSH also includes support for a tool called `secure copy`, which can copy files from system to system within the encrypted tunnel.

SSH consists of three primary components:

- A Transport layer protocol
- A user authentication protocol
- A connection protocol

The Transport layer protocol provides server authentication, confidentiality, and integrity. The user authentication protocol uses the Transport layer protocol for communications and provides client-side user authentication. The connection protocol serves to multiplex the encrypted tunnel into logical channels and uses the user authentication protocol.

SSH is designed to be extensible. Since its inception, the current version of the protocol (version 2) has added support for redirecting other application protocols through the encrypted tunnel created by the Transport layer subset protocol. This effectively turns SSH into a virtual private network (VPN) protocol.

Authentication with SSH can take place at a user level or at a host level. SSH enables strong authentication by supporting the public key encryption. DSS is usually used for key exchange, although SSH supports the use of other key exchange protocols as well.

SSH first establishes a connection and authenticates at the host level by exchanging host keys. After initial authentication is completed, SSH negotiates a symmetric encryption algorithm for the session. The available cryptographic algorithms for SSH follow:

3des-cbc	REQUIRED	3 key Triple DES in CBC mode
blowfish-cbc	RECOMMENDED	Blowfish in CBC mode
twofish256-cbc	OPTIONAL	Twofish in CBC mode using a 256 bit key
twofish192-cbc	OPTIONAL	Twofish in CBC mode using a 192 bit key
twofish128-cbc	RECOMMENDED	Twofish in CBC mode using a 128 bit key
aes256-cbc	OPTIONAL	AES (Rinjndael) in CBC mode with a 256 bit key
aes192-cbc	OPTIONAL	AES in CBC mode with a 192 bit key
aes1280cbc	RECOMMENDED	AES in CBC mode with a 128 bit key
serpent256-cbc	OPTIONAL	Serpent in CBC mode with 256 bit key
serpent192-cbc	OPTIONAL	Serpent in CBC mode with 192 bit key
serpent128-cbc	OPTIONAL	Serpent in CBC mode with 128 bit key
arcfour	OPTIONAL	Arcfour stream cipher
idea-cbc	OPTIONAL	IDEA in CBC mode
cast128-cbc	OPTIONAL	CAST-128 in CBC mode
none	OPTIONAL	no encryption - NOT RECOMMENDED

Notice that SSH protocol implementations are only required to support the 3des-cbc encryption algorithm. Recommended protocols are available in most cases. When configuring SSH, you can configure the server with a preference order for algorithms. SSH will attempt to negotiate encryption, offering algorithms in the preferred order.

For providing data integrity, SSH supports the following algorithms:

hmac-sha1	REQUIRED	HMAC-SHA1 (digest length = key length = 20)
hmac-sha1-96	RECOMMENDED	First 96 bits of HMAC-SHA1 (digest length = 12, key length = 20)
hmac-md5	OPTIONAL	HMAC-MD5 (digest length = key length = 16)
hmac-md5-96	OPTIONAL	First 96 bits of HMAC-MD5 (digest length = 12, key length = 16)
none	OPTIONAL	No MAC (NOT RECOMMENDED)

Finally, SSH uses the following public key algorithms:

```
ssh-dss            REQUIRED      Simple DSS
ssh-rsa            RECOMMENDED   Simple RSA
x509v3-sign-rsa    OPTIONAL      X.509 certificates (RSA key)
x509v3-sign-dss    OPTIONAL      X.509 certificates (DSS key)
spki-sign-rsa      OPTIONAL      SPKI certificate (RSA key)
spki-sign-dss      OPTIONAL      SPKI certificate (DSS key)
pgp-sign-rsa       OPTIONAL      OpenPGP certificate (RSA key)
pgp-sign-dss       OPTIONAL      OpenPGP certificate (DSS key)
```

After session negotiations have occurred, all subsequent communications occur using the random key and algorithms selected during negotiation. With the transport in place, other Application layer protocols can communicate with a remote system through the "tunnel."

Assessment

SSH has proven to be a reliable and secure replacement for the aging telnet and "r" protocols. The first implementation of the protocol was subject to a buffer overflow attack. The buffer overflow vulnerability was fixed as soon as it came to light. SSHv2 has proven to be both robust and secure. It is also a convenient tool for replacing protocols such as Telnet, FTP, Rlogin, RSH, and RCMD. Given SSH's strength, most vendors are starting to supply SSH support directly in their products (as appropriate).

IPv6

The procedures previously described integrate security mechanisms into the existing IP standard (IPv4), but IP version 6 (IPv6) follows a different route. This protocol, also referred to as IPng (next generation), is a completely new definition of IP and should replace version 4 in the future.

From a security standpoint, one of IPv6's interesting features is the modular structure of the new IP header, which replaces the rigid convention of IP version 4. To make room for future developments, no fixed-length header has been implemented; instead, space has been created for expansions with a simple chained list. Authentication (AH) and Encapsulation (Encapsulated Security Payload, encryption, ESP) headers, provided to protect the data traffic, contain information on the methods used for authentication and/or encryption. The last header in the chain is specially marked and followed by the payload data.

The new AH and ESP headers are part of the IPSec standard and are described in more detail later in this chapter.

Assessment

IP version 6 has a ways to go before it becomes a proper standard. Many implementation issues are still unclear. Above all, incompatibility with the old IPv4 standard, making it necessary to replace all network cards, has prevented its widespread use. One of IPv6's main advantages – larger IP address space – is no longer as relevant. Many companies configure their own internal networks with private network addresses (the former test addresses) and present themselves to the outside world through a firewall system. Because the AH and ESP mechanisms have now been integrated into IP version 4 as well, there is a danger that IPv6 will be downgraded to a peripheral development in the world of network protocols.

Internet Protocol Security Architecture

The Internet Engineering Task Force (IETF) has defined an Internet security standard known as Internet Protocol Security Architecture (IPSec). IPSec defines mechanisms to establish secure communications over IP. Currently, one of the most common implementations of IPSec is the vVPN, but normal network connections between two nodes are also possible.

IPSec was originally developed in the context of IP version 6 (IPv6). As the general implementation of IPv6 continues to be delayed because of its incompatibility with IPv4, the security mechanisms of IPSec have been integrated into IPv4. The new headers for authentication and encryption introduced under IPv6 are transformed in IPv4 into an extension of the data section of the IP packets, so that the headers are longer.

IPSec essentially offers two mechanisms: the Authentication Header (AH) and the Encapsulated Security Payload (ESP). IPSec is implemented on a computer system or a security gateway and protects IP traffic to and from this node. The precise protection specifications are stored in a separate database, called the Security Policy Database (SPD). The SPD can be viewed as a collection of rules, rather like the filter rules of a packet filter. It contains rules for all inbound and outbound packets, stipulating whether they should be handled using IPSec, sent on without IPSec, or discarded. If any packets are to be handled using IPSec, the SPD contains a reference to a Security Association (SA), in which the precise procedure is specified.

The Authentication Header

The IP Authentication Header checks the integrity and authentication of the IP datagrams. It also offers protection against unwanted packet retransmission and any resultant problems (replay attacks, for example).

However, the values of the fields in the IP header that change during data transmission, such as flags, cannot be protected by AH.

AH can be used alone or in combination with ESP. There are two modes of operation: transport mode and tunnel mode.

THE AH HEADER FORMAT

The AH header has IP protocol type 51 and is composed of the following fields:

- `Next Header` is an 8-bit field specifying the type of data behind the AH.
- `Length` is an 8-bit field specifying the length of the AH in 32-bit words.
- `Reserved` is a 16-bit field reserved for future use. It must always be set to 0.
- The Security Parameter Index (SPI) is a 32-bit value that, together with the IP destination address, produces a pointer to the associated SA.
- The sequence number is a 32-bit field containing a monotonically increasing numerical value. This enables the detection of retransmitted packets and the prevention of replay attacks.
- `Authentication Data` is a field of variable length that contains the integrity check value (ICV) for the packet. The authentication algorithm contains encrypted Message Authentication Codes (MACs) based on symmetric encryption algorithms or on one-way hash functions, such as MD5 or SHA-1. With this data, the integrity of the packet and the authenticity of the sender can be checked.

PROCESSING THE AH HEADER

As previously mentioned, AH can be used in two modes: transport and tunnel. In tunnel mode, a new IP header, which, for example, contains the address of a gateway, is inserted in front of the old one. The old IP packet, including its flags, is protected by the AH.

In transport mode, the AH is placed after the IP header, but in front of any ESP header. There are differences here between IPv4 and IPv6: under IPv4, the AH is placed between the IP header and the protocol of the higher layer (TCP, UDP, ICMP, and so on). Under IPv6, the AH appears as an additional extension header after the extension headers `hop-by-hop`, `routing`, and `fragmentation`.

In tunnel mode, the inner IP header transports the actual source and destination addresses, while the outer IP header contains, for example, the address of the security gateway. In tunnel mode, the AH protects the entire inner area of the packet, including the inner IP header.

PROCESSING INBOUND AND OUTBOUND PACKETS

The AH is only entered by the transmitter in an outbound packet if an SA requiring an AH has been found for the packet. This assignment is specified in the Security Policy Database (SPD).

When an AH packet is received, the receiver searches for a corresponding SA, based on the IP destination address and the Security Parameter Index (SPI) from the AH data section.

The SA entry reveals whether the Sequence Numbers field is checked, specifies the algorithms for the ICV calculation, and makes the necessary keys available.

If there is no SA for this connection (for example, if the receiver does not have a key), the receiver rejects the packet and enters the action in an audit log file.

Encapsulated Security Payload

The ESP header can also protect Ipv4 and Ipv6 IP packets. Like the AH, the ESP header is inserted after the IP header and before the header of the higher order protocol (transport mode) or before any embedded IP header (tunnel mode).

ESP enables confidentiality, authentication, and data integrity. As for the AH, the unwanted retransmission of packets is detected.

If the entire data flow, including the IP addresses, is to be handled in confidence, the tunnel mode must be employed. The original IP addresses are then encrypted and cannot be read. Tunnel mode is generally used on point-to-point connections such as firewalls or other security gateways.

THE ESP HEADER'S FORMAT

The ESP header has the IP protocol type 50. The meaning of the fields is the same as in the AH, with the following exceptions:

- The payload data is contained in a field of variable length. Apart from pure data, initialization vectors for the encryption algorithm can also be entered in this field.
- If certain algorithms are expecting a fixed data length, the payload data can be enlarged to the required value using the Padding field.
- The length padding indicates the number of preceding filler bytes.
- Authentication Data is a field of variable length containing an integrity check value (ICV), generated by the ESP header without the authentication data itself. This enables the ESP header to authenticate the packet.

> NOTE: Unlike the ESP header, the AH also refers to the preceding IP header (without the variable flags, and so on). Therefore, you can increase security by choosing a combination of AH and ESP.

In the IPv6 context, ESP is treated as an "end-to-end" data record that is always placed after the extension headers `hop-by-hop`, `routing`, and `fragmentation`. Additional extension headers can occur either before or after the ESP header. However, because ESP basically only protects the fields that follow the ESP header, it is desirable to place as much of the package as possible after the ESP header.

PROCESSING INBOUND AND OUTBOUND PACKETS

In transport mode, the transmitter includes only the information of the higher protocols in the ESP area. In tunnel mode, the entire old IP packet, including the IP header, is packed into the ESP data, and a new IP header is generated with the IP destination address.

ESP is used for outbound packets only in cases in which, in accord with the IPSec definition, it is specified in the SPD that the packet is linked with an SA and requires ESP.

To send an encrypted packet, the transmitter must do the following:

- Generate the area for the ESP payload data. This data covers the old IP packet's original payload data and the higher layer's protocol information, or the entire old IP header.
- Insert the necessary fill characters (padding), if required by the algorithm.
- Encrypt the results, such as ESP payload data, padding, and padding length, using the algorithm stipulated by the SA.

Inbound IP fragments are initially assembled prior to decryption. The receiver searches for the corresponding SA, based on the IP destination address and the SPI. The packet can then be decrypted and, if necessary, authenticated.

Security Association

A Security Association (SA) is a collection of keys and rules aimed at automating the processing of AH and ESP. For inbound and outbound packets, one entry is created for each communications partner (IP address), separated by AH and ESP. To protect a typical bi-directional communication between two hosts or two gateways, two SAs are required (one for each direction). If AH and ESP are used together, the number of entries increases to four.

Each SA is uniquely defined through the Security Parameter Index, the IP destination address, and the security protocol used (AH or ESP). The SPI must be entered in every packet sent.

Two SA types are possible, one type indicating transport mode and the other type indicating tunnel mode. Only the tunnel mode can be used for communications between two security gateways or between a host and a security gateway.

IPSec Databases

The Security Association (SA) is the link between an IP packet and the algorithms and keys for authentication and encryption. All system SAs are stored in the Security Association Database (SAD). For each packet handled using IPSec, a reference is generated by the previously mentioned Security Policy Database to the relevant SA in the SAD.

Key Management under IPSec

IPSec implementations allow both manual and automated key management. The IPSec protocols, AH and ESP, are largely independent of the SA management techniques, even if the relevant techniques influence some of the security services that are offered.

The simplest form of key management is manual: each system is configured with the keys and data necessary to ensure secure communications with other systems. Manual techniques are appropriate in small and static environments. For example, a small company could set up a VPN in security gateways using IPSec. If the number of security gateways is small, and if all security gateways have the same administration, key management can be manual. Manual key management is also appropriate in cases where only a particular part of the communication needs to be protected. The same applies to the use of IPSec within an organization that has only a small number of computer systems and/or security gateways. Manual key management often uses statically configured, symmetric keys even if other options are available.

In larger networks or in networks with several administrators, manual key management is generally not possible. IPSec supports a number of key management procedures; the standard method is ISAKMP/Oakley. In this two-stage procedure, the communications partners first authenticate themselves to each other with one of the procedures using public and private keys specified in the Digital Signature Standard (DSS). Keys for ESP encryption are then generated and exchanged using Diffie-Hellman. From the data exchanged during authentication and exchange of keys, the partners generate their SAs, with which the rest of the communication is then processed.

IPSec does allow other key management procedures – those introduced, for example, with the SKIP protocol. Here, a rapid, time-driven or data-driven key exchange makes it virtually impossible for eavesdroppers to follow the data traffic. Even in the unlikely event that a single key was decrypted, only a small part of the data stream could be converted to meaningful data. After the next key change, the hacker would be forced to start all over again.

ASSESSMENT

IPSec is definitely the most attractive of the standards for protecting network connections. However, the problem of secure key exchange remains unresolved. Nevertheless, many VPN and firewall systems manufacturers now support IPSec.

IPSec-capable devices produced by one manufacturer are not necessarily able to communicate securely with devices produced by other manufacturers. The possibilities envisaged in IPSec are so diverse that it is not possible to dispense with careful testing. However, progress is expected in this area in the near future. No manufacturer will willingly forego the possibility of placing his products in new markets by offering a problem-free integration capability.

Appendix B

References

[a Campo and Pohlmann, 2001] a Campo, M., and N. Pohlmann. *Virtual Private Networks.* Bonn: MITP-Verlag, 2001.

[Abrams et al., 1991] Abrams, M.D., J. Heaney, O. King, L.J. LaPadula, and I.D. Olson. *Generalized Framework for Access Control.* Proceedings of the 14th National Computer Security Conference, 1991.

[Aladdin, 1999] Aladdin. *Safe Internet Connectivity for the Home & Small Office.* White Paper. Seattle: Aladdin Knowledge Systems, 1999.

[Black, 2001] Black, E. *IBM and the Holocaust: The Strategic Alliance between Nazi Germany and America's Most Powerful Corporation.* Crown Pub, 2001.

[CCITT] CCITT. *The Directory – Authentication Framework.* Draft Recommendation X.509, Gloucester: 1987.

[CESG3] UK Systems Security Confidence Levels: *CESG Memorandum No. 3.* Communications-Electronics Security Group: 1989.

[Chaum, 1987] Chaum, D. *Security without Identification: Transaction Systems to Make Big Brother Obsolete.* Comm. ACM 28, 1985, S. 1030-1044.

[Cheswick and Bellowin, 1994] Cheswick, W. R., and St. M. Bellowin. *Firewalls and Internet Security.* Addison-Wesley Publishing Company, 1994.

[Chapman and Zwicky, 1996] Chapman, D.B., and E. D. Zwicky. *Building Internet Firewalls.* O'Reilly, International. Thomson Publishing, 1996.

[Comm, 1998] *Common Criteria for Information Technology Security Evaluation – Part 1: Introduction and general model.* ISO/IEC SC27 N2161: 1998.

[DTIEC] *DTI Commercial Security Centre Evaluation Levels Manual.* V22 Department of Trade and Security: 1989.

[Hughes, 1995] Hughes, L.J., Jr. *Actually Useful Internet Security Techniques.* Indianapolis: New Riders Publishing, 1995.

[ISO9798] Information Processing Systems – Open Systems Interconnection (ISO), Electronic Data Interchange for Administration, Commerce and Transport (EDIFACT) – Application Level Syntax Rules.

[ITSEC91a]	*Information Technology Security Evaluation Criteria (ITSEC).* Commission of the European Communities: Brussels and Luxembourg: 1991.
[NCSA]	*Firewall Policy Guide, NCSA Security White Paper Series.* NCSA. Carlisle: 1994.
[Santifaller, 1994]	Santifaller, M. *TCP/IP and ONC/NFS: Internetworking in a UNIX Environment (Data Communications and Networks).* Addison-Wesley Publishing Company, 1994.
[Standage, 1998]	Standage, T. *The Victorian Internet: The Remarkable Story of the Telegraph and the Nineteenth Century's Online-Pioneers.* Berkeley: Berkeley Publishing Group, 1998.
[Tannenbaum, 1998]	Tannenbaum, A.S. *Computer Networks.* New Jersey: Prentice Hall, 1998.
[TCSEC]	*Trusted Computer Systems Evaluation Criteria (TCSEC),DOD 5200.28-STD.* U.S. Department of Defense, 1985.
[Washburn and Evans, 1994]	Washburn, K., and J. Evans. *TCP/IP.* Addison-Wesley Publishing Company, 1994.

Appendix C

Glossary

3DES Abbreviation for Triple-DES. Triple-DES has largely replaced simple DES to increase the longevity of DES. Triple DES uses two or three DES keys and encrypts by using the DES algorithm three times. There are numerous variations of 3DES that use DES a little differently. 3DES EDE, for instance, uses key one to encrypt the data with DES then decrypts those results with a second key and re-encrypts the results of the second iteration with the first key again.

Access Control Security component that restricts what data users can view or change.

ActiveX Programming language developed by Microsoft in response to Java and JavaScript. The program code (an ActiveX control) is loaded by an ActiveX-capable browser from a Web server and executed on the local computer system.

AES (Advanced Encryption Standard) The recently ratified replacement for the aging DES encryptions algorithm. Rijandel is the mathematical algorithm selected as the new AES.

Algorithm A mathematical formula that takes information and performs a given calculation on it. Z = X*2 is an example of a simple algorithm.

AP (Authentication Process) The method used to determine the authenticity of a user or entity. The primary types of authentication are "what you know," "what you have," and "who you are." Examples of these three are passwords, physical security tokens, and fingerprints, respectively.

Applet Program code written in Java that is executed on the local computer system within a separate environment.

Application gateway A computer system on which one or more proxies are implemented.

ARIN (American Registry for Internet Numbers) The Internet group responsible for assigning IP addresses on the Internet.

ARPA (Advanced Research Projects Agency) A governmental group tasked with overseeing research projects of interest to the U.S. government; primarily defense and computer-related research.

ARPANET (Advanced Research Projects Agency Network) The first worldwide data network, based on packet-oriented data transmission. Today's Internet originated from ARPANET.

Asymmetric encryption Also known as Public Key System, this encryption system uses two different keys. The data or document is encrypted and/or signed with one of the keys, and decryption/verification can only be performed with the corresponding key. Algorithms derived from complexity theory are used in the implementation.

Asynchronous Transfer Mode (ATM) A data transmission technique that can considerably increase the available communications bandwidth. It enables the simultaneous transmission of data from different sources and can thus make optimal use of transmission capacities. This makes possible a bandwidth of up to 2.4 Gbps.

ATM See *Asynchronous Transfer Mode.*

Authentication The process of verifying (checking) the authenticity or identity of a person or object. Authentication can be performed in either a user-oriented (user authentication) or computer-oriented (using the computer address) manner.

Authenticode Control procedure for the use of ActiveX controls. A programmer of ActiveX controls has access to all the system resources and thus possesses the same rights as the user who is currently logged on. To prevent misuse, the Authenticode technology can be used to provide evidence of the origins of the ActiveX controls used through digital signature.

Bandwidth The volume of data that a given communications channel can transport per unit of time. An analog telephone line has a bandwidth of around 56 Kbps, an ISDN line manages 64 Kbps (or 128 Kbps in duplex mode), Ethernet 10 Mbps, and Fast Ethernet 100 Mbps. Finally, ATM achieves a bandwidth of up to 2.4 Gbps.

Note that bandwidth is often used to refer to the throughput of a system, but it is only indirectly related to throughput. Data rate or capacity is a better way to refer to the amount of data that can pass through a system.

Bastion An application gateway that is the only computer system that can be directly addressed from the insecure network.

Biometrics Procedures that use unmistakable physical attributes of the user, such as fingerprint or facial characteristics, for authentication.

Blowfish A symmetric encryption algorithm invented by Bruce Schneier.

Browser A software program that enables Internet pages to be viewed. The browser accesses Web servers using HyperText Transfer Protocol (HTTP). Documents are interpreted by the browser in HTML format and presented to the user, along with the image data. Common browsers include Netscape Navigator, Microsoft Internet Explorer, and Lynx.

Brute force attack When hacking cryptographic keys or passwords, one can proceed with varying levels of sophistication. For example, one can attempt to discover and evaluate clues. Brute force refers to the most primitive type of attack, in which one blindly tries every conceivable possibility. Such an attack is likely to be unsuccessful today; anyone who attempts to crack a 128-bit key with a brute force attack will probably need a period of time equal to several times the lifetime of the solar system.

CA (Certification Authority) An agency that issues user keys as certificates (electronic identity cards). The certificates are used for the authentic transmission of data and also to verify the identity of the sender.

CCITT Comité Consultatif International Télégraphique et Téléphonique, an international organization responsible for setting telephone system standards.

CERT (Computer Emergency Response Team) CERT acts as an Internet "fire brigade," responding quickly and efficiently to critical incidents, such as hacker attacks, security loopholes, and viruses, providing help and preparing and making available information.

CGI (Common Gateway Interface) Program interface between user data arriving at the Web server (for example, completed forms) and connected programs such as databases. Using CGI scripts, Web pages can be dynamically designed and provided with interactive elements.

Ciphering error A flaw in the design or implementation of an encryption algorithm. In general, the result of this type of error is that the keys generated are less complex. They may represent a smaller number of combinations than is technically possible.

Cipher-text Information presented in an encrypted form so that it can only be understood by those for whom it is intended.

Common Point of Trust The single link between different networks, viewed as trustworthy and implemented with the aid of a firewall system.

Compromise A general term referring to a breach of confidentiality.

Content security A term that refers to the vulnerability of Internet documents (HTML pages, e-mails, and so on) when threatened by malicious programs and malware.

Cookies Information, such as a customer number, that the Web server stores in the client browser. This information can be used to identify the user on his next visit to the Web site.

Corporate network A communications network established by an organization that contains nodes, routers, and multiplexers.

Cracker A hacker who penetrates other computer systems without authorization and tampers with or inspects stored data and programs with malicious intent – that is, with criminal energy and/or for personal advantage.

CRL (Certification Revocation List) A blacklist of revoked user certificates maintained in a trust center.

Cryptoanalysis The science of decrypting ciphers and codes. In electronic data communication, one can refer to cryptoanalysis as a form of hacking.

Cryptographic algorithm Every cryptographic procedure is based on transforming a comprehensible text into an incomprehensible sequence of characters, following certain rules. With electronic encryption, this is done following a particular algorithm, whereby the key length used in the algorithm determines how difficult it is for a hacker to decrypt the text, and thus how secure the encryption is. At present, for symmetric encryption algorithms, key lengths of 128 bits are regarded as secure.

Cryptographic protocol A cryptographic protocol is the specification of how specific cryptographic algorithms are used. Protocols are defined for interoperability between different systems.

Cryptography The branch of cryptology that is concerned with the development of procedures for encryption and coding. This science is very old – even the ancient Egyptians were concerned with ciphers. Today, cryptography refers primarily to mathematical encryption algorithms for electronic data communications. Digital signatures are also based on cryptographic procedures.

Cryptology A generic term for cryptography and cryptoanalysis.

Daemon A UNIX process that runs in the background and is only activated as required. Examples of typical daemons are ftpd (FTP-Daemon) and httpd (HTTP-Daemon).

Data confidentiality A term that refers to the protection of a message from being intercepted or read by someone for whom it wasn't intended. Encryption is the primary mechanism used to achieve data confidentiality.

Data integrity A term that refers to the accuracy and completeness of information. Security mechanisms promote data integrity by preventing the modification of data or by detecting the occurrence of data modification.

Data rate See *Bandwidth*.

DECNET A communications architecture for computer systems developed and used by the Digital Equipment Corporation (DEC).

Decryption The process of converting cipher-text to plain-text.

Denial-of-Service (DoS) A Denial-of-Service is any attack whose primary purpose is to prevent a service from being used by its legitimate users. A type of attack that aims to crash computers or paralyze particular aspects of their functionality, classic DoS examples are mail bombing – the planned overloading of an e-mail recipient with a huge number of e-mails – or sending *nukes*, IP packets that unceremoniously crash unprotected operating systems.

DES (Data Encryption Standard) One of the most well-known, used, and studied symmetric encryption systems. DES was standardized in the U.S. in 1976 (ANSI X3.92). The DES algorithm in its original version has a key length of 64 bits, 56 of which are significant. The DES algorithm is today generally used as Triple-DES with a 128-bit effective key length.

Digital certificate Anyone wishing to prove his identity remotely – for example, by using a smart card and entering a PIN – must refer to a trusted entity that can document the connection between him and the Smart card/PIN. This certification authority (CA) vouches for the authenticity of the cardholder and documents this with a certificate. This digital certificate is used by organizations that permit remote access, as a means by which users can identify themselves.

Digital signature The electronic equivalent of an ordinary signature that identifies the sender unambiguously and ensures that the data received has not been forged. In other words, a digital signature guarantees the origin of the software, messages, or other data. Digital signature technology is based on asymmetric encryption (that is, the public key system).

DMZ (Demilitarized Zone) An isolated subnet placed between the protected network and the insecure network.

DNS (Domain Name Service) Internet service that connects IP addresses of computers to their corresponding domain names, and vice versa. The databases that contain the addresses are administered by DNS servers.

Domain names Lower-level subdivision of the hierarchically structured and globally unique names of computer systems on the Internet. Domain names must be applied for at the relevant administrative centers.

DSL (Digital Subscriber Line) A technology that allows for high-speed connectivity to the Internet via standard telephone lines.

E-commerce, or electronic commerce A term that refers, in principle, to all stages of business processes that are performed by electronic means. Through e-commerce, consumers and businesses can obtain information about products for sale and place orders online. Payments made from home PCs will soon be a common aspect of e-commerce. With electronic payments, it is even more important than with orders that the customer is uniquely identifiable and that no unauthorized person obtains information on transactions.

Effective key length If encryption algorithms are run several times, it is not possible to simply multiply the key length. Cryptologists have thus coined the term "effective key length." For example, with an operation using three passes with a 56-bit key length, such as that employed with Triple-DES, the security of the procedure is not actually that of a single encryption pass using a key length of 3 x 56 bits = 168 bits, but is somewhat lower, with an effective key length of only 128 bits.

E-mail, or electronic mail The exchange of text messages and computer files over a communications network, such as a local network or the Internet.

Encryption The process of converting a message into cipher-text so that the information is protected against unauthorized inspection or use. Encryption systems are based on complex mathematical calculations (algorithms), whereby the key length and the quality of the algorithm determine the effectiveness of the security.

Ethernet A networking technology originally developed by Xerox for linking mini-computers in its Palo Alto Research Center. Ethernet is a networking standard covering the Physical and Data Link layers of the OSI model. Today, an Ethernet network is a widely used technique of connecting computers in a LAN.

Exploit The use of a vulnerability, such as a software bug, to compromise security on a system.

Extranet An intranet that has been selectively opened to a company's customers, suppliers, and mobile workers.

Finger An Internet utility for ascertaining and administering the user information of a computer system. The associated software is routinely part of every UNIX operating system.

FTP (File Transfer Protocol) An Internet standard for the transmission of files.

Gateway A service or device that serves as the portal between two networks or subnets – in other words, the "gate" through which data from the Internet reaches a local network. Gateways operate in layer 7 of the ISO/OSI model and can connect two or more networks with completely different protocols. For information security, the gateway is the sensitive point. One installs a firewall there, resulting in a "secure gateway."

GSM (Global System for Mobile Communications) A standard for digital mobile communications networks.

Hacker A general user who possesses a tremendous amount of knowledge relating to computer technology and programming, and who often devotes a large amount of time to these activities. The term is also frequently used for persons who gain unauthorized access to other computer systems. However, hacking is not the same as computer sabotage, computer espionage, or computer fraud. Many hackers are motivated by recreational or academic intentions. They often publish their findings, which can help with the development of security mechanisms. Unlike crackers, hackers are not motivated by criminal intent or by the desire to achieve personal advantage.

HIDS (Host-Based Intrusion Detection System) HIDS runs in a host and monitors its operation for indications of hacker activity.

HTML (HyperText Markup Language) Page description language with which elements (text, graphics, hyperlinks, and so on) in Web pages can be simply formatted. HTML is currently the most important file format used in the World Wide Web.

HTTP (HyperText Transfer Protocol) The Internet standard that supports the exchange of data between Web servers and Web browsers.

Hyperlink A cross-reference in a Web page to an information source in the World Wide Web, generated with HTML. By activating a link – for example, by clicking a mouse – the user is taken to this source; in this way, he can be linked from server to server in the Web.

ICMP (Internet Control Message Protocol) An Internet protocol of the Network layer that provides error correction and other information relevant to the processing of IP packets.

IDEA (International Data Encryption Algorithm) A symmetric encryption system with a 128-bit key length that was presented in 1990 by Lai and Massey as an alternative to DES.

Internet A worldwide, decentralized computer network based on the TCP/IP protocol. The Internet is the most popular network in the world, with over 350 million users as of March 2001. It offers its users numerous services, such as FTP, e-mail, and World Wide Web.

Intranet A computer network – based on Internet technology and the TCP/IP protocol – that is designed to meet the internal needs of an organization or a company.

IP (Internet protocol) A network protocol that defines the structure and address logic of data packets in TCP/IP networks.

IP address A worldwide unique address of a computer system connected to the Internet. The IP address consists of a numeric code of four numbers from 0 to 255 (for example, 192.168.1.2). The assignment of IP addresses is performed by ARIN.

IP spoofing The insertion of a false IP sender address in an Internet transmission. The aim is to gain unauthorized access to a computer system.

IPSEC (IP Secure) A VPN protocol designed to provide secure host-to-host, host-to-network, and network-to-network communications.

IPv6 (Internet protocol Version 6) An enhanced version of the Internet protocol, with enlarged address space and security functions.

IPX (Internetwork Packet Exchange) A network protocol used by Novell. In the OSI model, IPX is classified in the same layer as IP.

ISDN (Integrated Services Digital Network) A global digital communications network for the integrated transmission of voice and data.

ISO (International Organization for Standardization) An international organization of national standards bodies from some 130 countries, one body from each country. The ISO works on the worldwide standardization of technical standards, including the areas of communications and information exchange. ISO standards include the widely accepted OSI model.

ISS (Internet Security Systems) Manufacturer of firewall, intranet, and Web security scanners. The scanners test computer systems for weaknesses by carrying out known Internet attacks.

IT (Information technology) The computer systems and infrastructure that provide computing resources to an organization.

ITSEC (Information Technology Security Evaluation Criteria) Criteria specified by France, Germany, Great Britain, and the Netherlands for the certification of IT systems.

Java A platform-independent programming language for the Internet developed by Sun Microsystems. Java programs (applets) are transmitted from a Web server to the local computer system and executed there by a Java interpreter.

Java applet A small java program, typically embedded in a Web page.

JavaScript A script language defined by Netscape and integrated into the HTML syntax. JavaScript-capable Web browsers interpret the program code contained in a Web site and execute it.

L2TP (Layer 2 Tunneling Protocol) A carrier protocol designed to carry other protocols, primarily IPSEC.

LAN (local area network) A network that covers a relatively small, limited area, unlike a WAN.

LDAP (Lightweight Directory Access Protocol) A universal database protocol mostly used for directory services

MAC (Media Access Control) Protocol of the Network Access layer that controls packet delivery on the local physical network. MAC can also stand for Message Authentication Code, a one-way hash algorithm.

Mailbox A computer system, dialed by a modem, on which a program that enables the user to read messages from other users and to write messages to them runs. Normally, it is also possible to download or upload files.

Malware Programs, such as viruses, worms, and Trojan horses, that are intended to cause harm. When files are downloaded from World Wide Web documents or exchanged as e-mail attachments, there is a risk that malware will be sent along with the information itself.

MD5 A one-way hash function developed by Ron Rivest and used to support authentication procedures.

MIME (Multipurpose Internet Mail Standard) A standard for sending multimedia files in e-mails.

Modem Shorthand for Modulator/Demodulator. A device that enables the exchange of data over wire lines. Traditionally, modems used conventional telephone lines to establish a connection to the Internet and to send e-mail. However, modems can also use television cable, power lines, leased lines, and so on.

Modulation The conversion of a digital signal to its analog equivalent. Many data lines, such as analog telephone lines, carry a continuous signal – the so-called carrier. The actual information transfer is effected through modulation of the carrier signal.

MTA (Message Transfer Agent) A program responsible for accepting and forwarding e-mails.

Multiplex procedures Techniques that make it possible to transmit separate signals over a single line.

Network A group of computers and connected devices that are linked to each other through communications equipment. The network connections can be set up on either a permanent (via cable) or temporary (over a telephone or other communications link) basis and may be of different scales and extent.

NIDS (Network-Based Intrusion Detection System) Software and services that attempt to discover indications of malicious activity by monitoring network communications.

Non-Repudiation Security components that provide the ability to prove that a transaction occurred.

NNTP (Network News Transfer Protocol) An Internet standard with which news articles are transported.

One-way hash function A mathematical function that is applied to a message of variable length, generating a cryptographic checksum of fixed length (for example, MD5).

OSI Layer Model, or OSI Reference Model. A communications protocol developed by ISO that contains general rules for communication in networks.

OTP (one-time-password) A password that can be used for authentication only once.

PGP (Pretty Good Privacy) An encryption system based on RSA and IDEA developed by Phil Zimmerman.

Phreaker A person who wreaks havoc in telephone networks, telephone lines, answering machines, and voicemail.

PIN (Personal Identification Number) A numeric code assigned to an authorized user.

POP3 The current version of POP (Post Office Protocol). Standard for the transmission of e-mails.

PPP (Point-to-Point Protocol) A protocol used to exchange data packets by modem in the Internet. PPP is located one layer below TCP/IP and is concerned only with serial transmission and its structure.

PPTP (Point-to-Point Tunneling Protocol) A VPN protocol developed by Microsoft for secure communications to and from their Windows NT servers.

Private key system Also known as Symmetric Encryption. It uses a single key for both encrypting and decrypting information.

Proxy A software agent that acts on behalf of the server for the client and on behalf of the client for the server. Following authentication of the client or server to the proxy, the proxy works for both sides transparently. Proxies exist for the services HTTP, SMTP, FTP, and Telnet, among others.

Public key system Also known as Asymmetric Encryption. It uses a mathematically matched key pair to encrypt and decrypt information. What one key encrypts, the other key decrypts (and vice versa).

Remote Access A means by which mobile users can gain authenticated access to a computer system over a public network located some distance away. As remote access connections by their nature are particularly risky, security precautions must be taken to guarantee authenticity and confidentiality. Remote access can be protected with encryption and access control systems.

RFC (Request for Comment) An Internet publication that summarizes suggestions for or descriptions of standards.

RIP (Routing Information Protocol) A protocol used by a router to send IP packets to their destination.

Router A device used to connect different networks. Routers convey data packets on the most favorable route through the networks to their destination. They generally work in layer 3 of the ISO/OSI Reference Model.

RSA An asymmetric encryption system named after its developers: Rivest, Shamir and Adleman. RSA is the most well-known, tested, and studied asymmetric encryption system.

SATAN (System Administrator Tool for Analyzing Networks) A program for checking IP networks. It tests for weaknesses that an attacker from the Internet could exploit in order to gain unauthorized access to a computer system.

Secure gateway An access point is called a gateway if it links a local network with a public network. If the local network operator wants to control who should have access to services, and when and under what conditions the access is to be allowed, he sets up a gateway that is made secure through appropriate security measures. A secure gateway must, above all, be in a position to check the authenticity of users and to differentiate sets of access rights. A high-level firewall system, as the ultimate secure gateway, offers the maximum possible security.

Security policy A security policy constitutes the basis for security in organizations. Normally embodied in a document or documents, it should include, among other things, a definition of security objectives, an assessment of data protection requirements, and an analysis of communications structures.

Security token A data medium (for example, a smart card or diskette) with which the user can prove that he is authorized to gain access, provided he knows the correct PIN. The authentication is carried out using the challenge-response principle: the firewall system that grants access poses a challenge, to which the security token sends a response. If this response is correct, the user is authenticated.

Server A computer within a local network that makes information available to other computers in the network.

S/MIME (Secure Multipurpose Internet Mail Standard) The MIME standard extended to include mechanisms for authentication, encryption, and digital signature.

SMTP (Simple Mail Transport Protocol) An Internet protocol for the transmission of e-mail.

SSL (Secure Socket Layer) Protocol layer for the secure transport of higher Internet protocols such as HTTP.

Symmetric encryption Also known as Private Key System. An encryption system under which the same key is used to encrypt and decrypt data. The best-known symmetric encryption systems are DES and IDEA.

TCP (Transmission Control Protocol) The protocol within TCP/IP that controls the segmentation of data messages into packets and monitors their re-assembly at the receiver. This process includes checking the data packets for completeness and correctness.

TCP/IP (Transmission Control Protocol/Internet Protocol) Communications architecture used on the Internet and in intranets.

Trust center See CA.

UDP (User Datagram Protocol) A connectionless transmission protocol for the Internet. In contrast to TCP/IP, no checking of data messages is performed to ensure that they have been assembled correctly.

UPS (Uninterruptible power supply) An alternate source of electrical power (typically, a battery). A UPS is used with computer systems that have high availability requirements, to enable them to continue running during a power failure or, at the least, to provide enough operating time to permit the controlled shutdown of the computer systems in such cases.

URL (Uniform Resource Locator) A URL specifies the unique address of an Internet server or the source of particular information. It contains details such as the type of resource with which it should be connected (for example, FTP or Gopher), server address, and port number. A URL is entered in the browser or activated via a hyperlink in an HTML document.

User authentication Authentication that is specific to the user. With firewall systems, a number of different authentication mechanisms are possible, such as input of user ID and password, S/Key, token (challenge-response), and Smart cards.

Viruses Programs that propagate themselves unnoticed into other programs and, in general, execute destructive activities at defined times.

VPN (Virtual Private Network) A logical network within a conventional network, in which only encrypted connections between individual computer systems or subnets are permitted. Thanks to encryption, communications sent over the public network are confidential so that the connection is "virtually" private.

W3C (World Wide Web Consortium) An organization for the coordination of the further development of the WWW through the development of specifications and reference software.

WAN (wide area network) A network that extends to a large geographic area. A WAN is based on open standards so that different systems can all participate. The Internet is the largest WAN.

Web server A computer system that provides the WWW Internet service based on HTTP.

WWW (World Wide Web) The complete collection of hypertext documents stored worldwide on HTTP servers.

X.400 The OSI standard for e-mail systems.

X.500 The OSI standard for user tables.

Appendix D

Sample Security Policy

THIS APPENDIX CONTAINS EXCERPTS from a sample security policy. This can be used as a guide for your own security policy. The sample is more stringent than most organizations will want to employ. It is intended to give you a feel for the scope of issues that can be addressed in a security policy.

Security Policy

ACME Corporation's security policy contains the following sections:

- Computer usage guidelines
- Escalation procedures for security incidents

Computer Usage Guidelines

All computer equipment belonging to ACME Corporation is subject to the usage guidelines contained in this document. Any infraction of these guidelines is grounds for employee disciplinary action up to and including employee termination. All disciplinary actions are at management's sole discretion.

Unless specifically authorized by the appropriate management staff, personal computer equipment may not be used at ACME Corporation or connected to ACME Corporation's technical infrastructure. Any personal equipment authorized for connectivity to ACME Corporation computer resources becomes subject to the same computer usage guidelines as ACME Corporation's equipment for the duration of the connection or use.

The specific usage guidelines are as follows:

- Computers are for business use only.
- Data must be backed up to the central data server on a daily basis.
- Do not disable installed anti-virus software.
- Do not disable installed personal firewall software.
- Programs can only be installed or removed with proper authorization.
- User passwords are to consist of between six and eight characters, with at least one non-alphabetic character.

- Any posting to public forums, such as newsgroups, requires a disclaimer indicating that the view expressed is that of the employee's, and not necessarily shared by ACME Corporation.
- ACME Corporation client data is considered confidential and should be handled with the following guidelines:
  - Use and disclose client data only to the extent required to perform client activities.
  - Do not disclose client data to a third party without written authorization from the client.
  - Do not copy client data unless specifically authorized by the client.
  - Return or destroy any client data requested by the client.
- ACME Corporation data is considered proprietary and must not be disclosed, copied, or viewed without specific authorization from the data owner within ACME Corporation.
- You must comply to the fullest extent possible with any security investigations within ACME Corporation.

Escalation Procedures for Security Incidents

In the event you witness or discover any of the security incidents listed in this document, you must follow the steps outlined.

ILLEGAL BUILDING ACCESS

If an unauthorized individual is in a controlled access area within the building, do the following:

1. Call security at x911.
2. Escort the person out of the controlled access area.
3. Wait for security to arrive to complete incident handling.
4. Comply with security personnel requests.

SUSPECTED COMPUTER BREAK-IN

If you suspect a company break-in, do the following:

1. Begin taking detailed notes of everything done.
2. Notify computer security response team at x912.
3. Comply with computer security personnel requests.

LOSS OF PERSONAL PASSWORD/INABILITY TO LOG IN SUCCESSFULLY

To resolve password or login issues, do the following:

1. Call computer support at x913.
2. Identify yourself to computer support with your employee ID.
3. Answer verification questions from computer support personnel.
4. Computer support personnel will reset your password with a new random password.
5. Change your password immediately upon successful login.

ACME PROPERTY THEFT OR DESTRUCTION

In the event of property theft or destruction, take the following actions:

1. Call security at x911.
2. Wait for security to arrive to complete incident handling.
3. Comply with security personnel requests.

SUSPECTED OR CONFIRMED COMPUTER VIRUS

If you suspect or have confirmed a computer virus, do the following:

1. Call computer support at x913.
2. Comply with computer support personnel requests.

Index

continued

C

E

continued

G

H

I

continued

N

continued

O

P

continued

Q

R

continued

U

V

continued

X

Y

Z